Automobile Year

18

1970/71

EDITA LAUSANNE

Experiment and perfection.

Two cars – one concept. Because at Mercedes-Benz, experiment and perfection go together.

The search for trend-setting solutions. For the automobile design of the future. As exemplified today by the rolling test-bed, the C 111 – with new chassis, fiberglass body, and 4-rotor Wankel engine.

Then the detailed refinement of these ideas through long years of thorough development – until, from such experiments, a perfect new automobile results. Like the 280 S/SE, termed by critics "Europe's most finely balanced automobile."

Mercedes-Benz

078 Se

AUTOMOBILE YEAR No. 18 1970-1971 EDITION

contents

PUBLISHER AND MANAGING DIRECTOR: AMI GUICHARD
EDITOR: DOUGLAS ARMSTRONG
EDITOR OF GERMAN EDITION: GÜNTHER MOLTER
EDITORIAL SECRETARY: MARIANNE WUILLEMIN

CONTRIBUTING EDITORS:

FRANCE: JEAN FONDIN
GREAT BRITAIN: DOUGLAS ARMSTRONG
GERMANY: GÜNTHER MOLTER
BELGIUM: PHILIPPE DE BARSY
UNITED STATES: HUNTER FARNHAM

International Sporting Calendar 1971 8
Introduction 35
Day by Day in 1970 . . . . . EDOUARD SEIDLER 39
Riley was a Great Old Name . . . . . DENNIS MAY 47
Cars of the Year . . . . . JACQUES DETHURENS 55
GT = Comfort, Speed, Safety . . . . . AMI GUICHARD 89
Racing 1970 99
Drivers' World Championship
The Year of Jochen Rindt . . . . . JOSÉ ROSINSKI 100
Will the Big Manufacturers Ever Come Back? . . . . . GORDON WILKINS 105
Grand Prix Reports 107
Formula 1 Technique . . . . . GÉRARD FLOCON 159
What Makes a Champion . . . . . JACQUES ICKX 164
Manufacturers' World Championship
Porsche Reap what they have Sown! . . . . . HELMUT ZWICKL 176
Report on the Principal Sports-Prototype Trials 179
« Can-Am » — The 1970 Canadian-American Challenge Cup . . HUNTER FARNHAM 213
Indianapolis 500 Miles . . . . . HUNTER FARNHAM 227
Fastest on Earth for Blue Flame. Ist a Gas 231
Detailed Results of 1970 Championship Grand Prix Races 237
Final Classification of the Drivers' World Championship 251
Detailed results and final Classification of the European Trophy for Formula 2 252
Detailed Results of the Sports-Prototype Races 1970 254
Results of the Spa-Francorchamps 24 Hours 262
Results of the 500 Miles of Indianapolis 263
Results and final classification of the Canadian-American Challenge Cup 264
Results and final classification of the European Hill-Climb Championship 266
Results and final classification of the European Rally Championship 268
Photographic Acknowledgements 273

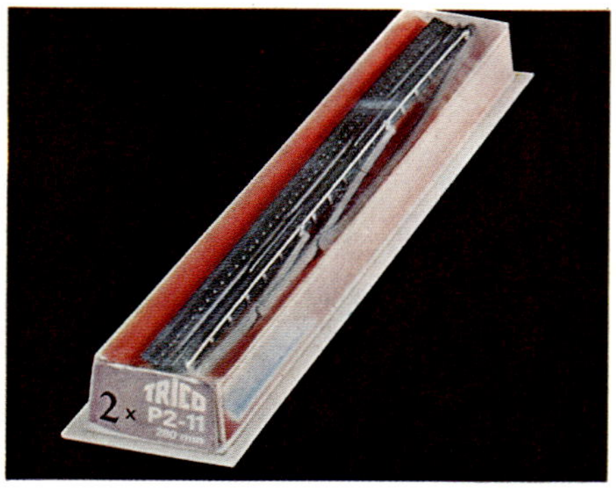

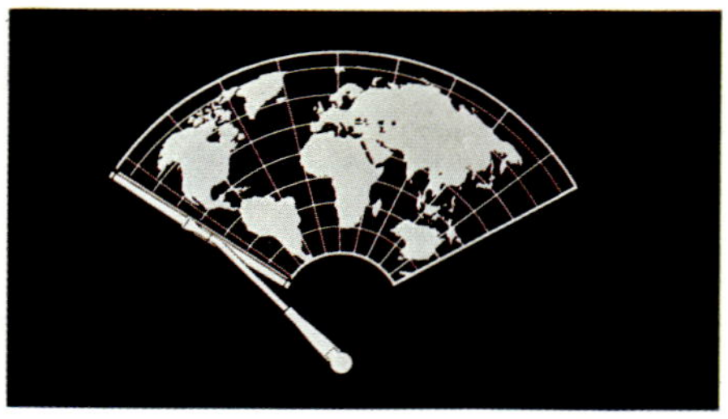

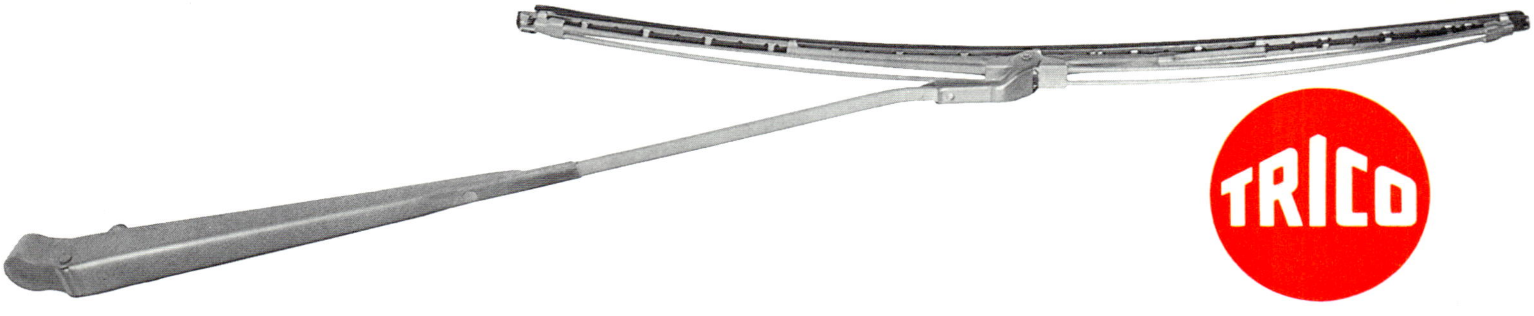

TRICO

A first-class example of
Italian coachwork
in Osaka was Pininfarina's
Ferrari 512/S
pininfarina

BERLINE FULVIA

International Sporting Calendar 1971

Drivers World Championship, Formula 1

March 6	Kyalami	South African Grand Prix
April 18	Barcelona	Spanish Grand Prix
May 23	Monaco	Monaco Grand Prix
June 6	Spa-Francorchamps	Belgian Grand Prix
June 19-20	Zandvoort	Dutch Grand Prix
July 3-4	Le Castellet	French Grand Prix
July 17-18	Silverstone	British Grand Prix
August 1	Nürburgring	German Grand Prix
August 15	Zeltweg	Austrian Grand Prix
September 5	Monza	Italian Grand Prix
September 18-19	Mosport	Canadian Grand Prix
October 3	Watkins Glen	United States Grand Prix
October 24	Mexico-City	Mexican Grand Prix
May 29	USA	* 500 Miles of Indianapolis

International Manufacturers' Championship (SP, S, GT)

January 10	Argentine	Buenos-Aires 1000 km
January 30-31	USA	Daytona 24 Hours
March 20	USA	Sebring 12 Hours
April 4	Great Britain	Brands Hatch 500 Miles
April 25	Italy	Monza 1000 km
May 9	Belgium	Spa 1000 km
May 16	Italy	Targa Florio
May 29-30	Germany	Nürburgring 1000 km
June 12-13	France	Le Mans 24 Hours
June 27	Austria	Österreichring 1000 km
July 24	USA	Watkins Glen 6 Hours
August 7	Canada	Canada 1000 km

European Rally Championship (drivers)

February 5-7	France	Rallye des routes du Nord
March 2-5	Germany	Stuttgart-Solitude-Lyons-Charbonnières
March 17-20	Germany	DDR Rally
April 2-3	Italy	Elba Rally
April 9-13	Great Britain	Circuit of Ireland
April 25-30	Holland	Tulip Rally
May 21-23	Germany	German Rally
June 3-5	Austria	Bodensee-Neusiedlersee Rally
June 5-10	Great Britain	Scottish Rally
June 16-20	Switzerland	Geneva Rally
July 2-4	Czechoslovakia	Moldau Rally
July 15-18	Poland	Polish Rally
August 12-15	Rumania	Danube Rally
August 19-22	Finland	Rally of the 1000 Lakes
August 26-28	Italy	San Martino di Castrozza Rally
September 18-28	France	Tour de France
October 7-10	Portugal	TAP Rally
October 15-17	Austria	Rally of the 1000 Minutes
October 22-24	Spain	Spanish Rally
November 6-7	France	Tour de Corse
November 11-13	Belgium	Tour de Belgique

European Rally Championship (makes)

January 22-29	Monaco	Monte-Carlo Rally
February 17-21	Sweden	Swedish Rally
March 15-17	Italy	San Remo-Sestriere Rally
April 8-12	Great Britain	East African Safari
April 28-May 1	Morocco	Morocco Rally
May 13-16	Austria	Austrian Alpine Rally
May 27-30	Greece	Acropolis Rally
October 17-23	France	Coupe des Alpes
November 20-25	Great Britain	RAC Rally

European Hill-Climb Championship

April 25	Austria	Austrian Grand Prix
May 23	Spain	Montseny
June 6	Germany	Berchtesgaden
June 19-20	France	Mont-Ventoux
July 4	Italy	Trento-Bondone
July 11	Italy	Cesana-Sestriere
August 7-8	France	Mont-Dore
August 29	Switzerland	Ollon-Villars

European Trophy for Formula 2

April 4	Germany	German Trophy
April 12	Great Britain	Thruxton
May 1-2	Germany	Eifel race
May 15	Spain	Gran Premio de Madrid
May 31	Great Britain	Crystal Palace
June 13	Sweden	Mantorp Park
June 26-27	France	Grand Prix de Rouen
August 22	Italy	Premio Mediterraneo-Pergusa
September 12	Austria	Tulln-Langenlebarn
September 26	France	Grand Prix d'Albi
October 10	Italy	Gran Premio di Roma

Canadian-American Challenge Cup

May 28-29	Canada	Mosport
June 26-27	Canada	St. Jovite
July 10	Canada	Klondike 200
July 25	USA	Watkins Glen
August 8	USA	Chesapeake
August 22	USA	Mid-Ohio
August 29	USA	Road America
September 12	USA	Bridgehampton
September 26	USA	Donnybrooke
October 17	USA	Laguna-Seca
October 31	USA	Riverside
November 7	USA	Searspoint

* = Non-Championship.
SP = Sport-Prototype; S = Sport; GT = Grand Touring.
N.B. This calendar may be modified during the season.

Another Rallye du Jour success for Edwin (Fangio) Threadfinger.

After sixteen gruelling miles, including new roadworks, old cars, careless pedestrians and reckless cyclists, commuter Edwin Threadfinger scores yet another brilliant victory, arriving home safely and in good time for tea.

With typical modesty, Edwin attributes his successes to the Triumph he drives and to the race-proved Lucas petrol injection system within it. (Lucas have, after all, powered 8 out of the last 9 Formula 1 World Champions to victory).

"We top drivers," he shyly explains, "use the extra power that Lucas petrol injection gives us to keep clear of trouble. Yesterday, for example, there was a bus. . . ."

Happy to have kept you safe, Edwin.

LUCAS makers of world-beating petrol injection and electronic ignition systems

Joseph Lucas Ltd., Birmingham, England

THE PININFARINA SHAPE
PININFARINA
cannot design all the cars in the world
— they can only be responsible for some of them.
But their ideas also influence the others.
And it has been like that for forty years.

UNIROYAL
L'HUILE

"Good

A certain way of taking the road and holding it. Effortlessly, because it has everything it needs just for that.

A certain calm way of facing turns, wet ground, and potholes. Knowing all about them, but not being afraid of them.

A certain pleasure in feeling the reaction of a powerful engine quick to respond, tenacious... in driving for miles without being bored and without getting tired.

A certain confidence based on mechanics, and on a conception of the automobile that proves its worth daily.
This is road behaviour: it's good behaviour.
Renault good behaviour.

RENAULT

PUBLICIS E827

5793 EZ59

The descendants of the first jet engines

Every designer has one ideal: an engine with perfectly smooth running characteristics. 27 years ago we reached this ideal for the first time, when making the engines for the world's first jet planes. But that didn't stop us from aiming at something similar for cars. Even though the principle of the piston engine — still the most reliable motor you can get — is seemingly opposed to absolutely smooth running. Our designers have made up for this by making ingenious combustion chambers that guarantee smooth and "soft" combustion. And by precise balancing of the crankshaft. So the motoring press calls the product of our endeavours "engines that run without any vibration; as smooth as a turbine". And so, we've done it again. Reached an ideal. As the drivers of BMW cars already know. Because they have one benefit just for themselves: the driving pleasure offered by their BMWs already starts under the bonnet.

BMW

For sheer driving pleasure — BMW

"Cream on Wheels."

Sunday Times

BRITISH LEYLAND **Jaguar XJ6**

Jaguar Cars Ltd, Coventry, England.

Deinhard

Symbol of Refined Taste

Patrons of Distinguished Taste
set a Special Value on
Deinhard Lila

175
YEARS
Deinhard
1794
ESTABLISHED AS
WINE TRADING
COMPAGNY
1843
INCLUSION OF THE
PRODUCTION OF
SPARKLING WINE

For more than 175 years, the House of Deinhard has been closely linked to the history of German wines. The friends of the House of Deinhard — like its owners — are individualists who have preserved their taste for the exceptional: Deinhard Lila. This sparkling wine deserves the highest recommendation. Patrons of Distinguished Taste set a Special Value on Deinhard Lila.

Available also
in Switzerland
and Austria

Economy,

transmission and engine of the 128

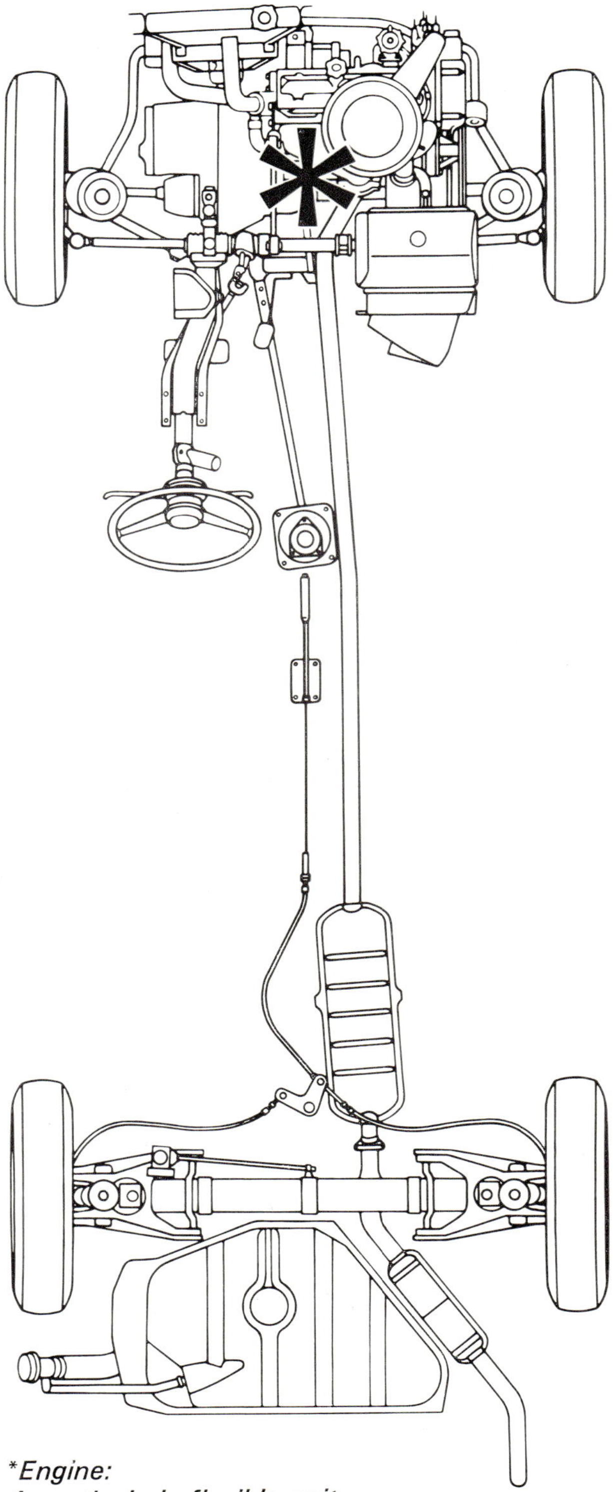

*Economy:
The 128's 1100 cc. engine produces a performance worthy of a much larger-engined car. And its economy is another of its advantages.

*Transmission:
Front-wheel drive with a transverse engine. Space available is thus fully exploited. Bodywork is simple, costs are lower. With no differential and gearbox to intrude on the interior, the luggage compartment can be larger. The passenger compartment can be made more rigid and more resistant to deformation and the bodyshell can be reinforced by longitudinal and cross-members.

*Engine:
A particularly flexible unit. High torque output at low engine speeds (3,000 r.p.m.). Gear ratios are planned to make the best use of top gear at low r.p.m., and allow high r.p.m. in the low gears. An optimum combination in terms of acceleration, speed, fuel consumption and engine life.

FIAT 128

GIRLING
STOP FAST
TO COME FIRST
In the sixties
7 out of 10 Formula I
World Championships were
won by Girling equipped cars.
With yet another season
of impressive victories in
1970, Girling are set for
another decade of progress
and success.
GIRLING DISC BRAKES

Porsche 917 - 24 Heures du Mans 1970 - 1st HERRMANN-ATTWOOD

Shell likes competitions and wins them

SHELL

Ferrari F1 G.P. Austria 1970 - 1st ICKX, 2nd REGAZZONI

Ferrari 512 S Chris AMON

J.P. JAUSSAUD Champion de France F3

SINCE 1907

SKF

HAVE BEEN EQUIPPING CARS

Today 2 out of 3 cars are fitted
with SKF ball-bearings.

Because of the quality of their steel,
because of their high-precision engineering
and their rigorous checking systems,
SKF ball-bearings can assure you
thousands of trouble-free miles

Jack Brabham's BT33 Brabham-Ford captures the South African Grand Prix at an average 111.700 Champion-sparked mph.

Jackie Ickx's Ferrari captures the Austrian Grand Prix at an average 129.269 Champion-sparked mph.

Pedro Rodriguez' BRM captures the Belgian Grand Prix at an average 149.942 Champion-sparked mph.

3 Grands Prix . . .
3 expert drivers . . .
3 makes of engines . . .

1 brand of spark plugs!

Grand Prix pros Jack Brabham, Pedro Rodriguez and Jackie Ickx are among those drivers who equip their cars with Champion spark plugs. And Champions have sparked each of them to a coveted international Grand Prix winner's circle this year.

Like engine experts the world over, Jack, Pedro and Jackie rely on Champion's spark for peak power—race-winning dependability.

Drive like a winner. Equip *your* car with Champions!

CHAMPION

A sports car that takes
that not all men

Because in this world there exist married men who crav
a sports car with the heated, frenzied passion of any bach
elor, we build the Javelin with enough room to seat four
There are two high-back bucket seats in the front, lik
most sports cars. (To hold a man and his woman in selfis
comfort.)
And unlike most sports cars, there's a wide cushione
seat in the back. (To hold a man and his woman's childre
and/or their dog.)
But in making the Javelin a family car, we didn't sacr
fice any of the performance characteristics of a sports ca
The Javelin has a standard 232 cubic inch engine tha
develops 135 horsepower. And optional V-8's that gene

ınto consideration are bachelors.

ıte even more. Up to a pulse-quickening 330.

The Javelin also has a standard three-speed, fully ›ynchromesh, floor shift transmission.

An optional heavy-duty 10 inch clutch.

A standard "twin-ball-joint" front suspension system.

And a list of other standards and options that will get he Javelin from 0-60 in less than 9 seconds.

All of which should make the Javelin as appealing to he single bachelor as it is to the married one.

American Motors Javelin

For the rugged Can-Am racing series, Jim Hall has designed and built the fastest-cornering car on earth. With several assists from GE silicones.

The 2J works on a vacuum principle, in which fans suck air out from under the car to create over 1000 lbs. extra downforce. This gives the car a 20% increase in cornering and braking effectiveness.

Performance like this puts a tremendous strain on all parts and materials. That's why Hall uses GE silicones for:

Potting. All vital electrical connections and instruments are protected against vibration, moisture and contamination by GE RTV potting compounds.

Seals. Automatic transmission and rear engine seals are special grades of GE silicone rubber with fantastic resistance to heat, oil and fluids.

Gaskets. GE RTV silicone rubber gaskets are formed in place to conform and adhere to mating metal surfaces of the engine and transmission—wherever there's a risk of oil, water or fluid leaks. GE RTV's won't harden, soften, crack or shrink.

Bonding. The adhesive strength of GE RTV is so reliable, even in extreme heat and moisture, that it's used to bond components such as water ducts and taillight assemblies to the car frame and body.

Insulation. Ignition wire and sparkplug boots are fabricated from GE silicone rubber. The rubber withstands temperatures up to 500°F, down to –150°F, fights ozone, has excellent dielectric strength.

Lubricating. To keep throttle linkage, skirt mechanisms and other components operating in any weather, Hall uses new GE Versilube® Plus lubricants. They're virtually invulnerable to water washout.

More information: write Section FU1342 Silicone Products Dept., General Electric Co., Waterford, N.Y. 12188.

GENERAL ELECTRIC

Ad No. 342—General Electric. This advertisement prepared by Ross Roy of New York Inc.—16746-0

The man without worries is the man with a Neiman
He knows that a Neiman anti-theft device is a guarantee of absolute safety. Over 35 million are made throughout the world because the Neiman, the only anti-theft installation with mechanical steering blockage, assures the most effective protection possible.
NEIMAN
Safety
49, Avenue de Neuilly - 92 Neuilly-France Tel.: 624.64.88

Automobile Year

published in English, French and German by
EDITA S.A. Box 121, 1003 Lausanne (Switzerland)
Tel. (021) 23 56 91 Cable address: Editasa
Managing Editor: Ami Guichard

If your bookseller cannot supply it, please write to one of the addresses listed below or to Edita S.A.

Argentina

Riverside-Litexsa, S.A.C.
Belgrano 2786/88

BUENOS AIRES

Australia

Universal Publications
45-47, Walker Street

NORTH SYDNEY, N.S.W.
Phone 92-0641

Belgium and Luxemburg

Etablissements VILO
27, rue Ginoux

PARIS XVe

Brazil

Agencia van Damme
Rua Goitacazes, 103 – Sala 1310
Caixa postal 1037

BELO HORIZONTE – MG

Denmark

C. A. Reitzel LTD.
Nørregade 20

1165 KOPENHAGEN – K

Finland

Suomalainen Kirjakauppa
Buchhandlung

HELSINKI 10

France

Etablissements VILO
27, rue Ginoux

PARIS XVe

Germany

Motorbuch-Verlag
Böblinger Str. 18 / Postfach 1370

7000 STUTTGART 1

Great Britain

Patrick Stephens Ltd.
9, Ely Place

LONDON E. C. 1

Hong Kong

The Good Luck Magazine Co.
42, Johnston Road
P. O. Box 49

HONG KONG

Italy

Libreria dell'Automobile
Via Hoepli, 6

MILAN

or

Via Marsala
Galleria Sara 14

ROME

107 Japan

Shimada & Co. Inc.
9-19, Minami-Aoyama 5-chome
Minato-ku

TOKYO

Malta

J. W. Micallef
34, Strait Street

VALLETTA

Netherlands

Meulenhoff-Bruna N. V.
Gebouw 106
Schiphol-Ost

AMSTERDAM

New Zealand

Modern Educational Publications Ltd.
82, Taranaki Street – Box 1324

WELLINGTON

North America

Walter R. Haessner & Assoc., Inc.
P.O. Box 89

NEWFOUNDLAND
New Jersey 07435
Phone: Area Code 201 – 697-3773
ISBN # 0-87799-008-5

Norway

J. W. Cappelens Bokhandel
Postboks 350

OSLO

Portugal

Livraria Bertrand S.A.R.L.
Apartado 37

AMADORA

Singapore

Marican & Sons
171, Middle Road
G. P. O. Box 69

SINGAPORE 7

Sweden

Importbokhandeln
Gävlegatan 12 A

11330 STOCKHOLM K

Thailand

Rainbow Specialty Co.
1170-1172 New Road
G. P. O. Box 101

BANGKOK

Uruguay

Editorial Nuevo Mundo
Casilla de Correo 1611

MONTEVIDEO

Venezuela

Librería del Este
Av. F. de Miranda 52
Edificio Galipán

CARACAS

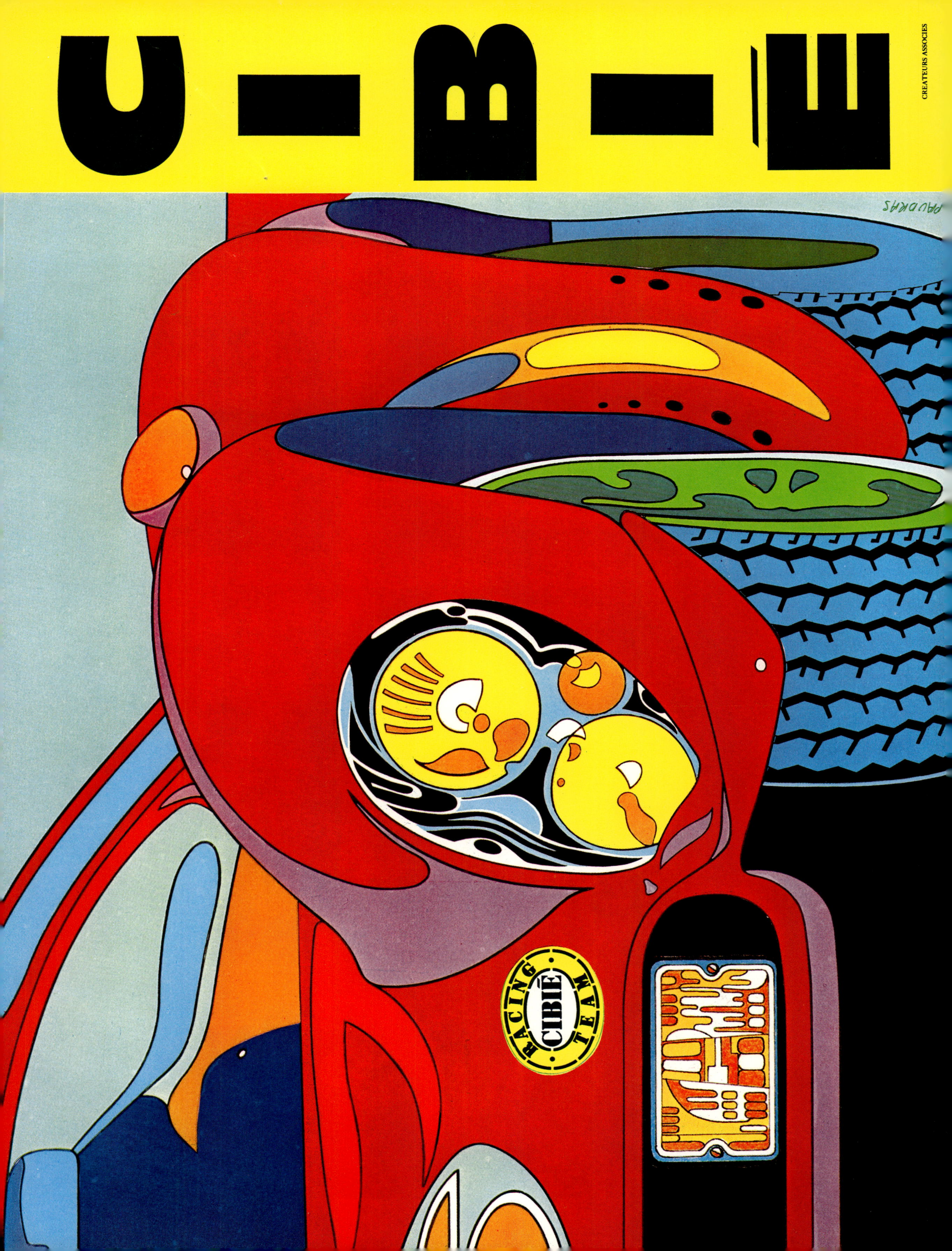
CREATEURS ASSOCIES
RACING
CIBIÉ
TEAM

The Po
It's not a racing tire - it just looks like one
It's a 60 series tire — only 60% as high as it is wide. A full eight inches of rubber on the road. Low cord angle, reverse molded construction, straight sidewalls and raised white letters. The Polyglas® GT— Goodyear's widest street tire yet.
Polyglas – T.M. The Goodyear Tire & Rubber Company, Akron, Ohio.
POLYGLA
GOOD

yglas GT
F60-15
YEAR

INTRODUCTION

The year 1970 cannot be recorded as one of great moment in the automotive sphere. Car production was thrown into chaos by social and labour problems in the United States, in Italy, and in Britain.

Colossal sums of money were lost due to the industrial upsets and lost production, and at the end of the year it seemed no great international panacea had been found.

In North America there was considerable disquiet over the progress that had been made by "foreign imports" from Europe and Japan—imports that had accounted for no less than 13.5 percent of the total market.

To counter the invasion, American Motors, General Motors, and Ford launched an interesting and competitively-priced breed of "sub-compacts" with engines that were small to American eyes, but with cleverly-planned internal dimensions, good performance, and economy of upkeep which had obviously kept directors, designers, accountants, publicity-men and production engineers awake at nights for a long time. The cars incorporated many attractive features and advanced technology, and in next year's *Automobile Year* it will be interesting to review their 1971 progress.

The US regulations against exhaust emission made the lot of the motor manufacturer more difficult, in practically every country, and the legislation is scheduled to become tighter still. It is significant that General Motors paid a vast sum of money, albeit in instalments, for the manufacturing and marketing rights of the Wankel rotary engine. After seventy years of the conventional piston engine, it may be the quest for clean exhausts which will bring a different type of power-unit to the ordinary motorist. Certainly 1970 suggested the steam engine will never become the man-in-the-street's prime mover. Speed limits tended to spread, if not by harsh laws, then by traffic jams and by the high and ever-increasing cost of fuel in many countries. Nevertheless, in the hope of attracting customers who might otherwise become disenchanted with motoring, many of the world's manufacturers introduced new sporting models of high performance, attractive appearance, and intriguing specification. When faced with a promising car the motoring enthusiast dispenses with logic!

The fact remains, more and more motoring obstacles are put in our way every year, suggesting that the freedom of movement which has been with us so long is in real danger of (literally) coming to a halt before many years have passed. In a year of tragedy for motoring sport, top drivers Bruce McLaren, Piers Courage, and Jochen Rindt perished. For the first time in the history of the Drivers' World Championship, the title was awarded posthumously.

The same year saw the 44-year-old Australian driver Jack Brabham retire after more than 20 years in the sport, and with three World Championship titles behind him. Wisely, he retired while still at the top of his form.

In addition to the traditional articles retracing the automobile events of the last 12 months, readers will find a fascinating analysis—the result of long and patient work by Jacques Ickx, celebrated motoring journalist and father of Ferrari driver Jacky Ickx—of the Driver's World Championship from its beginning nearly 21 years ago, to the present day.

The information and statistics which the writer uncovers are highly educational, and he brings to light facts which establish without doubt the superiority of Juan Manuel Fangio, and of Jim Clark. The article also brings into sharp focus the qualities which constitute the make-up of a World Champion. Jacques Ickx also outlines the dramatic effect "the British system" has had on post-war motor racing.

No new drivers were apparent in the 1969 Grand Prix season but 1970 was notable for no less than eleven newcomers to the scene. Two of them won Grand Prix races, and one of them finished third in the World Championship table!

The sport has never been healthier from that aspect but it has become alarmingly expensive.

Ami Guichard

Automobile Year day by day in 1970

by Edouard Seidler

January
Difficulties at Detroit

The beginning of the new year was marked by fresh offensives in the battle between American, European and Japanese manufacturers. During the preceding year, sales of imports reached over a million units in America for the second consecutive year and Detroit was preparing to react. Even before the first "American minis" appeared, symbolic news was being made in the United States: the US Steel works at Fairfield prohibited its 14,000 workers and all its visitors from parking a car of foreign origin in the company's parking lot. Reason advanced by US Steel was that Detroit manufacturers are their best customers and it is good policy to encourage the use of the client's products. This measure was to be dropped but it nevertheless bears witness to a protectionist state of mind which would henceforth worry onlookers.

Exposed to attacks from Europe and Japan, placed by the government under a regime of controlled liberty, affected by the beginning of a recession, the American automobile industry also experienced some difficult times on the domestic plane. Ralph Nader added yet another preoccupation when he had his disciples parade in front of the New York headquarters of General Motors to protest against air pollution by internal combustion engines. Hardest-hit of American manufacturers was Chrysler, which was going through serious financial difficulties and had appointed a new president, John J. Riccardo, a young financier of Italian origin whose job it is to put things right. News started spreading that Chrysler might liquidate its holdings in Europe and there was talk of a possible take-over of Simca by Fiat. These rumours were rapidly denied. Actually Simca was trying harder than ever to improve its trade image and to relaunch some of its oldest models, introducing a "rally" version of the Simca 1000 with a maximum speed of 94 mph.

Another new single-seater was conceived in Italy by the Argentinian A. de Tomaso, a car designed for Piers Courage. The tendency was still towards "special cars" with a sporty look. Ford announced the creation in Great Britain of the "Ford Advanced Vehicles Operation", an organization which will employ 250 people and will be charged with regrouping the output of all low-volume specialty cars. Symbol of the death of an era: 4,000 dwelling-places will be built on the site of the old Panhard factories.

The Monte Carlo Rally was a repetition of the 1969 edition. B. Waldegaard's and G. Larrousse's Porsches once again took the first two places in the tests, followed as in 1969 by an Alpine Renault, that of J.-P. Nicolas. The Argentine Temporada, the two races of which were fought out on the modern Buenos Aires circuit, finished in a draw between Matra and Alfa Romeo. J.-P. Beltoise and H. Pescarolo won the 1,000-kilometre test as if to celebrate the agreement drawn up between Matra and Simca, whose trade names will henceforth be linked on the blue car, while the Simca network will distribute Matra products. A week later A. de Adamich and P. Courage were to get their own back at the wheel of an Alfa Romeo 33/3 in the 200 miles race. The Alfa engine, having proved satisfactory, will be mounted in a Formula 1 McLaren for Andrea de Adamich. This rehearsal was successful for the Argentine organisers: their circuit was judged worthy for a manufacturer's world championship race in 1971.

March in February

World racing champion Jackie Stewart abandoned Matra for a completely new marque: March. An ambitious firm. Its engineer, Robin Herd, a transfer from McLaren, took only a few months to conceive and build the first of his single-seaters. Number one was ready in February for Stewart to test and five more were to be entered in the first Grand Prix of the season, in South Africa. Among the new marque's advertising sponsors is America's STP, which will finance the factory stable in order to provide a Formula 1 ride for its star, Mario Andretti.

De Tomaso, the new headman at *carrozzeria* Ghia and Vignale, negotiated an important agreement with Ford which will assure him of powerful backing.

The endurance race season started at Daytona with the first of a year-long series of matches between the 4.5 and later 5-litre Porsche 917 sports car and the 5-litre Ferrari 512s—both way ahead of the prototypes with a 3-litre displacement limit. Porsche, whose official racers are entered by the John Wyer team, took the first two places, with the Rodriguez-Kinnunen and the Siffert-Redman combines. But Ferrari had made a promising start with the Andretti-Merzario-Ickx team taking third place. It seemed that the support of Fiat would allow Ferrari to taste victory once more.

For its own part Fiat carried it off again in another kind of competition: after the 124, the 128 was named "Car of the Year" by an international jury brought together by the Dutch magazine *Autovisie*. Fiat's associate, Citroën, tried to relaunch the 2 CV. The new version of this car has a 602 cc engine developing 28.5 hp at 6,750 rpm. And the ancient "ugly duckling" proudly achieved a top speed of 69 mph!

Opel, also on the performance path, introduced a Commodore with electronic injection, the GSE, which reaches 123 mph. Less brilliant were the two new cars launched by American Motors in the US and Rootes in Europe. The Gremlin was promoted in Detroit as an "anti-Volkswagen". It is a compact car (13 ft. $2^5/_8$ in.) but is no more than a classical Hornet with the end cut off. The Rootes Avenger, a traditionally conceived car, will be welcomed above all in Great Britain. It was introduced in two versions of 1,248 and 1,498 cc developing respectively 53 and 63 hp. Its performance is, however, too modest and the selling price, after customs duties, too considerable to assure its success in the Common Market countries.

March Her Majesty Citroën

A great star at the Geneva Show: the Citroën SM coupe with a Maserati 2.7-litre V6 engine developing 170 hp. For weeks no one talked about anything but its revolutionary steering—but it will not have its first real tests until September. The key to this steering is a part about 5 inches high and 3 inches wide, a centrifugal regulator attached to the end of the gearbox and rotating in function with the speed of the car. This regulator controls the self-centering action. It works by means of a lever on a hydraulic slide-valve which regulates the pressure in the servo-direction circuit, so that the effort necessary to steer varies according to the speed. Very weak at zero, the necessary effort increases as the vehicle's speed accelerates. The straightening correction is always effective and assures the car the power to maintain a remarkably straight course. And so at the Geneva Show everybody thronged round the SM which, with a top speed of 138 m.p.h., claims to be the fastest front-wheel drive car in the world. Paradox: it was introduced at a time when France decreed a speed limit of 69 mph on 8,750 miles of main road!

Numerous novelties on neighbouring stands. The experimental Mercedes C 111 was introduced, six months after its debut at the Frankfurt Show, dressed up a little and with a four instead of a three-rotor engine.

Alfa Romeo exhibited its Alfa Romeo coupe, a rival to the Porsche 911. A new Lamborghini appeared, the Jarama.

The Jaguar XJ 6 received a new automatic gearbox. Bertone exhibited a BMW four-seater coupe. Matra tried to relaunch its 530 coupe as an "LX" version. Ford introduced two sports versions of known models, a 2.6-litre German Capri revised by Jochen Neerpasch and a British Escort with a 1.5-litre Ford-Cosworth engine.

Sporty cars, too, were launched a few days later at the New York Show. Under the *aegis* of Ford, de Tomaso introduced his Pantera, which is to take over from the Mangusta. The work of engineer G. Dall'Ara, creator of the first Lamborghinis, the Pantera is to be turned out at 5,000 units a year, and distributed essentially in the United States by the Ford network. American Motors launched a car that had also been conceived in Italy: the AMX 3, the first American car with a central (V8) engine, of which only two units will be built every month.

On the economic front, the main event was the partnership arranged between Dunlop and Pirelli. The new group has become the number one for rubber in Europe, close to the American giants Goodyear and Firestone.

In sport Datsun's triumph in the East-African Safari was noted. For eleven months the Japanese marque had prepared meticulously for the event and had spared no effort to win. Another firm which invested considerable capital to return to the limelight was at last rewarded for its perseverance: Ferrari beat Porsche at the Twelve Hours of Sebring when the Rodriguez-Kinnunen 917 halted in the last half hour of the race with a broken suspension. The final spurt of Mario Andretti, who came to lend a strong hand to Nino Vaccarella and Ignazio Giunti, gave the victory to Ferrari, by the skin of their teeth: partnering Peter Revson at the wheel of a Porsche 908 and driving with one foot in a cast, film-star Steve McQueen just missed winning. He finished the race less than a minute behind the victorious Ferrari!

April
Rush to the East

While, with the Wembley-Mexico Rally (the longest "race" in modern history), there was a spectacular rush of European cars towards South America, it was the "rush to the East" of the western manufacturers that dominated the economic scene. Mr Henry Ford II went to Moscow to negotiate the construction in the USSR by his technicians of an integrated factory capable of producing 150,000 trucks a year. At the same time one of the presidents of the American group, Mr Robert Stevenson, affirmed that "Europe is on the road to establishing a unique market, from West to East". Henry Ford and President Kosygin understood each other and were ready to come to an agreement, but the project was to have no immediate follow-up: Ford management, to whom Washington had officiously pointed out that the material constructed in the future factory could be used for strategical ends against the United States, feared hostile reactions in America and abandoned—provisionally at least—tentatives for co-operation with the Soviet authorities. The economic overtures set up in the East by Fiat and Renault were confirmed in no less spectacular a fashion.

In the United States itself the main worry remained the fight against the importers, whose penetration into the American market had reached 13.5 per cent for the entire country and 25 per cent in California, the Japanese launching base. John DeLorean, managing director of Chevrolet, revealed what would be the main Detroit weapon against foreign manufacturers: automation. For the "minis" prepared at Detroit, bodywork construction will be 80 per cent automatic, a rate never before achieved, and the cars are to be offered at a price equal to that of the Volkswagen beetles. At the same time attacks against Japanese protectionism were becoming more and more lively. To get out of the scrape Japan reduced customs duties on "compact" cars from 34 to 20 per cent and confirmed that from 1971 it will authorize partnerships between foreign and local groups on condition that the foreign participation does not exceed 50 per cent in the new enterprises, the creation of which will still need authorization.

In Europe the internal problems of Citroën were translated into the dismissal of the executive president, M. Claude-Alain Sarre, who was replaced by M. Raymond Ravenel, his assistant. Shortly afterwards M. Pierre Bercot was to announce his impending retirement: the new administrative council will be dominated by representatives of Michelin and Fiat.

Some of the leading manufacturers increased their interests in car-hire firms, at a time when hiring and leasing threaten gradually to replace personal car ownership. Thus in Germany Volkswagen bought back the Selbstfahrer Union (3,500 cars) while in France Renault took control of Europcars (13,000 vehicles).

On the circuits, Porsche reaffirmed its superiority over Ferrari after the Sebring interlude. At Brands Hatch Porsche 917s took the first three positions, victory going to this season's in-form team, Rodriguez-Kinnunen. These two drivers won again at Monza, but this time Ferrari put up a lot of resistance: three 512Ss finished on the heels of the victorious Porsche. British Leyland nibbled its way back into competition through the back door, using a Rover with its engine displacement increased by Traco from 3.5 to 4.5 litres and claimed to develop 345 hp. In the European Formula 1 season, which began with the

Spanish Grand Prix, Jackie Stewart gave March its first World Championship victory. Ickx and Oliver miraculously dragged themselves almost unscathed from an accident that could have had fatal consequences. The Scot, outgoing champion of the world, thus once again headed the world classifications. The rest of the season would, however, prove much less favourable to him, at the wheel of a car which would turn out to be disappointing after its misleading performance on the Jarama track. It would later be remembered that it was almost beaten that day by Beltoise's Matra, whose engine seized up as the French driver was attacking Stewart, the latter finally retaining the lead from start to finish.

♉ May
Second title for Porsche

Porsche, who in 1969 entrusted the defence of its colours to the John Wyer, the Salzburg and several private teams, picked up its second world title without even waiting for the 24 Hours of Le Mans, even though Ferrari had this time neglected nothing to bar its way. The German cars were practically invincible on every course. At Stuttgart a new model, the 908-3, was conceived at great expense for the single Targa Florio race, where Siffert-Redman and Rodriguez-Kinnunen again took the first two places—in front of the only Ferrari 512 S in the race, driven astonishingly well into third place by Vaccarella and Giunti. At Spa all the Ferraris finished once more but again a Porsche 917, that of Siffert-Redman, was in front of them. And the scenario was repeated at Nurburgring, where Porsche staked the 908-3s in order to carry off its second world title: at the wheels of these cars, Elford-Ahrens and Hermann-Attwood took over from the faltering John Wyer stable and preceded two Ferrari 512 Ss.

The manufacturer's world championship thus drew to a close while four races, including that of Le Mans, remained to be fought. The drivers' championship, on the other hand, was still in full swing. At Monaco, where Stewart led the race before being stopped by ignition trouble, Brabham seemed unapproachable until on the last bend he committed a novice's error and Rindt, dashing in from behind, triumphed at the wheel of a last year's car, the Lotus 49 C.

Dominated by sports competitions, this month of May also saw Al Unser win his battle at Indianapolis, two years after the success of his brother Bobby, and Ford asserting itself with its Escorts in the Wembley-Mexico Rally. Mikkola and Palm won in front of Culcheth-Syer (Triumph 2500 PI) and five Escorts figured in the first eight places of the test. It was a triumph of Stuart Turner's organization. Ford's main rivals, the Citroëns, had been overthrown: only one finished, in seventh position. Consolation for Citroën: while its Wembley-Mexico Rally cars were sailing on the Atlantic towards Rio de Janeiro, Neyret and Terramorsi won the difficult Morocco Rally for the French firm. Juan-Manuel Fangio was laid low by a heart attack and his life was thought to be in danger, but the robust constitution of the former world champion helped him get on his feet again. In the United States United Auto workers president Walter Reuther disappeared in a plane accident and all Detroit went into mourning: Walter Reuther was preparing to play an essential role in negotiations, due to open in the autumn, for a new collective convention. In Europe the process of industrial concentration continued with an important merger in the equipments sector: Ferodo (brakes, clutches) absorbed Marchal (headlamps, distributors, sparking plugs).

A major road project entered an active phase: the St.Gothard tunnel—which, with its 52,687 feet, will be the longest tunnel in the world—is likely to be open to traffic in 1975.

Finally two new cars made an appearance, an automatic version of the Audi 100 LS and a Simca 1100 "Special" equipped with a more powerful 1,204 cc engine developing 75 hp; the latter was greeted by the experts as one of the very best cars in its category in Europe.

♊ June
Tragic month

Bruce McLaren was killed at Goodwood while trying out his Can-Am car. A few days later Piers Courage lost his life at Zandvoort, during the Dutch Grand Prix. The death-toll continued at Rouen where two of the French hopes, Jean-Luc Salomon and Denis Dayan, both perished during the same Formula 3 tests. This succession of accidents was to bring about a series of retirements among top-ranking drivers. Servoz-Gavin hung up his helmet after the Monaco Grand Prix and was replaced by François Cevert in the Ken Tyrrell stable; Robbin Widdows decided to call it a day. And before the end of the season these two men were to be emulated by the American Gurney, the Australian triple-World Champion Jack Brabham, the Briton Brian Redman and the Germans Hahne, Ahrens and Herrmann.

The latter won at Le Mans, along with Richard Attwood, and so gave Porsche its first all-out victory on the Sarthe circuit. It was, however, an easy success for the German firm after four Ferrari 512S cars had been eliminated in the same collision. Two 917S models and one 908 took the first three places in a race rendered difficult by excruciatingly bad weather conditions.

In Formula 1 Jochen Rindt once again showed his form and beat Stewart and Ickx at Zandvoort; behind them appeared a talented novice, Swiss driver Clay Regazzoni. The Ferraris were coming back and prophecies began concerning the end of the V8 engine in GP racing. Rodriguez had paved the way for the return of the V12 by driving his works BRM to success on the ultra-fast Spa circuit.

A few new cars were unveiled. In London, Reliant introduced a toy car, the Bond Bug (three wheels, two seats, 81 mph). British Leyland launched the Triumph Stag, a pleasant but characterless car styled by the Italian Michelotti and equipped with a three-litre V8 engine developing 145 hp for a maximum speed of about 118 mph. In France, Renault introduced its Gordini version of the "12". The engine produced 113 hp and the car could reach more than 112 mph. This new front-wheel-drive car replaced the famous Renault 8 Gordini—to the great chagrin of its fans.

Renault, meanwhile, was getting ready to distribute shares worth 54 million francs to 45,000 of its employees as part of the shareholder-worker programme devised by the French government.

In Germany representatives of General Motors met with Professor Wankel to negotiate rights to rotary-piston engine manufacture which was attracting the interest of a growing number of enterprises.

Volkswagen management, apparently serene in spite of the American counter-offensive under preparation, celebrated the ten-millionth export Volkswagen to roll off its assembly lines. On another plane, however, the Americans scored a point: Dunlop, affected by the strikes that were slowing production in its British factories, announced its retirement from Formula 1 racing. This withdrawal left the two Akron giants Goodyear and Firestone facing each other at the top of racing. Michelin, whose official entry into the "Great Circus" of Formula 1 was rumoured from time to time, was content so far to test its racing tyres with Ferrari without ever taking the decisive step.

July
The Chrysler battle

The summer was dominated by Chrysler's difficulties. This third-ranking American group, whose subsidiary for hire-purchase sales ran into financial troubles, had to apply to a banking consortium for a loan of more than 400 million dollars.

Unlike General Motors and Ford, Chrysler did not take up the production of a "small American" car but decided to use European and Japanese weapons to join in the mini-battle. As a first step, it was to import Hunters produced by its English subsidiary and Colts from its Japanese associate Mitsubishi. Later, a small car is planned to be manufactured in Detroit, powered by an engine built in England.

Chrysler pulled out all the stops to reorganize its European subsidiaries and substituted its name for Simca, Rootes and Barreiros, which became no more than branches of the Chrysler-Europe organization. Another concentration movement made progress: Fiat obtained the French government's go-ahead to acquire 49 per cent of the shares of a holding company owning 55 per cent of the Citroën capital. Michelin, with 51 per cent of the shares, remained the major investor in the company, but Signor Umberto Agnelli's intentions were no secret: "We are going to run Citroën on equal terms with Michelin."

Fiat, on the other hand, was obliged to call a halt to its 1970 expansion: strikes continued to paralyse its Turin factories. Ford established itself in Italy taking control of the de Tomaso, Ghia and Vignale organizations. De Tomaso started building a new series of sport cars for the American market, including the Mangusta.

Volkswagen, Fiat's big rival in Europe, confirmed that it was going to take up the K70 project which started as an NSU, the firm now under Volkswagen control. The K70, to be introduced under the VW emblem, was the first front-wheel-drive and water-cooled car to be produced by the Wolfsburg firm. The development of this car was proof of the firm's intention to reduce the relative role of the Beetle in its productions.

On a sporting plane, Porsche once more demonstrated its supremacy in endurance racing. At Watkins Glen Rodriguez and Kinnunen chalked up their fourth success of the season, at the wheel of a Porsche 917, in front of their team-mates Siffert and Redman. The first Ferrari 512, driven by Andretti and Giunti, dropped out after three laps.

In Formula 1 the once-so-unlucky Jochen Rindt carried off two more unhoped-for victories. At Clermont-Ferrand Jean-Pierre Beltoise led the French Grand Prix, together with Jacky Ickx for 14 of the race's 38 laps, alone for the following eleven. But he had a puncture 11 laps from the end and had to cede the victory to Rindt. Two weeks later at Brands Hatch the Lotus leader triumphed again. This time he owed his success to Jack Brabham's running out of petrol just as he seemed to be winning, 300 yards from the flag. As at Monte Carlo Jack's misfortune was Jochen's lucky break... Brabham's bad luck so impressed the Guild of Motoring Writers that they were to make the ageing Australian their "Driver of the Year" for the third time.

Drivers, putting on pressure for improved safety measures on the tracks, refused to race at Nürburgring, and the German Grand Prix was transferred to the Hockenheim circuit. Elsewhere it was environment more than safety that was under discussion. After Buenos Aires and Rome, outlawing cars over the week-end, it was Tokyo's turn to prohibit a whole city sector to cars: every Sunday, from 10 a.m. to 5. p.m. a zone of 150,000 square yards was marked off in the heart of Tokyo for pedestrians. Will the car gradually be banished from the world's capitals?

♌ August
Return of Ferrari

Ferrari's return to the top, expected by the technicians and long hoped-for by the "tifosi", was at last assured and with it the revenge of the V12 engine over the Cosworth V8. At Hockenheim, Jacky Ickx threatened Jochen Rindt throughout the race and was on his heels to the end. The Austrian driver won his fifth victory of the season for Lotus, 7/10 of a second in front of the Ferrari leader, but Jacky Ickx was to have his revenge on Rindt's home ground when the Austrian Grand Prix was run at the new "Österreichring". The Lotus engine seized before half distance and the two Ferraris finished ahead, Ickx in front of Regazzoni. It was a great day too for the other cars with V12 engines, Beltoise' Matra and Rodriguez' BRM took high placings.

The outgoing champion, Jackie Stewart, continued to be in trouble with his March. His team manager Ken Tyrrell reacted energetically by putting a new car into production. The new model carried his name but the specialists soon rebaptised it "Tatra", so much did it resemble the Matra that Tyrrell had raced the year before.

The American counter-attack (objective: to throw Volkswagen back into the sea) developed with the presentation of two "small" cars conceived at Detroit: the Chevrolet Vega 2300, on which only the gearbox was imported from Europe, and the Ford Pinto, which uses engines and transmissions produced by the company's European subsidiaries. The experts' reactions were reserved. General Motors and Ford, launching a powerful publicity campaign for these new models, declared themselves ready to produce 400,000 of each a year. Many thought that these "mini-cars" would spell death for the "big American" saloons without actually reducing the share of importers (13.4 per cent) in the American market. Henry Ford II himself acknowledged that an era of automotive history had come to an end.

Ford gave up the idea of building a truck factory in the Soviet Union because of the pressure of American public opinion and was likely to be replaced in Moscow by Daimler-Benz and a consortium of other European firms. Following the treaty signed between the USSR and Germany, a Soviet delegation began negotiations with the management of Daimler-Benz. At the same time the danger of a "boomerang" effect in relations between the West and East European car industries became clear: the USSR launched an export campaign for its Moskvitch 412 (1,480 cc, 80 hp., 94 mph) and Poland was getting ready to sell to western Europe the "Polski-Fiats" built with the help of the Turin firm; both cars were being offered at very competitive prices.

Apparently insensible to these movements, the European manufacturers presented, from August on, a whole series of new models, so true is it that on a high competition level only novelties can maintain sales. Volkswagen developed a new version, the Super Beetle, equipped with MacPherson front suspension and with a lower floor which increased the boot capacity dramatically. Peugeot increased the displacement of its 504 from 1,800 to 2,000 cc and at the same time introduced a 304 "Break" and a 504 diesel. Volvo gave more muscle to its 142 and 144 models. The French subsidiary of Chrysler (Ex-Simca) introduced its 160-180 series: conventional cars equipped with a sophisticated ohc engine. They were greeted by the critics as the first "Poissy Americans".

French manufacturers were particularly prolific and introduced a 1,100 cc-engined Renault 6 and, most interesting of all, the Citroën GS. Already, many foresaw this model, described as a "smaller DS", as the 1970 "Car of the Year".

Meanwhile a batch of 1,000 Japanese cars was being unloaded in Italy, a country from which these products had always been banned. It was the result of a contract arranging for the exchange of Japanese cars for Italian woollen materials and typewriters...

♍ September
Death of a champion

Drama at the Italian Grand Prix: during practice, when he was beginning to brake at the approach of the Parabolica curve, Jochen Rindt lost control of his Lotus, thought by many to be because of a mechanical failure, and the car plunged under the safety barrier. Rindt died, cut down in his prime. The winner of five of the preceding Grands Prix, he was assured of the world title, which was to be given to him posthumously. Controversy then ensued as to how well Lotus racing cars are constructed. Ferrari's superiority was confirmed in the Italian Grand Prix: Regazzoni, in only his fifth Formula 1 Grand Prix race, took on Stewart, Beltoise, Hulme and Stommelen to drive to triumph in an atmosphere of general delirium. Two weeks later SEFAC Ferrari chalked up its third consecutive victory in the Canadian Grand Prix, where Ickx zoomed home in front of the same Regazzoni. The Lotus team had abstained from the race.

Matra, lucky neither in formula nor in endurance racing, "saved" its season by an effortless win in the automobile *Tour de France.*

The economic scene was dominated by the General Motors strike that broke out in the United States. The dispute was to be a long and costly one. G.M., for the first time since 1946, was to show a deficit for the second half of the year. At a time when their factories across the Atlantic had been forced to a halt, General Motors proceeded with a long-expected reconstruction of its overseas division. It was split into three regional units, with a European management which could—following the example already set by Ford and Chrysler—usefully coordinate the activities of the different subsidiaries of the group and give them a Continental strategy. This fundamental reorganization came at precisely the time when Opel was launching the "Manta", symbol of General Motors' efforts to catch up with Ford in Europe. The "Manta", originally designed to be the coupé version of a new series of Opel sedans, the "Asconas", had been hastily modified to reply to the Ford Capri, the success of which had caught Opel short.

Ford was moreover pursuing its policy of European integration by means of the renewal of its Taunus range in Germany, and Cortina range in Great Britain: except for a few sheet-metal differences, Ford was to produce virtually the same car ranges on either side of the Channel.

In the USSR the first Soviet Fiats came off the Togliattigrad production lines at long last. Twenty thousand units were to be produced before the end of the year and sold at triple the price at which equivalent models are offered in western Europe: 5,500 roubles or around £ 3,500 (approximately $ 9,000).

The month finished with an unusual coast-to-coast race in the United States. This "anti-pollution" race was between different prototypes with a low degree of pollution as the objective. Very few lasted the distance and the victory went, ironically, to a model propelled by a good old explosion petrol engine.

October
Salons for talking

The autumn auto shows confirmed that they were essentially meeting-places of economic and promotional professionals rather than technical manifestations: most new cars had already been presented in August and September. Two problems dominated the 1970 exhibitions: inflation and the increase in costs that preoccupied all European and American manufacturers, and the problem of social relations that weighed heavily on the London and Turin Salons. Numerous strikes continued to paralyse the British and Italian industries. Dottore Giovanni Agnelli declared that for Fiat 1970 would be looked back on as the year of lost opportunities. Even the Italian coachbuilders were this time unable to prepare all the innovations they had planned to exhibit at their show. For once Turin was not a "Fiat Salon" and the limelight returned to Opel who made use of the Italian exhibition to unveil its "Asconas", an intermediate range between the Kadetts and the Rekords.

A few minor novelties were, however, presented at the various Salons. In Paris former racing driver Guy Ligier launched his JS2 and announced a limited production plan. The coachbuilder Heuliez introduced a prototype based on the chassis of the Porsche 914. Renault launched a "Break" version of the "12". Vauxhall exhibited its new Vivas—disappointing—and Rover a face-lifted 2000 TC and 3500. In the coachwork department, Pininfarina unveiled a much-contested version of the Mercedes 600. But the most surprising car was not at the Salon: the Mercedes Laudaulet was exhibited only by the French importer of the marque. It was a "600" with special coachwork and luxury fittings, more than 20 ft. long. Its top speed is more than 125 mph and its price about £ 20,000 (approximately $ 50,000). This super-luxury model is already owned by the Pope and Mao Tse Tung—one each, that is!

In London, where last-minute novelties were equally rare, it was the "1750" version of the Austin Maxi that held attention. Displacement was increased by lengthening the stroke. The gain was 10 hp and it was felt mostly in the acceleration: the first version of the car was very unresponsive but it now accelerated from 0 to 60 mph in 15.5 seconds, an improvement of 2.5 seconds. It was still limited, however, to a top speed of 90 mph. British Leyland, plagued with work stoppages that affected both its suppliers and its own workshops, nevertheless managed to develop its integration of European distribution networks, measures preparing for the entry of Britain into the Common Market, etc. A surprise in the area of sport: a Lotus victory in the United States Grand Prix by Brazilian newcomer Emerson Fittipaldi (23), who had taken the place left vacant in the Chapman team by Jochen Rindt. But the season was to end with a new Ferrari double at the Mexican Grand Prix: Jacky Ickx drove to victory in front of Clay Regazzoni. The Belgian and the Swiss took second and third places in the Drivers' World Championship, behind the unfortunate Rindt, the first posthumous World Champion. It looked like 1971 would be a great year for Ferrari across the board: at Zeltweg, in the last race of the international manufacturers championship, a new and lighter Ferrari 512 led the pack before being stopped by a short-circuit in the alternator. At Bonneville Salt Flats, the record chase was resumed after an interval of five years. Gary Gabelich, a former astronaut candidate and dragster champion, for the first time went beyond the land speed of 622 mph at the wheel of the "Blue Flame", bettering the former record of Craig Breedlove (600.63 mph) with the Spirit of America in 1965). Less quick, the President of the French Republic, M. Georges Pompidou, inaugurated the completed Lille-Marseille *autoroute* driving his own car at a hundred miles an hour. The motorway is over 600 miles long with only one traffic light, south of Lyons, which was to be cancelled before the end of the year.

♏ ♐ November and December
End of overheating

The automobile industry drew up its balance sheets. Great Britain and Italy have marked time. Detroit has suffered from the long strike at General Motors and from the competition driven home from importers. Inflation was added to the other known causes to give priority to small and medium cars over the usual "living rooms on wheels" produced in the United States. The future was filled with more uncertainties by stronger government pressure on the industry. After giving priority to safety, Washington was now worrying about environment and pollution.

European manufacturers did not escape these pressures. The strongest firms seemed capable of meeting the official requirements in the prescribed time. But one wondered about the fate of the weakest.

On an economic level, the year was good for French and German manufacturers. The former took advantage of the effects of the devaluation of the franc and beat all their export records, in spite of a home market depressed by credit restrictions. The German manufacturers also reinforced their positions. French and Germans benefited notably from the production delays at Fiat, whose position in Italy was shaken—perhaps lastingly—by foreign manufacturers. But at the end of this year it was to be feared that the rhythm of expansion in the French and German industries would slow down in the future. It seemed, indeed, evident that Europe was going to emerge from the period of economic overheating it had known for several years. Competition was to become even more intense, to the profit of the best-structured groups. And the market was calling more and more for pleasant-looking and relatively low-priced cars rather than technically sophisticated vehicles. From all points of view the European automobile industry seemed to be going towards a growing "Americanization". The year 1970, which according to Henry Ford II marked "the end of an era", would seem to be the end of the golden age of the automobile.

Brockbank

6800

1904 Riley tricar with passenger somewhat hazardously located in front of the driver.

Riley was a grand old name

by Dennis May

Few British cars have done more than Riley to reinforce the credo of Scots economist John Stuart Mill that "all good things that exist are the fruits of originality". During a total life-span of seventy-one years, the genius of this enterprising *marque* was, for about its first four decades, richly innovative. True, the "firsts" commonly attributed to Riley weren't all classifiable as invention in the pure and unqualified sense; but at the lowest estimate they gave a practical and economically successful twist to ideas which other and more timid rivals had failed to exploit effectively.

The first Riley car ever built boasted a mechanically operated inlet valve at a date—1898—when the great majority of the world's designers were relying on piston suction rather than cam action for this vital function. Thus at one stroke a crippling impediment to rpm was eliminated.

It's a matter of debate among automobile historians whether the detachable wire wheel designed by Percy Riley, the family's engineering mastermind, and standardised on the 9 hp Riley in 1907, was first in its field. But certainly it scored a commercial success that was the envy of such competitors as Rudge and Sankey. Demand for the Riley wheel became almost world-wide, and no fewer than 183 makes paid for the privilege of using it; these included Rolls-Royce and Napier in Britain, Pierce-Arrow in the US, Benz, Mercedes, Renault, Panhard, Hispano-Suiza and Spyker in continental Europe.

In 1919 the first Riley model launched after World War one bristled with novelties, ranging from adjustability for the fore/aft position of the front seats *and* steering-column rake to turbo-cooled brakes with automatic take-up. At Olympia, London, in 1926, the sensational Riley Nine stood the Motor Show on its ear. Designed absolutely from scratch, its four-cylinder engine marked an epoch by bringing the race-proven advantages of the hemispherical combustion chamber within reach of prospective buyers of small, medium-priced family cars for the first time. The Nine also pioneered a form of rubber cushioned engine mounting no less than seven years before Plymouth in America launched its "Floating Power" system amid deafening explosions of publicity. The way the Plymouth admen told it—they'd probably never even heard of Riley—the interposition of rubber between an engine and its ferrous bed was NEW.

The Rileys of the *pur sang* era, although consistently outstanding for workmanship, finish and above-average performance for their class, didn't neglect mundane practicalities. Realising that in that day and age the majority of owner drivers did most if not all of their own maintenance and servicing work, Percy Riley applied his brains to minimising these chores; the result, in 1930, was a system of centrally grouped and easily accessible chassis lubrication nipples, connected to points of wear by enskeinments of pipework. This feature, like so many of the innovations that Mr. Riley pioneered, was subsequently counterfeited by her car makers in Britain and overseas.

The fortunes of the clan Riley, as far as they concern us here, were founded by William Riley Jr. in mid-Victorian times. He succeeded his father as head of the family weaving business at Coventry, in the English Midlands, in 1870, and sired five sons, Victor, Stanley, Allan, Percy and Cecil. With the progressive loss of weaving trade to continental countries where labour was cheaper, William Riley gave his old love the brush-off and bought a stake in the newly thriving bicycle industry. Himself, he would have been well content to devote his whole energies to cycle manufacture, but his sons, as they reached man's estate, saw further into the future and did their damnedest to persuade him to lay his wager on a different runner—the horseless carriage.

His opposition, however, was adamant, so much so that the first-ever Riley car, designed by Percy Riley, had to be built almost clandestinely, behind the old man's back. This one-off exercise, which can be seen in historical perspective as the starting point of a car making programme that would continue (albeit hesitantly at first) until 1969, was the upshot of an order placed by two high-up electrical engineers who were temporarily based on Coventry. Company archives reveal few details of Riley car number one, apart from the fact that its inlet valve (the engine was a "single") was operated mechanically.

But having dipped a toe in the water, so to speak, the Rileys didn't immediately take a headlong plunge into car construction, *per se*. First, for a period of some years, they dickered and compromised, designing and building motorcycles, tricars and quadricycles, none of them in very significant quantities. Finally, in 1902, three of the Riley brothers, Victor, Percy and Allan, raised a loan on their own initiative and formed a separate firm, the Riley Engine Co., to exploit Percy's power-unit designs. This concern had two outlets—father William's Riley Cycle Co. and the Singer company. The two other brothers, Cecil and Stanley, afterwards joined the Riley Engine Co. directorate. Percy Riley's services as designer were shared at this period by his father's firm on the one hand and the engine factory on the other; for the former he created a neat and robust two-speed constant-mesh gearbox for one of the early Riley oddities, a three-wheeled forecar, which gave the passenger the secondary role of buffer to protect the driver in the event of head-on collisions.

The first authentic Riley automobiles (as distinct from motor tricycles and quadricycles) to be produced *de serie*, appeared in 1905 and were powered by V-twin engines driving the rear wheels via single roller chains and three-speed gearboxes. It was on these 9 hp machines, two years after their debut, that Riley, for the first time anywhere in the world, standardised detachable road wheels. At a date when punctures were among the motorist's commonest ordeals, this facility gave automobilism an entirely new appeal for thousands of would-be recruits who'd been deterred by the dirty and difficult job of repairing flats with the tyre *in situ*.

Having demonstrated on their own wares the unarguable benefits of the detachable wheel, the Rileys were soon barraged with enquiries from independent car manufacturers throughout the

Left : The oval radiator'd Riley 12-18 had a twin cylinder engine and spanned the period 1911 to '13. Above : A V-twin engine and a radiator not unlike a Rolls-Royce's distinguished the 1907 Nine. Above right : The first-ever Riley, built during 1896/98, pioneered the mechanically operated inlet valve. Right : Another view (uninhabited) of the 1904 Riley tricar—a regular participant in the famous London-Brighton Run for veteran cars. 136-138

Far left : The history-making Riley Nine Monaco sedan, launched 1926. Left : Stelvio sedan of the early 'thirties, with 1622 cc hemispherical-headed 6-cylinder engine. Above left : Ultra-low Brooklands Riley, circa 1928 ; wire wheels were stud-fixed. Above : A consultant designer, Harry Rush, created this side-valve crossflow-ported 10.8 Riley in 1919. Below : A contemporary Riley Nine is timed in a test during the Bognor Trial of 1929.

automotive world (naturally the device was fully patented). This flattering show of interest nourished William Riley's optimism to the point where he personally was in favour of abandoning all other projects and staking the family's entire resources on the detachable wheel. Second-generation counsels prevailed, however, and the kinsmen committed themselves irrevocably to automobile manufacture, which was to run parallel with the wheel enterprise.

V-type engines were the common denominator shared by most of the Riley cars born in the make's formative phase. But whereas the 9 hp model recalled above had its cylinders fore/aft and its crankshaft set transversely, the later 12-18 and 10 hp lines reversed this configuration; also, they forsook chain transmission and used a cardan shaft instead. All three models were water-cooled V-twins with side valves, displacements being just over a litre for the Nine and approximately twice that for the 12-18; significantly, in view of much later trends in engine dimensioning, the intermediate-sized Ten engine was "square", bore and stroke both measuring 96 mm. Also presaging a fashion that was forseeable to few engineers of the Riley brothers' generation, the Nine featured a tubular frame with duplicated longitudinals.

These three Rileys, marketed concurrently, ran the whole gamut of body styles, from a lofty landaulette version of the 12-18 to a rakish two-seater edition of the Nine, known as the Speed Model. In hillclimbs and such dour tests of endurance and reliability as the Scottish Trials, the Rileys of the day were consistently to the forefront. Victor Riley himself was among the *marque's* outstanding competition drivers. As early as 1911, incidentally, the 12-18 Riley sported a refinement that most rival makes didn't adopt until years later—a carburetter intake silencer. In 1912 the Riley Cycle Co. died a voluntary death and a new firm with the title of Riley (Coventry) Ltd. succeeded to its assets and goodwill.

The bugbears which Ford currently abbreviate to NVH (noise, vibration, harshness), were beginning, in the early years of George V's reign, to exert a stiffening sales resistance. To exploit the new demand for quieter, smoother motoring, the Rileys turned over a whole new leaf, designwise, for 1913, ditching their range of twin-cylinder cars and announcing the first in-line fours in the companies' history. These were of two calibres, of which the larger, rated at 17 hp and with 86 × 127 mm cylinders (2,951 cc), made its bow first. The other was a 63 × 88 mm Ten, designed by Stanley Riley (the Seventeen sprang from Percy's prolific drawing board). Rather confusingly, the Ten powerplant was a product of yet another firm, independent but also founded and overlorded by a family member: Victor Riley's Nero Engine Co.

It had always been a Percy Riley tenet that a quiet transmission was among the greatest blessings of automobilism, and his 17 hp model translated this admirable theory into practice. The result was a four-speed gearbox with its helical-toothed top and third gears in constant mesh. Thus, from the noise point of view, third was indistinguishable from direct drive. Other notable features of the 3-litre Seventeen were torque-tube transmission with the shaft underslung to minimise overall chassis height,

Above : A derivative of the Brooklands Nine spins on a corner during a late-'twenties road race. Top right : 1933 Lincock hard-top coupé, powered by twincam Nine engine. Mid-right : Open sports 2-seater March Special Riley, with prettily flared mudguards and deep door cutaways. Bottom right : The fast MPH Riley offered three engine-size options in '34. Below : Amphibious WD model of 1933 was developed for African exploration. Bottom : This Riley six finished second overall at Le Mans in 1934—highest placement ever by a 1˙5-litre car. Another Riley was third.

worm type final drive, and simultaneous operation of the rear-wheel and transmission brakes by foot pedal.

In one respect particularly, the Seventeen's side-valve engine took a spectacular leap forward, for the cranskhaft, which incidentally was hollow, ran in five main bearings, anticipating a usage that many makers of four-cylinder engines were to acclaim as a startling advance in the mid-sixties. Visually, the appeal of this very clean and uncluttered engine was enhanced by cross-flow porting, with the carburetter on one side and the exhaust manifold on the opposite face of the detachable cylinder block. Like the V-twins that they had superseded, the 17 and second-generation 10 hp. Rileys were distinguished by a round radiator shell fronting an almost barrel shaped bonnet. Wheelbase and track of the Seventeen were 124 × 57 inches, the Ten's being 96 × 48 inches.

Due to the intervention of the first World War, these two Riley models had a shorter lifespan than their technical merit and practical excellence had seemed to promise. It is one of war's few redeeming features that it accelerates technological progress and, by the time the Armistice was signed, both the extant Rileys could be regarded as obsolete. Neither of the Riley family's creative engineers, Percy or Stanley, being immediately available for such work, the company made a break with tradition and chartered an outsider, a gifted operator by the name of Harry Rush, to design its first postwar offering.

This was an all-new voiturette officially rated at 10.8. hp under the British fiscal system but catalogued as the Eleven. Points in common with the immediate pre-war Rileys were four in-line cylinders with side valves, cross-flow porting and four-speed transmission. It was on the Eleven that, as mentioned above, Riley pioneered self-adjusting turbo-cooled brakes in the year 1919, plus fore/aft adjustment for the front seats of four-seater types and provision for varying steering column rake. The turbo-cooling device took the form of a ring of cup-like cowls, attached to the rear brake drums, which forced air into the brakes and out through orifices breached in the back plates; magnitude of the draught was of course proportional to road speed.

Rush, like Percy Riley, was much concerned with saving the owner-driver avoidable labour in the garage. To this end he used self-lubricating bushes at as many chassis points as possible, e.g., clutch pedal and hand brake pivots, etc. Only six grease nipples, requiring manual gunning once every six months, were tolerated. The Eleven's engine capacity—65.8 × 110 mm = 1,498 cc—slotted the car neatly into the 1.5-litre class, in which, as we shall see, several of its lineal descendants were to make racing and other competition history.

Again in the Percy Riley manner, Harry Rush was not the man to compromise on the quality of his materials in efforts to keep prices down. As Dr. A. T. Birmingham, the *marque's* leading historian, reminds us in his invaluable book, *Riley*, such items as road springs, propeller shafts and stub axles were made from 50/65-ton chrome vanadium steel, at a time when the majority of Riley's rivals were making-do with 28/30-ton stuff. His car, which broke new styling ground by abandoning a circular radiator (its nose was V-shaped and carried the diamond pattern Riley badge that the make would retain and cherish until its dying day), was the first-ever Riley to use semi-elliptic springs all round. Like so many of its contemporaries, the Riley company erred, if it did err, on the side of over-multiplication of body styles and types. These, counting variants that were added as the Eleven's production life progressed, included a four-door touring car, the so-called All-season tourer with four seats and two doors (this was catalogued in two separately priced editions), a cabriolet, a touring two-seater, a coupé, sports models in two- and four-seat versions, and a rig known as the Coach. In relation to the total build of Elevens, this, in hindsight, seems a ridiculous excess of diversification, but it nevertheless typified the mania for gap plugging which, at that time, had the British car industry in thrall.

A standout for looks among the many sub-types was the sports four-seater, panelled in polished aluminium. This car was normally fitted with bright red fenders, or "wings" in English terminology, and consequently became known as the Redwing. In 1924, a short-wheelbase Redwing, intended for competitions and lighter than standard, was added to the range. While Riley's heyday in racing and sporting events generally was yet to come, the Eleven in several of its guises racked up an impressive bag of competition successes, notably at Brooklands track and in the English trials that were then enjoying classic status—the Exeter, the Land's End, the Edinburgh and others. It was at a supper given for Riley drivers during the 1925 Edinburgh event that the Riley Motor Club was formed—with an initial intake of twenty-one. In the course of time this was to become the world's largest one-make motor club, with around 1,700 members.

If we discount the declining years of the Riley, when it was a mere chattel of, successively, the British Motor Corporation and British Leyland, and lost all pretensions to the individuality that had made it great, the history of the *marque* falls into two chapters. The first ended and the second began in 1926, the demarcation line being drawn by Percy Riley—with help from brother Stanley—when he presented the motoring world with his ever memorable Nine. The heart of a car is its engine, and Percy's *magnum opus* of 1926 established the norm for the top end of every Riley power unit built during the next thirty-one years.

The combination of a hemispherical cylinder head and steeply inclined valves was, of course, no new thing in 1926. It had, I believe, originated in 1904 on a Belgian car called the Pipe, while the elaboration of the concept by the use of dual overhead camshafts dated from 1912 and the Grand Prix Peugeots designed by the great Henry. Nearly all the high-performance motorcycles of the early twenties, too, employed hemi heads and inclined valves. But it was left to Percy Riley to introduce this formula for better respiration on a relatively inexpensive family car. And Mr. Riley sought the best of both worlds—the good breathing and efficient combustion associated with the race-bred head shape, minus the complication and resultingly high cost of camshafts mounted on the head rather than in the cylinder block. Fundamental to Percy Riley's masterpiece, then, was its hemispherical combustion chambers and rocker-actuated valves forming an

Famous shot of Fred Dixon's Riley leaving the road in the 1932 Tourist Trophy Race. Fred was tired after the customary all-night preparation, and nodded-off. In the top picture he switches-off the ignition before the landing!

Top left: Mrs Kay Petre with supercharged Riley six at Shelsley Walsh hillclimb. Left: 1936 Riley Kestrel sedan, a smart fastback. Below: 1935 Imp-Nine-engined cousin of the more powerful MPH. Two lower pictures: With the exception of No. 2, an Austin these are all Freddy Dixon-owned racing Rileys at Brooklands.

included angle of 90 degrees. The porting, reiterating a note that even the side-valve Rileys of yesteryear had struck, was of cross-flow type, with the intake and exhaust manifolds on opposing sides of the block.

Nines of all ohv vintages had plain-bearing crankshafts supported only at their ends, but whereas the cylinder block was detachable from the crankcase on the prototype batch, production examples combined these main units in a single casting. There were two camshafts, each with two splash-lubricated bearings, mounted high on opposite sides of the block, thus allowing the pushrods to be kept short and light. As an antidote to NVH, valve train loading was evened-out by fitting a "neutral" four-lobed cam at the midpoint of each camshaft, where it worked against a springloaded plunger. Early Nines had a single carburetter feeding forward into the tail of the manifold; later ones, using either one or two carburetters, depending on the engine's designed state of tune, had the gasworks more conventionally positioned at right-angles to the car's north/south axis, thereby shortening the induction tracts.

The cushioned engine mounting, briefly alluded to already, took the form of a rubber bushed bar that passed through a tunnel in the front of the crankcase, projecting at either side and with its ends seated on the chassis side members.

In the transmission department the Nine provided one of many examples of Riley's

weakness for technical vacillation. The 17 hp model of 1913 *et seq*, for instance, had featured torque-tube drive, this being abandoned by Harry Rush on his Eleven in 1919 in favour of the Hotchkiss open-shaft system; but now, on his Nine, Percy Riley re-embraced the torque tube. In the gearbox area again, students of design with long memories saw evidence of a similar double-switch: the Seventeen, you'll remember, had had what was known as a silent-third box. This vanished (temporarily) when Rush's smaller Riley took the stage in '19... only to reappear in a modified form on the Nine of 1926.

So far as I know, Percy Riley, unlike some of his brethren, never raced or indulged in competition activity personally, and indeed he was said to be out of sympathy with the sporting side of motoring. This seems to be borne out by the fact that the original Nine, in spite of its obvious potentiality for high performance, was catalogued as a sedan—the Monaco—and not as a fun car.

But the idea of coaxing more horsepower out of Percy Riley's intriguing twin-cam engine and building a far-out sports car around it immediately occurred to several well-qualified people without direct Riley affiliations. Among these was J. G. Parry Thomas, who had already broken the Land Speed Record three times and was preparing for a fourth attack on it. Thomas, the Welsh Wizard as he was called, was associated with the well known Brooklands firm of Thomson and Taylor Ltd., and also with Reid-Railton, who was later to design a whole string of Land Speed Record giants. This consortium, with the approval and support of the Riley company, evolved the hyper-sporting Brooklands Model in the winter of 1926/27, but before the job was finished Thomas unfortunately was killed while attempting his fourth Land Speed Record. On completion, the Brooklands Riley appropriately made its debut at Brooklands, where, driven by Railton in a race only about 6.5 miles long, it won by the sensational margin of one mile. The only flying-start lap of the 2.75-mile circuit that this event entailed was turned at an average of 91.37 mph.

The Brooklands Model, starting point in a process of evolution that yielded all the subsequent racing and high performance Rileys, developed about 50 bhp at 5,000 rpm, compared with the standard Monaco's 34 at 4,000. The chassis, lopped from 107 to 91 inches and narrowed at the rear, carried an ultra-light two-place body which was so low that the seated driver could easily touch the ground with the palm of his hand. To exploit the power bonus and drastic reductions in car weight and frontal area, the overall gearing was raised. Engine tuning measures included carburetter duplication, a raise in compression ratio and oil pressure and the use of special camshafts and a four-branch exhaust manifold. For many years, including a considerable time after its production had ceased, the Brooklands Riley in normal and modified forms won countless races and became the world's busiest record breaker in international Class G (1,100 cc). The firm also catalogued sporting Nines with more habitable bodies and in less advanced states of tune.

It wasn't only mechanically that the Monaco sedan marked an epoch. Its body styling too was an eye-opener. In Britain, at least, it pioneered what became known as the three-box shape, with a trunk that was designed into and harmonised with the general architecture. The original Monaco also set a fashion, albeit a bad one, for an exaggeratedly high beltline, resulting in slot-like side windows.

The 1926 London Motor Show, at which the Monaco Nine had its premiere, supplied yet another instance of the makers hedging their bets. Apparently not confident that the Nine would blow all opposition into the bushes (which it certainly did) Riley also exhibited a dressed-up version of an earlier model that the Nine was to render obsolete from the moment that the public viewed the two cars side by side. This was the 11-40 sports job (65.8 × 110 mm = 1,496 cc, same as Rush's old side-valve Eleven) with vertical ohv operated by normal length pushrods and a supercharger as standard equipment. The 11-40, which predictably never achieved any great fame, was the first British sports car to use a blower, which was of Riley design.

The development of the twin-cam Nine engine over the years makes too long a story to relate in any detail here; but it is worth recalling that the Nines entered for the 1931 Tourist Trophy race were fitted with four carburetters, one to each intake port. Also in 1931, carburetter quadruplication in a modified form was used by independent George Eyston on the 1,100 cc Riley with which he broke the Class G record for one hour at 108 mph. Wrongly, pioneership of the one-carb-per-port system on racing Rileys is sometimes credited to another of the *marque's* famous independent speedmen, Freddy Dixon. What *he* did, later in the thirties, was to improve on an already extant technique.

The first 6-cylinder Riley featuring the celebrated PR (Percy Riley) head made its bow late in 1928, fitted to a roomy family car with, again, no special claims to performance. The addition of two extra cylinders with the same bore and stroke as the Nine gave the six a displacement of 1,633 cc but, probably on account of asthmatical breathing resulting from poor inlet manifold design, it was certainly no fire-eater. Unlike the Nine, it had a three bearing crankshaft. Later, a Brooklands Six, naturally bigger in all main dimensions (track, wheelbase, etc.) than the corresponding four, but not unlike it in its taper-tailed shape, was added to the range.

Victor Riley, managing director of Riley (Coventry) Ltd. over a long and mostly fruitful period, laboured under the delusion that his company's sixes were inherently incapable of a competitive performance. In this he was proved doubly wrong. In 1934, ERA used drastically modified and supercharged derivatives of the Riley six as the basis for their brilliantly successful racing cars, in sizes ranging from 1,100 cc to 2-litres. Later, when the brainy and resourceful Fred Dixon proposed using unsupercharged but multi-carburetted Riley six engines for racing and record breaking, Victor Riley gave vent to his surprise and incredulity by making Dixon a present of a batch of these powerplants and a stockpile of appropriate spare parts. The results that this brash independent gained with his free gift, mostly at Brooklands, proved that a car manufacturer doesn't necessarily know better than a perspicacious outsider in such matters. About the Nines, however, nobody, inside or outside of the factory at Coleshill, Coventry, had the slightest doubts. And they were right. Commercially, they were consistently successful for over a decade. Technically, they were a phenomenon, no less. The highest output ever recorded by a Nine engine, supercharged at high pressure and admittedly modified almost beyond recognition by the introduction of a centre main bearing, was 183 bhp at 7,400 rpm (the car to which it was fitted was the Appleton Special, built and developed for a rich private owner, John Appleton).

The basic design of the Nine engine is sometimes attributed to a non-Riley man, Hugh Rose, rather than to Percy Riley. This is incorrect, though some confusion is understandable. In 1934 there were disagreements on technical matters between members of the firm's own design team. It had, however, been decided—notwithstanding the magnificent performance of the company' small sixes in that year's Le Mans, which we will come to later—that four was the optimum number of cylinders for engines *circa* 1½-litres. Victor Riley therefore chartered Rose, instructing him to base his new blueprint—so far as the engine was concerned—on Percy Riley's time-tested layout. This he did, retaining such basic features as the two high camshafts, 90-degree valves and hemispherical heads. Many years later, when he was resident designer to Lea-Francis, Hugh Rose adopted a closely similar top-end arrangement for this maker's engine. Designated the 12/4, the four-cylinder power unit resulting from the Riley/Rose marriage of minds had the classic bore and stroke measurements of 69 × 100 mm (1,496 cc), a three-bearing crankshaft and an unusual hotspotting system with a crosswise port cored right through the cylinder block to carry warmth from the efflux to the ingoing charge. The rocker shafts, unlike the Nine's, were mounted directly in the head instead of in separate rocker boxes.

This fine engine was fitted, *inter alia*, to a very pretty open tourer, the Lynx, and two equally attractive sedans, the Kestrel and Falcon. It later powered the Kestrel Sprite sports two-seater of the late inter-wars period and, post-war, carried over as propellent for the otherwise drastically redesigned 1½-litre sedan with which Riley made their first attack on the peacetime market.

Upper left: First post-World War II/Riley was the shapely 1.5-litre saloon with ifs. Botton left: Similar car in furious action during 1955 Monte Carlo Rally in the hands of Lyndon Simms.

In the general configuration of the cars, as well as in strictly engineering matters, yesteryear's Rileys reflected the makers' double-think tendency. At one stage in the thirties they made a big publicity outcry about the advantages of inter-axle seating, achieved, of course (at some sacrifice in back-seat legroom) by moving the rear passengers forward in relation to the axles. Less than two years later, however, they reversed this process, quietly forgetting the merits of within-the-wheelbase accommodation but strongly pointing up the newfound gain in leg and kneeroom...

Backtracking to the Nine in its many sporting and racing forms, this car had a brilliant Tourist Trophy career, filling the top three Class G places in the 1929 T.T., then winning outright at record speed three years later. Even this performance was surpassed at Le Mans in 1934, though, when six Rileys started and six finished—a survival rate that has seldom been equalled by so large a Le Mans contingent; four of these were Nines, and they occupied fifth, sixth, twelfth and thirteenth positions. The two remaining Rileys, both 1½-litre sixes, were, incredibly, second and third overall.

Last descendant of the Brooklands Nine was the Imp sports two-seater, launched in 1934 and characterised by strikingly flared mudguards. Of the same vintage, and similar in its distinctive styling, was the larger MPH model, with optional 1,458 and 1,633 cc six-cylinder engines.

Victor Riley, who had succeeded his father as head of the company when the latter died in the early twenties, was usually credited with a shrewd business sense. If, as one supposes, he dictated Riley's engineering policy, this claim is open to doubt, for the Coleshill firm was forever changing course designwise. There was never any lack of ideas but pursuing them to a logical conclusion seemed to be foreign to Riley thinking. Transmissions alone (apart from the systems already mentioned) illustrate the point. As early as 1932/3 the company experimented with the Salerni fully automatic transmission, an Italian invention; in theory it became a production reality, but although it was catalogued, no cars fitted with it were ever delivered. About two years later, Rileys using the new 12/4 engine offered a choice between, on the one hand, a centrifugal clutch in conjunction with a preselector gearbox and, on the other, an all-synchromesh box harnessed to a freewheel. Then, in 1937, yet another combination was listed: freewheel and automatic overdrive by Borg-Warner.

In an advertisement of the late thirties, Victor Riley confessed: "We make far too many models, of course, but then we have a pretty fertile design department." Among other examples of its fertility, in 1936, it made a minor sensation with a four-camshaft V8, essentially two normal Riley blocks set at 90 degrees on a common crankcase. The car that it powered, the Autovia, was Riley in everything but name, being built and marketed by a putatively separate company under Victor Riley's managing directorship. Commercially, the Autovia never really got off the ground.

Jokers used to say that that Riley listed more models than it built cars, and indeed one's head spins at the proliferation of type names and symbols. Going back no further into history than 1926, there was the 11-40, the Monaco, the Brooklands Riley in four- and six-cylinders calibres, the San Remo, the Lulworth, Deauville, Light Six, Stelvio, Sportsman's Coupé, Alpine, W.D., Plus Ultra, Gamecock, Overseas Nine, 12/6, 14/6, Ascot, March Special, Trinity, Falcon, Lincock, Lynx, Kestrel, Kestrel Sprite, Mentone, Winchester, Charlesworth, Edinburgh, Imp, MPH, Colonial Tourer, 12/4, Merlin, Adelphi, Continental, Big Four, Blue Sreak, Victor, Pathfinder... One-Point-Five, 4/Seventy-two and others that no doubt I've overlooked.

Victor Riley's admission that "we make far too many models" was uttered light heartedly, at a time when business was still brisk and he and his co-directors could afford light hearts. But there is little doubt that over-diversification was eventually responsible, at least in part, for the decline of the Riley fortunes. V.R. and his associates saw the red light, but not until it was too late. In 1937 the range was narrowed to two chassis–the Rose-begotten 12/4 and a new 2½-litre known as the Big Four—the former offering a choice of five body styles, the latter two. Then the blow fell. Trade, which had been on the downgrade for some time, slumped alarmingly. Coming to the rescue of what he perceived to be a still viable operation, Lord Nuffield purchased it out of his own personal fortune, then resold it advantageously to Morris Motors Ltd., of which he was already the head.

The two immediate pre-war engines survived, little else did, in Riley's first post-war offerings—outstandingly roadable 1½ and 2½-litre sedans with chassis featuring rack and pinion steering and one of the best independent front suspension systems of its day. The smaller of these cars, which has since acquired the status of a collector's piece, enjoyed a nine-year production run; the larger underwent a gradual metamorphosis until, under the name Pathfinder, it was all-but indistinguishable from its Nuffield Group stablemate, the Wolseley. When it was finally given a Wolseley engine to cement the bond, its power output dropped by 9 bhp inspite of the acquirement of two extra cylinders and a 200 cc displacement growth. Riley and Rationalisation, unaccustomed bedfellows, were in a mutual embrace at last, albeit it was to prove a fatal one. When Austin and the Nuffield Group makes fused to form the British Motor Corporation, Riley was part of the integration. And when BMC in its turn was swallowed up in the British Leyland take-over of 1968, Riley once again perforcedly tagged along—for the last time. The Rileys of the irrational yesteryear had given relatively few people a great deal of fun. Rationalised in the manner of the sixties, they became stereotyped, reliable transportation, and it wasn't enough. On July 9, 1969, British Leyland erased them from the catalogues. The car that had been "As old as the industry, as modern as the hour", in the words of the half-forgotten slogan, was as dead as yesterday's newspaper.

Right: Blue Streak of the late 'thirties features a 2.5 litre 4-cylinder engine. Below: At Montlhery, in 1955, five production BMC cars covered over 100 miles each in one hour. The result of these high-speed reliability tests was all the more remarkable because the weather was about the worst the drivers had experienced on the Montlhery track. This Riley Pathfinder, driven by Bob Porter, covered 103.03 miles in the hour.

Cars of the Year

by Douglas Armstrong

In spite, or perhaps because of, huge financial losses from many manufacturers in the capitalist world, 1970 was an automotive year of movement and vitality. There was a spate of new and modified models, and in spite of widespread industrial unrest the introduction of more sporting coupés underlined the ever-rising living standards in most manufacturing countries. Under the heading of performance and prestige came the Alfa-Romeo Montreal, Citroen SM, Triumph Stag, AMC AMX/3, de Tomaso Pantera, and the Monteverdi "hai" 450SS—expensive offerings from Italy, France, Britain, the United States of America, and Switzerland.

To bring the buyer of less affluence into the sporting sector, Opel introduced their Manta—GM's answer to Ford's highly successful Capri. Ford (of Germany) replied with their handsome Taunus coupé whilst continuing with production of the leaner, less-commodious Capri which was on the way to a production figure of half-a-million—on a basis of world-wide manufacture.

In north America too the smaller coupé was big news with both Ford and General Motors introducing "sub-compacts", mainly to stem the flow of incoming VW Beetles, but also indicating they knew the score if called upon to abandon one day the vast, traditional American Automobile. The American Motors Corporation also introduced a new sub-compact, the Gremlin, and got in early in the year because of the fact they used their existing 3.8 (and 4.2) litre in-line six-cylinder engine and running gear from the Hornet, but the lack of attractive lines and visibility did not make it a favourite with the American buying public.

The automotive year was also notable for a general continuance of the return of the engine to the classic position, and in most cases, with front wheel drive. Two new Citroens would of course be expected to have both, but a new VW (née NSU) with both front (water-cooled) engine and front-drive was an event indeed. The new European Fords retained their front engine position, but Cologne abandoned their front-drive models—even when they had got to the stage of sound sales.

Another very apparent trend was the non-spread of independent rear suspension amongst volume production cars. Even an expensive specialist machine like the Alfa-Romeo Montreal retained a live rear axle, although like so many Alfas of the past it used positive location for accurate steering geometry and good handling. The new Hillman Avenger (Sunbeam 1250/1500 in foreign markets) used a live rear axle with a "four-link" locating system, as did its close relative the French Chrysler 160/180. General Motors' Opel Manta and Ascona also utilised a live axle/link-location rear-end, and as expected, the US Ford Pinto and the GM Vega both used live rear axles, the latter also adopting four-link location.

Renault dropped the rear-engined "Gordini 8", and substituted a front-drive "Gordini 12" (with 1,565 cc TS-derived engine), leaving only one basic rear-engine/rear-drive model in a range of cars which was exclusively so only a few years ago. Dottore Agnelli announced that the Fiat 127 would be introduced early in 1971. It is known that the new model will be a front-drive, front-engine design, and that it will replace the 850 rear-engined model. It was also automotive knowledge in 1970 that Alfa-Romeo's new small, volume-production model, due to be manufactured in vast new works in the south of Italy, was to be front wheel drive.

But it wasn't just a year of technical moves. It was a year of ever-stiffening safety and anti-emission requirements from the US market, of efforts to standardise these requirements, of even greater moves towards rationalisation. Rolls-Royce announced they had a new diesel application of the Wankel rotary engine, and at the end of the year an official statement was made to the effect that General Motors had at last signed an agreement with Audi-NSU for the manufacture and marketing of Wankel rotary engines at a cost of about £18m (approximately $43.2m). The payments were to be made by instalments, and the GM-Audi/NSU agreement made the twentieth since Dr Felix Wankel announced his revolutionary power-unit.

The GM move has enormous significance, the US motor industry—indeed the world's motor industry—facing colossal difficulties in respect of the emission laws proposed

◄ *Elegance in fur, and steel. Well-clad lady prepares to enter her Citroen SM and find that three-star restaurant the Duc mentioned to her. With two shapes like those she is unlikely to pay the bill.*

by Washington for 1975 and beyond. If GM have paid out such huge sums of money for a different type of prime mover, it would follow that the vast company sees hope of beating the exhaust gas problems with the Wankel-type unit—even if it hasn't shown-up particularly well until now. Already many 1971 American cars, particularly the larger-engined types, have reduced compression ratios for satisfactory operation on reduced-lead fuels in an attempt to reduce exhaust emission. It has even been proposed that non-leaded fuels be used in future engines to further reduce emission, but inevitably power-outputs per litre will drop and many argue it is a shocking backward step. Charles Kettering undoubtedly made one of the discoveries of the age when he put lead in petrol in the early 'twenties, and in doing so solved the engine "knock" problem, dramatically raised power-outputs and promoted smoother running, as well as saving the motoring public enormous amounts of money. Other ways of beating the emission problem have been proposed by GM President Ed Cole, but his scheme of catalytic after-burners seem to require a greater amont of nickel than the world can supply and even if it could it would be too expensive. As a background to the 1970 emission problems, it seemed that American manufacturers abandoned, at least for the next few years, the possibility of steam cars. Electric "city car" developments also appeared to take a back seat, France adopted a 69 mph maximum speed limit on 9,000 miles of non-motorway roads—something that few ever expected to happen, Germany toyed with the idea of a maximum speed limit, and Britain's new Transport Minister John Peyton decided, after all, to drop the scheme of an 80 mph motorway experiment. Italy remained the last real stronghold of the enthusiastic motorist.

Australia and South Africa

The Australian scene continued to be a war between the American-owned giants, Ford, GM-Holden, and Chrysler, but signs of a British Leyland resurgence were evident when a restyled "1800" was spotted in embryonic form at the tail-end of 1969, and in near-production shape later in 1970. Unlike the British Austin 3-litre which utilises the "1800" unitary structure but is powered by a six-cylinder in-line engine mounted longitudinally and driving the rear wheels, the Australian car uses the basic 1800 structure, but with transverse ohc six-cylinder unit driving the front wheels. The engine is of 2,227 cc, brought about by the "addition" of two cylinders to the four-cylinder ohc 1500 engine. Hydrolastic suspension is retained, as are the servo-assisted 10 in. disc front brakes and rack and pinion steering, but a greatly extended luggage boot increases the overall length to 14 ft. 6 in. (compared to the 1800's 13 ft. 10½ in.). The plastic grille and twin rectangular headlights make for a neat front-end, and the tail treatment is pleasing. The facia is completely restyled, and it is expected the Australian car will be sold in "Tasman" (a less-expensive version) and "Kimberley" forms. The latter model will have twin carburetters, and is expected to sell at around A$3,100 (about £1,500 or $6,000). Already it has been dubbed "BL's Holden-beater".

Late in 1969, GM-Holden introduced a six-cylinder version of the sporty "Torana" with various power and transmission options for 1970, and early in the year Ford-Australia got the three-litre Ford Capri into production.

First of the true 1970 "Australians" however was Chrysler-Australia's introduction of the VG Valiant early in the year. The car used a modified body from the previous VF Valiant, but the four-litre "Hemi 245" six-cylinder (with pushrod overhead valves) was an all-Australian development, and was claimed to be "the most advanced six-cylinder power plant made anywhere in the world". Quite a claim.

It would seem that in Australia there is always a new Holden around the corner, but when the HG model made its appearance in the middle of 1970, it was virtually unchanged from the HT, except for minor grille changes and a new three-speed Trimatic automatic transmission. It was available with in-line six-cylinder or V8 engines, but its lack of novelty was perhaps explained by the fact that the rumoured Holden HQ for 1971 was due to have radically-changed styling, uprated engines, and revised styling.

End-of-1970 news was that GM-Holden would produce in 1971 an all-new Torana GTR-X—"Australia's first real GT coupé". The GTR-X will be based on the Opel GT coupé, a neat two-door model with flip-up headlights, and it is expected the power-unit will be a 160 hp edition of the three-litre Holden in-line "six". It should be good for more than 125 mph, and reflects the growing sophistication of the Australian market.

Ford-Australia's Falcons got a face-lift towards the end of 1970 but the main excitement was a new range of more powerful engines from six to eight-cylinders, and with power-outputs from 130 to 300 hp.

As one Aussie wag put it, "The year 1970 has been one of grilles and gearboxes for the Australian car industry"!

Big story of the 1970 South African motor industry was the Ford Perana—a Capri powered by a FX five-litre Ford V8. Developed by Johannesburg tuning expert and manufacturer Basil Green the prototype proved capable of 143 mph with 0-100 mph figures of 17.4 seconds. Bobby Olthoff dominated South African saloon car racing during 1970 with a hot Perana, and by late summer Green had put the promising car into series production with a 275 hp version of the V8 engine.

South Africa's own car, the GM Ranger, was joined by a new "SS" fastback in 1970. Powered by a 108 hp version of the 2.5-litre Chevrolet-based four-cylinder engine it was lively and exhibited typical GM lines. To confuse the issue, Rambler—built and marketed by Toyota SA, wholly-owned and controlled by South Africans—introduced the Hornet SST, a 100 mph car with 155 hp six-cylinder engine and "Very un-American roadholding". Chrysler standardised power disc front brakes on their 1970 Valiants, and the 383 appeared with "loop" bumpers surrounding head and tail lights. In a 1970 alliance with Mitsubishi, Chrysler also announced a range of five models for South Africa, all powered by the 1,088 cc 62 hp four-cylinder engine. For two months in succession Datsun-Nissan achieved record sales in South Africa. In April 1676 units were sold followed in May by sales amounting to 1801. Peugeot announced they were to set up a new R 700,000 (about £350,000 or $850,000) headquarters on a five-acre site at Isandro near Johannesburg. Renault Africa produced their 10,000th engine in the spring.

France

It was a notable year for France. A new Citroen is always good news, and 1970 saw two new models—front-drive of course—from the Quai André Citroen. Like so many motor industries, the French needed a shot in the arm, for although the year's production had increased some 10 percent (July 1969 to June 1970), it was mainly because of an extra quarter-of-a-million cars being exported. Home market figures revealed a drop of 30,000 cars. Renault, the market leaders with 30 percent, had interesting modifications but no really new models, and Peugeot, No. 2 in the French production table, had upped their 504 from 1.8 to two litres, and there was a new 2,112 cc oil-engined version. Chrysler-France (née Simca) with only 12 percent of the market entered the 1970 lists with the long-awaited four-door saloon models with overhead camshaft engines, and bearing a strong resemblance to the new British Chrysler saloons.

The first new Citroen appeared at the early part of the year, and was one of the stars of the Geneva Salon in March. Undoubtedly the fastest front-drive car ever offered to the buying public, the Maserati-engined "SM" featured a very aerodynamic two-door 2+2 body of modern appearance, yet with more than a suggestion of the 15-year-old "DS". The latter, in 1970, still could not be described as dated. Power-unit of the SM was a 90-degree V6 with twin overhead camshafts (chain-driven) per bank, and designed by Alfieri of Maserati. The engines will be built at Maserati's Bologna factory, itself part of the Citroen empire, the latter in alliance with Fiat.

The 2.7-litre 170 hp (net) engine gives the SM a top speed of around 140 mph, and of course in the Citroen manner there is self-levelling hydraulic all-independent suspension, and a completely new form of power-assisted rack and pinion steering which varies required driver effort according to cruising speed. With a home price of around £3,000 (about $7,300) it won't be everyone's car, but Citroen's scheme is to make France's first prestige car for years—and such a production sets a high-grade image and sells more of their "ugly ducklings".

Citroen's other new offering in 1970, the one-litre four-door "GS", was, in its class, as advanced as the SM. With a horizontally-opposed four-cylinder air-cooled engine (with a single belt-driven overhead camshaft to each bank), front-drive, self-levelling hydraulic suspension, and unusually commodious bodywork of high aerodynamic efficiency, it was a "family car" of great technical merit. The Citroen engineers had devised cylinder heads of great rigidity to achieve notably quiet running for an air-cooled unit, and the pleasing body shape was remarkable in that it offered really roomy accommodation for four, above-average baggage space, and a streamlining efficiency some 15 percent better than the "DS". The shapely French car in fact measured 13 ft. 6 3/16 in. in length, had a luggage compartment capacity of 16 cub. ft., yet would top 90 mph. The four-wheel disc brakes were power-assisted with double-circuit operation, and it was due to be put into volume production on such a scale as to sell in its country of origin at about £850 (approximately $2100) in *Confort* form—the less-lavish model.

Like the British Chrysler models, the new 160/180 saloons from the Poissy factories near Paris were of simple basic layout, but offering good performance from four-cylinder overhead camshaft engines in 1.6 or 1.8 litre sizes according to model. The same unitary steel body was utilised for all three cars, 160, 160GT, and 180. A reduced-bore engine was used in the least-expensive 160, but when fitted with the 97 hp (DIN) engine of the most-expensive 180 model, it became the 160GT. Smaller engined models featured disc front and drum rear brakes, but 1.8-litre-engined cars had disc brakes all-round. Like the new British Chryslers, the 160/180 range utilised a live rear axle and coil springs with wide radius arms and supplementary links for positive location. The new near-two-litre range offered good value in Common Market countries.

The increase in engine size for Peugeot's famed 504 improved both its power and smoothness. The extra capacity was gained by increasing the bore size of the four-cylinder push-rod ohv engine from 84 to 88 mm, which its 81 mm stroke made the unit even more over-square. Like the earlier 1,796 cc engines, the new ones were available in carburetter form (Solex) or with fuel-injection (Kugelfischer), the output of the latter increasing from 87 to 97 hp (DIN).

Regie Renault, the vast French nationalised network made a production switch when they introduced a pure estate version of the front-drive Renault 12 at the Paris Salon in October. For some years the *Regie* had concentrated, in the main, on "saloon/estates" which offered a choice of many roles and fitted-in well with the French way of life. The Renault 12 "Break" featured an attractively-styled four-door/tailgate estate body, powered by the standard 1,289 cc engine of 54 (DIN) hp, and driving the front wheels through the standard four-speed gearbox. A completely different version for 1970 however was the Renault 12 Gordini with 1,565 cc engine (from the "16") and a power-output in standard form of 113 hp (DIN). The power-unit was known to be highly receptive to special tuning—an output of nearly 150 hp being possible—and that fact plus the standard fitting of a five-speed gearbox made the 12 Gordini a potential favourite with the young *sportifs*. It also meant the end of the rear-engined Renault 8 Gordini.

Another power bonus in the Renault range was a supplementary version of the "6" (normally with 845 cc engine and front-drive) powered by the 1,108 cc unit of the rear-engined "8". With its "saloon/estate" attributes the front-drive model now with 45 hp (DIN) offered the sort of power required in such an all-rounder and made even more appropriate its pet-name of "the Poor Man's 16".

The Renault 16 and 16TL got a new 1,565 cc engine (was 1470cc) but although it developed 12 percent more power than the replaced unit it was fitted with a different cylinder head and carburetter to the high-performance 16TS which is also powered by a 1,565 cc engine. The 16 and 15TL's top speed went up to around 95 mph, and the TS got electric front windows as standard equipment. Since the 16 was introduced in 1965, three-quarters of a million had been manufactured by the end of 1970. The TL and TS also became available with Renault automatic transmission as an optional extra.

Quite the most interesting French car from the small manufacturers was the Ligier JS2, designed by Michel Tetu, and built by Guy Ligier at the Vichy works. Ex-Formula 1 racing driver Ligier names his cars after his old friend Joe Schlesser, killed driving the air-cooled Honda in the French Grand Prix at Rouen in 1968, and his second model features a steel backbone frame, shapely two-door, two-seat glass-fibre GT body, and rear-mounted 2.6-litre German Ford V6. The fuel-injected 165 hp engine is mounted ahead of the rear suspension and is in unit with a five-speed gear-box from the new front-drive Citroen SM. Suspension is independent all-round and there are four-wheel Lockheed disc brakes. Claimed top speed is 150 mph, and French price was expected to be about £3,800 (approximately $9,300). Ligier, also a works contractor of some magnitude, expects to make around a hundred a year.

Germany

West Germany's economic development continued powerfully upwards in 1970, but prices as well as production increased in car factories, mainly brought about by successful wage demands. The first half of 1970 saw car figures up to 995,785, an increase of 3.5 percent over the same period in 1969. Exports rose 3.7 percent, but there was strong revival of domestic turnover. The workers were obviously buying new cars with their fatter wage packets!

The big activity where new models were concerned came from the VW Group, and from General Motors-Opel in 1970. It was more than usually interesting to observe VW "stretching" their ubiquitous and controversial "Beetle" to Super dimensions and increasing power-output to keep it in the sales race, but also to note the entry of another product bearing the VW badge, obviously insurance as against possible ultimate demise of the long-run Beetle. We refer to the VW K70, introduced in the late summer of 1970, and the first-ever water-cooled front-engined VW. It was of course originally the NSU K70, and was to have been launched with that particular badge at the Geneva Salon in 1969, but the take-over talks which had been going-on for some time between VW and NSU suddenly came to a head, went through, and the new front-drive NSU was put on the shelf. Before taking it off the shelf, VW cleaned-up the bodywork slightly, but in launching it as the VW K70 it was little changed. The 1.6-litre four-door saloon is roomy, light and airy, and has a near-100 mph performance. Handling and ride are excellent and it will undoubtedly prove popular in European Common Market countries. No plans exist at the time of writing to export the K70 to the USA, the Beetle still being relied upon to remain the big foreign export. If the 90 hp edition of the K70 does find itself in the USA its 9:1 compression engine wouldn't be at all happy on unleaded fuels.

VW's I302 Super Beetle still looked like a Beetle but was in fact the nearest thing ever to a new Volkswagen. Gone were Dr Porsche's rear swing-axles, and gone too were his front torsion bars. Instead, the front-end sported the celebrated MacPherson struts which had been introduced by Ford almost twenty years ago—and abandoned on their new Cortina and Taunus models for 1970! Rear-end of the Super Beetle was still independent but the swing-axles had gone in favour of the double-jointed axle and semi-trailing arms which had been fitted to semi-automatic Beetles up until then. The new combination transformed the handling (to good) and the MacPherson struts freed forward space to almost double the luggage capacity—and the boot took on a pre-natal look. With a 60 hp (SAE) version of the VW 1600 engine, through-flow ventilation, widened track, and lengthened wheelbase, it looked as though Wolfsburg had done it again—and with a 7.5:1 compression ratio the I302 had no fear of unleaded fuels.

General Motor's two Opel offerings were more closely-related than perhaps the general public realised. The sporty Manta coupé with two basic engines (in Europe) and variations of tune was actually launched first, and it was obvious it was brought to the market place to do something about Ford's equally sporty Capri which had sold in quite indecent numbers since its introduction in early 1969. In the first place however, the Manta was to have been a coupé version of the 1.6-litre Ascona family car (two and four-door sedans and three-door estates) which was in fact introduced a few weeks later. The same base-plate, running gear, and basic ohc engine were used for Manta and Ascona models, but the former became the "family sports car" when the manufacturers realised they had anti-Capri potential "in stock", and Opel's Chuck Jordan restyled the front-end. It was a good effort and Opel expected to make 125,000 in 1971, and to export around 30,000 to the United States where it would sell as Buick's Opel 1900.

The Ascona, like the Manta, had front suspension by coil springs and double wishbones, and a live axle rear-end with coil springs, trailing links and a Panhard rod. Handling on all models was good, as was equipment, and luggage space. The Ascona 16 had the 80 hp 1.6-litre engine as standard (same unit as the standard European Manta), and would better 95 mph. The Manta with 1.9-litre "S" engine was a 102 hp (SAE) car which was good for 110 mph. An interesting exercise which will be worth watching in 1971. The Manta offers a little more luggage space than the Capri, and its lighting equipment is better, but the GM car betrays its family car background by its greater height, but they are only a few points and it's the buying public who will provide the ultimate story.

Ford of Cologne's new Taunus was a revival of an old name but a very new car. It graphically illustrated the "Euro-car" concept in that it was virtually identical in chassis, and running gear to the new British Ford Cortinas, but it used a more angular body. The new engines of 1300 and 1600 cc used belt-driven overhead camshafts and were both reduced-capacity versions of the two-litre Cortina/Pinto engine. For their two-litre Taunus the German factory adhered to the well-proven V6 ohv (pushrod) from the 20 M. There was also a handsome fastback coupé. It was said the top brass from the British and German Ford factories were shown a selection of saloon-body shapes for the new ranges, and they each chose which they thought would be best. It is also said that when Cologne first saw the finished Cortina, they wished they had said yes to it. It would made for even more rationalisation too!

Mercedes-Benz and BMW were quiet in 1970, although the old-established Stuttgart firm unveiled their four-rotor Wankel-engined coupé—more as a one-upmanship demonstration than as a future production basis we fancy. In a world of engulfments and rumours of engulfments, automotive chatter still suggested a VW take-over of BMW, even though they were doing fine. Or because of it!

Great Britain

For Britain 1970 was a year of substantial and record losses for many motor manufacturers, labour disputes, strikes, and wage increases continuing to take priority over production. There was no inactivity in the design, production planning and costing departments however, for new models appeared from Rootes (later to become Chrysler UK), Rover, Triumph, Vauxhall, and Ford amongst the major manufacturers, and a new Marcos was evident from the smaller constructors. Austin-Morris introduced a more attractive version of the controversial Maxi, with an optional 1750 cc engine, and Rolls-Royce, unobtrusive as ever, increased the cubic capacity of their RR-Bentley "saloon" engine from 6.2 to 6.7 litres.

On a basis of chronology, the Hillman Avenger was the 1970 new model leader, appearing in February and illustrating the American-owned company's resolve to present a roomy four-door saloon with simplified production methods , and a "stepped" performance with choice of two engine sizes, 1248 and 1498 cc. Luxury increases were also offered through de Luxe, Super, and Grand Luxe options, and, in the American manner, there was a vast list of equipment variations and permutations. The rear suspension was non-independent but used trailing arms and links for positive location, and the engine, rather surprisingly as it was a brand-new design, adhered to pushrod operation of its overhead valves. The formula seemed a good one however, for sales were brisk until strikes of one sort or another halted the production lines. Chrysler UK ended the year with a 1969/70 loss of nearly £11m (about $27m). The Range Rover from the old-established Warwickshire company was a refreshingly different vehicle. With well-styled cubist bodywork of great roominess (for people, goods, or animals), the vehicle featured permanent four-wheel-drive, a 3½-litre light-alloy V8 engine detuned to operate satisfactorily on low-grade fuels, and in spite of its fantastic cross-country performance and shape would cruise the (Continental) motorways at 90 mph with a reasonably low noise level. With 12 inches ground clearance, self-levelling non-independent suspension (nine-inch movement), two sets of forward and reverse gear ratios, and an instantly-lockable pneumatic differential, it was a car that would appeal to businessmen and fun-pursuers alike. Ventilation had been well designed, but there was provision also for a very advanced air-conditioning system. Just as at home on the Range as outside the Savoy.

An exciting GT car from British Leyland's Triumph Motor Company was the three-litre Stag with 90-degree V8 engine based on the inclined four-cylinder unit the Company had been producing for the Swedish Saab 99 since 1968. The V8 used a longer stroke and a smaller bore than the four-cylinder, but the Stag's power-unit was still very much oversquare. Chain-drive was used for the overhead camshaft actuation (one per cylinder block), and with twin side-draught Stromberg carburetters the engine developed 145 hp (net), besides exhibiting remarkable flexibility and quiet running.

Production costs had been very carefully studied, for the Michelotti-styled Stag used many body pressings from the Triumph 2000 and 2.5PI saloon models. Much ingenuity went into the 2+2 with a built-in padded roll-bar which also lent much rigidity to the unitary structure, and an optional hardtop which converted the open model (with retained soft hood) to a handsome coupé. There were electric windows as standard, an electrically-heated rear window automatically made contact when the hardtop was clipped on, and the all-independent suspension provided a most acceptable ride allied with high cornering capabilities. Power steering was also a standard fitting on this near-120 mph model. Triumph also made two interesting "modifications" for 1970, announcing a new Toledo model in August —a two-door, rear-drive saloon which had been derived from the four-door front-drive 1300. The 1300 was discontinued as such, but was replaced by a four-door front-drive 1500 which used an lengthened-stroke version of the same engine, and at the same time had almost six inches "inserted" into its length to extend the luggage capacity and tail.

The Toledo was obviously intended to replace the ageing Herald, and surprisingly the new model featured a live rear axle in constrast to the Herald's i.r.s. The Toledo was due to be produced at Triumph's new £11m plant at Speke near Liverpool. Sales were good but industrial upsets stopped production in the middle of the year, albeit temporarily.

Vauxhall, General Motors' British factory, introduced a third-series Viva, the HC, at the Paris Salon in October. The emphasis was on more room and more car for the buyer's money, but the basic 1159cc three-bearing power-unit was still the main prime mover, although slightly uprated. With wider bodywork and track, plus a little more length the new range offered greater arm and leg-room, but the same suspension was utilised. Boot capacity was up 25 percent, but the extra power was absorbed by the weight increase of some 60 lb. Frontal area was also greater. The 1159cc Vivas, with choice of two or four-door bodywork, came in both standard 59 hp (gross) and 72 hp ("90" specification) forms, and there was also a 1.6-litre overhead camshaft version, the motor being from the Victor series. The two-litre Viva GT had been dropped, at least temporarily. Good-looking "fastback" estates with all the engine options made up the new Viva range. Like all GM cars, the new Vivas incorporated a huge number of built-in safety features, and much work and money had been devoted to quiet-running. In fact the 1.2-litre Viva was a notably quiet car for its modest engine capacity. Vauxhall lost £3m (about $1.2m) in the first six months of 1970.

Ford of Britain announced their third series Cortinas just nine days after Vauxhall's Vivas, and surprised many with the "coke-bottle" lines of the new cars—lines which Vauxhall had featured on their Victor FD range for some three years. With a choice of engines from 1.3 to two litres (there was also an 1100cc model for export only) the new Cortinas were the stars of the London Motor Show, and motoring journalists sang the roadholding praises of the car after trying them on a searching course in Belgium.

Not only had Ford adopted two new overhead camshaft engines (belt-driven) of 1600cc and 2000cc for the new range but they had abandoned their celebrated MacPherson strut-type independent front suspension after a twenty-year run. Most European manufacturers, even Volkswagen, had adopted the MacPherson front-end, and Ford's switch to coil springs and wishbones must have given a few designers furiously to think. The well-behaved Cortina live rear axle was also coil spring-suspended and well-located by a four-link system. Ford had made the new model much roomier but the overall length (14ft.) was the same as the outgoing model. Front and rear track had been increased, and the body was 2.1 inches wider, although 2.7 inches lower. The two overhead camshaft models were capable of more than 100 mph, and with the attactive two and four-door salooons, plus the four-door estates, the Cortina range added-up to 35 basic versions. Catalogue specifications varied from Cortina through "L", "XL", and "GT" to "GXL". In an extremely busy year, Ford of Britain introduced an "E" version of the Capri 3000 V6, a 16-valve Escort Twin-Cam with Cosworth-developed BDA engine of 109 bhp (net), and the Escort "Mexico", a two-door clubman's rally car, powered by the uprated crossflow "Cortina" engine of 1,600 cc.

Specialist manufacturer Jem Marsh introduced a fast Marcos GT 2+2 with above-average room for rear seat occupants, and powered by a 2.5-litre Triumph in-line "six" with Lucas mechanical fuel-injection. The unusual glass-fibre two-door body was styled by Dennis Adams, and the 150 bhp output (net) suggested a 120 mph maximum. The separate steel chassis featured a live rear axle, but positively-located by "A-bracket" for accurate steering geometry.

Best-selling British car at the end of 1970 was still the Austin-Morris 1100/1300, but due to industrial disputes and component manufacturers' strikes, the volume division of British Leyland faced substantial losses. Lotus Cars too finished the year with a dismal balance sheet.

Jaguar officially announced their new engines would appear in 1971, and it was confidently expected the new Jensen-built Healey sports car would be introduced at the London or Paris Show—probably with a two-litre ohc Vauxhall engine.

Italy

Italy certainly had no glut of new mass-production models in 1970, although motor industrial prospects began to improve after the grim industrial strikes and violence of the previous year. From January until September 1970 Italy's car production of 1,241,532 was 2.47 percent better than the previous year, and exports had increased 3.32 percent. With Agnelli's Fiat empire either controlling, part-controlling, or having a substantial interest in Autobianchi, Ferrari, Lancia, Maserati, and OM (as well as Citroen in France), Fiat can be said to constitute the bulk of the Italian motor industry, and some of the problems that still exist can be gauged by the fact that every day 180,000 people fail to turn up for work at Fiat plants! The one absolutely new car from Italy in 1970 was from small manufacturer Lamborghini who produced the intriguing 2.5-litre "Urraco" at the Turin Show in late October. The beautiful rear/mid-engined 2+2 was Bertone-styled with sharp nose and characteristic "venetian blind" rear treatment.

The power-unit was mounted transversely ahead of the independent MacPherson-type rear suspension, and sported single overhead camshafts per bank, both belt-driven. The vertical valves were set in Heron-type combustion chambers, and with four twin-choke Weber carburetters the claimed maximum power-output was 220 hp (net) at 7800 rpm. A pump for the air-conditioning system was driven by normal V-belt from the crankshaft nose.

The transverse engine was in unit with a new five-speed gearbox which transmitted engine power through final-drive gears and unequal-length half-shafts. A beautiful little projectile with realistic space for two plus baggage, which was expected to sell in Italy at around the same price as the mid-engined Ferrari Dino 2.4-litre. Earlier in the year Lamborghini introduced the four-litre "Jarama", a new model to replace the older separate-frame models but using the existing V12 engine. The Jarama was front-engined, Bertone-styled, and used a unitary body/chassis unit. With 2+2 seating and a top speed of 160 mph, it was for the wealthy industrialist who likes to cut a dash. The lines were beautiful and weight was 2,760 lb. Before the end of the year however, Ferruccio Lamborghini was reported to be in financial trouble due mainly to slowing sales of tractors from his factories. He was also reported to be seeking take-over talks with Henry Ford II.

Nearest approach to new volume-production models came from Fiat when the 1,438 cc, 80 (net) hp twin overhead camshaft "coupé" engine was offered in a sporting version of the ubiquitous 124 saloon, renamed 124T. Although ten horsepower down on the 1½-litre Sport Coupé Fiat, latest 124 variant could exceed 100 mph, and displayed the customary nimble handling and complete equipment of this highly successful model.

During 1970 Fiat had adopted General Motors' Strasbourg-produced automatic transmission on 124 and 125 models as optional equipment. The GM automatic had quickly gained a reputation for smooth, effective operation—as well as a low price. It was said the prestige Fiat 130 V6 would also eventually be equipped with the GM box.

Alfa-Romeo's 1970 new-model contribution was the Montreal two-seater coupé with 2.6-litre four-cam V8 engine mounted at the front. The engine, based on the *Tipo* 33 racing unit, develops 230 (SAE) hp as installed in the coupé, and drives the rear wheels through a five-speed gearbox and live rear axle.

Bertone styled the Montreal, the name emanating from Expo 67 which was staged in the Canadian city, and where Alfa-Romeo and Bertone collaborated to exhibit cars to symbolise modern automobilism. In spite of its claimed top speed of 135 mph the Montreal looked dated in 1970, and its capacity for two occupants only rather limited its usefulness.

Alfa-Romeo also inserted their amazing 1,290 cc twin overhead camshaft "GT" engine into the four-door Giulia saloon for 1970, rechristening it the Giulia 1300 Super. Billed as "The most powerful 1,300 cc saloon in the World", it is certainly no sluggard with 103 (SAE) hp.

Not to be outdone, Lancia introduced a "Series 2" edition of the Fulvia 1300, the front-drive V4 being given a five-speed gearbox.

Italy's brilliant but dwindling band of coachbuilders—which in that country means artist/engineer/stylist—firmly put the "wedge" configuration before the eyes of the public—and the manufacturers. Contributions from Pininfarina (the Ferrari-based "Modulo"), from Bertone (the Lancia-powered "Stratos"), from Ital Design (the

VW-Porsche-based "Tapiro"), and from Francis Lombardi (the special NSU 1200SS) clearly indicated our not-so-distant future motoring is to be wedge-shaped.

The house of Zagato produced an intriguing, massive two-door, four-seat saloon, designated "NART" (after the North American Racing Team), powered by a vast Oldsmobile Toronado engine/transmission unit in the tail of the car. Amazingly, but typically, Zagato had managed to retain a Toronado look about the car, although it was completely Europeanised. The equally incredible de Tomaso presented a new Ghia-bodied (who else?) four-door saloon designated "Dauville" with lines suggestive of a Jaguar XJ6 but powered by one of de Tomaso's overhead camshaft conversions on the five-litre (or 5.7 on option) Ford V8. The enterprising manufacturer also exhibited two V12 engines, both with twin overhead camshafts, and one with modified manifolding and fuel-injection for competition. In this day and age it could only happen in Italy!

Yet another product of great interest from de Tomaso was a backbone chassis frame with transverse/rear Ford 16-valve DBA engine and a de Tomaso gearbox and final-drive.

As ever, there was no shortage of engineering and artistic ideas from the Italian motor industry in 1970, but it cannot be overlooked that every year names disappear or are engulfed into other vast groups.

Japan

Japan held her place as the No. 2 World Producer of cars, and clearly demonstrated she intended to retain the position. Since 1961 Japanese car production had doubled every two years, and in 1970 output totalled more than 2.8 million. The Japanese industry exhibited enormous virility, and new models which had great potential in world markets—particularly the North American—as well as in its own.

Quality, design, and buyer-appeal increases with every new generation of Japanese cars, just as it did with her cameras and motorcycles. Neither of those industries made it first time, or even for a number of years, but in the end they both dominated world markets.

The annual Tokyo Show, staged in November, has quickly gained a similar reputation to the Turin Salone, with masses of way-out "prototypes" and special models being displayed as well as new volume-production cars. The 1970 Tokyo Show presented a bewildering display of prototypes and new models, amongst the latter being two brand-new offerings from Toyota, the Carina and Celicia. Unveiled only a week before the Show opening, the new cars shared the same basic engine with options of 1.4 or 1.6 litres. Surprisingly the engine relied on pushrod gear for its valve operation, but nevertheless the hottest version of the Carina 1600 five-bearing unit developed 105 hp. The Carina had its live rear axle located by four links and a Panhard rod, and was available as a two or four-door saloon. The Celicia featured stylish two-door hardtop coupé bodywork, and was also available with a twin ohc version of the 1600 engine, developing 115 hp, promising a very high performance. A five-speed gearbox could be specified on all 1600 Carina/Celicia models.

In Japan the twin ohc Celicia GT with five-speed box could be delivered for the equivalent of £1075 (about $2550). Mitsubishi's Colt Galant GTO was another 1970 Japanese car of 1½ litres, cast in the sporting mould, and offering high performance with a reasonable price tag. The well-established Japanese manufacturer entered into an agreement with Chrysler in the late summer, Mitsubishi to hold 65 percent of the stock, the American corporation to have 35 percent. The Galant was to be sold in the USA as the Dodge Colt through Dodge dealers, and with a price tag of around $2250 (about £945) would undoubtedly be a good temporary "sub-compact" for Chrysler to sell until their own car is on the US Market, maybe in 1971.

The Galant came in two and four-door form, with five-bearing overhead camshaft engine, developing 95 hp in "Saturn" form and 105 hp in "Grand Sport" tune with twin SU carburetters and a 10:1 compression ratio.

The 1970 Tokyo Show also co-incided with a mass offensive by the rest of the US motor industry to gain at least a foothold in the Japanese industry. Ford were working on a scheme to invest up to 20 percent of Mazda's (Toyo Kogyo) total capital, and GM were jockeying for position to gain a similar deal with Isuzu.

Mazda are traditionally very go-ahead, and the 1970 Tokyo saw a way-out RX 500 prototype with mid-mounted two-rotor Wankel engine, and also an EX-5 bubble runabout with constant-speed Wankel engine driving a generator which fed electric current to separate wheel motors. Mazda's production of their three Wankel-engined "catalogue" models, the R100, Cosmo 110S and R130 had gained realistic figures, and the Company also introduced a "Capella" 1175 cc piston-engined version of the R100 coupé with a reputed 120 hp and a top speed of 120 mph.

Nissan-Datsun introduced the neat "Cherry" front-drive model with 1000cc engine and choice of two or four-door saloon bodies, or a three-door estate. With 58 hp under the bonnet the single-carburetter engine was installed transversely with four-speed gearbox under the crankcase. Very good-looking, the Cherry was quite a bit larger than a BL Mini, and there was also a 1200cc version with 80 hp motor. Datsun's old one-litre range was upgraded to 1200cc in January 1970. Datsun's 240-Z sports coupé with 2.4-litre (2-litre only on Japanese home market) overhead camshaft six-cylinder engine and all-independent suspension began to assert itself as an international rally car.

Honda introduced a coupé version of the 1300 front-drive model with 110 hp available from its air-cooled, four-carburetter engine. The famous Japanese car/motorcycle manufacturer also unveiled a "2 + 2" coupé on the little 360cc structure, with 31 hp, and there was even a racey GS version with 36 hp and five-speed gearbox.

The Japanese industry was certainly on to sport-Orientation in 1970, and with its propensity for developing innovation, it seemed poised to bring the Wankel engine to popularity, plus reliability and volume production.

Switzerland

Not normally classed as a motor-manufacturing country, Switzerland nevertheless had two 1970 offerings, one of them amongst the world's fastest cars. Monteverdi of Basel drew the crowds at the Geneva Salon with his mid-

engined 450SS "hai"—a Bertone-styled GT bomb with 6.9-litre 450 hp (net) Chrysler V8 ahead of the Dion rear axle. With a claimed 0-60 mph in 4.8 seconds and a top speed of 180 mph it was sheer fantasy. Strictly for sybarites it carried a Swiss price of about 100,000 francs (approximately £10,000 or $24,000).
The other car was a GM product, assembled at the Bienne plant for the Swiss market and christened "Ranger". Using Opel engines (1.9 or 2.5 litres) and running gear as well as bits and pieces from Vauxhall and South Africa's GM Ranger, it looked much the same as an Opel but sold for a trifle less.

U.S.A.

The big happenings in the North American automobile industry in 1970 were the "minis" from AMC, GM, and Ford. Amongst the "traditional-sized" cars, there were of course sheet-metal changes, and as usual several of them added inches in length and width. Even the "Compacts" got bigger, but perhaps the most noteworthy technical move in the world's largest and most productive motor industry was the switch to lower compression ratios as the unleaded fuel campaign got under way. The US anti-emission laws, and the even tougher ones to come, certainly tax the designers—and the accountants—in every corner of the world. After nearly fifty years Kettering's fantastic discovery looks like being thrown away—and it is by no means certain at the moment of writing, that unleaded fuel is to be the answer to emission problems.
The signing of an agreement late in the year between General Motors and NSU-Audi in respect of Wankel rotary engine production was loaded with significance, and gave some idea of the forward-planning, expense—and risk—involved in meeting never-ending motoring legislation. The GM giant is well-fitted to remove fume and production problems from Felix Wankel's controversial power-unit, and if anyone can make a viable proposition of it, it is the huge American business.
The year 1970 was the one in which American industry decided to take steps to stem the menace of the small imported car. The year of Beetle-squashing, the manufacturers hoped.
First of the new "sub-compacts" to appear was the AMC Gremlin in the early part of the year. Although the smallest of the American manufacturers, AMC got sharply off the mark because they employed existing components to constitute their odd-looking coupé with 128 hp in a package 2 ½ inches longer than the Volkswagen. It was also ten inches wider, seven inches lower, and 765 lb. heavier. The two-passenger model with all rear space for baggage etc., cost around $1879.
The new GM and Ford sub-compacts hit the streets around the same time, in mid-year, the Chevrolet Vega 2300 having the bigger engine, but the Ford Pinto offering two different units, one of 1600 cc with pushrod overhead valves, the other a two-litre with a cogged-belt driving an overhead camshaft. Both cars expressed the way the American industry's top brass was thinking. Imports were stealing 10-11 percent of a colossal market, so a home product of similar broad outline had to be offered—with what the industry hoped would be a superior specification, and operation prospects, at a competitive price. It was a tough assignment. The industry faced the fact they were competing in a field where the German worker earned about 50 per cent of his American counterpart, and the Japanese about 25 percent. Added to which many Japanese cars are sold in the USA at a lower price than in their country of origin. GM made full use of their vast facilities (and capital) to put automation to work in a big way. Whereas a normal car uses about 18 percent automated welding on the many hundreds of welds needed, the Vega is up to 80 percent. This helps to cut costs dramatically. The light-alloy four-cylinder overhead camshaft engine (with two power options) also represented a technological break-through as well as pointing to cost-reduction in machining time. The cylinder block contained a high silicon content, employed no liners, and the zincate/copper/tin and hard iron-coated pistons were in contact with the light-alloy walls.
Ford got around some of the cost problems by having the Pinto's power-units made in their British and German factories. They also ended the import of the British Ford Cortina as a part-insurance against competition and marketing complication. Both the 1600 and two-litre engines were cast iron, yet light in weight due to modern foundry techniques.
The Pinto provided more leg, hip, and shoulder room than the Beetle, both front and rear, but less headroom in the front. In nearly every direction the new American "minis" seemed one-up on the German car.
The Vega used coil springs all-round with positive rear axle location, the Pinto relied on semi-elliptic leaves for the live rear axle. Both cars handled well. GM offered a three-speed manual as the standard transmission, but there was an optional four-speed, as well as a two-speed automatic and a two-speed semi-automatic. Ford's Pinto came with standard four-speed manual on either engine, and there was a single three-speed/torque-converter automatic option for the two-litre model.
Vega was introduced with options of standard two-door sedan body, GT Coupé (same body with 110 hp engine), Wagon, and there was a commercial van as well. The Pinto came in one body style only, with choice of two engines and two transmissions. Both were well-styled and good-looking, both had been planned for simple servicing and easy replacement of body parts in the event of damage. It remained to be seen whether the new American minis would beat the imports and/or lower the sales of the more traditional US cars.
Chrysler didn't get into the US mini-market as a manufacturer in 1970 but entered into agreement with Mitsubishi, Japan's fourth-largest car producer, to import and distribute "Colt" models into the USA. Chrysler's own sub-compact is to come later. Japanese manufacturers have avoided agreements with US companies in the past for fear of domestic criticism of accepting foreign capital. Mitsubishi, which made 340,000 cars in 1970, felt that as Chrysler weren't as big as Ford or GM, they were pretty safe from take-over at a later date, and decided to go ahead. Wonder if Rootes felt the same way a few years ago! Chrysler themselves went deeply into the red in 1970, GM lost $77m, and AMC $82m. Industrial upsets and strikes had badly affected the US industry but there were signs they were taking sensible steps to recover.

As well as having internal accommodation quite out of keeping with a one-litre car, the Citroën GS has a 16 cubic foot luggage boot in its square tail—and a lift-up rear bumper. The "flat-four" can truly be said to be a fast Grand Touring car, even if its engine capacity is modest. Suspension is hydropneumatic, and overall length 13ft. 6.3/16in.

A typical unconventional exercise from Citroën, the new 1015cc GS, unveiled at the Paris Salon, is capable of 93 mph. With the customary front wheel drive, the GS also has all-independent self-levelling suspension giving it exceptional ride and handling qualities. Amazingly, its very aerodynamic four-door bodywork is 16 percent more efficient than the slippery DS. The horizontally-opposed four-cylinder air-cooled engine—a new departure for Citroën—has a belt-driven overhead camshaft to each bank of cylinders, and sets high standards of quiet-running by the use of very rigid cylinder heads. The motor develops 55.5 bhp (DIN) from fractionally more than one litre and such is the aerodynamic efficiency that only 30 bhp is needed for 75 mph. The engine is designed to run for 60,000 miles without major overhaul.

Citroën produced 500 examples of a prototype M35 coupé powered by a "995cc" Wankel rotary engine, and released them to selected French buyers at about £1000 ($2400) each. Powered by a single-rotor version of the Wankel engine, the M35 had a claimed 90 mph top speed, and utilised several panels from the ugly duckling Ami 8. The fastback coupé used a simplified hydropneumatic suspension, and power-output of the water-cooled rotary engine was a claimed 49 bhp (DIN). An interesting evaluation exercise which may have its effect on later Citroëns.

Impressive front view of the advanced Citroën SM reveals the six tungsten-halogen headlights, all of them automatically-levelled by links with the front and rear suspension. The inner pair, connected to the front wheels by a hydraulic link, turn with the steering for "around the corner" illumination. Height of the SM is 4ft. 4in. (6in. lower than the DS models), and the aerodynamic shape is of a high order.

Driving compartment of the Citroën SM is functional but comfortable with cross-pleated seats adjustable for fore-and-aft position height, and backrest rake. Headrests are fitted, and the central console contains switches for the electric windows. The small diameter, well-padded steering wheel is evident, as is the short lever for the five-speed manual gearbox. Windscreen rake is considerable, and legroom generous.

CITROËN SM

Bearing more than a passing resemblance to the "DS", in spite of its two doors, the Citroën SM is an ultra-high performance 2 + 2 with V6 engine of Maserati design and manufacture. Although of a modest 2.6 litres (to take advantage of the French fiscal system) the engine which has twin overhead camshafts to each bank of cylinders will propel the 16ft-plus car up to a maximum of around 137 mph. With three double-choke Weber carburetters, the power-output is 170 bhp (DIN) at 5500 rpm. The long, low, purposeful SM can accelerate from zero to 60 mph in less than nine seconds, and from zero to 120 mph in less than 40 seconds. Overhang at both front and rear is considerable, but all contribute to the streamlining and to the commodious luggage boot. The V6 engine is installed well back in the structure, and of course, front-drive is employed.

The Maserati V6 engine of the Citroen SM is a 90-degree unit with twin overhead camshafts per bank driven by duplex chains from a central jackshaft. The cylinder heads are interchangeable. The three double-choke Weber carburetters can just be seen between the cylinder block "V", and the two distributors are mounted at the front of the engine. The massive inboard disc brakes are mounted ahead of the engine, behind the five-speed all-synchromesh manual gearbox. Bore and stroke dimensions of the engine are 87 mm by 75 mm, the exact cubic capacity being 2570cc.

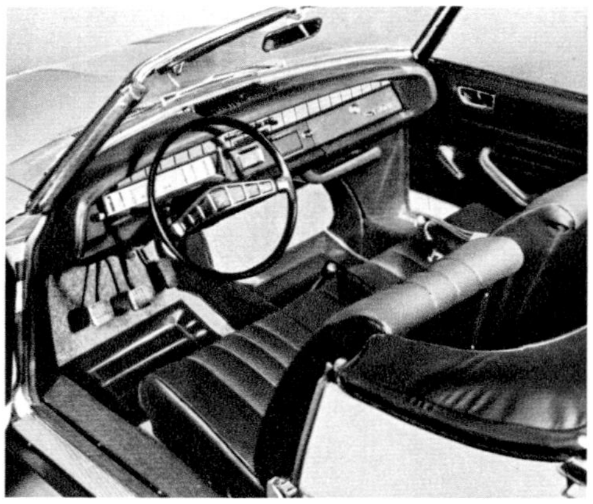

Classed as a "2 + 2", the Peugeot 304 cabriolet doesn't have much space for an adult in the rear compartment. But the luggage boot is large, so two can travel in millionaire comfort. All 304s have servo brakes, discs at the front.

Presented at the Paris Salon in October the Peugeot 304 "Break Super-Luxe" utilised the same underpan and running gear as the 304 saloon, but offered enormous carrying capacity as well as a high degree of luxury.

Peugeot was the only French manufacturer to produce coupé and cabriolet models at realistic prices in 1970. The 304 main structure was not changed but the lowered and swept roofline improved the aerodynamics and raised the top speed to around 93 mph. The front-end retained the familiar 304 saloon grille and trapezoidal headlights which gave it a very definite likeness to the more expensive 504. A good-looking front-drive car.

First French Chrysler, the four-door 160/180 created a good impression with semi-fastback looks, and roomy interior. Three models were introduced just before the Paris Salon, and all were powered by a basic four-cylinder overhead camshaft engine. The 160 model was equipped with a 1639cc engine, whereas the 160GT and 180 models came with a 1812cc motor. Power-output was 80 bhp (DIN) for the smaller unit and 97 bhp for the larger. The 160 models had disc/drum brakes, but the larger-engined cars had discs to all four wheels.

At the Paris Salon the Regie Renault deviated from their recent pattern of saloon/estates and introduced an elegant "pure" estate on the Renault 12 structure. With wheelbase lengthened some 2,5 inches, the rear platform offered a load length of 5 ft. 5 in. when the rear seat back was folded. A useful estate car with a maximum speed of 88 mph.

The Renault 8 Gordini, for so long the mount of the enthusiastic French driver—and others—was replaced by the front-drive "12 Gordini". The basic car, normally propelled by a 1300 cc motor, was a veritable bomb with the 1565 cc "TS" engine, lifted to 113 bhp (DIN) for the new model. Interior trim and instrumentation were very "sportif", and the brakes were servo-assisted discs to all four wheels. An all-synchromesh five-speed gearbox was standard equipment and top speed was around 115 mph. The engine could be tuned to higher outputs.

The Renault 6, "poor man's 16" received the option of the 1108 cc engine from the rear-drive "8", but mounted at the front and driving the front wheels. Already well-established as a useful five-door load carrier, the 45 bhp (DIN) motor transformed its performance and capabilities. An invaluable work-horse, with a new maximum speed of around 85 mph, and the highly desirable attribute of a low-octane fuel requirement. Nine-inch disc front brakes.

In June, Simca-Chrysler introduced a fast version of the front-drive "1100", designated "1204". Powered by a 1204 cc transverse engine with two twin-choke Weber carburetters and developing 75 bhp (DIN), the ultimate in small "estates" could exceed 100 mph. Interior trim and amenities were of a high order and the new model could be recognised by the two rectangular quartz-iodine supplementary lights.

Guy Ligier's new JS 2 made its debut at the Paris Salon and revealed itself as a good-looking glass-fibre coupé, mounted on a "backbone" frame and powered by a fuel-injected 2.6-litre Ford-Cologne V6. The engine is mounted ahead of the rear suspension, and is coupled to a five-speed gearbox from the Citroen SM. Designed by Michel Tetu, the target production is 100 cars per year at the Vichy works. Claimed maximum speed 150 mph on 165 bhp.

The 914-6 VW-Porsche was a 1970 favourite with special coachbuilders, and this one, the "Murene" by Heuliez is not notable for good looks. Finished in grey and beige, the Murene was introduced at the Paris Salon and featured two seats and a roofline which contributed to a generous luggage capacity. Unfortunately the curved waistline rather gave it an appearance of having had something heavy dropped in the middle. The Heuliez company is situated south of Nantes in France.

Co-operating with the small-series manufacturer CG, Simca produced a mid-engined competition prototype with glass-fibre coupé bodywork. The four-cylinder motor was of 2.2 litres with an output of 175 bhp—a very high power-to-weight ratio. Light weight and a small frontal area made it an interesting proposition for competition, and its first showings suggested a small production series by Chrysler-France. The engine is an enlarged overhead camshaft 160/180.

Year by year the Volkswagen Beetle gets more power, more luxury—and better suspension. Yet it manages to keep its original appearance. In October 1970 reconstituted Beetles were announced, the 1300 model receiving a 52 bhp (SAE) engine, through-flow ventilation, and a maximum of 78 mph. Also introduced was the "Super Beetle" with 1.6-litre engine, new MacPherson front and double-jointed axle/trailing arm rear suspension. There was also a wider track and larger luggage compartment.

VW's new K 70 started life as the NSU K 70 and was to be introduced in March 1969 but take-over talks between the two companies brought its future to a halt. Re-introduced in September 1970, as the VW K 70, the 1605 cc front-drive saloon had been cleaned-up externally, but was basically the same near-100 mph model with water-cooled engine on top of the transmission. The base is a shortened NSU Ro 80 floorpan, and the K 70 was obviously launched as an "insurance" model for possible Beetle fade-out.

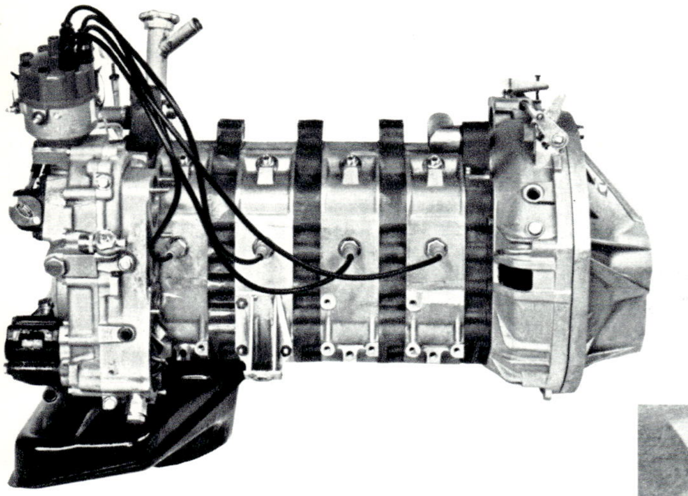

Mercedes-Benz impressive "second-generation" Wankel rotary engine was unveiled at the Geneva Show. With four rotors and a rated cubic capacity of 4.8 litres, the engine developed 350 hp at 7000 rpm. The motor in effect was a later edition of the three-rotor C-111 unit introduced at Frankfurt in 1969.

Parked beside the earlier Mercedes C-111 rotary coupé (left) the revised C-111/1970 model with four-rotor engine exhibits different grilles and tail treatment. Maximum speed said to be about 186 mph. No production plans.

In adopting Bosch electronic fuel-injection equipment, Opel lifted power-output of their 2.5-litre "Commodore" six-cylinder engine to 150 (DIN) hp. The Commodore GSE illustrated had its top speed increased to 120 mph. The manufacturer also put into small-scale production a Commodore 2000 with special engine prepared by rally/race driver Henri Greder, with an output of almost 300 hp. This very potent model was produced for rally drivers and lovers of extra high performance.

Using the Manta under-pan and the 1.6-litre version of the Manta engine, the Opel Ascona was officially unveiled at the Turin Show in late October. Available with two or four-door saloon bodywork, or as a three-door "Voyage" estate, the Ascona 16 had 90 (gross) hp and a top speed of around 96 mph. Of rather dull appearance, the saloon nevertheless offered unusually complete equipment including two-speed heater fan, two-speed wipers, electric cigar lighter, safety belt attachments, seats adjustable for angle, coat hooks, electric clock, collapsible steering column etc. The saloon offered seating room for five.

At the Paris Salon in early October, Ford-Cologne launched their new Taunus models. Sharing suspension and running gear with the new Ford of Britain Cortinas, the German models had more square-cut Teutonic lines, and belt-driven overhead camshaft four-cylinder engines from 1.3 to 1.6 litres in two stages of tune. The largest power-unit in the new range was the two-litre V6 from the 17 M/20 M model which remained in production. Like the British Cortinas the new Taunus models had discontinued MacPherson strut front suspension, and had adopted coil springs and wishbones. The live rear axle was also coil spring-suspended and positively located by the "four-link system". The range included two and four-door saloons.

General Motors' long-awaited "Manta", the "anti-Capri" coupé, arrived in the autumn of 1970 and exhibited well-balanced lines. The two-door bodywork offered realistic leg and kneeroom for rear seat occupants, and a good-sized boot. The shapely tail incorporated a "spoiler", and four round headlights were standard. Powered by a four-cylinder "cam-in-head" engine with a choice of either 1.6 or 1.9 litres, the Manta proved itself to be a fast "family GT" with excellent handling, notable comfort and surprising fuel economy. In spite of its sporty appearance the Manta was endowed with generous headroom, front and back, the latter being achieved by use of torque-tube and radius arm-located rear axle which in turn permitted a relatively low seat pan to be fitted. Engines were derived from the Opel Rekord, the different capacities being obtained by bore variation.

Exciting car of unusual capabilities, the Range Rover with permanent four-wheel-drive and 3.5-litre light-alloy V8 engine, had the ability to cruise at 90 mph on the lowest grades of fuel. Internal comfort was high, and the nine-inch suspension movement gave it an exceptional cross-country performance.

Rootes introduced a new model, the Hillman Avenger, early in 1970, a 1250/1500cc model which bore the name Sunbeam on the European Continent. Later the manufacturer's name was changed to Chrysler UK. The new car was made in four-door saloon form only, and later a GT version with twin-carburetter 75 hp (DIN) 1500 engine was added to the range. Bearing a strong resemblance to the Chrysler-France 160/180 models, the British-made car was launched with a highly competitive price tag.

Vauxhall's third generation Viva, the "HC", displayed new, wider bodywork, a much larger luggage boot, lengthened wheelbase, and widened track. The accent was on more car and more space for your money, but the same basic three-bearing 1159cc engines were employed, although slightly uprated in power. Also available was a 1600 version with the overhead camshaft unit from the Victor series. Much attention had been paid to noise minimisation, and the 1159cc models offered unusually quiet running for a model of such modest capacity. The HC Vivas retained the coil spring/wishbone front suspension of the previous model, and also the live axle rear suspension with location by the "four-link" system. Available with two or four-door bodywork.

Estate bodies on the new Vauxhall Viva featured three doors and a pleasing fastback. Like the saloon models, the estate cars came as standard with 1159cc engines and drum front brakes, but high-output or 1600 power-units were available as options, and servo-assisted disc/drum brake layouts.

Ford of Britain's third series Cortina was launched at the London Motor Show in October and seemed set to become another sales record-breaker. The new bodywork incorporated the "coke-bottle" kick-up in the rear quarters, but was no longer than the earlier model. It was wider however, as well as lower, and the track, front and rear had been increased. Wheelbase had been lengthened 3.5 inches.

Ford Cortina XL on test at the vast Lommel proving ground in Belgium. The two headlights indicate that this is either an L or XL model. Four headlights distinguish GT and GXL.

Ford Cortina 2000 GXL, the most powerful and luxurious model in the new British range. With two and four-door saloon options, plus four-door estates, the 1970-71 Cortinas offered 35 basic versions. Engines ranged from 1300cc pushrod ohv to the new two-litre four-cylinder with belt-driven overhead camshaft, virtually identical to that the of American Ford Pinto sub-compact. MacPherson front suspension was discontinued in favour of a coil spring and wishbone arrangement, and the live rear axle was positively-located by a "four-link" system. The GT versions employed a 1593cc edition of the overhead camshaft engine, and that model, with two or four doors was fitted with front seats incorporating built-in headrests as standard.

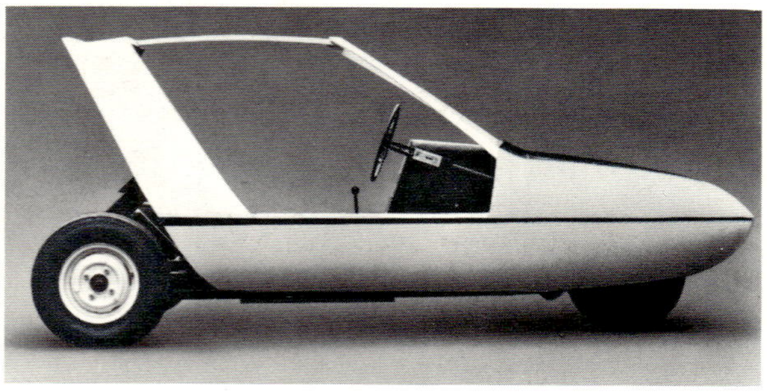

Fun car from Bond, the "Bug" three-wheeler had a moon-shot appearance with glass-fibre bodywork and lift-up top. Strictly for the young it was powered by the 700cc water-cooled light-alloy four-cylinder engine from the Reliant Regal three-wheeler (Bond Cars are part of the Reliant Group), and was capable in its most potent (32 hp) form of 80 mph. The front-mounted engine drove the rear wheels through a four-speed all-synchromesh gearbox. The car was marketed with inclusive insurance—a package deal for the young. A vast range of accessories was also offered.

Exciting new three-litre V8 2 + 2 from Triumph, the Stag featured Michelotti styling and a built-in, padded roll-bar which could be covered by a shapely hardtop, or soft folding hood. Independent suspension to all four wheels.

The British Triumph Company also introduced the 1300cc Toledo, a two-door saloon based on the previous four-door "1300" but with rear-drive and a live axle. A well-finished small car, it was obviously intended as a Herald replacement. A new front-drive 1500 was introduced at the same time with enlarged Herald-type engine, four-door bodywork, and extended boot. Rectangular headlights were fitted to the Toledo, four round lamps to the 1500, the former being produced at the new Liverpool plant.

Marcos' latest high-performance offering was the "Mantis" with really roomy 2 + 2 glass-fibre bodywork styled by Dennis Adams. Powered by a fuel-injected 2.5-litre Triumph TR6 engine, the British car was capable of 120 mph with a range of 350 miles. The live rear axle was positively-located by "A-bracket".

Way-out mid-engined GT from Swiss manufacturer Monteverdi appropriately appeared at the Geneva Show in March, styled by Peter Monteverdi himself and built by Fissore. The seven-litre 450 (SAE) hp Chrysler "hemi" V8 was installed ahead of the rear suspension, and the "hai" (shark) had a claimed maximum of 180 mph. The big engine permitted only two occupants.

◂ *Czechoslovakian Tatra 603, after 14 years of manufacture, was restyled by Vignale, and the rear-engined, air-cooled 3.5-litre V8 took on a modern look. It is unlikely the restyled car will reach production until 1972, and then in small numbers, for high-ranking Communists.*

Another car of interest from Czechoslovakia was the prototype Skoda Sport Coupé 1100 GT with wind-cheating bodywork, flip-up headlights, and powered by a raised-compression (12 : 1) engine developing 75 (DIN) hp. Maximum speed said to be 110 mph.

Lamborghini pensioned-off the old front-engined V12s and presented the monocoque Jarama at Geneva. Styled by Bertone, the new 2+2 had its four-litre 350 hp V12 at the front. Lamborghini does not support racing, and the designation "Jarama" does not refer to the Spanish track but to the town where the best fighting bulls used to be bred. Coil and wishbone suspension all-round and a maximum of more than 160 mph.

Lamborghini Urraco's transverse water-cooled V8 sports a single overhead camshaft to each cylinder bank, driven by cogged belt. The air-conditioning compressor is driven by a V-belt. The five-speed gearbox and final-drive is by Lamborghini, and MacPherson strut suspension is used front and rear. Disc brakes outboard all-round.

Lamborghini's "mini", the rear/mid-engined Urraco bears the unmistakable stamp of Bertone in its styling. The tail incorporates venetian slats for rear visibility and protection from heat and glare, and the aggressive front has flip-up headlights. The basic profile is "wedge" with excellent air-penetrating qualities but headroom is restricted—also legroom in the rear compartment. The rear/transverse V8 engine is in full view of the Urraco's occupants through a thick glass pane. The new 2.5-litre was designed to muscle in on the Ferrari Dino market, and is expected to cost about the same in Italy.

Bertone-styled Alfa-Romeo Montreal was introduced at the Geneva Show, powered by a front-mounted 2.6-litre V8 derived from the Tipo 33*—although the hind treatment suggests a rear engine. Not one of Bertone's happiest shapes, the 230 hp two-seater GT offered enormous performance. The name was derived from Montreal's Expo 67 where Alfa and Bertone exhibited.*

Bertone got in on the buggy act with a Simca-powered car, first shown at the Paris Salon. The chassis base-plate was Simca 1000, and the power-unit a 1200S with full rear nudity. Web-type seats provided surprising comfort, besides being the ideal, easy-to-clean equipment for this fun car. Roll-bar is massive, and there is extra steel tube protection for side damage, and for the engine.

Front view of the Bertone beach buggy looks like some sort of sea serpent —which must prove something. Roll-bar acts as prop for headlights and twin windtone horns. It is absolutely forbidden to turn this car over! With 75 (DIN) hp on tap it should be one of the faster pebbles on the beach, and deep-grip tyres are perfect for the job, but back-draught should pull much sand into the motor.

Lombardi of Vercelli produced a rather bitty coupé on the VW 1600 structure, the paintwork lending a wedge theme of sorts. On the credit side there was good visibility through the generous glass area. Flip-up headlights and sharp nose contribute to reasonable aerodynamic shape.

Lombardi's wedge treatment of the NSU 1200S was altogether better, and the neat coupé had electric windows, flip-up headlights, reasonable luggage space, and an oil radiator for the air-cooled motor. Signor Lombardi hopes to put this model into small-series production in 1971.

The Pininfarina Modulo, on the Ferrari 512 S chassis was, according to its makers, an expression of culture. It was little more than three feet high, and composed of two body shells placed one upon the other and separated by a groove surrounding the entire far-out shape. As in a modular object, the car, in theory, could be changed from saloon to coupé, and from coupé to convertible, simply by eliminating one or more panels. Strictly an "idea car", it would nevertheless be a very potent one with 550 hp of fuel-injected V12 under its shapely tail panels. The Modulo was first shown at Geneva in March, and in modified form in Turin in October.

Bertone's "Stratos" was a last-minute surprise at the Turin Show, and well-characterised the exhibition, and the art of the Italian coachbuilder. The incredible wedge was three-feet high, with a lift-up windscreen/door, movement of which raised (or lowered) the jointed steering column and wheel. Instrumentation was very moon-shot, and visibility wasn't of the best. The driver's seat was a reclining affair, and the power-unit/transmission was a Lancia 1.6-litre Fulvia HF, normally a front-drive unit, set ahead of the rear suspension and driving the rear wheels. The chisel nose incorporated a band of ten small headlights, and at the rear there was a cluster of red lights set in a ring around the tail. Radiator for the V4-cylinder engine was also tail-mounted.

De Tomaso's "Dauville", a massive four-door saloon powered by a Ford V8 engine with de Tomaso overhead camshaft conversion, in five-litre, or 5.7-litre form. General shape was reminiscent of the Jaguar XK6. ▸

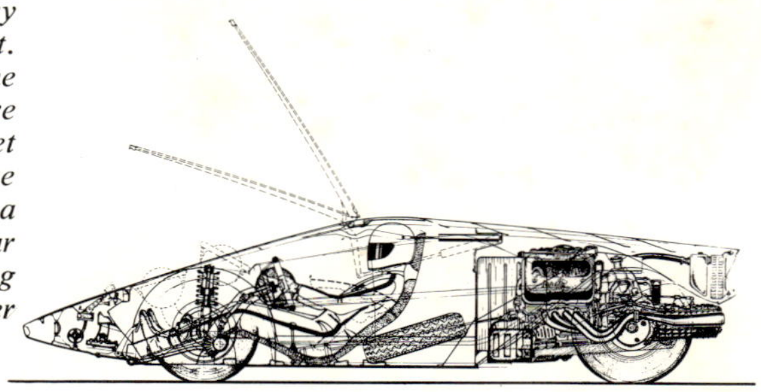

Zagato, the old-established Italian coachbuilder, produced this interesting rear-engined four-seat NART saloon at the Turin Show. Bearing more than a passing resemblance to the Oldsmobile Toronado, it did in fact use the V8 engine and automatic transmission from the American front-drive car in the tail, and driving the rear wheels.

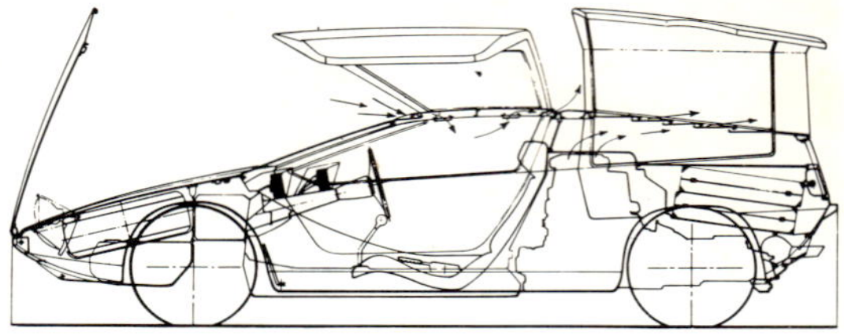

Using the VW-Porsche 914-6 as the basic structure, ex-Bertone stylist Giorgetto Giugaro produced a good-looking gull-wing coupé under the Ital Design banner, designated "Tapiro". Visibility was reasonable and there was a little baggage space over the engine and transmission. The engine had been enlarged to 2.4 litres and power-output was up to 220 (DIN) hp. ▸

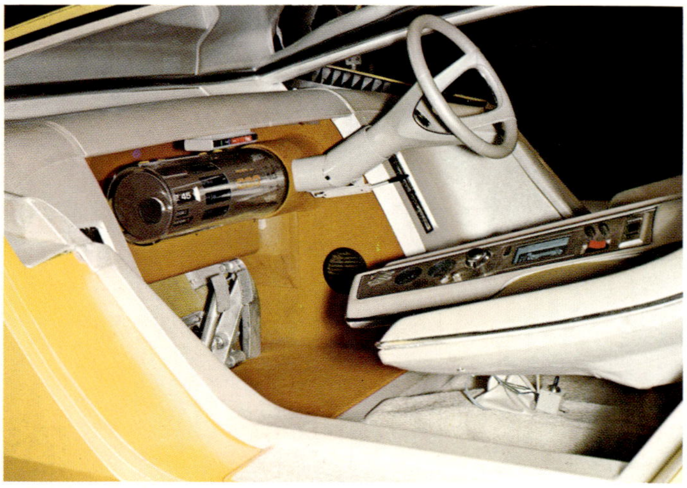

Toyota's EX-7 'wedge' was based on the ex-Group 7 V8 with five-litre four ohc engine. The two-seater coupé featured a vast glass area, electric up-swing doors, and space-type instrumentation. The two seats lifted for access to the rear compartment, and steering wheel diameter was very Japanese.

Honda Z, new tiny coupé based on the 360 was presented in standard form but also as a 'GS' with 36 hp twin-carburetter engine, five-speed gearbox, servo disc front brakes, radial tyres and what else. The 360 cc class is hotly contested in Japan and Honda cut back normal production to introduce the 'Z'.

Nissan's 'dream car', the 126X was classed as an inter-city car for the nineteen-eighties. Wedge-shaped, it was a four-seater with a mid-mounted six-cylinder power-unit and electronic fuel-injection. The automatic transmission and anti-skid braking were also electronic. Power-output was said to be around 180 hp.

Datsun's 270 X is a wedge that might happen, with production-based 1.2-litre four-cylinder engine mounted transversely at the front, driving the front wheels. Based on the "Cherry" engine it also has electronic fuel injection, and the general shape suggests high top speed. The two occupants gain access through the front-hinged canopy roof. Nose radiator is fully ducted, and height of car is a mere three feet. Sideways/rear vision restricted.

Isuzu Bellett R 6 Spider is a mid-engined competition car with central seat, and cooling arrangements at each side, as well as at the rear. Roll-bar is correct height for Japanese drivers! No performance figures available.

Isuzu's Bellett MX 1600 is a mid-engined prototype of attractive shape and undoubted aerodynamic efficiency. The engine is mounted transversely ahead of the rear suspension. Vision through the rear quarters is obviously difficult, as witness the stalk-mounted wing mirrors. Tail slats a la *Bertone assist with aft vision as well as with general engine cooling.*

Tail view of the "Nissan 126 X" reveals the convex nature of the rear slats and engine cover. Also the underbody cooling louvres.

Four lamps are set in the grille, and the stream-lined headlights are in the wings. ►

Mazda's RX500 is the Japanese manufacturer's reply to Mercedes' CIII. Strictly experimental, its thick rear quarters house a twin-rotor Wankel engine of unspecified capacity, with temporary Weber induction arrangements. The wind-cheating bodywork has two seats, and the chassis is pure "racer". Rather indecent rear display reveals special silencing arrangements, and great attention has been directed at exhausting hot air from engine compartment. Like the Europeans, the Japanese are adopting the wedge form in their experimental cars.

Toyota's new Celicia sports coupé is a 2+2 which shares the power-unit of the Carina. The engine is available in two sizes, 1.4 and 1.6 litres, with respective power-outputs of 100 and 105 hp.

Honda's latest edition of the 1300 cc air-cooled model has seating for five, and a slightly less powerful engine than its predecessor. The "77" develops 95 hp (SAE) at 7000 rpm in contrast to the earlier car's 100 hp 7200 rpm. The four-cylinder transverse motor drives the front wheels and the suspension is all-independent. Although air-cooled, the Honda engineers have achieved quiet running with the power-unit, due to the use of a double-wall cylinders.

Jolly little town car by Toyota from the drawing board of former racing chief Kawano has electric motor built-in to the single front wheel. Power is supplied by a large-capacity lead-acid battery. Seats for two, and just the thing for Nipping around Tokyo.

Mazda's EX-5 is a bubble of outstanding interest with Wellsian look and a little Wankel engine running at constant speed and driving a generator which supplies current to four electric motors, one to each wheel. The constant-speed running of the rotary engine means its emission is at its minimum, and well suited to city work. Turning circle is unbelievably tight.

The Datsun Cherry is an attractive front-drive model which comes in three styles, two and four-door saloon, or three-door estate. Suspension is independent all-round, and there is a high-output 1200 X-1 model with twin carburetters and 80 hp output.

Galant GTO by Mitsubishi is a good-looking fastback coupé with 1.5-litre, 105 hp engine. Under the Chrysler-Mitsubishi banner, the Galant will be marketed by the Dodge Division in the USA but will be known as the Colt. The Galant is very much in the Capri/Manta mould, and could perhaps capture some of the would-be Pinto and Vega buyers. Hottest model has a twin o.h.c engine.

In its coupé form the Honda 1300 is designated "9", and claims a 105 hp output (at 7300 rpm). The air-cooled transverse engine drives the front wheels, and top speed is around 112 mph. The two doors are wide and seating capacity is for four. Luggage capacity is generous and the general shape pleasing. Like the saloon model, the engine is unusually quiet-running for an air-cooled unit. Honda is Japan's third-largest car manufacturer, and also the biggest motorcycle producer.

Ford restyled their Mustang in a big way for 1971 with longer bonnet, new roofline, and a rear slope angle of only 14 degrees. The rear visibility aspect wasn't its strong point, but the Kamm tail and general masculinity of it all made it a favourite with youth sectors. Front wheel track was widened three inches to make room for the seven-litre V8 with "stagger valves".

Chrysler Corporation's Plymouth Satellite exhibits pleasing, uncluttered lines, and although it cannot be seen in this view, the front-end features a "loop" grille with bumper encircling the nose. The Satellite came in two and four-door hardtop form and a great deal of rubber damping material was employed in the rear suspension to insulate the body from road noise.

For 1970, Cadillac's Eldorado featured an entirely new body and a longer wheelbase. The V8 engine of 8.2 litres featured a compression ratio of 8.5:1, making it a proposition for the new reduced-lead fuels. Front drive was retained, but rear suspension switched from leaf to coil springs and trailing arms. Computerised rear wheel braking control optional.

American Motors' Javelin AMX (top) wasn't all-new but there was enough that was to make it interesting. The AMX/3 on the other hand was an exciting mid-engined GT, built in Italy by Giotto Bizzarini. With 6.4-litre V8 ahead of the rear wheels, and with all-independent suspension it was one of AMC's most potent projects. Limited production, and a 0-60 in 5.5 seconds !

American Motors were first away with their sub-compact, the Gremlin, because they used their standard Hornet six-cylinder engine, front and rear suspension, steering gear, wings, inner sheet metal and what else. With long wheelbase/short overall length formula, it wasn't the prettiest of cars, but the (optional) lift-up rear door made it useful.

Ford Pinto, "the Model T of the 'seventies", was designed to squash the Beetle, and to out-do General Motors' Vega on every count. With an overall length of 13 ft. 7 in., the Pinto was 2.8 inches longer than the German car, and 8.4 in. wider. The engine, of cast-iron with two-litre belt-driven ohc (optional 1600 cc pushrod ohv) developed 95 bhp at 5700 rpm, and was German-built. The optional 1600 cc unit was the British-built Cortina engine. Suspension was simple and there was an excellent turning circle of 31.5 feet with 4.2 steering wheel turns.

A three-speed Ford automatic was available on the two-litre Pinto, but the 1600 came with four-speed manual only. Trim was good for a car with a target price of $1850 (about £830).

With 2.3-litre (light-alloy) engine only, GM's Chevrolet Vega sub-compact measured 14ft. 1.7in. in length, and was 5 ft. 5.4in. wide. The die-cast cylinder liner-less engine had a belt-driven overhead camshaft and was available in 90 or 110 hp form. Standard transmission was a three-speed manual, but a two-speed Powerglide automatic was an option. The sedan came with a sloping fastback rear window, the coupé with a lift-up window-hatch, and an estate version featured an opening rear tailgate. Rear live axle suspension was positively located by four links.

GT = COMFORT SPEED SAFETY

The term "GT" has become incredibly confused over the last few years, being attached to anything from a relatively inexpensive volume-production-based saloon, to a certain type of racing car. The real meaning of the designation, which derives from the fast, luxury cars of the past—the "Grand Tourers" like Rolls-Royce, Hispano-Suiza, Isotta-Fraschini, Bugatti and so on—is a vehicle of high performance which at the same time provides comfort, baggage space, creature amenities, and a good range. In more spacious days, when Milord and Milady set off on the Grand Tour, they would of course have been chauffeured by Hoskins—"such a reliable fellow"—and would have probably been accompanied by a couple of close friends. Today it is different. Hoskins would probably find it difficult to accommodate his peaked cap within some of the modern "GT" cars, and in any case his boss probably likes driving good cars so much he would want to be at the wheel. In any case real Grand Touring cars of the "seventies are hard-put to seat four in comfort, so the Grand Tour is usually made with two adults and luggage. These impressions of four modern "GT" cars are unusual in that they deal with engines of virtually the same capacity but all have different configurations. *Automobile Year* has so often been amazed to try cars which were classed as "GT", yet which couldn't be used for long journeys. So often the engine was noisy, the ventilation inadequate, the luggage space laughable. Fast driving is one thing, but covering the ground at high average speeds in comfort, with ample luggage, and without exhaustion is another. Who needs a powerful engine if its operational noise promotes fatigue, and what use is a high-performance power-unit if its heat is not efficiently taken away from the cockpit? The subject of these impressions is not to test maximum performance, but to evaluate the cars as Grand Touring machines. All of them are classed as such in present-day parlance.

From experience gained with the four cars it is obvious that the mid-engined layout provides superior handling and roadholding to both the classic front engine position and the true rear engine. The configuration however has distinct disadvantages for the Grand Touring car—disadvantages of heat, both in the cockpit and in the luggage compartment, and of noise. But arguments always ensue wherever automobiles are discussed—cars, like drivers, are very different, and the permutations are endless!

Fiat Dino Coupé's lines by Bertone are handsome with large glass area for visibility, and plenty of headroom. From the front the four-headlight equipment can be seen, and the four luxury bucket seats are visible. No shortage of instruments but the rev-counter was often hidden by driver's hand.

Typically Ferrari, the Dino 246 with Pininfarina coachwork is an eyeful on any road. Radiator intake size is kept to the minimum in the interests of good aerodynamics, and frontal area is small. Note air-intakes in rear "wings" for tyre cooling. Transverse/rear engine mounting has made possible a short tail, but surprisingly the Dino is longer overall than the Porsche 911. With its air of masculinity the Dino 246 GT is a female trap of the top rank, but only lightly-laden ladies can be given lifts. Swiss driver on right is emitting oaths as he discovers the shapely female in need of transport has a tent with her. Or is it a pointer?

GE 1634

DINO 246 GT

As a car the Dino-Ferrari 246 is fantastic. It is almost impossible to find superlatives to use in relation to the performance. The roadholding is quite incredible, like a racing car, the transverse mid-engine providing perfect weight distribution. Corners and bends can be taken at unbelieveable speeds, and although a top-flight racing driver could undoubtedly find the car's cornering limit, it was quite impossible for a normal motorist (with sporting inclinations!) to discover the breakaway point.

The Dino GT 246 uses the same four ohc V6 engine as its close relative the Fiat Dino, but it is installed transversely at the rear, ahead of the (independent) suspension, instead of longitudinally at the front. The 2.4 litre engine is identical in both cars, but the 246 has larger carburetters and delivers another 15 hp, its maximum output of 195 (DIN) being sufficient to propel it at 146 mph.

With *Berlinetta* two-door coachwork by Pininfarina it is a thing of beauty—lithe and animal-like. For the affluent motorist who would attract admiring glances from the opposite sex, the Dino 246 must be a good bet.

It is very much a two-seater. The seats are well-shaped but surprisingly (particularly in view of the price tag) they are upholstered in PVC. Although comfortable enough, a run of almost any distance, particularly during the summer, would find the occupants stuck to the seats. Ventilation arrangements are inadequate, and a great deal of heat is transmitted to the interior by the engine which is very close to the cockpit.

Apart from the space provided for two occupants, there is room for precious little else! There are no map pockets (the Grand Tour, remember?) and nowhere to put one's jacket in hot weather. There is a reasonable-sized luggage compartment aft of the power-unit but the engine heat transmitted into this area actually melted the inside of a plastic suitcase during *Automobile Year's* "ownership".

In spite of the racey nature of the 246 GT, its engine displayed no temperament whatsoever, and it never stalled or fouled a plug in traffic, and although immensely powerful it displayed amazing docility. Two thermostatically-controlled electric fans take care of water temperature, and these worked like a charm.

Sitting in the Dino 246 had the effect of making the driver feel like a racer. The driving position was perfection, the instrumentation complete, and the stubby gear lever projected from a neat "gate" marked-out for five forward speeds and a reverse. If the clutch was dropped with 5,500 rpm on the tachometer, the Dino performed like a racing car! The gearbox was a joy to use, and there seemed no limit to the machine's capabilities. What is more, it was an entirely manageable car and appeared to have no vices at all. The engine was powerful yet docile, the performance more than satisfying, and the ride relatively soft.

For performance and high-speed control the Dino 246 GT cannot be faulted, but it must be classed as a performance-first car. To extract the best from it, and to minimise noise it is necessary to drive with the windows closed, so the heat problem is a very real one—particularly in summer. In hilly country the handbrake is useless. It will not hold the car on a steep gradient, and in countries like Switzerland it presents a big problem. When the luggage compartment lid is opened in or after rain, the top of the panel pivots inwards and deposits water over the baggage.

No-one who has any sort of enthusiasm for motor cars could fail to enjoy driving the Dino 246 GT. It is a powerful projectile, yet with its relatively soft suspension, good driving position, fantastic handling, light gear-change, it falls short of being a Grand Touring car. It is exciting and enormously satisfying to drive fast, like at horoughbred motorcycle, but by the same token it would be a perfect car to keep for Fun. The engineering is splendid, but we feel it would spend a great deal of time in its owner's garage while he or she used a more suitable car for long runs.

Nevertheless, in spite of the 246 GT's shortcomings, we shall go slightly green with envy when one passes! Either way!!

Ferrari's Dino 166P with 1600 cc 200 hp engine was the precursor of the 246 GT. The original car finished fourth in the 1965 Nürburgring 1,000 kilometres.

Pininfarina Berlinetta, 2 doors, 2 seats.

Engine: Ferrari-Fiat. V 6 (65 deg.) transversely-mounted ahead of rear suspension, in unit with gearbox and final-drive. Bore 92.5 mm. Stroke 60 mm. Cubic capacity 2418 cc. Compression ratio 9 :1. Twin ohc per cylinder bank. Three double-choke Weber carburetters. Coil ignition, and alternator. Power-output: 195 (DIN) bhp at 7600 rpm. Max. torque 166 lb. ft. at 5500 rpm.

Transmission: Rear engine, rear drive. Manual gearbox, 3.79, 4.98, 6.75, 9.39, 13.62. Reverse 11.80. Top gear per 1000 rpm, 18.5 mph. Limited-slip differential.

Chassis and Suspension: Welded steel tubular frame with independent suspension all-round by coil springs and wishbones. Servo-assisted Girling disc brakes to all four wheels. Rack and pinion steering.

Dimensions: Wheelbase 7 ft. 8.2 in. Track, front, 4 ft. 8.1 in., rear, 4 ft. 7.1 in. Width 5 ft. 7 in. Length 13 ft. 9 in. Height 3 ft. 8 in. Ground clearance 5 in. Turning circle 44 ft. Unladen weight 2376 lb. Fuel tank capacity 15.4 gallons (Imp). Tyres 185-14.

Maximum speed: 146 mph.

Prototype of the 246 GT had its V6 engine mounted longitudinally in the chassis ahead of the rear suspension. Good car as it was, the transverse layout of the current mid engine has greatly improved the handling.

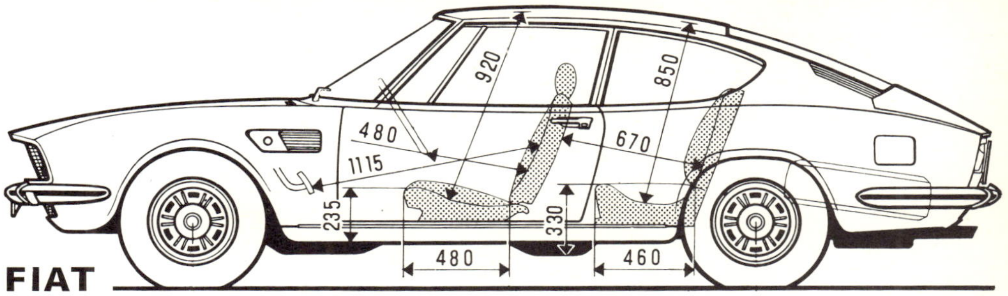

DINO FIAT

In 1969 the Fiat Dino had its V6 engine increased from two to 2.4 litres, and its cylinder block was cast in iron instead of light-alloy. The new block was standardised to simplify manufacture (the old light-alloy block had separate cylinder liners which had to be inserted) and to ensure against water leaks as the engine aged. At the same time the rear suspension was changed from that of a well-located live axle and semi-elliptic leaf springs to a fully-independent system of coil springs and double-jointed half-shafts. With almost half-a-litre more engine, the Dino was transformed from a racey car which needed to be "driven on the rev-counter" to a high-performance GT with the emphasis on torque increase more than on maximum power. The two-litre had been fitted with a five-speed Fiat gearbox, but the greatly-increased torque of the new engine prompted the Torinese manufacturer to fit a new ZF box with first speed position isolated from the four upper ratios which are used once the car is on the move. The Fiat Dino was originally introduced in Pininfarina "Spider" form at the Turin Show in 1966, but the Bertone coupé followed in 1967 at the Geneva Salon, and it is with the latter model that we are concerned as it is the true GT model of the range, and has the longer wheelbase necessary for comfortable rear passenger habitation. The Dino series-production engine came into being due to Enzo Ferrari's desire to enter his ex-racing Dino (named after his son who died in his 'twenties) V6 engine in the 1967 two-litre Formula 2, and his need for homologation as a production engine. With Fiat producing the engines for a catalogue model his entry was assured. With its wheelbase of 8 ft. 4 in., and overall length of 14 ft. 97 in., the Fiat Dino Coupé is commodious as well as extremely handsome. All four seats are true "buckets" which provide excellent lateral support during fast cornering, and all are upholstered in a rough-textured cloth which is extremely comfortable and breathes well. Although mounted longitudinally at the front, the Fiat Dino engine is identical to the Dino-Ferrari, except that smaller carburetters reduce its power-output 15 hp With its maximum output of 180 (DIN) hp and an unladen weight of 3,042 lb., it is anything but a sluggard.

The increased torque of the enlarged engine has a dramatic effect on the Dino. The two-litre power-unit produced 126 lb. ft. at 6,000 rpm, the latest 2.4-litre unit provides 159 lb. ft. at *1,400 rpm less.* Whereas the older car demanded racing car technique to produce results, the 2.4 Dino leaps forward like a bull in all gears from relatively low revs, but will also trickle along in fifth speed at 25 mph and accelerate strongly without changing-down, and without a snatch. The steering is fairly heavy with the large tyres, and there is no servo-assistance, but the steering wheel is not of the fashionable mini-variety and there is never any real difficulty. The car will cruise tirelessly, if not quietly, at 110 mph, and fourth speed will lift the speed to 120 mph for swift overtaking.

The gearbox was a delight to use, first being selected by placing the lever to the far left and back, the remaining four speeds being found in the usual "H" position. Second speed could be engaged like lightning after take-off, and the others went through like a hot knife through butter. Every time a new gear was selected the acceleration hit occupants in the back and the engine note rose in a stimulating manner.

The Dino Coupé was tried over several days during which time it covered more than 1,200 miles, 900 of them being devoured on the trip to and from Le Mans (from Lausanne) to cover the 24 hours race. The trip embraced almost every sort of going, and the car soon revealed itself to be a true Grand Tourer with impressive performance, great comfort, space for maps and *bric-a-brac*, and a realistic luggage capacity. The four-wheel disc brakes were immensely powerful.

A true GT car, and if there are any criticisms at all they can be levelled at an engine which is hardly quiet (but which emits an exciting Ferrari-type whine), and rev-counter which was hidden most of the time by the driver's hand.

Luxury interior of Fiat Dino Coupé has well-shaped bucket seats trimmed with cloth. Rear seat knee and legroom is good for type of car.

Fiat Dino's boot was of the "up-and-over" variety but capacity was generous. Body dimensions in fact are the same as the older two-litre model, but in every other direction it is a completely different car.

Bertone Coupé, 2 doors, 4 seats (also Pininfarina Spider with shorter wheelbase and lighter by 220 lb.)

Engine: Fiat V6 (65 deg.) longitudinally front-mounted, in unit with five-speed gearbox. Bore 92.5 mm. Stroke 60 mm. Cubic capacity 2318 cc. Compression ratio 9 :1. Twin ohc per cylinder bank. Three double-choke Weber carburetters. Electronic ignition, and alternator. Power-output 180 bhp (DIN) at 6600 rpm. Max torque. 159 lb. ft. at 4600 rpm.

Transmission: Front engine, rear drive. Diaphragm clutch, manual gearbox, all-synchromesh. 4.14, 4.77, 6.20, 8.38, 14.26. Reverse 17.50. Top gear per 1000 rpm 17.1 mph. Limited-slip differential.

Chassis and suspension: Unitary construction with all-independent suspension by coil spring struts, at the front, and by coil springs and diagonal trailing arms at the rear. Double-jointed half-shafts and fixed differential casing. Servo-assisted Girling disc brakes (outboard) on all four wheels. Steering by worm and roller.

Dimensions: Wheelbase 8 ft. 4 in. Track, front, 4 ft. 6½ in., rear, 4 ft. 5.2 in. Length 14 ft. 97in. Width 5 ft. 7.3 in. Height 4 ft. 3.9 in. Ground clearance 4.7 in. Turning circle 40 ft. 8 in. Unladen weight 3042 lb. Fuel tank capacity 14½ gallons (Imp). Tyres 185-14.

Maximum speed: 125 mph.

S-W 4883

The clean lines of the Porsche 911 2 + 2 are a familiar sight in most countries. Introduced as the 901 in 1963 it is still one of the world's finest Grand Touring cars—and one of the few that measure up to requirements.

It is an easy matter to remove the roof panel of the VW-Porsche for maximum light and air, but turbulence spoils the car when it is detached and stowed in the rear boot. There is surprising baggage capacity fore and aft, but the instrumentation is rather limited for a car of its type. The pop-up headlights are actuated by electric motors, both of which can be seen in the view of the opened front luggage compartment. A complete toolkit wallet is stowed in the front boot which, like the rear, is carpeted. The 914-6 doesn't look particularly aerodynamic but fuel consumption and speeds suggest it is far better-streamlined than it appears.

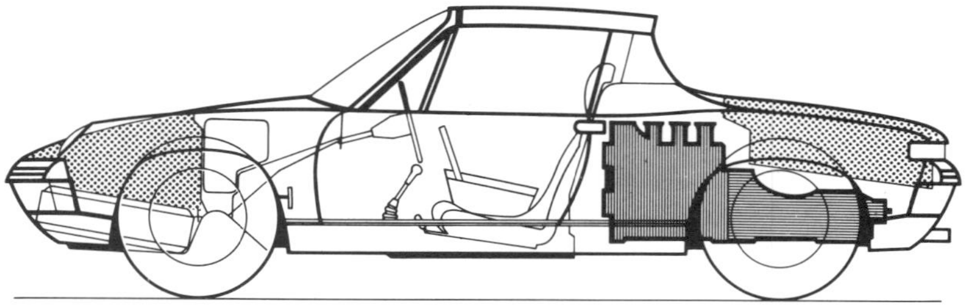

VW-PORSCHE 914/6

After years of co-operation, Volkswagen and Porsche decided to launch a "combined" sporting car in late 1969. Bearing the name VW-Porsche the new car was mid-engined, with an option of the 1.7-litre electronically-injected four-cylinder VW engine, or the two-litre Porsche "911" "six". Both engines of course are horizontally-opposed and air-cooled. The 914 has the four-cylinder engine and the 914-6 the "flat-six", the former being assembled by VW, the latter by Porsche. The car features a lift-off roof, the aft section of the body forming an anti-roll bar. It is of ultra-low build, has luggage compartments fore and aft, and flip-up headlights. In appearance you either like it or loathe it—it is squat and powerful-looking, but rather angular. Its performance however is never in doubt.

Unlike other Porsche (and VW) production road models, the VW-Porsche is mid-engined, the configuration inevitably making the car a two-seater. The seats don't look comfortable but in fact are well-shaped and provide good lateral hold. The dashboard is dull with a minimum of instruments for a car of this type. Driving position is good.

Road view ahead is excellent with the fall-away nose, but the three-quarter-rear sections of the bodywork form blinker-like screens, which due to their nearness to the driver's eyes, will block large objects from his view. The two-litre version of the six-cylinder Porsche engine has two three-choke Weber carburetters, a useful power-output of 110 hp, and the car is extremely lively. It would easily attain 110 mph and hold this speed happily, and there was a maximum of 120 mph. The ride is good, the independent four-wheel suspension soaking-up road irregularities in an impressive manner, and the mid-engined configuration assists with extremely rapid cornering capabilities. The 914-6 corners as though it is on rails, and there seems no limit to cornering speeds. Finally, the limit can be reached, then all four wheels break away together rather untidily but bearing witness to the very even weight distribution. The engine is smooth, flexible, and very responsive, but being mid-positioned its presence is never in doubt. The noise is tiring on long runs, as we found with our testing programme of 1,500 miles. The five-speed gearbox has excellent synchromesh, but the floor lever doesn't provide the precision of selection one would expect on a car of this type and we found it all too easy to engage third instead of fifth, even after a lengthy period of acquaintanceship.

There is a good deal of transmitted heat within the cockpit, but although it is not a cramped area there is still nowhere for occupants to put jackets etc. Removal of the roof certainly admits air and light, but there is too much turbulence for comfort at high cruising speeds.

Unusually, the VW-Porsche has two luggage compartments, one on the nose, and another aft of the engine. A great deal of baggage can be stowed away with a little planning, but the car suffers from the seemingly inevitable bugbear of mid-engined cars in that the rear compartment is always hot. One presumably packs one's pyjamas into the boot most suitable for the time of year! And the chocolates!!

The 914-6 is a fast, smooth car with ride and handling characteristics that deserve the highest praise, but in other directions it falls short of being classed as a Grand Touring model. It does not fascinate.

Rear upper flanks of the 914-6 form a safety roll-over section, even with roof panel detached.

Coupé with removable top, mid-engined, 2 doors, 2 seats. (also 914 model with 1.7-litre four-cylinder, fuel-injected Volkswagen engine).

Engine: Horizontally-opposed six-cylinder, air-cooled. Bore 80 mm. Stroke 66 mm. Cubic capacity 1991 cc. Compression ratio 8.6 :1. Two three-choke Weber carburetters. Electronic ignition and alternator. Power-output 110 bhp (DIN) at 5800 rpm. Max torque 116 lb. ft. at 4200 rpm.

Transmission: Rear engine, rear drive. Five-speed all-synchromesh manual: 3.36, 4.10, 5.40, 7.86, 13.68. Reverse 13.84. Porsche "Sportomatic" (optional extra semi-automatic/torque converter): 3.80, 5.53, 6.86, 10.61. Reverse 11.15. Top gear per 1000 rpm 21.8. mph. Limited-slip differential.

Chassis and suspension: Unitary body and all-independent suspension. Front, longitudinal torsion bars, rear, coil springs and semi-trailing arms. Four-wheel disc brakes (ATE). Rack and pinion steering.

Dimensions: Wheelbase 8 ft. 0.25 in. Track, front 4 ft. 5.5 in., rear, 4 ft. 6.4 in. Length 13 ft. 0.7 in. Width 5 ft. 5 in. Height 4 ft. 0.5 in. Ground clearance 5.2 in. Turning circle 36 ft. Unladen weight 2070 lb. Fuel tank capacity 13.7 gallons (Imp). Tyres 165-15.

Maximum speed: 120 mph.

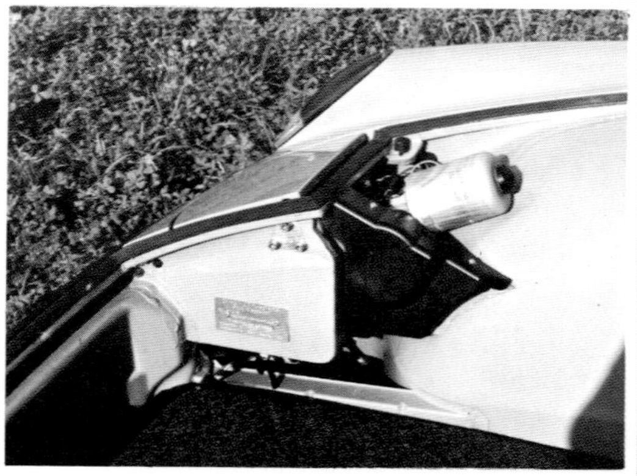

Close-up of one of the electric motors which operate the retractable headlights. Fixed halogen lights are fitted in the front bumpers for daylight flashing.

PORSCHE 911 T

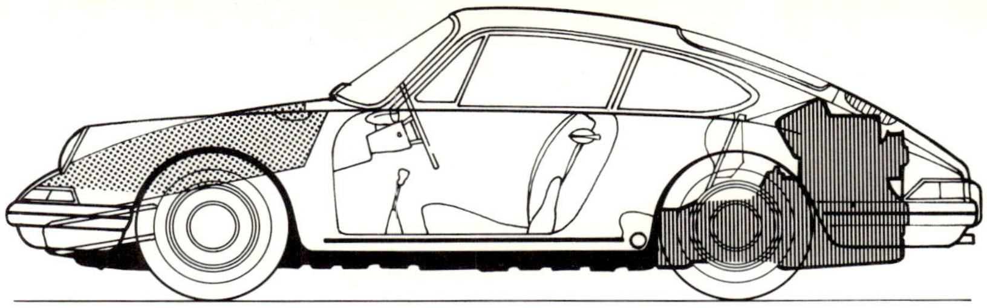

The Porsche 911 needs little introduction to readers of *Automobile Year*. It is a low-built two-door coupé of excellent aerodynamic shape, powered by a six-cylinder air-cooled horizontally-opposed engine mounted aft of the (independent) rear suspension. It carries a high price tag in any of its model forms, but it is built to exacting standards by the well-known German manufacturers who have dominated the endurance racing and rallying scene of late, and who have participated in competition for many years since the war.

There are three basic versions of the 911, all of which have the 2.2-litre engine, the capacity of the motor being increased from two litres in 1969 when the smaller size was chosen as the production unit for the VW-Porsche 914-6. The "Model T" develops 125 (DIN) hp, the "E" has fuel-injection with power up to 155 hp, and the "S" (also with injection) has the impressive output of 180 hp. Models T and E have a choice of four or five-speed manual gearboxes, as well as the four-speed semi-automatic (two-pedal) Sportomatic transmission. The 911S has the five-speed manual as standard equipment.

We have no hesitation in saying the Porsche 911 is a car which is designed—well-designed— for travel. Best roadholder of the series is the "S" which has stiffer suspension than the two less-sporting models, but the handling and ride of the "T" and "E" are perhaps the most favourable compromise. Most striking aspect of the "T" and "E" models, both of which we have extensively tested, is the low noise level inside the car—even though the air-cooled engine sounds noisy outside. The 911 can be driven all day at an indicated 180 kph (110 mph) with just a murmur from the rear engine bay. At all times the six-cylinder *boxermotor* is turbine-smooth and responsive. Both cars under test were equipped with the optional semi-automatic transmission, although the gear-change is a little slower, and there is reduced engine braking effect on the over-run, the disadvantages are well outweighed by the advantages. The four speeds enable the engine to be exploited, and the lack of clutch pedal and smoothness of the torque converter take the misery out of traffic driving. On the main roads and byways the 911 Sportomatic could be driven with zest, but when towns and traffic were encountered the two-pedal control made for effortless acceptance.

The seats are well-shaped with material options but the test cars were equipped with cloth contact surfaces and PVC "edges"—an ideal arrangement. The material was cool in the summer weather which prevailed during the test periods, and would be warm in winter conditions. Like most rear seats in 2+2 cars, they were little more than a joke. More suitable for children, they could be folded forward to provide extra luggage space, and used as a two-seater with seats folded the interior was commodious. The nose of the car also had a shallow but long compartment which would swallow a surprising amount of baggage. The back seat would accommodate one adult but even then for only short trips.

The driving position was first-class and could be adjusted to suit almost any size man or woman. Ventilation was excellent, as was visibility. In keeping with GT performance the four-wheel brakes were immensely powerful and unfadeable. The handbrake would easily hold the car on steep gradients—a particularly important feature if the Grand Tour is to include mountainous country. Porsche achieve such good results with their handbrake system by employing two small auxiliary internal-expanding drum brakes incorporated in the rear discs.

Handling was superb at high speed with light steering. Basic characteristic was oversteer but this was controllable and predictable, it being possible to place the car to a hair. Through fast curves the handling was a joy, both steering and throttle contributing to control.

The Porsche 911 is a genuine Grand Tourer and although it is expensive wherever it is sold, the number that are seen on the roads of the world is a measure of the car's fitness for purpose.

Neat four-spoked steering wheel is good to hold and provides a clear view of the rev-counter and speedometer—most of the time.

Two-door 2 + 2 Coupé (also Targa Cabriolet, and more powerful engines are available in models 911 E (155 bhp DIN), and 911 S (180 bhp DIN).

Engine: Rear-mounted aft of suspension. Horizontally-opposed six-cylinder, air-cooled. Bore 84 mm. Stroke 66 mm. Cubic capacity 2195 cc. Compression ratio 8.6 :1. Two triple-choke Weber carburetters. Electronic ignition and alternator. Power-output 125 bhp (DIN) at 5800 rpm. Max torque 130 lb. ft. at 4200 rpm.

Transmission: Rear engine, rear drive. Five-speed all-synchromesh manual gearbox: 3.36, 4.1, 5.4, 7.86, 13.68. Reverse 13.84. (optional Porsche Sportomatic semi-automatic/torque converter transmission: 3.31, 4.34, 5.9, 9.26. Reverse 9.80) Top gear per 1000 rpm 21.6 mph. Limited-slip differential.

Chassis and Suspension: Unitary body and all-independent suspension. Front, longitudinal torsion bars and anti-roll bar (self-levelling), rear, transverse torsion bars and semi-trailing wishbones. Four-wheel disc brakes (ATE/Dunlop) with double hydraulic circuit. Rack and pinion steering.

Dimensions: Wheelbase 7 ft. 5.3 in. Track, front 4 ft. 5.5 in., rear 4 ft. 4.8 in. Length 13.8 in. Width 5 ft. 3.5 in. Height 4 ft. 4 in. Ground clearance 6 in. Turning circle 35 ft. Unladen weight 2250 lb. Fuel tank capacity 13½ gallons (Imp). Tyres 165-15.

Maximum speed: 125 mph (911 E 137 mph; 911 S 140 mph).

DUNLOP
elf
elf
elf
DUNLOP
1
Tyrrell
elf
elf

RACING

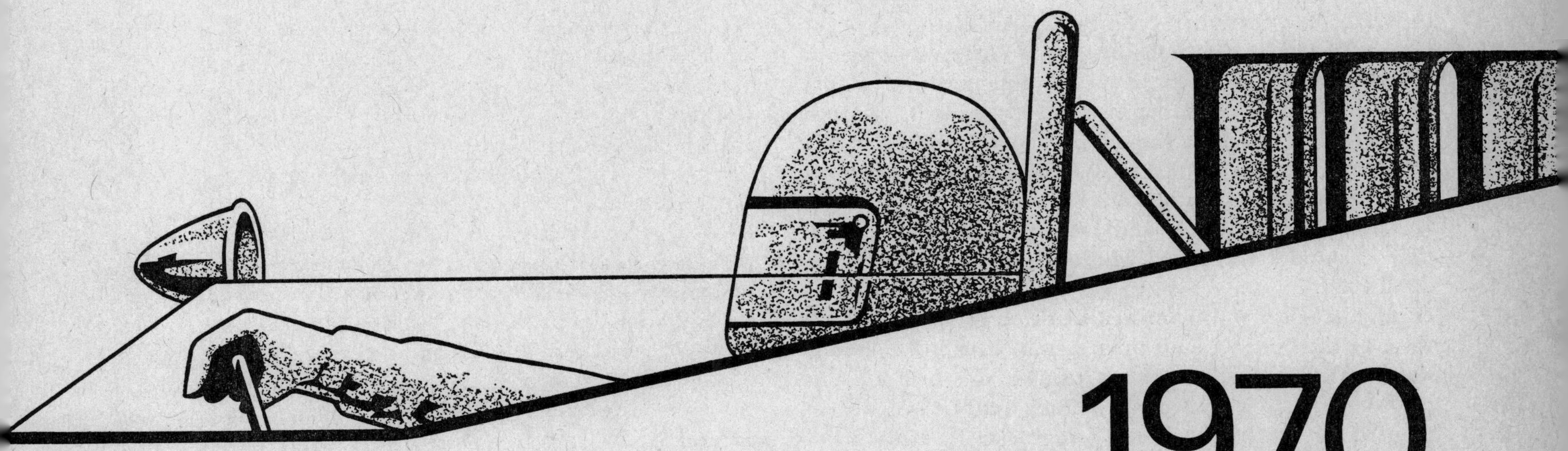

1970

◄ *An impressive photograph of Jackie Stewart at the wheel of the Tyrrell-Ford during the United States Grand Prix practice.*

Drivers' World Championship

The year of Jochen Rindt

by José Rosinski

In 1970, the "three-litre" Formula, instituted four years earlier, began to reach the heights. There was considerable expansion on both technical and sporting planes, but it was a year of drama and tragedy as well. Instead of being a year which should have been remembered as one of splendid accomplishment, it will always be coupled with the untimely deaths of Formula 1 drivers Bruce McLaren, Piers Courage and Jochen Rindt, although the New Zealander was killed whilst testing a CanAm car at Goodwood.

To say that they will be missed and that motor racing will never be the same without them sounds trite and commonplace. Written words cannot express the emotion and grief one feels, but it will be a long time before we will be used to not seeing Bruce's merry face, Pier's spare frame, and Jochen's pursed lips on the scene. It is sad that motor racing cannot be a permanently joyous affair.

Under the normal five-year span the three-litre Formula 1 should have finished its term at the end of 1971. Instead the Sporting Commission of the *FIA* decided to prolong it so there was a chance of "consolidation" in a sport which was becoming ever-more expensive. In 1969 the Grand Prix fields had often thinned to the point where the race organizers had real cause for anxiety, but in 1970 there was a score of steady and reliable entries for each event. At the same time the teams announced that their financial demands would be greater to which the organisers replied they were unable to accept the demands on a basis of quantity *or* quality. How could the deadlock be broken? Representatives from both sides met in an attempt to find common ground, and the outcome of their discussions was the "Geneva Agreement".

Far from being an agreement, it caused bitter controversy and confusion.

What was it actually all about? The system that had prevailed until then had been based on starting money, and invitations. Before any new season opened, organizers and manufacturers agreed on the sum the former were to pay the latter. The scheme was based on the prestige of the team in question, and the reputation and record of the drivers involved. The scheme assured each Grand Prix of a field which included the leading drivers, while the latter in turn were assured of their rewards, and that their cars would participate in all the principal events. The last-mentioned clause was the most important for in this commercial age most teams are tied to one or more companies (directly connected with the sport, or not) by contracts that are obviously based on the regular presence of the team cars in Grand Prix races.

For instance, Players Gold Leaf, the tobacco firm which backs the Lotus team, or Yardley toilet preparations which sponsor BRM, would certainly not hand out the same amount of money to see their cars taking part in three, five, or twelve events.

Chief attraction for members of the Formula 1 Manufacturers' Association was the start guarantee. Each of them —Lotus, BRM, Matra-Simca, McLaren, Brabham, and March—agreed they would each have one driver qualified *ex-officio*. A place was also reserved for Ferrari, although not a member of the Association, and one each for past or existing World Champions who did not belong to works teams, namely, Stewart, Surtees, and Hill. (At the beginning of the 1970 season Surtees had bought a 1969 McLaren which he drove in World Championship races until he produced his own TS7 for the British Grand Prix in July.) All other competitors had to qualify on the basis of times attained during practice, to gain available places which varied from circuit to circuit. Starting money was abolished in favour of a system based on results. Three classifications providing prize money for all competitors down to the last-placed were established for one-third distance, two-thirds distance, and for the entire race.

It so happened that the earlier races of the season—except for Kyalami where the South Grand Prix was staged to the old formula—were the shortest, and consequently those which could accommodate fewest competitors. The grids at Monaco and Jarama were restricted to 16, which with ten places reserved *ex-officio* left only six to be competed for in the qualification runs. To add complication the new formula needed to be "run-in" and very complex calculations were called-for. It all led to weeping and gnashing of teeth, to interpretations and counter-interpretations, wrangling and so on. In fact, to utter confusion from which neither justice nor the ethics of the sport emerged unscathed.

Fortunately, things came right in the end, either because of the fact the larger circuits could accommodate a greater number of competitors, or because some organizers decided, as at Brands Hatch and Zeltweg, to raise the stakes in order to make room for all drivers who had participated in the trials.

Another bone of contention that stirred-up the 1970 Grand Prix scene was circuit safety. As a result of the storm two events were not staged at venues originally selected. One change took place "on the quiet", at considerable cost to the organisers: the Albi circuit was not homologated under existing conditions by the *CSI* who demanded big alterations entailing expense too great for the organizers to bear. As a result, Albi was obliged to withdraw in favour of the Charade circuit near Clermont-Ferrand where the French Grand Prix had taken place the year before.

There was no great drama where the French Grand Prix was concerned—public opinion was not stirred-up because the general view was that it was all for the best as Charade provided a more searching test than Albi, but the affair of the German Grand Prix created uproar, even amongst people of the most equable disposition. It is a long time since the *GPDA* (Grand Prix Drivers' Association) first became preoccupied with the subject of safety. Early in the 1970 season it announced its members would boycott the Spa-Francorchamps circuit, where the Belgian Grand Prix was scheduled to take place unless their safety recommendations were carried out. At first the *GPDA* made recommendations then as little had been done, they changed them to demands. In the end, the organisers agreed to adopt a "moving scale" of starting times under wet conditions, to avoid visibility and aquaplaning hazards on that very fast track. The subject had already resulted in hot-tempered discussions between upholders of tradition, notably Jacky Ickx and Pedro Rodriguez, who on that occasion at any rate, turned their backs on their fellow-members, and those who sided with the Association.

In the event, there was no drama as the race was run in fine weather, but emphasis was lent to the controversy by the tragic death of Bruce McLaren, killed a few days earlier whilst testing his CanAm car at Goodwood.

Tragedy struck again two weeks later at Zandvoort when Piers Courage crashed in Frank Williams' de Tomaso and was killed. The car burned as the competing cars passed lap after lap, and drivers were mostly of the opinion that a guardrail on that wide bend might well have saved the unfortunate Briton's life. Perturbed and ill at ease, the *GPDA* decided to take a tougher line with circuits where, in their opinion, the safety arrangements were inadequate. A programme of modifications, planned to be spread over a number of years was already under way at Nürburgring, but Association members demanded its completion in time for the 1970 German Grand Prix. The organisers reply was that with only one month to go they could not possibly comply. The drivers refused to race on the Eifel track and suggested the race be held on the Hockenheimring, an uninteresting circuit where Formula 1 cars had never before raced, but which was considered safe. What an outcry that raised!

Stewart, Rindt, Beltoise, and their associates would not surrender, although called a variety of rude names from piddling to cowardly. They had dared to offend the name of the legendary "Ring" which had witnessed the great exploits of their illustrious predecessors. Shades of Caracciola, Nuvolari, and Fangio were invoked, and Moss declared that stripped of danger, motor racing didn't make sense. If the drivers may be blamed for the manner of their actions—they had decided on their attitude very late in the day—their basic thinking was right.

It is quite unreasonable to suggest that Stewart—to name but one—is even the slightest degree less-courageous than the great champions of the past. Few will forget his fantastic performance on the Nürburgring in 1968 when he outdrove all his rivals in a fog so dense one could not see the pits from the main grandstands! Nor had Rindt any need of an advocate, for his closing laps on Brabham's tail in the 1970 Monaco Grand Prix were heroic stuff.

It must be said that in 1970 a racing driver's job was far more dangerous than it had ever been before, except perhaps for the early days of the first "city-to-city" races. There has been an enormous increase in the power and speed of the modern Grand Prix car, and it means that circuit improvements must keep pace with the machines or the risks will increase out of all proportion. In 1970 the circuits didn't keep pace with the cars. In modern times a Formula 1 driver enters a given bend, brakes, say, at 50 yards and turns at 110 mph, to be subjected to a centrifugal force of 1.5 g. Fifteen years before, a driver reaching the same bend braked at 100 yards and cornered at 85 mph. The driver of yesteryear had no less skill, but it is a fact that his chassis and tyres were less-efficient. It is also a fact the lower potential provided a safety-valve in effect, for if something untoward occurred, there was time for the driver to react, and there was room for him to slow-down before hitting a bank or tree, or turning-over in a ditch.

The roadholding capabilities of the modern single-seater have reduced the safety margin almost to nothing, hence the reason for safety devices which do not reduce the accident risk but merely make them less likely to be fatal, and then only up to a point. The opinion put forward by some that greater safety will drive away the big spectator crowds who flock to the circuits for excitement, is therefore superficial and quite unjustified.

As for calling the colleagues of McLaren, Courage, and Rindt cowardly, as I have both read and heard, the less said about that the better. In my mind's eye I can still see Stewart at Monza practice, less than an hour after his close friend's death, his face was still wet with tears. It was typical of the man that he climbed into his car, improved on his best practice lap time, and put himself in amongst the "invincible" Ferraris.

Safety arrangements on the circuits are only one aspect of the problem however. During 1970, in the opinion of many experienced observers of the motor racing scene, the cars were getting too fragile, particularly the Lotus 72. When the new car first appeared at Jarama, Chapman's latest machine marked an advance on the technical plane no less important than the Types 25 and 49 had done in their day. With typical enterprise and non-conformism, Chapman took advantage of every nook and cranny in the rules. While the other manufacturers advance step by step, improving each year on the previous year's models, he alone dares to go forward in leaps and bounds, sweeping away all preconceived ideas, and building something entirely new. In so doing of course, he takes risks and lays himself open to possible attack. Did Chapman go too far with the 72? It certainly seems a possibility that Rindt's crash may have been due to a mechanical failure, but that possibility cannot be set aside in the cases of McLaren and Courage either. Contrary to all appearances, Lotus has no monopoly of suspension breakages, and in that connection I shall merely say that even a serious, objective technician cannot be sure "at sight" whether or not the dimensions of such and such a component on the Lotus 72 are compatible with safety. Nevertheless, the Lotus has gained a reputation for fragility, but at one time or another during the season other constructors experienced serious suspension failures.

The inescapable conclusion must be that steps should be taken to strengthen Formula 1 cars. An appreciable minimum weight increase would undoubtedly enhance safety, and a decision should be taken without delay. Such an increase would enable constructors, whilst still maintaining the current ratio of suspended and non-suspended masses, to calculate the latter far more generously. It would also ease tyre problems which have just about reached the limit of compromise between size and weight. In the opening paragraphs of this article I referred to the notable technical expansion of Formula 1 in 1970. In fact, 1970 saw the end of the Ford-Cosworth V8's "invincibility". It is no exaggeration to say that for two seasons, a car equipped with any other power-unit just didn't stand a chance. The situation led to the establishment of what came to be known as the "success formula"—a classification of the elements required to win a Grand Prix, in order of importance. The engine headed the list—Ford-Cosworth of course—followed by driver, tyres, team manager, and last of all, the chassis. One of the consequences of that thinking was that in the "dead season" between 1969 and '70, World Champion Jackie Stewart and his manager Ken Tyrrell decided to quit the marque with which they had been associated for two very fruitful years. The main reason was that J. L. Lagardère, Matra's general manager, had announced his company's Formula 1 cars would all be equipped with French-built V12 engines at the beginning of 1970. It meant that Ken Tyrrell's Matra International team could no longer be supplied with a bare chassis into which they could insert their Ford-Cosworth V8 engines, and also it meant they would have to use the French V12s if they wanted to continue with Matra. Stewart and Tyrrell moved heaven and earth to change Lagardère's mind, but nothing would persuade him. He told them he would be pleased to supply them with Matra V12 engines, but Tyrrell and Stewart were convinced the Ford-Cosworth was unbeatable, so they started to look for another chassis manufacturer. Their departure from the Matra scene put the French constructor on the spot, for Stewart left a void that was not easy to fill. A number of established drivers were approached with offers to back-up Beltoise, among them Chris Amon who had already intimated he would like to leave Ferrari. The New Zealander however had no more faith in the V12 than had Stewart—his main reason for wanting to leave Ferrari was to drive a Ford-powered car. Looking back on the 1970 season one has no difficulty in grasping how bitterly Amon must have regretted his decision. As this article is written he has still to win his first Championship Grand Prix.

Be that as it may, when the season dawned both Stewart and Amon were still looking for a manufacturer capable of supplying a competitive machine designed around the Ford-Cosworth engine. Manufacturers Brabham, Lotus, and McLaren were unwilling to supply their latest models to Tyrrell, and none of them were to offer Amon a drive. Nor had any of them had any desire to hand Stewart a weapon with which to effect their defeat, for each wanted to gain the title for his own team, and not with Stewart as the "middle-man". All three teams had their No. 1 driver's place filled, the respective positions being occupied by Jack Brabham himself, who for all his 44 years made no secret of his ambition, by Jochen Rindt whose short-lived tiff with Chapman was already over, and by Denny Hulme.

So the marque March came into the picture. When the new firm's plans were revealed in the winter of 1969/70, the scheme had already been in the air for several months. The project revolved around three people, all of whom were well enough known to offer a serious chance of success and efficiency. At the beginning of 1969, Alan Rees a former and successful racing driver (and team-mate of Jochen Rindt) who had been responsible for the almost invincible Winckelman Formula 2 team, and Max Mosley, were convinced there was room for a new racing car manufacturer.

The basis of their thinking was that whereas almost anyone could obtain a perfectly good Ford-Cosworth V8 from the manufacturers, no-one could get delivery from the established constructors of a new chassis absolutely identical to a works car. With those convictions in mind they joined forces with talented designer Robin Herd who had an aeronautical background and had also been responsible for the 1968 McLaren M7A. The alliance was formed, not merely to sell chassis, but also to form a March works team. Indeed the two objectives were very definitely linked since if they wanted to race, they needed both men and money, and they would get both only if the number and calibre of their potential customers came up to expectations.

In many ways the operation was unique. It was virtually unheard-of for a brand-new constructor to start off in business and yet hope to attract the top drivers and teams to their cars, and products of March Engineering had to "saleable" while still on the drawing board. There is no doubt this sort of start precluded the company from launching the first March Formula 1 chassis as a way-out design. Rather the 701 had to be straightforward, not too sophisticated, reliable, and capable of "working" from the outset. And they didn't have much time.

March Engineering's basic plans were completed by April 1969, and they were shown around at the Spanish Grand Prix of that year, at Barcelona. They made an excellent impression and serious agreements were concluded with Tyrrell, who even at that stage foresaw difficulties with Matra. Another who was impressed was American Mario Andretti, anxious to participate in European Formula 1 racing in 1970. Colin Crabbe also ordered a new 701. In all, six March 701s were ordered for 1970, three for Tyrrell, one for Andretti, one for Crabbe (for Peterson to drive), and one for German driver Hubert Hahne who never raced it and failed to qualify at Hockenheim. A total of nine chassis were built including the three assembled for the works team, to be driven by top men Amon and Siffert.

Once they had made sure of an adequate number of customers and drivers of the first rank, the astute promoters of the marque March were able to launch their ambitious undertaking. Unfortunately, in spite of—or rather, because of—the technical precautions taken at the outset, the cars failed to keep their promise. In fact, Herd had restricted himself to conservative design for the reasons already outlined, and the 701 was out of date before it was built—an early 1969 car for the 1970 season. It was far too heavy, with an excess of unsprung weight despite modifications to the rear suspension introduced at the beginning of the season, which consisted mainly of mounting the rear brakes inboard.

If the March did succeed, in winning the Spanish Grand Prix, it was due to Stewart's inspired driving. In spite of the car's shortcomings it is only fair to point out that for any brand-new marque to win a World Championship Grand Prix in the first year of its existence is an event of some magnitude. It was the fact that such high hopes had been placed on the March, and such noteworthy people had bought it, that overshadowed the win. Such big things had been expected that the result was a bitter disappointment.

Nevertheless, it would be grossly unfair to blame all the reverses suffered by Stewart, Amon and Siffert on the shortcomings of the March chassis. No doubt, on some "specialised" circuits, notably Brands Hatch, the 701B was totally outclassed. At Spa and Monza however the chassis is not the vital factor. On those high-speed courses it is the engine that counts, which brings us to another basic feature of the 1970 season—the Ford-Cosworth's loss of the monopoly it had so long enjoyed.

It would be hazardous to infer, as indeed many have, that the V8's day is over and that the V12's victory era has dawned. There can be no doubt the Ferrari Formula 1 engine—a "flat-12"—develops more power than the famous Ford, which is three years its senior. The results of the second part of the 1970 season are proof enough of that, besides which, on more than one occasion the BRM and Matra V12s got the better of the British V8s.

It does not mean however that Cosworth has no option but to follow the example of BRM, Ferrari, and Matra, and change over to 12 cylinders, for it would be quite wrong to overlook the fact that the mishaps suffered by the British V8 manufacturer in 1970 were due far more to practical than to technical causes. Indeed, the chief reason for Cosworth's stagnation first and failure later was the success the engine had achieved. The engine was raced by no less than 15 drivers, a situation which meant the little Northampton works were forced to tackle the overwhelming task of keeping some fifty engines in operation. It is not difficult to appreciate the fact that under such conditions Cosworth Engineering was kept busy by mere maintenance, with no time left for research and development. Previously the engine had enjoyed such a degree of superiority that they could be set-up with a safety margin which averted all risk of disaster. But as the competition finally grew hotter and hotter, and rivals launched stronger and stronger attacks, the situation was suddenly reversed and the Ford-Cosworth mortality rate reached catastrophic proportions.

Does it imply the V8 engine is out of date, out of wind, and good only for the scrap heap? Supporters of the 12-cylinder power-unit have always held that, in theory, theirs was the best solution and that the "multi" could not fail to assert its superiority once it had reached a certain stage of development. Costin and Duckworth deny the theory and in 1971, with the aid of a radically-changed organization, aim at proving they are right.

It is interesting to reflect that three different engines, based on three different design principles, won at least one Championship Grand Prix in 1970, and these facts alone bear witness to the maturity attained by Formula 1—but not of any definite superiority of any type, V8, V12, or horizontally-opposed 12.

It is also of interest that one cannot trust the power-output figures claimed by the makers, whose equipment, instruments, and recording methods are not comparable. Ferrari claimed 460 hp, BRM 435, and Matra and Cosworth 430. According to Aubrey Woods, BRM's chief engineer the figures would be 440, 435, 425-430, and 410 respectively (*Autosport* 17 September 1970) if taken off the same test bench, and not those of Maranello, Bourne, Northampton, and Vélizy.

Certainly the power balance, as a rule, in 1970, revealed a more balanced situation on the tracks. In other words, the Grand Prix races were decided by narrower margins and consequently provided keener interest than is usual in Formula 1 events. Never were prognostics more fragile; never before were the favourites more strenuously opposed. If the Championship was apparently decided in Rindt's favour after the German Grand Prix, it was due no less to an amazing series of untoward events which influenced results, rather than to the superiority of the great Austrian driver and his Lotus 72. By and large the 1970 season can be divided into three phases. The first ended with the Belgian Grand Prix and comprised four extremely open races each of which was won by a different driver and a different marque. The second phase extended from the Dutch to the German Grand Prix and was marked by the triumph of the Rindt/Lotus combination which chalked-up four victories in a row and was thus practically, if not mathematically, assured of the World Championship. The third phase was the Ferrari era which opened with the Austrian Grand Prix.

One may say with certainty, that if it had not been for the catastrophe of Monza, Rindt would have become a living World Champion—a title he undoubtedly deserved. Yet, except for Zandvoort, he never had an easy win. And if Ferrari's superiority was beyond question towards the end of the season, it was hotly disputed by Stewart thanks to a combination of his personal talent, the new Tyrrell car, and a particularly powerful Cosworth-Ford engine. All in all, though divided quite clearly into three different acts, the season bears all the elements of a thrilling drama—at one full of uncertainty yet entirely coherent.

It is relevant to speak of the actors who took part in the great drama, for in 1970 we witnessed a phenomenon that rarely occurs on so vast a scale. After years of the established cast, 1970 saw the accession to Formula 1 of an unusual number of new, young drivers. Traditionally, entry to the "club" is difficult, conservatism and prudence having always been the rule. This time there was a spring tide of novices who stormed the magic bucket seats without a trace of diffidence—no less than nine newcomers including Regazzoni, Giunti, Stommelen, Peterson, Gethin, Fittipaldi, Wissel, Cevert, and Schenken. Two of them won World Championship races in their first season!

Clay Regazzoni took his place among the cracks at the start. In his first Formula 1 race he finished fourth (Dutch GP), and when he won the Italian Grand Prix at Monza little more than three months later, it was the fifth Formula 1 Grand Prix in which he had competed. His success was due to great talent of course, but also to the fact he joined the Ferrari team just when the 312B's development began to reach fruition, and it started to display a certain advantage over its rivals. No less accurate and cool in Formula 1 than he had sometimes been excessively exuberant in the lesser formulae at the wheel of lower-powered cars, the Swiss driver was undoubtedly the revelation of the year. The authority and confidence he demonstrated at the wheel of a Formula 1 machine were quite amazing.

The same observations apply to Emerson Fittipaldi whose rise was even more meteoric and set a record that will be difficult to surpass. The young Brazilian was quite unknown when he made his European debut in Formula Ford, only the previous year. Towards the end of the 1969 season he was promoted to Formula 3, and in 1970 to the Lotus Components Formula 2, a semi-works car. He was offered his first Formula 1 drive by Colin Chapman in the British Grand Prix, the car being a rather out-dated Lotus 49c which had been driven up until then by John Miles. On his second F 1 outing, in the German Grand Prix, he notched-up his first Championship points with a fourth place. Finally, at Watkins Glen, he won the United States Grand Prix—his fourth Formula 1 race! His team-mate Reine Wissel took third place in the same event—his first Formula 1 Championship race.

Not one of the novices proved a disappointment, in fact quite the reverse. If Cevert and Peterson took less of the 1970 limelight than Regazzoni and Fittipaldi, they too displayed a truly astonishing adaptability in view of the briefness of their racing careers. The events suggest that drivers' skill in every category has increased enormously, and that the age at which they now reach maturity is steadily falling. It is also noteworthy that youngsters like Stewart and Ickx give the impression of being men of experience—which they undoubtedly are. If this decade of Formula 1 ended tragically with the death of three great champions, the new one started with...

Will the Big Manufacturers Ever Come Back?

by Gordon Wilkins

Grand Prix racing is passing through a phase when it seems to have less and less relevance to any cars we can buy and use. Many people wonder if it serves any useful purpose at all except to provide entertainment for the public and some incidental publicity for those who take part in it or support the competitors. The sponsors may be manufacturers of brakes, brake linings, oil or fuel; they may be manufacturers of cigarettes or toilet preparations but only three car manufacturers are directly involved, Ferrari Matra and Lotus and their production of road cars is relatively tiny. Some Grand Prix cars are simply built to exploit the talents of a particular driver with no purpose other than winning races. Car manufacturers who have supported motor racing in the past find it a daunting spectacle which seems to have about as much to do with moon rockets as with automobiles. Perhaps this is not an unfair analogy for Maurice Phillippe of Lotus, who was trained as an aeronautical engineer, maintains that Grand Prix car design is closer to aircraft than to motor cars.

Even Rudolf Uhlenhaut, who drives as fast as ever and is still capable of testing a racing car himself, says privately that he hopes Mercedes Benz do not have to re-enter motor racing for a while yet, because there is such a big development programme to do on production cars, complicated by ever increasing safety regulations and increasingly stiffer rules on exhaust pollution.

I recently asked Sir David Brown whether he felt the time was coming when Aston Martin would have to renew their prestige by going back into racing. He said "It's possible. I don't think the time has arrived yet. Personally, I rather hope it won't. Once one is out of racing it is difficult and expensive getting back. You probably have to serve an apprenticeship again before you are successful."

Yet while the giants hesitate to get involved, young engineers seem to come from nowhere and start designing racing cars with apparent ease. Robin Herd, after four years with McLaren and Cosworth tackled the design of the March with great confidence and sufficient conviction to induce Ken Tyrrell to buy one for World Champion Jackie Stewart. When it proved slow in getting results Tyrrell produced a new car out of the hat, designed by Derek Gardner who had four years on transmissions with Hobbs Transmissions followed by a long spell at Harry Ferguson Research first on transmissions, then moving to racing cars via the Ferguson Novi for Indianapolis, the Lotus turbine car for Indianapolis and the Matra Ford four-wheel-drive car. Tony Southgate, the new man at BRM, came to motor racing via a design apprenticeship at Dowty, makers of aircraft undercarriages, followed by a spell with Eric Broadley at Lola then some experience with Brabham and a period working as chief engineer on Dan Gurney's Eagle.

Maurice Phillippe served his apprenticeship at the De Havilland Aircraft Company and was ten years in the aircraft business, so it is not surprising that when he built his first racing car for his own use it had a monocoque structure. He seems to be one of the rare Grand Prix car designers who has been involved with ordinary cars, having done a stint on car design and production engineering at Ford before being invited by Colin Chapman to go and start designing Lotus racing cars.

A major car manufacturer trying to enter Grand Prix racing today would therefore need the help of a designer who is in touch with the special problems involved but he would also need to achieve some technical break through to score decisively over the opposition. I remember the excitement when we got our first look at the Mercedes Benz W 196 single-seater in 1954, saw the single pivot swing axles, then got a look at the engine and hastily went away to swot up the history of desmodromic valve gear. That engine was developed to give over 290 bhp from 2.5 litres at 8,000 rpm or 116 bhp per litre and the car weight was eventually brought down to 4.75 lb/bhp. Fifteen years later, 3-litre Grand Prix engines are delivering about 440 bhp at around 11,000 rpm with conventional valves and valve gear, and pump fuel, yielding about 147 bhp per litre in cars which weigh only about 3.8 lb/bhp. But many of the cars are virtually kit cars are assembled from standard components. Details vary, but the most important factors are the driver and tyres. Since the championship winning Mercedes Benz single-seaters were retired into the museum at Stuttgart-Unterturkheim, the design of the Grand Prix car has changed out of all recognition. British designers showed how to obtain a decisive reduction in weight and frontal area by putting the engine at the back and letting the driver lie down on the job. Eric Broadley evolved the radius arm rear suspension which is now adopted generally, although there are countless detail variations.

De Tomaso and Cosworth established the engine as a part of the chassis. But the greatest advance of all has been in tyres, aided by aerofoils which help to get the best out of them.

Just to illustrate the importance of tyres, Uhlenhaut got a 15-year old Mercedes-Benz Formula One car out of the museum, fitted it up with a set of modern wheels and tyres and had a go on their steering pad. The car and especially its suspension were literally museum pieces but it held a 2g lateral acceleration just like the moderns.

Robin Herd quotes some figures which illustrate the influence of tyre development in the space of three years. When Jim Clark won the Dutch Grand Prix at Zandvoordt in 1967 on a Ford-Cosworth he used 28 gallons of fuel. Today a Cosworth engine uses over 40 gallons in winning a Grand Prix. The reason is mainly that present-day tyres, aided by aerofoils to increase the grip, allow the driver to use full throttle for a large part of the time. In fact, Herd says "The primary aim of chassis design is to make the best use of the tyre's performance." You start with the wheel and tyre dimensions, then lay out the front and rear suspension geometry. Though different cars may look alike, there is an infinite choice of possible variations which can influence success or failure; track width, swing axle length, roll centre and movement of roll centre, camber change, spring rate and suspension travel. Do you put the spring-damper units inboard for neatness and low drag or outboard for light weight, easy access and better cooling? Should the brakes go inboard to reduce unsprung weight and permit the use of smaller wheels and tyres (with a further saving in unsprung weight) or are you daunted by the possibility of disaster if a shaft or universal joint should break?

There is an impression that racing car design is just a process of trial and error and one well konwn designer did tell me light heartedly "I have never done a stress calculation in my life. I wouldn't know how to." But mistakes can cost drivers' lives and the most methodical practitioners use computers, strain gauges, photo-elastic analysis and any other modern tool which cuts down the risk of error. One car may weigh 100 lb. less than another and there may be a spread of 25 bhp between the output of the various engines on the starting line but most of this can be cancelled out by differences in the grip of the tyres and the ability of the drivers. The designer is struggling to save tenths of a second and to do it he often has to spend money like a drunken sailor, ordering £8,000 engines, half a dozen at a time or £60 magnesium wheels by the dozen. It is a strange, bizarre world for an engineer from a big car factory, who spends his life trying to save pennies, and is told that he must not fit an exhaust system which could be guaranteed not to rust through in twelve months because it would cost an extra five shillings.

Between the Race of Champions at Brands Hatch and the British Grand Prix, Jackie Oliver's lap time in a BRM was cut by 0.6 seconds. This was considered a good result for months of development work but when they got it, it was difficult to say exactly what was most important in achieving it. Details are constantly being changed between one race and the next.

Fitting the same front tyres on to narrower rims for the Monza race cut the wind resistance at a critical point and probably yielded an extra 100 rpm on the straight but it is difficult to tell exactly, when the driver has so many other things to attend to.

Even the really big changes, which seem to offer decisive advantages can turn out disappointingly when the racing begins. Then only long experience backed by round-the-clock work can save the situation. The Lotus 72 was a good example. Wind tunnel tests with a detailed scale model at MIRA. showed that the new shape with its sharp nose and rear-mounted radiators would give a drag reduction of around 10 per cent, which was ample to justify going ahead with the project. As the car developed, it was given an anti-dive geometry in the front suspension and anti-squat characteristics at the rear. It looked like the big break-through, as even rival constructors agreed, but in its first appearances it was a load of trouble. There were problems with wheel bearings and radiator air ducts. All the efforts to eliminate the lack of feel and response in the steering which is the bugbear of anti-dive geometry had failed and the anti-squat rear end was allowing the inside rear wheel to lift and spin on corners. The front end was hastily re-jigged with parallel wishbone pivots and during the season there were actually five different variations of rear suspension in use. There was also the problem of cooling the inboard front brakes. With the brakes mounted outboard the heat from the disc can seep into the metal mass of the hub when the car stops but on the inboard discs the heat had nowhere to go, so it simply burned the grease out of the bearings and electric air blowers had to be popped on to the brakes at every pit stop until a brake assembly with a greater mass of metal could be produced. All this has to be done at a speed which is right outside the experience of big factories whose work is geared to the lengthy tooling procedures required to turn out parts by the million. It would occupy the time of large numbers of engineers who could not get on with their normal work and it is not surprising that even Daimler Benz have to pull out after brief incursions into Grand Prix racing in order to resume work on their normal cars.

Even in a small factory the priorities between racing and production must be carefully watched. Colin Chapman told me "The racing cars do interfere with production. When a body for a single-seater has to be produced quickly, it brings the other work in a glass fibre shop to a standstill and when we wanted to get the first 72 on to the surface table we just had to call in a fork lift truck to remove the prototype of our next production car."

So the car manufacturer trying to enter Grand Prix racing really does enter a world where his previous experience is of little value. He has to find new people to cope with subtle new problems and must by-pass the time-consuming procedures of his normal factory routine. He will also have to operate on a much larger and more expensive scale than most existing Grand Prix teams because for prestige reasons he cannot buy his engines and gearboxes outside. He will be expected to introduce new and important technical advances.

Lotus, who buy engines and gearboxes from outside, get by with 32 people in their racing department, but this does not tell the full story, because they rely on a group of smaller firms, maybe of only one or two people, who do machining and other work for them, working all night or right through the week-end to deliver on time.

BRM, who make their own engines and gearboxes, employ about 75 people and even this would not be enough for a big manufacturer committing his reputation to a Grand Prix team. After all, Cosworth have 130 people designing and building engines alone.

But before he gets involved, a manufacturer has to consider very carefully what effect Grand Prix racing may have on his normal products. This applies to any kind of racing, because there is still a widespread belief that racing experience must be reflected in the design of production cars and there may be some disappointment if it is not. Four years ago, Jaguar built a mid-engined sports car for a new challenge in the Le Mans 24-hour race. It was tried out by two racing drivers at Silverstone and showed great promise but Sir William Lyons decided not to go ahead, because it was feared that buyers would stop ordering E-types and would wait for a new mid-engined production sports car which he had no intention of building.

Though an eventual return to sports car racing is not ruled out, Jaguar will not get involved in Grand Prix racing, but there some people within the group who feel that British Leyland as a whole might well reinforce its prestige by a foray onto the Grand Prix circuits. "Trades union rules alone would kill it if you tried to do it within the organisation. If I had to do it I would hire Jack Brabham and Ron Tauranac to run it", said a British Leyland director.

South African Grand Prix

Kyalami, March 17, 1970

The 1970 Grand Prix season opened with a bang when Jack Brabham won the South African GP at record speed with a brand-new car, and shared the new lap record of 113.614 mph with John Surtees who was driving a McLaren M7c. It was the Australian driver's first GP victory since the 1967 Canadian Grand Prix.

It is certainly worth recording that there were no less than five of the new marque, March, entered for the 204-mile race on the Kyalami circuit near Johannesburg, and by and large, it seemed that most followers of the sport expected the new Herd-designed machines to win—first time out, as far as a full-scale GP was concerned.

Lotus, like March, had five cars entered for the race, but Stewart's string of six 1969 Championship victories at the wheel of a Tyrrell-guided Matra-Ford, undoubtedly influenced may race-fellowers' minds, as well as the "force of numbers" thinking. To add weight to the theory, Stewart and Amon, both on March-Ford 701s, fronted the 3 × 2 grid with fastest practice times of 1 m. 19.3 s. The official lap record for the Kyalami circuit before the start of the race was held by Stewart at 1 m. 21.6 s., a speed of 112.50 mph.

One of the "shocks" of the proceedings however was the 1 m. 19.6 s. best practice lap of the incredible 44-year-old three-times World Champion Jack Brabham—a run that also gave him a place on the front row of the grid. Although the pundits were already filling in the results sheets with a flotilla of March-Fords, brand-new as they were, it was also worthy of the record that Brabham's Tauranac-designed BT 33 (BT for Brabham-Tauranac) was equally new. The new BT 33 used a monocoque-type main structure, the first time the Brabham équipe had gone for this form of construction in their Grand Prix cars—in the past both Brabham and Tauranac had always opted for simplicity, and ease of repair. Now the weight-reduction race had caught up with them, but typically, they had produced a new car that was obviously very light. There was another BT 33 for the German driver Rolf Stommelen who was to be entered throughout the season by the magazine *Auto Motor und Sport*, but

The start, and Stewart takes the initiative, followed by Ickx (17), Rindt, and Siffert.

Kyalami marked the first competition appearance of the Formula 1 March-Fords, but although the marque was numerically superior to any other in the race, save Lotus, their best placing was third. That position was taken by Jackie Stewart (above).

On the 20th lap Jack Brabham who had been slowed by a mix-up with Rindt on the first corner, took the lead from Stewart, and stayed out front for the remaining 60 laps. The race marked the first competition appearance of the new monocoque Formula 1 Brabham.

which was, to all intents and purposes, a works car. So with two new cars and one old (a BT26 entered by the Rhodesian équipe, Team Gunston, for Peter de Klerk) entered for the race, Brabhams, like BRM and McLaren had three cars each on the grid. The new Matra-Simca MS 120s numbered two, and there was one Ferrari 312b for Ickx, although it had been rumoured that local-driver Basil van Rooyen might drive a spare car. It didn't materialise.

Twenty-three cars in fact got away on the hot afternoon of the race. As the flag fell it was Brabham who initially grabbed the lead, but some difficulty with the gear-shift held him back and it was Stewart with the new March who led into the first corners. It looked black for Black Jack when Rindt hit both he and Amon, and rode over one of the Australian's front wheels. The Austro-German slid on to the grass, and Stewart led from Ickx, Beltoise and Oliver. Brabham had dropped to sixth. Stewart pulled away from the Ferrari, but Brabham had made sure his car felt right after the incident, then started to pile on the pressure. On lap 4 he passed McLaren and Oliver, on lap 5 it was Beltoise in the Matra who had to bow to the determined Aussie, and on the next lap he shot past Ickx. He was 17 seconds behind leader Stewart, but Jack and his new car were the quickest combination on the circuit, and after 17 laps he was but one second behind the reigning World Champion. Hulme had blasted his way into third place, but was 12 seconds behind the new Brabham. By that time the first of the March cars had retired when Amon's works machine went out with over-heating, and by lap 27 Andretti's STP-March was out with the same fault. Four laps before that, Brabham had wrested the lead from Stewart, and immediately began to pull away in a most convincing manner. Hulme and McLaren were running tight in third and fourth, and behind them there was a real dice taking place between Ickx, Surtees, Siffert and Beltoise. Rindt had got going and was holding ninth a long way behind the Matra. Graham Hill, making his first race appearance since his accident in the US Grand Prix with far-from-well legs, and Rob Walker's Lotus-Ford 49c.

On lap 39 Piers Courage, making the first Grand Prix appearance of the new de Tomaso-Ford in Formula 1 racing, hit a kerb and damaged the suspension too much to continue. McLaren's engine died and he fell from fourth place, and Surtees moved into that position. There were 19 cars running at half-distance (40 laps), but in another 20 laps six more cars had disappeared. Hulme had passed Stewart into second, but Brabham was 12 seconds ahead of him for the bulk of the remaining laps. He eased right off however for the last two laps, and finished 8.1 seconds ahead of the New Zealander.

"Good on yer, blue'', says four-year-old David Brabham after his Dad has shown the opposition the way around Kyalami. An ardent fan.

Good placing for the new Matra-Simca MS 120 with V12 engine when Jean-Pierre Beltoise netted fourth at 110,474 mph. The revamped 12-cylinder engine demonstrated good power and torque characteristics, and the latest car was obviously lighter than its battleship appearance suggested.

After only making the third row of the starting grid, Denis Hulme went on to an impressive second place, 8.1 seconds behind the winner Brabham. The New Zealander passed Stewart into second place on lap 39 and stayed put for the rest of the race. His team-mate and patron Bruce McLaren wasn't so lucky for his engine blew-up on the same lap. Only eleven cars were running at the end out of 23 starters. Race organisation was voted first-rate.

Denis Hulme listens attentively to "the Guv'nor" Bruce McLaren during practice. McLaren finished second in the race—for the second year running!

Cor, don't it make yer tired? Chris Amon found practice tiring, going by appearances, but he was a seeded driver and assured of a grid place.

Graham Hill studies the programme during practice, thankful he is a seeded driver. His Walker-Oxo-Brooke Bond Lotus 49c was however bothered by overheating oil. Hill finished fourth after a steady drive, and collected two Championship points.

Gran Premio de España

Jarama, April 26, 1970

The new marque March justified its existence by winning the Spanish Grand Prix at Jarama—the second Championship race in which it had participated. The winning car, one of two entered by Ken Tyrrell, was driven by Jackie Stewart who led from start to finish. It was the second time the Spanish Grand Prix had been staged on the 2.11-mile Jarama circuit near Madrid, and Stewart won at record speed.

Although the Scottish driver led for all of the 90 laps, he had anything but an easy race. On the very first lap, Oliver's works BRM P153 broke a stub axle and tangled with Ickx' Ferrari 312b. The melée resulted in a serious fire but both drivers escaped without serious injury. The BRM blazed for the remainder of the race on the outside of *Esses Bugatti*, where floods of water and foam from the fire-fighters covered the track and made progress difficult for competitors.

The fire-fighting was abysmal, only water being hosed on the burning cars for the first twenty minutes, and even after foam equipment had arrived the BRM continued to burn for the rest of the two-hour-plus race. Stewart said after the race it was one of the most tiring contests in which he had taken part—the soaking wet corner had forced him to exercise the utmost restraint through that area, for it would have only too easy to spin—and the amazing Brabham was ever-present. Brabham, fresh from his win in South Africa indicated his victory had been no flash in the pan by making fastest practice lap at 1 m. 23.9 s., and by setting a new official race lap record at 1 m. 24.3 s.

The two-day practice period was notable for qualification arguments, and a crash involving Piers Courage in the de Tomaso-Ford 505 which had been lightened and modified since it ran in the South African Grand Prix.

Mario Andretti, the Italo-American driver came over from the USA to race the STP-March but had a most unhappy practice period with handling and cooling problems. The period was also notable for the new McLaren M7a powered by an Alfa Romeo T33-3 V8 motor, and driven by Italian Andrea de Adamich.

There were 22 competitive starters but only 16 were permissible, and the "qualification"

▲ *Jarama, scene of the Spanish Grand Prix for the second time, took on a lonely look as the race progressed. Only five cars finished out of 16 starters, and the organisation was poor. This is Rampa Pegaso, uphill to Virage Ascari.*

Mario Andretti made his second 1970 Grand Prix appearance, drove the STP March-Ford well to take third place, and earned himself four Championship points. It was a particularly good effort.

Bruce McLaren was well down the field for the early part of the race, but consistent driving and a heavy car mortality rate finally brought him up to second. Stewart led from start to finish and gave the marque March its first Championship race victory. The Scot found it a tough and tiring contest.

Opening laps and Hulme, in second place, leads Brabham, Rodriguez, and Ickx. Hulme held second for nine laps, then retired with ignition trouble. ▸

Jackie Stewart and the marque March won its first Formula 1 race at Jarama. The reigning World Champion's time was a record, but the lap record went to Brabham.

runs developed into such a farce that everyone was heartily sick of it all by the Saturday evening. Even on the morning of the race arguments persisted as to who was to run and who was not. There was even talk of 20 starters being allowed after all, and in fact that number took their places on the grid, but finally non-qualifiers Siffert, Miles, de Adamich and Soler Roig were ordered off.
With Brabham, Hulme, and Stewart on the front row the flag finally came down and Stewart made one of his copy-book starts, never to be headed. Hulme, Brabham and Rodriguez shot after the Scot. The first-lap accident upset the field somewhat but the leaders stayed unchanged. Amon, who had tried a clutchless getaway on the starter rumbled round with a very rough engine. As the drivers took the second lap the burning Ferrari started to roll across the track and Jackie Stewart was only just able to miss it. After that the Scot drew away from Hulme and Brabham, but BRM team manager Tim Parnell wisely called-in Rodriguez in case there was a recurrence of the stub axle failure that had affected Oliver. The move put Pescarolo's Matra-Simca V12 into fourth. Brabham then started to go motor racing, pulled-up on Hulme, then spun-off on the skating rink by the burning BRM.
After 10 laps Hulme was only five seconds behind the leader, but electronic troubles in the ignition system, caused the Cosworth motor to die. The New Zealander fitted another rotor, managed another two laps, but the engine stopped again. Rindt, giving the Lotus 72 its race debut, also had ignition failure at 10 laps and retired, reducing the field to 10 cars.
Stewart's lead was 12 seconds, in front of Brabham. Beltoise (who made fastest lap with a Tyrrell Matra-Ford in the 1968 race) pressed-on, passed Brabham and got within ten seconds of the leader. Surtees in the McLaren-Ford M7c started to gain on Pescarolo in fourth place.
Beltoise was going well and reduced Stewart's lead to 6 ½ seconds in another four laps. Brabham, trying to catch the Frenchman, spun again. The Australian set off again after Beltoise—and Stewart!
Then the Matra seized and Brabham was second. Pescarolo's Matra blew-up in the second-biggest cloud of smoke seen at Jarama that day, and reduced the field to eight. Surtees was third, ahead of McLaren. At half-distance Brabham was only five seconds behind the leader, and Surtees was about to be lapped.
Stewart was doing all he knew to stay in front of Brabham, only a few yards separating them. Sudenly the Brabham slowed—the engine had blown-up, and Stewart eased-off to win by 4.2 seconds from Bruce McLaren. The same two drivers finished 1-2 in the 1969 Spanish Grand Prix—at Barcelona!

Drama on the first lap when Ickx's Ferrari and Oliver's BRM collide on the second corner. The BRM split the Ferrari's fuel tanks and both cars were engulfed in flames, and here as Amon passes the holocaust burning fuel runs across the track. Oliver was quick to vacate his car, but Ickx was unable to get out quickly. He finally emerged with his overalls on fire, ran across the road where the flames were put out by a soldier. His petrol-soaked overalls were left on him and he suffered uncomfortable fuel burns, but escaped serious injury. The accident occurred because of a stub axle breakage on the BRM, and the other works car driven by Rodriguez was withdrawn a safety measure. The accident created race havoc, not only the visibility being dangerously reduced for drivers left in the contest, but the flaming petrol constituted another hazard. The fire-fighting was abysmal, vast quantities of water being hosed on the flames for a long time—a procedure which caused the magnesium elements to 'gas' and flare-up time and time again. The BRM was still burning at the end of the race, but miraculously no-one was hurt. The five finishers were probably the filthiest racing cars ever seen.

BARDAHL
elf elf elf elf
DUNLOP
26
28
21

Streaming down from "Station" towards the tunnel on the second lap, the crocodile is led by Stewart. Behind him is Amon, and in third position, Hulme. Stewart led for 27 laps, then his ignition went sour and eventually he dropped out.

◄ *Brabham leads Ickx, Beltoise, and Hulme towards the* Tabac *in the early part of the race. Out of the bunch only Hulme survived the race, taking fourth place behind Pescarolo who tried really hard with the Matra-Simca MS120.*

Gutter shot of Amon in the works March 701 at "Station Hairpin". The young New Zealander held second place for 33 laps and was going well when a bolt detached itself from a rear wishbone, and he had to retire. He had made the front row of the grid in practice—shared with Stewart in his Tyrrell March.

Grand Prix de Monaco

Monaco, May 10, 1970

In its 41 years of existence the Monaco Grand Prix has been the scene of many drama-packed incidents, but surely none will ever surpass the 1970 race when Jack Brabham who had led for two-thirds of the event, was pipped on the last corner of the last lap.

The sensational occurrence was packed into the last few yards and seconds of the race when Jochen Rindt with a works Lotus 49c was able to pressure the wily Australian into making a mistake in the last-lap "traffic" at *Virage Gazometre*. Brabham had also been experiencing brake troubles, both in practice and in the race, and everything built-up to an excursion into the guard rail, while Rindt went on to take the victor's flag. Brabham extricated himself as quickly as possible, and with nose-fins awry, blasted after the Austro-German driver to take second place. Only nine cars were running at the end of the 156-mile contest, but eight were classified as finishers.

The Australian driver's second place however put him at the top of the World Championship table with a total of 15 points—six added to the nine he had already gained with his South African Grand Prix win two months previously. Rindt, in his efforts to catch Brabham on the last lap set a staggering new lap record at 1 m. 23.2 s.—a speed of 84.36 mph.

Henri Pescarolo underlined the new-found speed and torque of the Matra-Simca V12 by finishing third. His team-mate Beltoise had held fourth place until a final-drive breakage put him out on lap 22.

"Qualification" was of course a pre-race feature at Monaco but although the organisers had received no fewer than 26 entries for the 16 grid places, they were soon reduced to 22. Ferrari decided to send one car only for Ickx, and Andretti, Bell, Moser, and Soler Roig scratched.

Both Gold Leaf Team Lotus entries for Rindt and Miles were Type 49s brought up to "C" specification as the revolutionary "72s" were giving development troubles, but the old cars were using the new three-layer aerofoil. Five-times Monaco winner Graham Hill, driving the Walker-Brooke-Bond-Oxo Lotus brought the marque strength up to three, but his car was also a 49c, sporting a 72-type aerofoil like the works cars. There were no new-*type* cars at Monaco, but Colin Crabbe appeared with a brand-new March-Ford 701,

(Above) In a fantastic finish, Jochen Rindt took the lead from Jack Brabham on the last few hundred yards of the last lap, and scored Lotus' first 1970 Championship GP victory. Early in the race the Austro-German had been lying 8th, and even at half-distance he was only 4th. (Right) Alone in the centre of the track a jubilant Jackie Stewart welcomes his victorious helvetic neighbour.

Brabham rushes to grab his second place after distentangling himself from the barriers on "Gasometer Hairpin". He led for two-thirds of the race, then did it all wrong on the very last corner, and Rindt snatched the lead—and the race. The Australian had suffered brake trouble for a great deal of the race, and he was getting very tired.

finished in "Antique Automobiles" yellow and red (Antique Automobiles is a vintage car sales firm owned and run by Colin Crabbe in London) for the quick young Swedish driver Ronnie Peterson who won the Formula 3 race at Monaco the previous year. It was to be the Swede's first Formula 1 race. Fastest in practice were Stewart (1 m. 24 s.) and Amon (1 m. 24.6 s.) both on March-Ford 701s. Thursday's weather was good but Friday was streaming wet. Stewart was fastest in all three sessions. In the end it was Miles (Lotus), Stommelen (Brabham), de Adamich (McLaren-Alfa), Eaton (BRM) and Servoz-Gavin (March) who were eliminated. It is an ill wind that blows nobody any good for Hill crashed in practice and was able to borrow Miles' Lotus 49 for the race—the same car with which he had won the 1969 race! It had been raining most of the preceding night but it was dry when Paul Frére dropped the flag on Sunday and Stewart led Amon and Brabham up towards the Casino on another sort of gamble.

The Scot pulled away and behind him Brabham was trying hard to find a way past Amon. After 20 laps Stewart was 11 ½ seconds in front of the New Zealander and Brabham was only a second behind the works March. Stewart continued to pull away, broke the lap record at 1 m. 24.6 s., but after 27 laps the Cosworth-Ford engine went ragged. Brabham had passed Amon five laps earlier, and as Stewart went into his pit for attention, Brabham was in the lead. Stewart rejoined the race after two laps had been lost to a "black box" change. He went as quickly as ever but the engine again went ragged, and he pulled-out on lap 58.

Brabham now led, but Amon was pressing him hard. Hulme was third with Pescarolo never far behind. Then suddenly Rindt started to come into the picture. He forced his Lotus past Hulme on lap 40, and when Amon's rear suspension collapsed on lap 61, the Austro-German was second.

Rindt was 13 ½ seconds from Brabham, and Siffert started to pile on the pressure to catch Rindt. The Lotus driver had just broken the lap record at 1 m. 24.3 s., but the Swiss replied with 1 m. 24.1 s. Then the March started to falter with fuel starvation. Brabham, signalled by his pit of the impending danger, kept about 13 seconds ahead, but then Rindt started to close at two seconds a lap. With four laps to go Brabham was balked by Siffert who was swerving about trying push fuel into his pumps, and Rindt caught-up dramatically. Brabham kept the Lotus at bay—as only he can—but as the two cars entered their last (80th) lap Rindt was on top of the Brabham. Brabham took the inside line at "Gasometer", left his braking too late and had all four wheels lock. While he slid into the guardrail, Rindt whipped the lead, and took the chequered flag!

Grand Prix de Belgique

Spa-Francorchamps, June 7, 1970

Round five of the World Championship brought into sharp focus a fact that had been thrusting itself more strongly upon the motor racing world with each of the preceding 1970 Grand Prix races. The fact that the 12-cylinder cars were getting faster and faster—whether the circuit was twisty and undulating, or whether it was a 'fast' course.

There is no faster road circuit in the world than the fantastic 8.76-mile Spa-Francorchamps course in the Ardennes near the German border, and the 1970 Belgian Grand Prix, held after a cancellation in 1969, proved a very convincing victory for Mexican driver Pedro Rodriguez and the BRM P153.

There were four 12-cylinder cars in the first six at the finish, and out of eight classified finishers, five were 12-cylinder machines, from BRM, Matra-Simca, and Ferrari.

The classic 'Belgian' had been in doubt for some weeks as the Grand Prix Drivers' Association had wanted an 'adjustable'' 11am start—an arrangment that would have made it possible to alter the starting time according to the weather. The infamous Spa weather can produce sunshine at one end of the circuit and pouring rain at the other, and the drivers wanted to make the race as safe for themselves as possible. In the event the organisers agreed to a 1pm start, and at a pre-race press conference supplied a weatherman who predicted dry conditions for the

Away from "Eau Rouge" and up towards Les Combes, *the crocodile is led by Rindt's Lotus 49c after the start. Already the leading trio, Rindt, Amon and Stewart, are pulling away from the rest. Brabham "leads" the main phalanx.*

morrow, with just a possibility of light rain in the afternoon. It was agreed the race would go on in light rain conditions, but that it would be stopped if heavy rain manifested itself. Rodriguez was on the third row of the grid with a best practice time of 3 m. 31.6 s compared to Stewart's best 3 m. 28 s with the Tyrrell March. The Mexican driver was considered a sound bet however by reason of his amazing performance some three weeks earlier when he had lapped one of the JW Porsche 917s in an almost unbelievable 3 m. 16.5 s (160.30 mph) on the same circuit in the 1000-kilometre "sports car" race. The circuit for the sports car event had been

Jean-Pierre Beltoise drove a well-judged race to take third place with the Matra-Simca MS120, and to underline the growing potential of the latest 12-cylinder cars—on all types of circuit. Both Matras finished—that of Pescarolo in sixth place.

Chris Amon actually led the field on laps 1, 3, and 4, but thereafter shadowed eventual winner Rodriguez, in second place. There were times during the race when it looked as though the March would again take the lead but the Mexican was master.

Pedro Rodriguez drove the GP of his life on the Spa-Francorchamps circuit he knows so well. In the 1970 Grand Prix of Belgium he was the fastest man in the fastest car and no-one could do anything about it. Here he corners at La Source *hairpin.*

◄ *It was Ignazio Giunti's first-ever Grand Prix, and he justified Enzo Ferrari's faith in him by taking fourth place—and three Championship points!*

Jo Siffert takes a wide line at La Source *where the surface became very slippery with oil. The Swiss driver took seventh place with his works March.*

Rolf Stommelen, formidable sports car driver, entered by Auto Motor und Sport, *brought this works-prepared Brabham into a good fourth.*

Looking as though he could manage another Grand Prix, Pedro Rodriguez holds his victor's garland aloft. Second-man Amon is on the left with third-man Beltoise on the right. It was the Mexican's second Grand Prix victory.

left wide open, but for the GP cars a "chicane" had been included in the Malmedy straight—not a genuine chicane for it was in fact a diversion around the grass-covered road junction island outside the village. In spite of the "safety hazard", Amon clipped 2.8 seconds off Surtees' old record set up in the Honda V12 in the 1968 Belgian GP. Fastest practice times were set by Stewart (3 m. 28 s), Rindt (3 m. 30.1 s), and Amon (3 m. 30.3 s), and these three drivers occupied the grid front row.

Ronnie Peterson added colour to the pre-race proceedings by getting himself clapped in jail for driving to the circuit in a somewhat uncontrolled manner and for striking a *gendarme*. Never the best way to go motor racing on the Continent! He was released just before the start of the event.

Stewart hung back with wheelspin when the starter dropped the flag, and as the pack came around the first time it was Amon's red works March ahead of Stewart, Rindt, and Rodriguez. Stewart took the lead on lap 2, with Rindt third and being pressed hard by Rodriguez. The next lap Stewart again headed the 17-car field past the grandstand/pit area, but the engine was losing its edge and on lap 4 Amon again got out front, but only for that *tour*. Rodriguez was flying in the BRM and he wrested the lead away from Amon on the next lap—and was never again headed. New-boy Giunti spun his Ferrari at *La Source* but quickly got back into the fray, and Brabham was working his way through the field in characteristic manner.

By lap 18 five cars had expired and the leaders had lapped Graham Hill in the Oxo Lotus. Stewart had blown-up in front of the pits—the height of exhibitionism, as one wag described it. Brabham had got into third place by lap 15, held the position for five laps, then pulled out with excessive vibration which turned out to be a disentegrating clutch. Rindt's Lotus 49c had gone eight laps earlier with a broken engine, so the Australian driver knew he still led the World Championship. By half-distance Rodriguez and Amon were 20 seconds ahead of the next batch, and still they were scrapping like terriers. *La Source* was very slippery with oil, and Peterson spun there, but got going again. Rodriguez was blowing cement dust into Amon's face as the two cars rushed into La Source each lap—due to the drying dust spread by the marshals. But it didn't slow the New Zealander. Ickx pulled out on lap 22 due to fuel dripping on to his thigh and causing him pain.

Amon made his great effort on the last lap at 3 m. 27.4 s, but he couldn't pass Pedro. The Mexican won magnificently and gave BRM their first Championship GP victory since Monaco in 1966 when Stewart won with the two-litre V8. Last 12-cylinder GP win had been by Ickx for Ferrari in the 1968 French Grand Prix.

Grote Prijs van Nederland

Zandvoort, June 21, 1970

After a period of uncertainty due to financial troubles, the Dutch Grand Prix was finally put on when the Netherlands Government came to the assistance of the organisers. The Zandvoort race proved to be the first winning-place for the Lotus 72, and also provided Rindt with his second victory of the season. It was a tragic race however, for British driver Courage died in Frank Williams' de Tomaso-Ford after a crash on the 23rd lap. It was the first death ever in a Dutch GP. Some drivers had travelled to Zandvoort even before the official, practice periods, to test cars, tyres and so on. One of those drivers was Jack Brabham who suffered a puncture when testing Stommelen's car, and left the road in a big way. The BT 33 knocked-down posts, and was completely wrapped in wire from the safety netting, the unfortunate driver being trapped inside, unhurt, for nearly an hour. Tyre troubles were a feature of the race and of the practice periods. Rodriguez also left the road at high speed on the first day of official practice with his BRM P 153 when a tyre punctured. The BRM hit a traffic light and was written-off, but by a miracle the little Mexican was unhurt. Later, during the second day's practice Rodriguez again had tyre trouble when a cover pulled over its security bolt and deflated, but this time the car came to rest with no damage. At the start the 20-car grid had only 3 ¼ seconds variation between the fastest and slowest qualifier, and Rindt had proved the fastest with a best time of 1 m. 18.50 s. suggesting the Lotus 72 was at last beginning to go. Stewart was second-fastest with the Tyrrell-March at 1 m. 18.73 s., and the Scot, with Ickx' Ferrari (1 m. 18.93 s.) made up the front row of the 2 × 3 grid. The 1969 lap record set by Stewart in the winning Matra-Ford had been 1 m. 22.94 s. Rindt had also had an unofficial practice lap on the Wednesday before the race and had circulated at an incredible 1 m. 17.6 s. (more than 120 mph) on the tight little circuit with the Lotus 72. Everyone on the grid had recorded a faster time than Stewart's 1969 record! Ickx tore into the lead at the start and once again emphasised the 312 b's potential.

Jochen Rindt comes into the pits after winning his second 1970 Grand Prix, but he does not register joy, for Piers Courage, killed during the race, was an old friend. Rindt won at record speed.

Up until about quarter-distance a tremendous battle ensued between John Miles in the second works Lotus 72, Piers Courage in the de Tomaso, Beltoise (Matra), Pescarolo (Matra), Gethin (McLaren), Brabham (Brabham), Surtees (McLaren) and Siffert (March).

Reigning Champion Stewart had to fight hard for his second place. The Scot was third, behind Ickx in his Ferrari, until the Belgian stopped for a new wheel after a puncture. Stewart still led the World Championship with 19 points after the race.

Ickx was third-fastest in practice, and in the race demonstrated the growing potential of the Ferrari 312 b. He held second place for the greater part of the 208-mile race but was unlucky enough to puncture a tyre. Despite the stop he finished third.

Stewart laps Beltoise but the French driver took the 12-cylinder Matra (No. 23) through to fifth place, and his team-mate Pescarolo finished eighth. There were three 12-cylinder cars in the first six at the finish of the race.

Clay Regazzoni put up an unusual performance by finishing fourth in his first Grand Prix, and earned himself three Championship points! Better-known in Formula 2, the Swiss-Italian finished one place behind his Ferrari team-mate Ickx.

Piers Courage, tragically killed in the Dutch Grand Prix, was a driver of great promise. An 'amateur professional', the 28-year-old British racing motorist and started his serious competition career in Formula 3 but was soon amongst Formula 1. ◄

Stewart made a bad start as Rindt occupied second place, followed by Oliver's BRM.

The Ferrari headed the pack for three laps, then Rindt (who had broken the lap record, with full tanks, at 1 m. 19.19 s.) took the lead and kept it for the rest of the 110-minute race. After ten laps Rindt was followed by Ickx and Stewart, and the BRMs of Oliver and Rodriguez. The third BRM, George Eaton up, was back in 18th place. Amon had been left on the start-line, had got under way slowly, then come in with a defunct clutch and retired after two laps. Two McLarens were running, the first time the team had appeared since the tragic death of Bruce McLaren at Goodwood a little more than two weeks earlier. Drivers were Californian Dan Gurney, who at that time was reported to be joining McLaren for the rest of the season, and Formula 5000 champion Peter Gethin. Hulme was a spectator, his hands not being fully healed from his Indianapolis crash. Another spectator was Basil von Rooyen from South Africa who had at one time been in line for a drive with the Tyrrell équipe after the surprise retirement of Frenchman "Johnny" Servoz-Gavin. The French Elf fuel company which partly sponsored Tyrrell's stable, not unnaturally wanted another Frenchman in the team, and so François Cevert was making his Formula 1 debut at Zandvoort in one of the blue March-Ford 701 s.

Gurney was out of the race by the third lap when his engine failed, and 16 laps later his team-mate was out after spinning off.

The Lotus 72 with Rindt at the wheel was displaying enormous performance, helped on the twisty circuit by its special Firestone tyres. At half-distance Ickx had a tyre deflate and had to pit-stop to change a wheel. The stop dropped him to third and Stewart moved up to second—but he was still some 30 seconds behind Rindt. Brabham had to stop twice for tyre changes—punctures possibly being caused by pieces of magnesinim from poor Courage's car which had crashed on the 23rd lap and was burning furiously.

Clay Regazzoni, up-and-coming F 2 driver, was holding fourth place in the second of the works Ferrari 312 bs—in his first Grand Prix!

By half-distance the field had thinned considerably—both Siffert's works March and Cevert's Tyrrell-March had blown-up. Oliver and Eaton's BRMs had retired for different reasons—and Ickx had set a new lap record of 118.383 mph.

With ten laps to go but 12 cars were left and only Rindt and Stewart were on the same lap. Rindt came in the winner, more than a minute ahead of Stewart but he didn't smile during the presentation, for Courage had been one of his best and closest friends. The organisers cancelled the remaining saloon car race, and the prize-giving party—normally a traditional part of the festivities.

In the opening laps Ickx streaked into the lead with the Ferrari 312b, followed by Beltoise (Matra), Stewart (March), Amon (March), Rindt (Lotus), and Pescarolo (Matra). The Scot was displaced by Amon on the fourth lap when the March-Ford developed ignition trouble. Ickx was out on lap 14 with a burned valve.

The crowded 2 × 2 grid unleashes its gaggle of blaring cars at Clermont and fastest-man-in-practice Ickx leaps into the lead (extreme right). Beltoise occupies most of the camera's lens in second place, and Stewart is close behind with the March. Fifteen cars finished. ►

Lotus designs make a habit of 'coming good' at Zandvoort, and Rindt's victory in the 1970 Dutch Grand Prix was no exception. The unconventional '72' justified its existence by finishing around half-a-minute in front of Stewart's March 701. ►

Ken Tyrrell (centre), Jackie Stewart's entrant, seems to be ticking-off driver after the French Grand Prix. And Winner Rindt seems to approve!

Grand Prix de France

Clermont-Ferrand, July 5, 1970

Originally scheduled for the Albi circuit, the French Grand Prix finally went to Clermont-Ferrand, for the second year in succession. The Albi organisers hadn't the finance to carry out the necessary safety modifications, so it was back to the picturesque 5.005-mile Charade circuit in the Auvergne.

Once again the 12-cylinder cars demonstrated their potential, both in practice and in the race, a Ferrari and a Matra occupying the grid front row and both dominating the race for 25 of the 38 laps. But it was Rindt who again won, at the wheel of a Gold Leaf Team Lotus 72, with Chris Amon in second place with a works March some 7 ½ seconds behind. It was Rindt's third Championship victory of the year and he enjoyed his almost customary slice of luck to achieve his win.

At the start of the 190-mile race Ickx shot into the lead with the Ferrari 312 b and stayed there for 14 laps, although menaced closely by Beltoise in the Matra-Simca—both 12-cylinder machines. When the Ferrari failed with a burned-out valve, the little Frenchman took over the lead to the delight of the partisan crowd. A French driver led the French Grand Prix in a French car!

For five laps Stewart had held third place but he had had to pit-stop for a change of ignition "black box", and Amon and Rindt had taken third and fourth place respectively. When the reigning World Champion re-entered the race he was 18th. Oliver retired his BRM with timing trouble, and de Adamich's MacLaren-Alfa was making pit stops with cooling derangements. Rodriguez, who had been holding sixth place, was forced out with a fourth gear that wouldn't disengage.

Rindt passed Amon into third place before Ickx dropped out, so when the Ferrari retired he was second. Rindt and Amon battled away whilst Beltoise kept well ahead from them and at half-distance the Frenchman had a 16-second advantage. Hulme was trying hard to overtake Brabham in fourth place.

On lap 25 Beltoise had the bad luck to collect a rear tyre puncture and Rindt and Amon roared by even as he made his way to the pit. By the time the wheel had been changed the blue car was down to 10th. Rindt and Amon, only a few seconds apart, continued their battle with renewed zest, and Siffert slid into a guardrail, bending his works March but not doing himself much harm.

DUNLOP

10
TEAM

LEAF
LOTUS
GIRLIN

elf
21
MATRA
SIMCA
elf
elf

◄ *After Ickx' departure from the lead, Beltoise took over and drove a well-judged race. It looked as though the French car and driver would win the French Grand Prix, but after eleven laps he was forced into the pits with a puncture.*

In the early part of the race, Amon (March) was ahead of Rindt. Here the New Zealander holds third place on the fifth lap ahead of the eventual winner. Rindt passed Amon on the seventh lap on his climb through the field.

For lap after lap Brabham, Pescarolo and Hulme battled in a close bunch. Finally, Hulme passed the Matra driver, and in spite of his still-burned hands, menaced Brabham strongly. Brabham kept ahead in third place however and set a sensational new Charade lap record of 99.68 mph. The fourth car is driven by Peterson who was forced to retire on the 17th lap.

Siffert never climbed very high on the lap charts, his best position being ninth at 23 laps. His works March was beset by gearbox troubles and he finally hit a guardrail after a brake locked, retiring on lap 24. The Swiss driver wasn't fast in practice either, making only the eighth row of the grid with a best time of 3 m. 03.78 s., and making rather rude remarks about the 5.005-mile circuit in the hills.

Victory grins. Lotus chief Colin Chapman, his No. 1 driver Jochen Rindt and Nina Rindt all register delight after the win. It was the Austro-German's third GP victory of 1970 and the second in a row for the Lotus 72. John Miles finished eighth in the other works Lotus 72. A good day out.

The 12-cylinder cars had disappeared from the lead scene, in fact the "leading 12" was Pescarolo's Matra in fifth place! Twelve cars were in fact on the same lap as the leaders at that stage—with eight laps to go, and Rindt had a five-second lead over Amon. The New Zealander was still trying hard, and Brabham started to go really fast again. The Australian had already broken the Charade lap record at 3 m. 0.75 s. and started to close on the leaders. Hulme had another go at passing him, but he was in pain with his tender hands, although he got within a second of the Brabham.

Gurney, in sixth place with the McLaren, was trying hard to take Pescarolo and as the cars entered the last lap the Californian was slip-streaming the blue car through the pit/grandstand area. He was unable to make it however.

After lively closing laps Rindt took the flag 7.61 seconds ahead of Amon, and Hulme made a last lap effort and again got within one second of Brabham. Pescarolo was working very hard to keep Gurney at bay, and that is how they crossed the line. Stommelen drove well to take seventh, Miles was next with the other works Lotus 72 ahead of Stewart. The reigning World Champion passed Hill on the last lap to take place—as Hill's engine blew-up and he free-wheeled the Brooke-Bond-Oxo 49c over the line! Rindt's win had hoisted him to the top of the Championship table with 27 points, to Brabham's 19. The 12-cylinder cars had once again displayed great speed and it was hard luck that neither Ickx nor Beltoise had their taste of success.

The story behind Ickx' retirement was worthy of the record in that he was second-fastest in practice with a very fast time, then his 312b was found to have a poor compression on one cylinder due, it was thought, to a stone being induced from the very gritty Charade paddock. The Ferrari mechanics went to work to try and restore the compression by turning the valve on its seat (without dismantling the engine) but when they had finished, the compression was no better. On the morning of the race the drivers were allowed an exploratory lap, and Ickx took out the spare 312b with the idea of using it in the race. When he returned to the start area he told Ferrari team manager Forghieri that the spare car didn't handle as it hadn't been set-up for the circuit, and that in spite of the defective valve he would rather chance the other car. Forghieri had the other car brought out from the paddock, and Ickx shot into the lead—and held it—for 14 laps!

Suprisingly, out of 20 starters 15 cars finished, and the only incident in the entire event was Siffert's contact with the guardrail. There were five different makes of car in the first five, and it was only the fifth that wasn't powered by a Ford-Cosworth engine.

RAC British Grand Prix

Brands Hatch, July 19, 1970

The British Grand Prix at Brands Hatch proved to be another of the extraordinary Brabham-Rindt duels that ended in a lucky victory for the Austro German driver on the very last lap. In an almost unbelievable finish, Brabham freewheeled over the line, out of fuel, to be pipped, as at Monaco, by Rindt, who was amazed that such a thing could happen again. As if that were not enough, the Lotus driver was disqualified soon after the race-finish due to a protest about his car's aerofoil not being to regulations, then, before the evening was out, being reinstated!

The British Grand Prix, staged for 1970 at Brands Hatch (it alternates annually with Silverstone), was the most ambitious ever held in Britain, with the Royal Automobile Club guaranteeing a start for all-comers, without the necessity of "qualification". In the end, 22 formed the starting grid—only one less than in the South African Grand Prix. The RAC also organised a two heats and final Formula 3 event on the second day of practice, thus making the meeting a two-day affair—Friday and Saturday. The tricky 2.65-mile circuit 20 miles south-east of London, had, as its lap record-holder before the meeting, Jack Brabham, with a time of 1 m. 25.8 s. (111.19 mph). The Australian set the record in the Race of Champions the preceding March—another race which he looked all-set to win, but failed with ignition trouble only three laps from the end.

First day's practice for the British Grand Prix indicated that Rindt was to be one of the fastest with a best lap of the day at 1 m. 24.8 s. (112.50 mph), but Brabham characteristically rushed round a few minutes before the end of the last session and officially equalled the Lotus 72's. time.

Sharing the front row of the grid with Rindt and Brabham was Jacky Ickx who had once again demonstrated the enormous potential of the 12-cylinder *boxermotor* Ferrari with a fastest practice lap of 1 m. 25.1 s. Hulme and Oliver were on the second row with McLaren and BRM respectively, the latter putting one more 12-cylinder car amongst the fastest contenders, and adding-up to five different makes of car.

A crowd of 75,000 watched Brabham get away initially as the flag fell, but Ickx was alongside as the 21-car pack rushed into the tricky Paddock Bend and although he had to take to the grass, the Ferrari driver came through in the lead—and drew away. The young Belgian drove superbly and headed the field for six laps, then pulled into the back pit road with a broken final-drive. Brabham had been holding second place, but as Ickx was slowing, the Lotus driver got through into first place as both he and Brabham passed

First lap and Ickx leads the field followed by Brabham, Rindt, Oliver, Hulme, Regazzoni and Stewart. Ickx had four laps of leadership.

During the opening laps Stewart (left) and Regazzoni duelled hard. Here the Scot locks a brake as he tries to pass.

Cevert (foreground) and Surtees fought a battle but finally the British driver retired his new TS7 on lap 52. Cevert finished seventh.

For lap after lap Brabham breathed down Rindt's neck, then on lap 69 passed and seemed all set.

On the very last lap Brabham runs out of fuel, and as at Monaco, he takes second place.

Brabham leads Rindt at Druids Hill, and soon pulls away from the Lotus. Drama was to come.

the Ferrari. Oliver was third with the BRM, followed by Regazzoni's Ferrari, Stewart and Beltoise.

Rindt stayed about one second in front of Brabham, but the Australian seemed content to stay second—for the time being. Oliver was 6 ½ seconds behind, and at the back a colossal struggle was going on between six cars for 11th place!

At 20 laps the two leaders were still a second apart and Oliver still occupied third place, but Stewart, Beltoise and Regazzoni had caught up with Hulme and Andretti took eighth as Pescarolo pit-stopped with a puncture. On lap 20 Siffert retired his March with hub failure, and one lap later Mario Andretti was out with the same trouble.

Beltoise' Matra also had to pit-stop with a puncture, and Peterson started to have clutch trouble after an impressive run during which he had led both works March cars in his privately-entered one. Stewart dropped back with handling troubles, and Regazzoni forged on to get close to Hulme in fourth place. Surtees, in his brand-new TS 7, had worked his way steadily upwards, getting into seventh place by just after half-distance.

Still Rindt and Brabham lapped in close company and still Oliver held third. Hulme was being pressed by Regazzoni. On lap 52 Surtees drew into the pits and retired with no oil pressure—but it had been a convincing debut. Next lap Stewart came in with a puncture and while the wheel was being changed hydraulic fluid dripped on to the exhaust system and the resultant small fire caused the car's retirement.

Emerson Fittipaldi, the young Brazilian driver from Formula Ford, 2 and 3, had been given his F1 chance in the Lotus team's old 49c and was holding eighth place with no fourth gear and a broken exhaust manifold. Oliver was out on the 55th lap when the engine died, so now the fight between Hulme and Regazzoni was for third place.

With eleven laps to go Brabham made his bid, and passed Rindt coming out of South Bank. He pulled away dramatically and illustrated how much he had in hand. In four laps he put a ten-second lap between himself and the Lotus and put in the race's fastest lap at 1 m. 25.9 s. It looked as though Rindt had resigned himself to second place, and the crowd got ready to applaud Brabham, but on the very last lap the wedge-shaped Lotus was seen to be coming through Clearways, and the Brabham was crawling! There was confusion as Jochen Rindt took the victor's flag, and Jack Brabham coasted into second place, out of fuel.

It was a bitterly disappointed Brabham who got out of his car, and a surprised Rindt who spoke over the PA system. Later, Rindt was disqualified over a seemingly needless aerofoil wrangle, then after 3 ½ hours reinstated.

Jochen Rindt, winner of the "British", with his lovely model wife, Nina. She is a racing driver's daughter.

The winner discusses the amazing win with Lotus chief Colin Chapman (right). Then there was a protest...

Ickx led the race for more laps than anyone else, and here he blows dust into Rindt's face.

Grosser Preis von Deutschland

Hockenheim, August 2, 1970

The 1970 German Grand Prix was preceded by much argument, unrest, and finally a boycott of the Nurburgring circuit by members of the Grand Prix Drivers' Association on the grounds of safety. The drivers refused to drive at the "Ring" unless protective steel barriers were erected all around the 14.17-mile circuit, and fire-fighting equipment was greatly expanded. The *Automobil Club von Deutschland* maintained they had not been given sufficient notice and that the modifications could not be carried out in time. So the drivers refused to race at the traditional „Ring", and instead went to the 4.218-mile Hockenheimring near Heidelberg. The circuit had never enjoyed much of a reputation for safety—Jim Clark had died there in 1968 after leaving the track and striking a tree—but much work had been carried out since then, and there was protective barrier all around the course.

It was the first Formula 1 race to be staged on the relatively new circuit, and on the first day of practice Regazzoni displayed his knowledge of the course (he had participated in, and won F2 races there) and the potential of the Ferrari 312 b by making fastest time at 1 m. 59.8 s. Rindt was second-fastest, but a good second down on the Swiss driver. Next day Ickx took his Ferrari through to fastest practice time at 1 m. 59.5 s., a run which gave him pole position on the grid. At the end of the practice sessions there were three drivers who had broken two minutes (Ickx, Rindt, and Regazzoni) and one who had returned two minutes dead (Siffert). It was the first time cars had circulated the Hockenheimring at less than two minutes. The McLarens seemed down on speed, and Brabham was another driver who seemed unable to make his customary quick times. The Australian hadn't in fact driven at Hockenheim before, nor had Stewart, Amon, Andretti, Surtees and Ickx.

Non-qualifiers were Redman (de Tomaso), de Adamich (McLaren-Alfa) Moser (Bellasi-Ford), and Hahne the German F2 driver who was entered in a brand-new March 701 sponsored by newspaper mogul Axel Sprin-

The Hockenheim phalanx. Rindt leads Ickx, Regazzoni, and Amon. All but Amon led the race at one time, the New Zealander and Regazzoni eventually retiring.

Busy bunch, with Fittipaldi's Lotus 49c in the foreground. Surtees in centre and Stommelen to the right. Fittipaldi finished fourth, Stommelen fifth.

Hulme (foreground), Peterson, and Beltoise, in very close company. Only Hulme finished, in third place. His McLaren was a new, more rigid car.

Andretti's STP-March was much-modified by McNamara but was not impressive, and retired on lap 16 with a gearbox selector breakage.

Regazzoni and Amon kept close company for much of the race, the Swiss always ahead of the March until the Ferrari broke its transmission.

ger. Andretti's STP-March had been much-modified by McNamara in Germany, particularly with respect to the rear suspension. The great grandstand with nearly 100,000 "seated" spectators saw Ickx out-accelerate everyone into the first right-hander. Rindt was second, with Regazzoni and Siffert close behind. Brabham was left on the line with gear selection troubles, and it was 30 seconds before he blasted after the field. First time around it was Ickx out in front and going well, followed by Rindt, Siffert, Regazzoni, Pescarolo, Amon, Rodriguez and Stewart. Regazzoni soon passed Siffert, and Brabham got going like a bomb (and smoking rather like one!) to set the first official lap record at 2 m. 3 s., but on the fifth lap had to retire with lubrication problems.

Just before the halfway mark (25 laps) Regazzoni swung out and led for two laps, and Ickx dropped to third place behind Rindt, but by lap 26 Ickx was back in command, although the Lotus was close behind. Only driver still on the same lap as the leaders was Graham Hill in the Walker Lotus 49c. Rindt and Regazzoni fought over second place, but Amon managed to grab third place when the Swiss driver had a moment on the right-hander before the pits straight. By the second part of the corner the Ferrari's gearbox had seized and Regazzoni's great effort had come to an end. Four laps later Amon was also out, with a broken camshaft. Rindt was back in the lead but Ickx was battling hard — only half-a-second separated the British and Italian cars, and Surtees was third in his near-new TS 7. Rindt and Ickx continued their ferocious scrap, and on the last ten laps the lead changed no less than five times. Surtees blew up and Hulme, still with tender hands, moved into third place. Fittipaldi went up into fourth, and Stommelen, to the delight of the partisan crowd, was fifth. The final laps had the huge crowd (estimated at 150,000) in an uproar, and on the last lap both leading drivers pulled out all the stops. Ickx had had to shut-off on the previous lap when Rindt got on to the grass—just in case the Lotus should spin in front of him—so the Austro-German driver went on to win, but only by seven-tenths of a second.

The *AvD* staged their own Formula 2 "Grand Prix of Germany" on the same day as the Hockenheim race, but there were many who regarded the smaller circuit, with its vast grandstand accommodation and nearness to the Frankfurt *autobahn*, as more suitable for Germany's premier race than any other course. Jacky Ickx married a few days after his fine run in the German GP, and rumours started to fly about his intending to retire from racing at the end of the season. It was also being said that Rindt, who had been very affected by Courage's death in the Grand Prix was also contemplating retirement.

Grosser Preis von Österreich

Zeltweg, August 16, 1970

Ferrari scored a terrific comeback in the Austrian Grand Prix at the *Ostereichring*, the new circuit built near the old airfield site at Zeltweg. Ickx and Regazzoni dominated the entire 60-lap race, the Italian cars never being challenged, and the young, newly-married Belgian proving the victor. It was Ferrari's first Championship GP win since the French GP of 1968—when again Ickx had been the driver. It was also an enormous triumph for the 12-cylinder cars, for "multis" finished in five of the first six places.

Jochen Rindt, leading the World Championship by a handsome margin had four consecutive Championship wins behind him, and was obviously anxious to put on a good show in front of his compatriots. In spite of being fastest in practice (it was the first F 1 race ever on the picturesque, mountain-dominated course) he was never higher than third, then broke his engine in front of the pits on lap 22. Stewart covered only one lap, then had to call in with a broken fuel pipe (in the cockpit), soaked in petrol and was forced to change his clothing. He eventually retired on lap 8.

The organisers took the unusual step of having three days of practice, sessions which added-up to no less than eleven hours of work for drivers and cars. In view of the Cosworth-Ford engine shortage prevailing at the time, it was perhaps not the best of ideas.

Rindt proved the fastest in practice with the works Lotus 72 at 1 m. 39.23 s, but the amazing Regazzoni was close behind at 1 m. 39.70 s with the Ferrari 312 b, and obviously found the tricky circuit to his liking. The grid was a 2 × 2 so the Lotus and the Ferrari shared the front row. Before the meeting the lap record had been held by Jacky Ickx with a three-litre Mirage "sports car" at 1 m. 46.6 s. (124.02 mph). Graham Hill was expected to race Rob Walker's new Brooke-Bond-Oxo Lotus 72, but in spite of two of his own mechanics working with the Lotus engineers at the Hethel factory, the new car couldn't be readied in time. By then the race was too close for the old 49 c to be prepared, so Walker withdrew.

Jochen Rindt, Austria's national hero, signs autographs for countless fans. His Lotus blew-up.

The flag went down a little after 3 pm, and Regazzoni made a splendid start, pulling away from Rindt. As the cars streaked into sight on the first lap, Ickx had taken second place, Rindt was third, and Giunti was holding fourth with the "No. 3" Ferrari. Amon was fifth, and Beltoise sixth. Even at that stage 12-cylinder cars were dominating. Stewart pulled into his pit, and Stewart's team-mate Cevert blew-up on the same lap.

On the second lap Ickx took the lead from Regazzoni, and from then on the 1-2 order stayed for the rest of the 220-mile race.

After five laps Beltoise was close to the Ferraris, and this threesome pulled well away from the rest of the field. Giunti was leading the second batch, in close company with Rindt, Brabham, Amon, and Hulme. The pace was immense, and Brabham managed to pass Amon under braking and started to press Rindt. The Austrian driver finally passed Giunti but was by then ten seconds behind the 12-cylinder trio. Andretti went off the track through a fence with a stuck throttle, but was unhurt.

After 18 laps Rindt had picked-up nearly four seconds on the leaders, but his engine seized and he pulled-off at the pits. The Lotus driver's disappearance put Giunti once again in fourth place, so Ferraris were 1-2-4. Surtees, who had been going well in his TS 7, broke a valve spring on lap 28 when in sixth place. Two laps earlier, Australian Tim Schenken, having his first F 1 drive, had blown-up in Frank William's De Tomaso. Hulme's McLaren also blew-up—the Cosworth-Ford engines were disappearing fast ! The leading Ferraris began to pull away from Beltoise. Brabham, holding fifth place, had to pit-stop with a holed radiator—which his crew changed in five minutes. His "team-

◄ *The ageless Brabham held fifth place for a lengthy period, but was forced to stop for a complete radiator change after a stone had caused a water leak. The Australian was classified 13th.*

▲ *Apart from the two opening laps, Ickx led the Austrian Grand Prix at Österreichring from start to finish. It was the first Formula 1 victory for Ferrari since 1968, at Rouen.*

For almost the entire 60-lap race, the order was Ickx and Regazzoni in the two Ferraris, followed by Beltoise in the Matra-Simca. With three laps to go, the Frenchman ran short of fuel. ▼

Feverish activity in the Matra pit when Beltoise rushes in for fuel on lap 57. The driver stayed at the wheel while about five gallons were quickly put in, then he tore back into the race and finished sixth. Until the fuel drama he had been holding third place behind the two Ferraris.

Tussle between Rodriguez, Stommelen, Gethin and Siffert. The BRM driver is ahead here but Stommelen got past and took third place with the Brabham BT33. The Mexican driver took fourth place followed by his team-mate Oliver who worked his way through the field. Siffert and Gethin finished 9th and 10th.

During Saturday's practice, Siffert had a tyre deflate, causing the March to hit a guardrail. Damage was slight, only the nose and the exhaust pipe suffering. Here the Swiss driver runs along on the rim, en route for the paddock, and repairs. He made only the tenth row of the starting grid.

mate" Stommelen was holding an impressive fifth place, then Giunti had to make for his pit for a wheel/tyre change, so the German was fourth. Amon was fifth but in all sorts of damper and brake trouble, and he was finally overhauled by the BRM pair, Rodriguez and Oliver. With 11 laps to go the leading Ferraris lapped Amon, and with three laps to go poor Beltoise had to stop for fuel. By the time he rejoined the race he was sixth, and Stommelen had taken third place for Brabham. At the finish the vast Italian crowd broke down the fence, rushed down the track like an invading army, flags and banners aloft. Ferrari team manager Forghieri was showered with congratulations—and the revels continued long into the night, which was just as well for the traffic jam was about the biggest ever seen in Austria. It had been a big day for Ferrari and for the "multis", and every one of the nine retirements had been V8-engined. The tents ran out of beer—but the band kept playing!

Worm's eye view of Ickx and Siffert. Ickx led the race for the three opening laps but retired with transmission trouble. Siffert broke his engine.

Even with fastest practice time and pole position, the newly-married Ickx finds time for a few sweet nothings before the race. L'amour, eh?

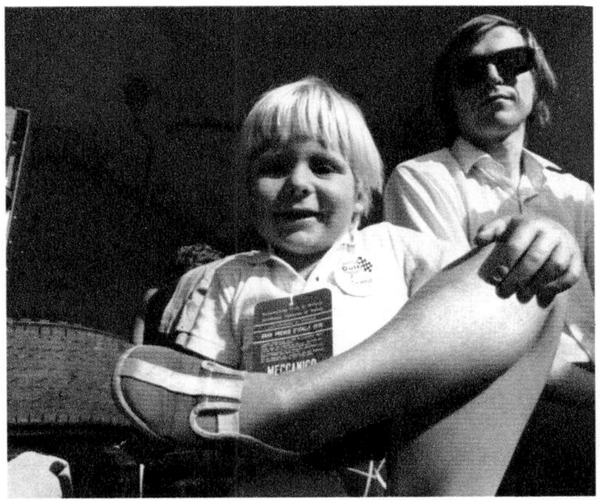

Denny Hulme has been married longer than Ickx and his four-year-old son Martin wears a mechanic's pass to prove it.

Jean-Pierre Beltoise does the frontal nudity bit, absorbs the Milanese sun, and exhibits some of his impressive motorcycle accident scars.

Gran Premio d'Italia

Monza, September 6, 1970

The 41st Italian classic gave Swiss driver Clay Regazzoni his first Grand Prix victory—an amazing performance in view of his debut in the category less than three months earlier, in the Dutch Grand Prix. The 31-year-old Ferrari driver also gave Maranello their first Italian Grand Prix win since 1964.

The race was as fast-moving and exciting as ever, but was overshadowed by the tragic death of Jochen Rindt in practice the day before. His Lotus 72 went out of control at the *Parabolica* whilst braking from about 200 mph, and the unfortunate driver died soon afterwards. It spoke volumes for the dedication and courage of the other drivers in general, and Jackie Stewart in particular that the Sunday's race took place with no reduction in pace or professionalism. The other two works Lotus 72s were withdrawn, as was the brand-new 72 of Rob Walker which Graham Hill was to have raced for the first time.

Practice had indicated once again the speed of the 12-cylinder cars on the 3.57-mile circuit, five out of six in the first three rows having that form of power-unit. The sole V8 in the first three rows was the March 701 of Stewart, the Scot and Ken Tyrrell electing to use the well-proven car in preference to the new and promising Tyrrell-Ford as fuel-feed problems were not fully resolved.

Stewart did not practice at all after Rindt's Saturday crash, but kept his fourth-fastest time and place on the second row of the grid. The prospect of a Ferrari victory brought a colossal crowd into the circuit on the Sunday morning— a typical Italian Grand Prix Sunday of tropical heat and animation. Jacky Ickx, as the fastest practiceman occupied pole position, alongside Pedro Rodriguez in one of the three works BRM P153s, and as the flag came down it was the young Belgian who led away the field of 20. For three laps past the pit/grandstand area Ickx headed the pack, then the contest became the usual Monza demonstration of slipstreaming, late braking, and high-speed gamesmanship. In ten laps the lead changed four times, Ickx, Rodriguez, Stewart, and Regazzoni all taking a turn. Stewart's driving was immense, for his car could not be considered as fast as the Ferraris and BRMs on that ultra-fast circuit, and the events of the day before must have had an effect on his enthusiasm for the race. Jochen Rindt was a very close friend and neighbour of Stewart, and the Scot had helped to extri-

FINA

Third lap and Ickx' Ferrari is in the lead, followed by Rodriguez, Regazzoni, Stewart, Giunti, Oliver, and Brabham. Siffert retired on that lap. After Ickx fell back (second picture) Rodriguez took the lead with the BRM P153 on lap 3, shadowed by Stewart, Ickx, Regazzoni, Oliver, and Giunti. Picture 3 and the typical Monza cut-and-thrust continues with Stewart in the lead and Rodriguez in close attendance. Third is Regazzoni, followed by Oliver, then Stommelen, Hulme, and Ickx. Right-hand picture—as they finished, with the victorious Regazzoni ahead of Stewart.

It was Regazzoni's first Grand Prix victory in his first Grand Prix season. He won for Ferrari at the record speed of 147.07 mph.

Clay Regazzoni, 31-year-old Italian-speaking Swiss drove like a master to win the Italian Grand Prix, and his win for the "home team" Ferrari brought crowds of Italians and Swiss out on to the circuit after the 100-minute race. The Swiss "new-boy" also set a new Monza lap record at 150.96 mph with the Ferrari 312b, but was the only survivor of the three-car team from Maranello.

cate the unfortunate driver the day before. Poor Surtees (he won the race in 1964 and '67) stalled his engine on the line, and was forced to retire after one lap due to a flat battery which was fitted after a rush to repair a leaking fuel tank before the start.

The battle on the sun-soaked concrete was Monza at its best. Every time a Ferrari led, the partisan crowd went mad. During the 1 h. 40 m. race the lead changed at least 28 times, Stewart, Ickx, Regazzoni, Rodriguez, Hulme, and Oliver taking their turn at heading the contest. At half-distance (34 laps) Regazzoni led Stewart, and seemed to have power in reserve. The Swiss contingent was very excited. By that time Ickx's Ferrari had retired with a broken transmission. Oliver was going well in third place with the BRM, but his team-mate Rodriguez was out with a blown engine, and the third BRM driver, Eaton, was out with an overheated motor. Eaton's engine was fitted with the new-type BRM cylinder-heads, but they had proved porous and troublesome.

Regazzoni continued to impress, and from then on only Stewart got ahead of him, and then for but two laps.

With 18 laps to go Stewart somehow forged ahead of Regazzoni, but it wasn't to last and the Ferrari was back in the lead on lap 54, and stayed there until the finish.

The pace had accounted for half the field, and Brabham had had a very lucky escape on lap 32 when his car went out of control leaving the *Parabolica*, and was destroyed. The Australian was unhurt, was in eighth place when the incident occurred, and claimed his engine had cut-out as he came out of the difficult corner. Regazzoni was uncatchable. He equalled Beltoise' existing lap record of 150.96 mph, and won the race at the record average speed of 147.07 mph. Hulme pulled out all the stops and passed Stewart, only to be repassed three laps later. Unlike the close 1969 finish, Regazzoni brought the Ferrari 312b through to the chequered flag 5.8 seconds in front of Stewart. His win put him in fifth place on the World Championship table with 21 points. Stewart's second place brought his points total to 25, equal to Brabham, but Rindt's score of 45 points was still head and shoulders above them all.

The win by an Italian-speaking Swiss in an Italian car had the effect of sending the crowd wild. Vast hordes of them invaded the track, and the roads from Monza were jammed for hours. After the race the equal points score of Brabham and Stewart seemingly put them in line for the Championship, but a few days after the race the *F.I.A.* announced that Jochen Rindt would be awarded the title posthumously if his score of 45 points was not exceeded during the remainder of the season. The situation has never risen before.

Stewart built-up a big lead in the early stages of the race with the Tyrrell-Ford, but a stub axle broke, and here he signals his retirement.

Canadian Grand Prix

Mont-Tremblant, September 20, 1970

After their tragic Monza, Lotus stayed away from St. Jovite-Mont. Tremblant, but Ferrari continued with their winning streak and finished first and second, Ickx notching the Italian marque's third successive victory in a Championship Grand Prix. Only half the field of twenty starters officially finished the race on the 2.65-mile circuit which is about 90 miles from Montreal, and extremely hard on suspensions and running gear.

In fact, a smoother course could have easily resulted in a different winner, for Stewart, after making a very fast practice time in the Tyrrell-Ford, which at that time had yet to participate in a Championship Grand Prix, chose to drive the new car in preference to the March, and led the race from the start until put out with a broken stub axle on lap 31. From that moment on, Ickx who had held second place throughout, took the lead and pressed on to another Ferrari win, backed-up by his skilful team-mate Regazzoni who made it a 1-2 for the red "flat-12s". Practice indicated that cars were to have a tough time in the race, for the rippled surface of the track made braking difficult, put a tremendous strain on chassis and transmissions, and resulted in a never-ending vibration which was bound to break brackets and so on. In spite of all sorts of practice troubles, it looked as though the Ferraris had the upper hand with Ickx managing a best 1 m. 31.6 s., and Regazzoni a 1 m. 31.9 s., in spite of brake troubles. These were the two fastest times until the final practice day when Stewart, after stopping out on the circuit after a wheel bearing had seized on the March, ran across the fields, leapt in to the Tyrrell, and recorded the fastest time at 1 m. 31.5 s.—on the very last permissible practice lap. So at the last minute the reigning World Champion snatched pole position (his best time in the March had been 1 m. 31.9 s.), and because of it he chose to drive the new car in the race. During the proceedings Hill's new Brooke Bond Oxo Lotus 72 (the only 72 at the circuit, and fitted with solid front brake shafts) caught fire, Amon's March broke a rear upright, and the Brabhams of Jack himself and Stommelen had handling problems which turned out to be due to seized roller bearings in the rack and pinion steering assemblies.

Regazzoni drove well on the rough circuit and backed-up winner Ickx for most of the race. His second place took him to 27 amassed points in the World Championship table—only one down on Ickx. It was a convincing day for the marque Ferrari—a first and a second in the third consecutive win.

Pescarolo (24) and Gethin (6) were in close company for most of the race, but the Briton finally took sixth place with the works McLaren ahead of the Frenchman in the works Matra-Simca. It was Gethin's first Championship point.

◄ *Chris Amon finally took third place after a lengthy scrap with Cevert. Here the New Zealander hurries the works March in characteristic manner. Only the first three cars were on the same lap.*

Ickx on full song in the victorious Ferrari 312b. The young Belgian had run second to Stewart from the start but took the lead when the Scot retired on lap 31. Ickx won the previous year's race, at Mosport, but for the Brabham team.

Rodriguez stopped for fuel and a suspension check with four laps to go but kept his fourth place. Dunlop's Ian Mills (left) surveys the tyres.

Cevert had the appalling luck to break a damper on the Tyrrell-March after holding fourth place for half the race. He finished ninth.

Surtees worked his way through the field with his near-new TS7 and took fifth place, a lap ahead of sixth-man Gethin.

Even on race morning a half-hour familiarization session saw Hill's clutch disintegrate, and Stommelen's rear sub-frame break, but both were repaired in time for the race—in fact all cars were good and ready for the "off". At the start Stewart was quickly away and even after one lap he had a clear lead from Ickx, Rodriguez, Surtees, Cevert and Regazzoni. The Scot just increased his lead as the laps were completed, and it seemed his car, new Dunlop tyres—and his style—had an affinity with the Canadian track.

Surtees' TS7 was going extremely well (the near-new car had won the Gold Cup race at Oulton Park less than a month earlier against Formula 1 and F5000 cars) in fourth place, but he had to stop to investigate a misfire which suddenly manifested itself. He set off again in 17th place.

Siffert's March was the first casualty when it blew up on lap 22, and on the next lap Stommelen called it a day (amongst other things) when his steering stiffened-up too much to continue. Hill stopped with a loosened rear wishbone, but continued later. Stewart still led convincingly with Ickx all on his own in second, and Regazzoni having to fight to keep ahead of Amon and Cevert. Then Stewart went missing, but managed to crawl in with his breakage. The two Ferraris now occupied the most desirable positions but Regazzoni was still scrapping with Cevert and Amon. Rodriguez was fifth, Hulme, sixth Gethin seventh and Surtees had worked his way up to eighth. Surtees kept going great guns and passed Gethin and Hulme.

Ickx was well ahead and eased-off to save his car but Regazzoni was still hard at it, and set a new lap record at 1 m. 32.2 s. with 15 laps to go.

The Swiss driver had put such efforts into his closing laps that he finally got away from Amon and Cevert. Cevert had to head for his pit on lap 76 with a broken damper, and although the Tyrrell staff were able to replace it and get their French driver back into the race, he was down to ninth place. As the race drew to its conclusion Beltoise fell out with a broken clutch, and Rodriguez was forced to refuel his BRM.

Ickx and Regazzoni continued on their winning way and collected the chequered flag, but Stewart had demonstrated that the Tyrrell-Ford was a potent force in Grand Prix racing. Only the two Ferraris and Amon's March were on the same lap at the finish. The result of the Canadian Grand Prix brought into sharp focus that Ickx with his Championship point score of 28 was the only driver who could exceed the late Jochen Rindt's total of 45 points. With two races left, a victory in each for the Belgian driver would have meant he could amass 46 points, but he sportingly remarked after St. Jovite that in his eyes Rindt would be the 1970 World Champion.

Rodriguez led the US Grand Prix for 18 laps, then had to stop for fuel. With a 17-second lead he managed to rejoin the contest and finish second behind Fittipaldi. It was the second consecutive race in which the Mexican had to take on fuel.

United States Grand Prix

Watkins Glen, October 4, 1970

The United States Grand Prix at Watkins Glen was fantastic in every way. Lotus made a tremendous come-back with first and third places with a two-car team; their drivers were both "new-boys"; Stewart again led the race for a considerable distance untul put out by engine failure; and Rodriguez looked a certain winner in the closing stages of the race when he had to pull into his pit (as at St. Jovite) for fuel. The Mexican managed to finish second. Ickx finished fourth thus ruining any chance of him exceeding the Championship points score of Rindt.

Watkins Glen victor was Emerson Fittipaldi, the 23-year-old Brazilian driver, in his fourth Championship Grand Prix. He had made his European debut only the year before in Formula Ford, and not so long before that had been racing go-karts. His new team-mate, the Swedish driver Reine Wisell, was making his first-ever appearance in a Championship GP, altough he had raced a Formula 1 car once before. His was a close third place, and only the first three cars were on the same lap.

After missing the Canadian Grand Prix, Team Lotus arrived at Watkins Glen with two Type 72s, both with larger-diameter, thicker front brake shafts than hitherto. Fittipaldi's car was the one in which he had crashed at Monza in practice, but it had been completely rebuilt. Stewart's Tyrrell-Ford had new-type front uprights and stub axles since the St. Jovite incident, and the works Brabhams sported revised steering and lower

▲
Stewart and Ickx blast away at the start, leading the big field of 24. Rodriguez and eventual winner Fittipaldi are in the second row. Unusually, the holders of the first two grid rows all held the lead at one time or another. Stewart led for the first three-quarters of the race.

Ickx, Regazzoni, and Amon passing the stands in an order that persisted for the early laps. The Swiss Ferrari driver lost ground dramatically when he was forced to stop for a front tyre change and for ignition trouble.

After trying both March and Tyrrell in practice, Stewart eventually made second-fastest time with the Tyrrell-Ford, seen here with new-type stub axles, and suspension uprights. The car revealed enormous speed, and in the race pulled away from everything. Stewart had lapped everyone except Rodriguez when he retired.

Emerson Fittipaldi, driving in his fourth Championship race, won at record speed and clinched the World Constructors' Championship for Lotus. He took the lead on lap 101.

wishbones. For the first time Surtees fielded two TS7s, one for himself, and another for Derek Bell. BRM entered a four-car team, the extra driver being ex-hill climb star Peter Westbury who had at one time exploited a four-wheel-drive BRM, and had lately competed in Formula 2. Westbury didn't qualify.

Star of the practice sessions was Ickx with a sizzling 1m. 03.07s. (existing lap record was held by Rindt's 1969 figure of 1m. 04.34s), but Stewart tried both Tyrrell March 701 and Tyrrell-Ford, finishing-up with second-fastest time at 1m. 03.62s. The grid was 2 × 2, and with Regazzoni and Fittipaldi on the second row, there were four different marques in the two front rows—with three different engines. The race started 25 minutes late, but the field of 24 was led by Stewart when the flag did come down. The twisty course obviously suited Stewart, the Tyrrell, and the new-type Dunlops, for

in one lap he pulled clear of Rodriguez—who was being harried by Ickx.

By one-third race distance Stewart was out on his own, and had lapped everyone below sixth place. By that time Surtees, Eaton, Oliver, and Hutchison had retired for divers reasons.

By half-distance Stewart had lapped Fittipaldi (who was to win!) and Regazzoni who had held third place for a long time, had fallen back due to a stop for a new front tyre, and another for ignition problems.

Ickx was holding second with Rodriguez in third, but sudenly the Belgian Ferrari driver shot into his pit with a fuel breather squirting petrol all over the place, and Ferrari hopes were dashed. Ickx was 12th when he rushed back into the fray.

Stewart looked set but on the 70th lap his engine began to trail smoke and it all appeared ominous for the Scot. He slowed down in an effort to save the motor—he could well aford to do so as he was more than 30 seconds ahead of Rodriguez' BRM. Another three laps and the car blew-up and Stewart was out of the contest, but not before he had once again demonstrated the enormous potential of the car—and of the driver when he has a mount worthy of his skill.

So with 25 laps left it now looked set for Rodriguez who was driving well in a crisp-sounding car, and who had a lead of some 17 seconds over Fittipaldi. Wisell was 30 seconds behind his team-mate, in third position. The BRM pit had lost their other cars but it seemed they might repeat their Spa win, with the same driver. On and on went the race and then with seven laps to go, the BRM tore into the pits for fuel—just as it had to do in Canada—and the mechanics tossed some in. The Mexican blasted his way back into the race but Fittipaldi had gone by and taken the lead.

Rodriguez was still in second place but he had to drive hard to prevent Wisell from moving in. Fittipaldi showed not a trace of nervousness and went on to take the victor's flag in his first year of Formula 1. His win also clinched the Constructors' Championship for Lotus. Fourteen cars were running at the end of the 248-miles race.

Fittipaldi certainly picked the right race to win for it was the best-paid Formula 1 event ever, the young Brazilian netting $50,000 in prize-money.

Jackie Stewart once again didn't finish but in view of his peerless performance while he was in the race, was selected as "Man of the Race" by working journalists—a title which gave him the BOAC Trophy and around $5000.

The United States Grand Prix, penultimate event in the 1970 World Championship series, had settled the question of whether or not Jochen Rindt's score of 45 amassed points could be surpassed, and Lotus had broken the string of Ferrari victories.

Team Lotus' other find was Reine Wisell, driving in his first Championship Grand Prix. He finished third, on the same lap as the winner, in the Lotus 72. A day of surprises.

German Prince Paul von Metternich of the FIA stands between Swiss drivers Siffert and Regazzoni, with Paul Blancpain and Maurice Baumgartner on either side. Just to show that Switzerland can produce noblemen, Baron de Graffenried joins in.

Jackie Stewart implores the spectators to go back behind the rails before the start. Most of them refused, and after a delay of 75 minutes the race started with the crowd lining the track edge. There could have been tragedy.

Gran Premio de México

Mexico City, October 25, 1970

A chaotic race in which Ferrari scored another 1-2 victory with a two-car entry, the winner Jacky Ickx finishing the season with more World Championship points than any other living driver. To ram home the superiority of the Italian marque, Regazzoni finished with 33 points, second only to his team-mate's 40 points. Only one works Lotus finished the race, that of Wisell, in tenth and last place. Fittipaldi retired on the first lap with vanished oil pressure, and a tightening engine.

Jack Brabham had announced the Mexican Grand Prix was to be his last race, the 44-year-old Australian veteran and three-times World Champion deciding to hang up his helmet—as he put it—after more than twenty years in motor racing, and 14 Grand Prix victories behind him. Unfortunately he was forced to retire when in third place, with only 13 laps to go. Still one of the world's fastest drivers, Brabham had won the 1000 kilometres race at Montlhéry the weekend before, with François Cevert, at the wheel of a Matra-Simca MS660. One of motor racing's greats. It looked for a considerable time as though Brabham wouldn't have a Mexican Grand Prix in which to participate, for crowd control was non-existent, and its size was officially estimated at more than 200,000 people. Spectators swarmed on to the track—renamed Ricardo Rodriguez Autodrome in honour of Pedro Rodriguez who was killed practising a Lotus for the 1962 race—and the police were afraid to get tough in case there was a riot. The start was delayed for more than an hour whilst efforts were made to get the crowds back behind the fences but it was useless, and finallly the drivers made several exploratory laps to determine whether or not to race.

Practice saw an incredible number of engine breakages—not to mention Brabham having a moment in the opening minutes of the first day when a rear damper unscrewed itself. The Australian slid to halt past the pits without damage to himself or his car—and finished the sessions with fourth-fastest time. The amazing Regazzoni hadn't even seen the circuit before, but was the fastest within an

▲ *By lap 2 Ickx had taken the lead and he stayed there for the rest of the race. He won last year for Brabham, and holds the circuit lap record.*

The crowd, officially estimated at more than 200,000, was completely uncontrollable, and took up positions in unbelievably dangerous places. ▼

Jacky Ickx drove magnificently under very dangerous conditions but did not break the lap record. It was a demonstration of restrained high-speed. ►

hour of practice starting. Ickx later made a quicker time leaving the Swiss driver second-fastest, but by the end of the sessions Regazzoni was again fastets at 1m. 41.86 s.
The high-altitude (7400 ft. above sea level) circuit outside Mexico City, as usual, played havoc with induction systems and cooling, and Stommelen's Brabham was fortunate to escape real damage when an electric light fitting fell into a tray of fuel and ignited it in the Brabham garage. The car was quicky pushed out of the flames and suffered only a little blistering. The Lotus 72s of works drivers Fittipaldi and Wisell, as well as the Brooke Bond Oxo car driven by Hill, had reverted to the old-type front brake shafts as the heavier pattern as fitted at Watkins Glen had caused damage to fourth and fifth gears. All three cars were fitted with new engines and extra oil coolers the night before the race, and Surtees too fitted an extra oil cooler.
At last the race started, 75 minutes late, and was run through the crowds who sat at the circuit edge. Many crossed the track during the event.
It was the Swiss Regazzoni who led away at the start, closely followed by Stewart, but by the second lap Ickx had passed both of them. Stewart stayed with Ickx for several laps, but Regazzoni fell back when he hit his ignition switch during a gear-change. Siffert was out by the third lap with a blown engine, and Cevert was out after eight laps for the same reason. Brabham was running fifth.
After 14 laps Stewart called at his pit to have a loose steering column bush attended to, and when he rejoined the race he was 12th. Brabham was then third, but Stewart started working his way through the field. The two Ferraris were way out in front and Hulme passed Beltoise to take fourth place. At half-distance Ickx was 15 seconds ahead of his team-mate in second place, and the Swiss was 15 seconds ahead of Brabham. Stewart had made fastest lap up until then but then had the appalling luck to hit a straying dog which damaged the Tyrrell's front suspension and forced him to retire.
Brabham still held third and when Regazzoni's engine started smoking it began to look as though the Australian might have a rewarding final appearance. On the 53rd lap however Brabham's engineblew up, and he retired—in every sense of the word.
Hulme took over third place but Amon was trying very hard to catch his compatriot. There was only a second between them but try as he might Amon could not get the March past the McLaren. Apart from the first lap Ickx had led from start to finish, and as he crossed the line he was hard put to miss the spectators who were running across the track. Ten cars out of 18 starters were running at the end, and many were saying it was unlikely there would be another World Championship Mexican Grand Prix.

3

HINCHMAN
NOMEX
GOODY

BRABHAM

Jack Brabham and Ron Tauranac adhered to full steel-tube space-frame construction with their Formula 1 cars longer than anyone else in the top league. The two Australians (based in Britain) were enthusiasts for the relative simplicity of construction and the ease of repair the system offered, but in the end the superiority of the monocoque won, and there was a Formula 1 Brabham with this form of main structure on the drawing board by the beginning of 1969.

Due to pressure of work and racing, the BT33 (BT stands for Brabham-Tauranac) as it was designated, did not take the stage until 1970, but when it did it immediately demonstrated it was indeed a potent proposition — particularly with the redoubtable Jack at the wheel. There had in fact been a monocoque Brabham before, but that had been the 1968 Indianapolis car, rather a different proposition.

The monocoque obviously provided greater rigidity than the space-frame, but due to the fact the car had originally been designed for the 1969 F1 it was not built with the mandatory rubberised fuel bags in mind. For 1969 it was to have had the side pontoons sprayed with sealing compound, the fuel to be contained within the sealed areas. With fuel bags becoming compulsory in 1970, the rubberised bags were inserted into the same spaces and fuel capacity was drastically reduced. The first car had a capacity of only 40 gallons (Imp), but later cars were given a wider monocoque which increased capacity to around 45 gallons. It still wasn't enough in the British Grand Prix at Brands Hatch!

Besides being the first F1 monocoque Brabham the BT33 also showed a change from customary Tauranac designs by changing to inboard-mounted front suspension instead of the scuttle-pivoted and forward-pivoted lower arm system. The Cosworth-Ford DFV V8 was again employed and was a self-supporting unit, the combination of a short engine and monocoque nacelle making for a very rigid structure.

The monocoque was an uncomplicated design built-up of 18-gauge NS4 aluminium alloy, with a straight-sided inner "box" within curved outer panelwork. Extra stiffness was imparted by square-section mild steel bulkheads fore and aft, by curved panels under the driver's legs, and by the seat tank which was curved upwards across the rear of the chassis. The monocoque structure proved to be 60 lb. lighter than the earlier space-frame of the BT26.

The Cosworth-Ford engine was attached to the rear bulk-head by two bolts on the lower part of the crankcase, and by two plates on the cambox covers. Rear suspension was mounted on a steel tube cage bolted to the Hewland DG300 gearbox, and no loads were transmitted to the engine. The rear suspension was virtually the same as the space-frame BT26, featuring single top links, reversed lower wishbones, outboard coil spring-damper units, an adjustable antiroll bar, and twin tubular radius arms (per side) anchored on the aft end of the monocoque. The rear hub carriers were identical to those used on the BT26, as also were the 11 in. outboard solid Girling disc brakes.

Transmission drive-shafts were fitted with two Hardy-Spicer universal-joints, and one Metalastik rubber "doughnut" per side. The huge cylindrical oil tank was mounted on one side of the gearbox, and the 12-volt battery on the other. The oil cooler was sited above the gearbox.

Front suspension of the BT33 featured lower wishbones, top cantilevers and inboard coil spring/damper units. The cantilever pivoted on needle-roller bearings. The rack and pinion steering gear, fire extinguisher bottle etc. can be seen behind the radiator mounting.

With the Ford-Cosworth engine wheeled away the Tauranac-designed monocoque exhibits its bluff stern, and also the rear suspension radius arms attached to it. The main rubberised fuel bags are contained in the bulbous sides and the disconnected radiator water pipe dangle from the lower sides of the 'body'.

The rack and pinion steering gear featured an integral damper and was low-mounted with fire extinguisher bottle, master cylinders and fluid reservoirs positioned below it. The Serck radiator was forward-mounted on outrigger stays, coolant being passed and fro the engine via external pipes. The glass-fibre nose incorporated fins, and the small aerofoil at the rear of the car used a slotted flap and end-fins which produced as much down-thrust as the old high-mounted strut-aerofoils.

The Brabham BT33 won the 1970 South African Grand Prix on its first competition appearance. It looked all set to win the Monaco and British Grands Prix but was pipped at the post on both occasions. It was undoubtedly one of the fastest 1970 cars, but luck was not always with the team.

BRM

British Racing Motors' P153 won a Championship Grand Prix in 1970, came within an ace of winning another, and demonstrated it could keep up with the fastest marques. The 1970 victory at Spa-Francorchamps came about because Rodriguez just couldn't be approached on that ultra-fast circuit, and it was at that moment that the P153 and its V12-cylinder engine had really arrived. After the BRM shake-up of 1969, Tony Southgate joined the Bourne équipe as chassis designer, and Aubrey Woods returned as chief engine designer. Stokes the gear wizard stayed with BRM so it was a strong team. Pedro Rodriguez, perhaps the most-improved driver of 1970, became No. 1, and Jack Oliver stayed with the team. Canadian George Eaton also drove the Formula 1 cars in some Grands Prix. Southgate's monocoque for the P153 weighed a mere 68 lb, the outer skin being of 18 gauge NS6 aluminium alloy. That material was difficult to work so it was cut longitudinally along a centre-line, and the two sections were later welded together. The inner skin was of L72 aluminium alloy, and bulkheads numbered only three in the interests of minimum weight. The seat tank mounting and leg panels also lent strength to the structure. Front suspension was by coil spring/damper units, double wishbones and anti-roll bar. In the BRM manner the springs and roll-bar were beautifully made in titanium. Rear suspension utilised reversed lower wishbones, single top links, coil spring/damper units (outboard), and double radius arms. Brakes were 10 ½ in. Girling discs (outboard) on all

The revised BRM engine with Woods-arranged porting. The exhaust ports face outwards, and the inlets and injection system are located in the area between the cylinder block "V". There are four valves per cylinder and four overhead camshafts.

At the German Grand Prix the P153s appeared with new positions for the oil tank and radiator. The new mounting was used mainly to achieve the most efficient circulation of lubricant. The rear suspension is also visible in this view, and the installed engine which was not designed as a load-bearing member.

At the front, as at the rear, the disc brakes are outboard. The dampers are mounted at a steep angle, and the wishbones are tubular.

◄ *"Its been a good 15 years' Grand Prix racing, and I'm thankful for all that its brought me". Jack Brabham bows out gracefully and still on top form.*

four wheels with Mk 4 AR calipers. Wheel diameters were 13 in. all-round, the front rims being 11 ½ in. wide, and the rears 17 in. wide. Front and rear uprights were cast in magnesium. The 60-degree V12 engine was designed originally as a sports/racing unit and the limit was intended to be around 350 bhp. BRM had at that time settled on the H16 engine as their Formula 1 unit, but when it became obvious it was to fail, the V12 was pressed into service. Woods rejoined BRM in mid-1970 and soon found the maximum power-output was around 370 bhp. It was also unreliable. He revised the inlet and exhaust systems, locating the exhaust ports in the sides of the cylinder heads—where they had been in the first place—reshaped the combustion chambers, modified the valves and seats, and introduced a more generous system of water passages. The lubrication system was also modified, and the engine was stiffened by using a crossbolted block to enable it to be partly stressed. Misfiring troubles were overcome by fitting Marelli ignition, but if 11,000 rpm were exceeded the connecting rods wilted. Stronger con-rod bolts were then used but oil surge wrote-off several engines on long, fast left-hand bends at Brands Hatch. Gradually the problems were overcome and late in the 1970 season the P153 engine was developing around 430 bhp on the bed. New-type cylinder heads were tried without success. The BRM five-speed gearbox was virtually trouble-free in 1970.

FERRARI

Regarded by many as the best-looking car of 1970 Formula 1 racing, the Ferrari 312b was also very successful, and the fact it was the only "flat-12" in the contest made it an even more interesting design. The 312b was only one victory inferior to the Lotus 72 in 1970 Championship GP races, winning the Austrian, Italian, Canadian, and Mexican Grands Prix—four races to the British car's five. As early as the Spanish Grand Prix in April the horizontally-opposed Italian car began to assert itself, but reliability wasn't too good. The 12-cylinder machine repeatedly demonstrated great speed in practice and in part of the race, but it wasn't until the Austrian GP that reliability was found.

The 312b is largely an engine story—Ferrari had always depended on more power than his competitors, rather than better handling and roadholding—and the "flat-12" certainly developed more power than any other engine in 1970 Formula 1. The engine was suspended from a beam on the rear of the monocoque's bulkhead (similar to the Honda air-cooled V8 F1 car of 1968) and produced a great deal of power from the start, but there were many problems through the earlier part of the season. At the outset there were piston troubles, then the valve inserts repeatedly worked loose. By the middle of the season a fuel distribution fault manifested itself at speeds above 10,500 rpm but Mauro Forghieri finally overcame the problems, and the boxermotor (for which the "b" designation stood) was not only the most powerful engine in GP racing, but possessed unusually good torque as well. Although Ferrari built-up his reputation with V12-cylinder engines, the "flat-12" was by no means a new configuration to the Maranello équipe, a 1½-litre Formula 1 engine of that type having been used in 1965, and a two-litre version of it powered the victorious 1969 European Hill-climb Championship Ferrari.

The monocoque was actually a reinforced space-frame, the structure not relying on the engine to lend stiffness. In fact, although at the time of writing no details of the engine's internal construction had been officially revealed, it is thought the crankshaft may have had only two or three main bearings, and this may well be part of the reason for the high power-output. A 12-cylinder engine, all things being equal, will always develop more all-out power than a unit with fewer cylinders, but a great deal of the extra power disappears through the frictional losses of extra pistons, bearings and so on. Ferrari's boxermotor was said to overcome this disadvantage by the use of the minimum number of bearings, and indeed could do this because of the excellent balance of the "horizontally-opposed" cylinder layout. In addition, the fact that the unit wasn't part of the chassis meant that torsional stresses through crank-case and cylinder blocks were lessened. In short, the construction enabled the engine to run "free", and this feature plus the low internal fractional losses meant a very high power-output. The low mounting of the "flat-12" engine not only made for good handling, but contributed to the animal good looks of the car. Whereas most of the current GP cars possess a naked, untidy appearance due to the completely exposed rear engine, the 312b's power-unit being set low made it not only unobtrusive, but the outrigger and panelling cleaned-up the rear of the "bodywork". Even the oil coolers were handsome with trumpet-shaped ducts at the rear of the car, fanning-out to the matrix and blending with the body lines. No space was wasted, the oil tanks being mounted underneath the coolers, and wedge-shaped to fit the areas. The snake-like exhaust system had to be twisted through the suspension parts, two final pipes per side emerging by the rear-mounted oil tanks. The 12-volt battery sat horizontally between the oil coolers, atop of the starter motor and five-speed Ferrari gearbox.

Suspension was conventional, at the front by reversed lower wishbones and fabricated top wishbones connected to inboard coil spring/damper units, and at the rear by single top links, lower wishbones, twin tubular radius arms (per side), outboard coil spring/damper units, and the usual adjustable anti-roll bar. Outboard disc brakes were fitted all-round (ducted at the front).

Various modications were made to battery, oil tank and other mountings during the 1970 season, and different suspension geometry was utilised for Monaco, but five virtually identical cars were built during the season. Ickx' 312b was completely destroyed in the Jarama first-lap fire.

Rear-mounted oil coolers of the Ferrari 312b featured trumpet-shaped ducts which blended with the general shape of the car. The five-speed Ferrari-made gearbox, horizontal battery, and outboard rear disc brakes can also be seen in this view.

Ferrari's space-frame-reinforced structure supported an outrigger at the rear of the aft bulkhead, from which the horizontally-opposed 12-cylinder engine was suspended. It made for a neat and handsome car. The conventional suspension system, front and rear, is visible in this photograph of a partly stripped 312b, and also the tortuous exhaust layout. Throughout the 1970 season Ferrari used a small aerofoil at the rear, and adjustable nose fins for stability. Fuel was carried in rubberised bags within the main structure, and the water radiator was also fully-ducted although the nose panelling is removed in this view. Brakes are outboard all-round, lack of space precluding rear inboard installation.

LOTUS

Colin Chapman has been an innovator for years. Ever since he got into competitive motoring some 20 years ago he has revealed a flair for extracting the maximum benefit from any set of regulations. From his Austin 750 Formula days he literally left others behind by exploring every nook and cranny of the rules, and by taking advantage of them. Whereas the majority of racing cars are subjected to year-by-year development, Chapman's Lotus machines have always strode forward in leaps and bounds.

Shown to the motoring press in early April 1970, the Cosworth-Ford DFV-powered Lotus 72 incorporated nothing that hadn't been seen before, but the fact that so many advanced features were incorporated in one car made it stand out. Designer of the new wedge-shaped machine was Maurice Phillipe, directed by Chapman, and it was immediately obvious the Lotus Indianapolis turbine cars had greatly influenced the shape of the new Formula 1 challenger. To achieve the wedge shape (and minimal frontal area), side radiators had been used, and there were many observers who prophecied trouble for the layout. With radiators in a vacuum area, they said, there would be insufficent through-draught to cool a racing engine. Gone too were the coil spring/damper units of the preceding Lotus 49 and in their place were compound torsion bars. As first introduced the "72" had powerful "anti-dive" and "anti-squat" characteristics built-in to the suspension. This feature proved unsuccessful in that it made high-speed handling difficult, and during the season Rindt's car was modified to "parallel" front and rear suspension, but the No. 2 car, driven mostly by John Miles, retained antidive front suspension. Inboard disc brakes (with solid discs) were employed, both front and rear, and great cooling problems were experienced with the front brakes. The brakes received cooling air through two inlets in the glass-fibre nose, the hot air being exhausted through two "chimneys" further back in the panel. It was insufficient however, and the amassed heat would melt grease out of the bearings, so portable electric fans had to be dropped on to the cooling slots during pit stops for a part of the season.

The new aerofoil regulations prompted Chapman to adopt a neat single-piece tail unit which incorporated three adjustable foils. It was also used on the works 49s (and on the Rob Walker 49) until some of the bugs had been removed from the 72 and it became an active racer. Fixed-angle wing root stubs were embodied in the nose of the car, and alternative blades could be attached to them to gain the required adhesion and stability.

The monocoque structure's outer panels were fabricated from 18 gauge NS-4 aluminium-magnesium alloy, and 20-gauge L72 aluminium for the inner panels. A $^{5}/_{8}$ in. square-section steel sub-frame reinforced the front of the structure, and also accepted front suspension loadings. Particular care was taken to present a smooth outer surface. Front and rear suspension was by compound torsion bars, the inner solid and outer tubular bars deflecting under torsion. Externally splined at their free ends they connected by light-alloy couplings. Upper and lower wishbones at the front of the car were fabricated from nickel-chrome-molybdenum alloy steel sheet, but at the rear there were wide-based tubular steel lower wishbones. The upper rear suspension links were reversed wishbones, coupled by push-pull rods to the torsion bars. There were top tubular radius arms which, typically Lotus, were attached through their ball-joints to the brackets which secured the engine's cylinder heads to the monocoque. Dual-purpose and weight-saving.

The general shape aimed at down-thrust, and the weight distribution of 65-35 front-rear was adopted to gain maximum traction. Rubberised fuel cells within the monocoque had a capacity of 45 gallons (Imp), and the saddle oil tank, mounted over the Hewland DG 300 gearbox, held three gallons.

The Cosworth-Ford DFV V8 engine was a fully-stressed member of the structure, transmitting the power through the five-speed Hewland box and double-jointed half-shafts. During the season the radiator position did give trouble but it was quickly put right by modifying duct-shape. The front brakes also gave trouble but this too was overcome

Rear suspension of the Lotus 72 in its latest 1970 form with the dampers mounted at an angle. Originally the rear dampers were tucked inside the exhaust pipes in an almost vertical position where, not surprisingly, the fluid boiled. The radius arms, one per side, are attached to the brackets which bolt the Ford-Cosworth engine to the monocoque. The upper and lower suspension links are of the wishbone type, normal at base and reversed at the top. One compound torsion bar is visible under disc brake.

The front inboard brakes, doubtless inspired by the four-wheel-drive Type 63, release suspension components from colossal brake torque reaction. The "drive-shafts" transfer torque from disc to wheel.

At the British Grand Prix the Lotus 72 appeared with rear-end modifications including the placing of the oil cooler to the left of the tank, and the battery had been moved from the front to the extreme rear.

by the use of the already-mentioned electric portable cooling gear. The handling problems were more drawn-out, but experiments continued throughout the season, and the Lotus 72 won more Championship GP races than any other car in 1970. The Monaco win with the old "49" boosted the total, and Lotus was also the Manufacturers' Championship winner.

MARCH

The marque March was brand-new for 1970, yet besides its own works team drivers Chris Amon and Jo Siffert, it was also raced by Jackie Stewart, Ronnie Peterson, François Cevert, and Mario Andretti in European and American events. Stewart won the Spanish Grand Prix at Jarama in April with the March 701, but this proved to be the only Championship event victory for the marque. In view of the number of good drivers handling the car it is too easy to regard its success list as poor, but it should also be said that it is quite exceptional for a brand-new marque to win even one important race during its first season. It must be added that designer Robin Herd had a sizeable problem to contend with when he set the first F1 March on the drawing board, namely that he was forced "to play it safe" and not delve too much into the unconventional. In a first year it is best to adhere to well-tried principles, but if he had had one successful season behind him he would have undoubtedly produced a much more radical machine.

The youthful Herd had achieved the highest academic honours, was involved in the aeronautical field and was reponsible for some of Concorde's design before getting into the world of racing cars. He designed the McLaren Formula 1 M7a, the Can-Am M6a and also the Cosworth four-wheel-drive F1 machine before throwing in his lot with the new March enterprise with workshops near Oxford.

The March 701's *monocoque* was of 18-gauge LM72 alluminium-alloy, tied at the front by two cast magnesium bulkheads. At the rear there was no bulkhead but a chamber divided to form three fuel cells provided the required rigidity. The hollow longerons also accommodated fuel bags, the total tankage adding-up to more than 40 gallons (Imp). The Cosworth-Ford DFV V8 and Hewland gearbox formed the rear structure, the reversed-lower wishbone/single top link suspension being attached to it. Later the rear suspension was modified. Two radius arms per side located the suspension longitudinally, and exposed coil spring/damper units were used all-round. Front suspension was by tubular wishbones, and although the cars first appeared with outboard disc brakes all-round, Stewart's car was converted to inboard rears for the Spanish Grand Prix, and consequently all F1 March cars were changed to that specification. The truth was that the 701 was overweight for 1970 racing, and the conversion not only reduced weight, but unsprung weight at that. In spite of the fact the Tyrrell équipe produced their own F1 car late in the season, and soon concentrated on it to the abandonment of the March, the latter car embodied many sound features and gave promise of what the marque could produce in the future.

Beautiful workmanship and simplicity of construction were features of the March 701, fitted with the aerodynamic "down-thrust" auxiliary fuel tanks. The later rear-end utilised inboard disc brakes to reduce both all-up, and unsprung weight. The lower wishbones were also replaced by two parallel links. All F1 Marches were later converted.

MATRA

With one of the most-lavishly equipped constructional plants in motor racing behind them, Matra-Simca entered a two-car team of MS120s with V12 engines in 1970. The cars were extremely workmanlike, but in spite of promising performances here and there, the team of Beltoise and Pescarolo never won a race. Matra MS120s did net third places at Monaco, Kyalami, and Monza, and Beltoise looked for a while an almost certain winner in the French Grand Prix.

The Matra enterprise entered a new V12-engined Formula 1 car in 1968 races, but it did not come up to expectations, so the factory withdrew their works cars for 1969, loaning their factory driver to Ken Tyrrell. Tyrrell ran two Matra MS80-Fords for his drivers Stewart and Beltoise during 1969.

During the 1969 season *Engins Matra* worked on the "all-French", V12-engined Grand Prix and sports prototype cars, the Formula 1 machines being kept out of racing until they were considered *au point* for the 1970 season. Matra really went French in 1970 Formula 1, refusing to supply Tyrrell with engine-less chassis for Stewart to drive, and announcing an all-Gallic driver team—Beltoise and Pescarolo—for their new MS120 V12s. When the cars appeared they were very different from the 1968 MS11 machines with longer wheelbase, and the *monocoque* was unpartitioned. The new monocoque had a battleship appearance due to the many visible rivets in its construction, and was formed of two main pontoons which contained the rubberised fuel bag tanks. It was also evident that much design change and thinking had been put into the 2,993cc 60-degree V12 engine. Externally it was immediately obvious the induction arrangements had been completely revised with inlet ports in the centre of the cylinder block "V". The new port angles made possible the use of much lighter pistons, but with the same bore and stroke dimensions (79.5×50 mm). The crankcase, cast in AS9 KG (an advanced aluminium-alloy in keeping with the missile and space vehicle background of *Engins Matra*) was completely new, stressed so that it could be utilised as a load-bearing chassis-member. The crankshaft, supported in seven 52 mm main bearings was unchanged, as were the titanium connecting-rods with their 44 mm big-end bearings. As announced, the engine had a much-improved power curve and a claimed minimum power-output of 425 bhp.

Matra's aviation knowledge had enabled them to construct the unsectioned monocoque while still distributing the loads evenly throughout the structure. The car's profile was dictated by the V12 engine, which due to its 60 degrees cylinder bank angle presented a smaller frontal area than the Cosworth-Ford. It was also said at the Vélizy works that the V12 was lighter than the British motor, although this assessment was probably made before the ancillaries had been added.

Suspension was similar to the MS80, except that the lower front wishbones were narrowed at the base to ensure sufficient steering lock in view of the larger tyres. The front suspension uprights were of magnesium and incorporated the brake caliper housings. This saved space and permitted the use of a good-sized brake pad even with the restricted space brought about by the 13 in. wheels. The lower wishbone/top link rear suspension was similar to the MS80, but the radius arms were bolted to the diaphragm section aft of the driver. All coil spring/damper units were fully exposed to the air-stream, but rear brakes were inboard to reduce unsprung weight and make possible the use of 13in. rear wheels.

The oil tank was incorporated within the monocoque, and the oil coolers were mounted above the Hewland FG 500 five-speed gearbox. The gearbox, clutch and fuel injection were all British, but practically everything else was French. The half-shafts and

universal-joints were manufactured by Matra, but for 1970 the équipe adopted Goodyear tyres.
As introduced in February 1970 the Matra-Simca MS120 weighed 1208 lb. with oil and water. It displayed good low-speed torque during its 1970 performance—a characteristic which had been sadly lacking in 1968. A non-French driver, Chris Amon, was signed-up late in 1970 for 1971, and more power had been reported for the new season.

One of the distinguishing features of the 1970 Matra V12 engine was the use of new cylinder-heads with induction between the "V" of the blocks. The inlet valves (two per cylinder) were inclined at 16 degrees and the exhausts (also two per cylinder) at 17 degrees, 30 minutes. This view shows close-fitted camshafts.
Another feature of the 1970 Matra was the ingenious front brake caliper housing, built-in to the suspension upright. The arrangement saved space and weight, and permitted the use of an adequate brake pad in spite of the 13in. wheels.
The inboard disc brakes are just visibile ahead of the two oil coolers, also the massive rear suspension uprights in magnesium. The gearbox is Hewland and the tyres Goodyear. Half-shafts and universals by Matra.

McLAREN

The McLaren team used the Herd-designed M7 for two years as a first-line works machine, and it won four World Championship races. For 1970 they introduced the M14a which was really a logical development of the earlier car, but there were certainly no radical departures from the orthodox. The M14a didn't win a Championship race in 1970 but second places in the two opening events, Kyalami and Jarama, indicated the cars were competitive at least at the beginning of the season.

The team suffered an enormous loss when Bruce McLaren was killed, both from the driver and driving force aspect, and the marque was also handicapped as the season progressed by retarded tyre development. The monocoque of the original M14a was fabricated from 18-gauge L72 aluminium-alloy, further strengthened by mild steel bulkheads and the Ford-Cosworth DFV engine which was a fully-stressed member. Elimination of intermediate bulkheads made possible the use of two rubberised fuel bags per side, providing a fuel capacity of about 45 gallons (Imp).
The M14a's front suspension uprights were new and lighter than the M7's, and the longitudinal links in the lower front wishbones were forward-facing to provide more lock and at the same time the fuel bays were increased in length by eliminating a bulkhead. Tubular anti-roll bars were adopted, also as a weight-saving measure.
Coil spring/damper units were fitted outboard all-round, but the rear disc brakes were mounted inboard, close-up to the Hewland gearbox, and short tubular half-shafts with metal universal-joints transmitted the power to the 15in. rear wheels.

The beautifully-executed detail work of the M14a, and the simple front suspension are obvious in this photograph. Battery, fire extinguishing equipment, and master cylinders were accessible through separate nose panel.

Although at first sight the half-shafts appeared to be of fixed length, in fact the stub axles gained elongation by in-out movement on pair of roller races. The front-end of the car carried a larger light-alloy radiator than the M7, and the battery and fire-extinguisher bottle were also located in the same area, and were accessible via a panel. The oil tank and cooler were located at the rear.
McLaren started 1970 with the intention of using 15in. wheels all season so that their large 11.6in. front brakes could be used. Before the year was out however, they had experimented a good deal with 13in. front wheels in an effort to lower frontal area and to find more speed. An Alfa-Romeo V8-engined car was also entered for the Italian Andrea de Adamich to race during 1970, and he started the season with an M7, but later the M14 monocoque was modified to accept either motor. De Adamich's car then became an M14d.
At the German Grand Prix at Hockenheimring Denny Hulme appeared with a brand-new M14a which used thicker 16-gauge light-alloy for its monocoque. The structure weighed only 8lb. more but the increase in torsional rigidity was dramatic. The suspension material was changed to T45 steel at the same time—a metal almost as strong as chrome molybdenum but considerably less difficult to work. Throughout the season, workmanship was always of a very high standard on the cars, but the unfortunate loss of the founder seemed to have taken some of the steam out of the Formula 1 side of the enterprise.

SURTEES

John Surtees finally made his own car. An admirer of the Brabham/Tauranac philosophy he sought simplicity for effectiveness, and made the "TS7" a continuation of the successful Surtees Formula 5000 car. A full monocoque structure was built for the first car, mainly of 18 gauge L72 aluminium alloy but with the top panel in 20-gauge material. The second car utilised L72 for the inner panels only as it is a difficult material to work, and the softer NS4 was used for the outer skins. Three bulkheads, one in aluminium alloy (front), and the others (centre and rear) were made of rectangular steel tube. The panels were bonded and riveted, the latter being of an American aircraft type. Rubberised fuel tanks were fitted into four different areas, one under the driver's knees, one in a seat cavity, and the two largest in the side pontoons. Capacity was 47 gallons (Imp), and non-return flap valves were incorporated. The monocoque terminated behind the driver's seat where the Ford-Cosworth DFV V8 is bolted as a fully-stressed member. Rear suspension was by lower reversed wishbones, single top links, coil spring/damper units and single upper radius arms anchored to the engine camboxes. The rear hub carriers were Italian and cast in Zirconium, and the half-shafts were Japanese with friction-free ball-bearing splines. Front suspension was by one-piece upper rocking arms with inboard coil spring/damper units and wide-based lower wishbones. The anti-roll bar was attached to the inboard ends of the rocking arms.

Lower inboard mountings of the TS7's rear suspension are attached to a small sub-frame under the Hewland DG300 gearbox. Rear brakes are inboard, and the wheels are the celebrated Surtees split-rim type with "adjustable" width.

The cockpit has a high standard of finish and typifies the first-class engineering.

DE TOMASO

Encouraged by his cars' good showing in 1969 Formula 2 races, Alessandro de Tomaso decided to enter the Formula 1 lists in 1970. Ex-Maserati engineer Dall'ara designed the car which was completed at high speed, work not starting until after the Grand Prix of Rome in October 1969. It was shown to the press at the Modena works in early February 1970, and in a few days was testing at Vallelunga. Entrant was Frank Williams and the driver Piers Courage, the British pair planning to contest the Championship races. Displaying beautiful workmanship, the de Tomaso featured a monocoque of AT16 aluminium with front and rear bulkheads cast in magnesium. The centre bulkhead was in light-alloy. The Ford-Cosworth DFV engine was fully-stressed and a fabricated bearer over the Hewland DG300 gearbox supported the top suspension links and coil spring/damper units. As introduced the de Tomaso weighed 1217 lb., and 46 gallons (Imp) of fuel were accommodated in the bulbous sides of the monocoque. Outboard Girling disc brakes were 10 ½ in. ventilated at the front and 11 in. solid at the rear. Front suspension was by angled-back top wishbones, and angled-forward lower wishbones. Rear suspension was by single top links and reversed lower wishbones, with tubular radius arms and anti-roll bar.
The original car was written-off in a practice crash at Jarama (for the Spanish Grand Prix) and Courage appeared with a 65 lb. lighter car for the Monaco GP. The "Jarama" car was later rebuilt with new monocoque wider track, and other modifications.

TYRRELL

The Tyrrell rear-end looks unusually neat, for in the interests of favourable weight distribution the battery and oil tank are positioned centrally.

Front brakes are outboard, rear brakes inboard, but all are 10½ in. Girling discs. Top mounting of the front wishbones is similar to Matra MS80. The steel sub-frame supporting the radiator can be seen, also the rack and pinion steering assembly. Construction is light yet strong, the finished car being only 20 lb. over the Formula I minimum weight requirement. Complete car about 100 lb. lighter than the March.

Few motor-racing followers had visualised Ken Tyrrell as a constructor, but with typical canniness he had built a car and "kept it up his sleeve" just in case the March 701 didn't come up to expectations. Bearing more than a passing resemblance to the Matra-Ford with which the Stewart-Tyrrell partnership won the World Championship in 1969, the new car was designed by Derek Gardner, late of Hobbs Transmission, and Harry Ferguson Research. Main objects of the exercise were to reduce weight, both sprung and unsprung, to a minimum, and to evolve a good aerodynamic shape. The monocoque, of 18 gauge aluminium was stiffened by fabricated steel bulkheads, and the roll-bar was an integral part of the car. Great efforts were also made to amass as much weight as possible towards the centre to gain a favourable distribution, and good handling. The Cosworth-Ford DFV V8 was a fully-stressed member of the structure, and supported a bolted-on steel sub-frame to which the rear suspension was attached. Another sub-frame at the front carried the radiator and the forward lower wishbone attachments. Front suspension was by coil spring/damper units and double wishbones, whilst at the rear it was by twin parallel lower links, coil spring/damper units, single top links and twin radius arms. Anti-roll bars, front and rear, were both tubular. The Tyrrell didn't win a race in its first season, but it led both the Canadian and US Grands Prix until put out by irritating troubles.

SPECIFICATIONS

BRABHAM Type BT 33
Engine: Ford-Cosworth DFV V8. Transmission: Hewland DG 300 5 speeds + reverse
Brakes: Girling
Type: Goodyear. Front, 13in., rear 15in.
Dimensions: Wheelbase 7ft. 11¹/₄in. Front track 4ft. 9⁷/₈in., rear 5ft. 1in.

BRM Type P 153
Engine: BRM Type 142 V12. Transmission: BRM 5 speeds + reverse
Brakes: Girling
Tyres: Dunlop 13in., front and rear
Dimensions: Wheelbase 8ft. 0¹/₈in. Front track 5ft. 0⁵/₈in., rear 4ft. 11in.

FERRARI Type 312b
Engine: Ferrari Type 312b. 12 cylinders, horizontally-opposed. Transmission: Ferrari 5 speeds + reverse
Brakes: Girling
Tyres: Firestone. Front, 13in., rear 15in.
Dimensions: Wheelbase 7ft. 9³/₄in. Front and rear track 5ft. 1³/₄in.

MARCH Type 701 (701b with inboard rear brakes)
Engine: Ford-Cosworth DFV V8. Transmission: Hewland DG 300 5 speeds + reverse
Brakes: Girling
Tyres: Firestone (works and STP), Dunlop (Tyrrell equipe). Front, 13in., rear 15in.
Dimensions: Wheelbase 8ft. 4in. Front and rear track 4ft. 11in.

LOTUS Type 72
Engine: Ford-Cosworth DFV V8. Transmission: Hewland DG 300 5 speeds + reverse
Brakes: Girling
Tyres: Firestone. Front 13in., rear 15in.
Dimensions: Wheelbase 8ft. 4in. Front and rear track 4ft. 8³/₄in.

LOTUS Type 49c
Engine: Ford-Cosworth DFV V8
Transmission: Hewland DG 300. 5 speeds + reverse
Brakes: Girling
Tyres: Firestone. Front, 13in., rear 15in.
Dimensions: Wheelbase 7ft. 11¹/₄in. Front track 5ft. 1³/₄in., rear 5ft. 0¹/₄in.

MATRA Type MS120
Engine: Matra Type MS 120 V12
Transmission: Hewland FG 400. 5 speeds + reverse
Brakes: Girling
Tyres: Goodyear. Front 13in., rear 15in. (13in rear wheels sometimes used)
Dimensions: Wheelbase 8ft. 2³/₈in. Front track 5ft. 4⁵/₈in., rear 5ft. 3in.

McLAREN Type M14a
Engine: Ford-Cosworth DFV V8
Transmission: Hewland DG 300. 5 speeds + reverse
Brakes: Lockheed
Tyres: Goodyear. Front and rear 15in. (13in. fronts sometimes used.)
Dimensions: Wheelbase 7 ft. 10⁷/₈in. Front track 4ft. 9¹/₈in., rear 4ft. 11in.

SURTEES Type TS7
Engine: Ford-Cosworth DFV V8
Transmission: Hewland DG 300. 5 speeds + reverse
Brakes: Girling
Tyres: Firestone. Front 13in., rear 15in.
Dimensions: Wheelbase 7ft. 11³/₄in. Front track 4ft. 10¹/₄in., rear 4ft. 11⁷/₈in.

DE TOMASO Type 505/38
Engine: Ford-Cosworth DFV V8
Transmission: Hewland DG 300. 5 speeds + reverse
Brakes: Girling
Tyres: Dunlop. Front 13in., rear 15in.
Dimensions: Wheelbase. 7ft. 10¹/₂in. Front track 4ft. 11⁷/₈in., rear 5ft. 2³/₄in. (Track dimensions after widening)

TYRRELL Type F1/70
Engine: Ford-Cosworth DFV V8
Transmission: Hewland FG 400. 5 speeds + reverse
Brakes: Girling
Tyres: Dunlop. Front 13in., rear 15in.
Dimensions: Wheelbase 7ft. 9³/₄in. Front track 5ft. 6⁷/₈in., rear 5ft. 4⁵/₈in.

FORMULA 1 ENGINE COMPARISONS

	Cosworth	Ferrari	Matra	BRM	Alfa Romeo
TYPE	V8	"Flat-12"	V12	V12	V8
DESIGNATION	DFV	312/b	MS120	142	300
BORE/STROKE (mm)	85,7 × 64,8	78,5 × 51,5	79,5 × 50	74,7 × 57,1	86 × 61,4
CUBIC CAPACITY	2992 cc	2991 cc	2993 cc	2998 cc	2993 cc
VALVE ACTUATION AND NUMBER	4 ohc 32 valves	4 ohc 48 valves	4 ohc 48 valves	4 ohc 48 valves	4 ohc 32 valves
INDUCTION	Lucas indirect injection	Lucas indirection injection	Lucas indirect injection	Lucas indirect injection	Lucas indirect injection
POWER-OUTPUT	435 bhp at 10,000 rpm	460 bhp at 11,500 rpm	435 bhp at 11,000 rpm	450 bhp at 11,000 rpm	430 bhp at 10,000 rpm

Farina

Ascari

WHAT MAKES

Twenty-one years of the Drivers' World Championship

P. Hill

Fangio

Clark

Hawthorn

G. Hill

Stewart

JACQUES ICKX

During its 21 years of existence the Drivers' World Championship has been fought out in 186 GP races by 347 drivers. The latter figure is impressive in as far as it seems to indicate that in those 21 years one driver out of 1500 must have reached the top rung. The proportions thus obtained are so favourable that a fault in the system can be suspected. There is no doubt that it would be incorrect to consider as a GP driver anyone who happened one day to be in the racing line-up. Such a qualification would be more realistically based on a certain degree of experience or success. One could, for instance, single out only names that have figured in the World Championship points list, still a very modest requirement since in any case to do so only involves obtaining one sixth place in a GP. But this simple discrimination is sufficient to reduce the number of GP drivers from 347 to 128, which is in turn impressive in an inverted sense, and brings us to the proportion of one driver in about 4500. The honours list can be seen elsewhere in these pages. It is surprising how it revives many dozens of names that have been almost completely lost to sporting memory, lost because they made no mark at all at the time. On reading it, it becomes clear that the term GP driver needs to be given a more rigorous definition. The gradings that follow will be based on the consideration that this definition can be applied to anyone who has a victory to his credit. The application of such a test leaves us with 32 names in all, which gives us one driver in 18000. But here an objection can be raised. A certain element of chance is by definition connected with the competition phenomenon and a single success cannot be taken as a sign of proved value. And so we can eliminate any drivers who have not confirmed their initial victory by a second one...

But this only leaves us 22 in all for 21 years of Championship racing, in other words one GP driver for approximately every 25000 licence-holders.

We should also add that during this time only 13 drivers have got as far as five victories and seven have just about reached the ten-victory mark. Finally one only, Jim Clark, raised himself to the level of 25 victories.

A CHAMPION

Brabham

Rindt

An Experiment

Let us come back to our selection. How does one become this one driver among 5000, 10 000, 25 000 others?
Is the champion a man set apart from birth? Or does one become a champion by sheer strength of will and brain, at the cost of considerable personal effort?
In 1964 the prevailing opinion in Belgian automobile sporting circles was that it all came around to a matter of favouritism. Among dozens of equals only he could succeed who was lucky enough to be taken in hand, for reasons that had nothing to do with his worth, by a manufacturer or a powerful team.
A noted sportsman, Count R. van der Straten-Ponthoz, decided to give a practical demonstration of this. In order to do so he created the *VDS* team, the aim of which was to make Le Mans winners out of two drivers with no claim to fame by giving them the opportunity to complete one season of Mini racing, one with Alfa GTAs and one with two-litre Alfa 33s, and one or two with Alfa 33-3s.
The Count's appeal to non-graded drivers turned up 57 candidates of whom 17 were rejected straight away because they were young people with no racing experience. A jury presided over by Lucien Bianchi was to make a two-stage track selection from the remaining 40. It would leave nine men for the final Mini-season test from which were to emerge, according to the plans, the four drivers who would be called upon to form the definitive *VDS* team. But at the end of the year only two of the nine tested drivers were judged capable of making it, a snag which caused Count van der Straten to amend his original plan and complete his team with two of those very drivers whose artificial reputations he had wished to expose. At the beginning of the third year the Alfa 33s were not yet available and so the *VDS* drivers raced another GTA season. At the end of this additional exercise only one of the original "guinea-pigs" was left and to the objective observer it was painfully obvious that he would never make a racing driver. But Count van der Straten was still determined to pursue his experiment to the bitter end and launched the survivor at the wheel of the 33-2. It was finally the driver himself who in mid-season was wise enough to abandon a sporting task for which he no longer felt cut out.
And that was the end of that. The experiment had at least the great merit of establishing clearly the fact that you cannot produce a champion to order.
Which, in turn, establishes clearly that, in spite of the immense importance of experience and training, you have got to start off with talent.

What is Talent?

Can talent be distinguished by innate driving ability? This widespread notion is one of the biggest fallacies that exist.
To start with innate driving ability is a fairly common thing, especially in the young contemporary generation. But its range is relatively limited in the case we are dealing with, for high-level competition driving is an extremely specialized business and demands the patient schooling of the best elements.
This schooling (which one has to give oneself, discovering little by little things that no one can teach you) plays such a large role in the final success that one can even become a champion without having the famous innate talent. So true is this that the alert observer can pick out the "born drivers" among champions from the rest.

This leads us automatically to the conclusion that it is on the level of character that we shall find the clearest definition of championship qualities.
Important scientific work has already covered this area and has revealed numerous constants that can be found without fail in the make-up of a champion.
But to discuss them would be a fastidious and sterile exercise for these are only marginal traits, satellites around a single fundamental characteristic: the NEED to win.
If we use this word and make it appear in capitals, it is to convey the intensity, the completeness and the persistance of the will to win that animates the being of a champion.
Already in the time of Liège-Rome-Liège and Liège-Sofia-Liège it was unanimously agreed that if at the start it had been possible to measure the teams' wills to win, the victor would have been known in advance.
But in the case of a champion's career it is no longer a question of feeling this need to win during a period of four consecutive days and nights but for a dozen or so years. What is more, the extent of this desire will still not be sufficient to indicate to us the outcome of a contest. An enormous degree of will-power, though indispensable, is not in the present case the be-all and end-all.
To start with it has to be backed up by a faultless means of execution. It is hard to imagine the number of promising careers that have aborted because the driver's nerves were not on the same level as his will.
This is why Ken Tyrrell, who is universally acknowledged as the greatest talent scout, has put the major emphasis on impassibility in his selection scheme. As far as performance goes he is happy with "adequate" times. But adequate times, a fierce will to win and nervelessness are still not all. And nothing shows this better than in the case of Ken Tyrrell who, even if he has launched more champions than anybody else, has not managed to make them all his nurslings.
We can put our finger on the other thing that is needed by making a digression and citing the case of Professor Anon, Nobel Prize Winner in physics for his work on the atom.
Forty years ago young Anon was a prep school pupil. Maybe he was top of his class and maybe he wasn't. He probably wasn't and if he was it was only ever by a small margin.
From his teacher of the time the most we learn is that he was one of the good pupils who would automatically go on to further studies. It is very probable that this teacher, with the experience he had behind him, would not even have been willing to bet that Anon would necessarily be successful. Professor Anon probably gave his teachers a few surprises during his school life but none of them suspected the future that awaited him, a future that only began to be glimpsed in the last years of his university career.

What distinguished Professor Anon from the millions like him at the various states of his pupil and student life? A character that none could suspect since it was not shown in his appearance and defied prediction: an almost limitless ability to acquire new knowledge.
In this very specialized field one can do no more than offer the results as proof. But even as these results start to be seen, what will follow is still impossible to predict. The ceiling will inevitably be reached one day, perhaps tomorrow.
The case of the champion racing driver is identical to that of Professor Anon. The secret lies in a capacity to achieve ultimate success, a faculty that is not necessarily manifest at the present moment.
This is why even those who best know the party refrain from making predictions as to a driver's future beyond the next rung on the ladder. And indeed this they do reluctantly.
One last word. It is quite probable that those former co-disciples of Professor Anon who were as good pupils as he in the prep classes today remark to anyone who wants to listen: "If I had been the son of Mr Anon Senior I would be the winner of the Nobel Prize for physics!" They are wrong.

Are They Born in All Countries?

If the phenomenon of the champion is, as has just been said, a natural phenomenon, he must then, as exceptional as he is, be distributed fairly evenly over the world. We all know that it works like that for the vertical scale of social classes. GP drivers are from all levels of society, from the most modest or the most elite, which automatically destroys a widely-held belief that there is only room in automobile competition for well-heeled young people.
Is it the same one a horizontal plane? In other words, are champions born in every country?
If we look at the lists for the 1971 World Championship we notice that 13 countries are represented, hardly a negligible number certainly, but not particularly varied for a list of 25 names.
This territorial limitation of the GP driver phenomenon can be seen even more strikingly in the total list for the 21 world championships where 103 extra names produce only seven more nations. This automatically accentuates the gap between the most and the least represented nations.
Here then are the numbers of drivers, by countries of origin, who have figured in the success lists:

Great Britain	41	South Africa	2
Italy	20	Spain	2
France	15	Mexico	2
United States	9	Sweden	2
Germany	6	Australia	1
Argentina	6	Austria	1
Belgium	6	Monaco	1
Switzerland	5	Netherlands	1
Brazil	3	Rhodesia	1
New Zealand	3	Thailand	1

And so we see that there are some countries which stand out in this particular field. But the privilege of certain countries does not automatically reflect their population level. If we establish a ratio between the number of GP drivers from a given country during the past 21 years and the number of its inhabitants, even without taking into account the special case of Louis Chiron who represented a proportion without equivalence to the Principality of Monaco, even more striking differences appear:

New Zealand	1/ 0.9 million
Switzerland	1/ 1.2 million
Great Britain	1/ 1.4 million
Belgium	1/ 1.6 million
Italy	1/ 2.6 million
France	1/ 3.3 million
Argentina	1/ 3.8 million
Rhodesia	1/ 4.5 million
Sweden	1/ 5.25 million
Austria	1/ 7.3 million
South Africa	1/ 9.4 million
Germany	1/10.0 million
Australia	1/11.75 million
Netherlands	1/12.6 million
Spain	1/16 million
United States	1/22.2 million
Mexico	1/22.8 million
Brazil	1/31.7 million
Thailand	1/32.7 million

The Time Factor

This said, if we bring the time factor into play in the distribution by countries of origin of our 128 drivers—which is expressed by Table 1 below (where the countries figure in order of appearance, as it were, while each annual Championship list is represented by one column) we get an even greater surprise. Here is, in fact, what we arrived at line by line.
France, so well represented in 1950, went into a decline immediately afterwards, steadied herself on a more moderate level between 1954 and 1959 only to disappear completely from the table for the following seven years (with the exception of the purely episodic return of Maurice Trintignant) and then make rapid progress in the last four years.
Italy was the object of massive representation from 1950 to 1956. After which came a period of doldrums from which she has not even yet emerged.
For Great Britain, apart from a thrust that was not followed up in 1952, the take-off was laborious. Then all at once came the ascent and 15 stable years at a level that no other country has ever reached.
The case of Argentina is quite unusual. We see her on the scene for nine consecutive years and even high-ranking from 1953 to 1955, only to disappear completely and finally from the table in 1961.
We pass over the exceptional cases of Monaco and Thailand which were both single-driver countries. There then comes a second group of countries whose representation was never very high but which alternated periods of stability with periods of absence from the table. Thus Switzerland was present for three years, absent for nine, and present again during the eight most recent years. For Belgium there were four active periods, the first three separated by one-year intervals,

TABLE 1 **NUMBER OF DRIVERS PER COUNTRY**

	50	51	52	53	54	55	56	57	58	59	60	61	62	63	64	65	66	67	68	69	70
France	6	2	3	1	3	2	3	3	3	3					1			1	2	2	4
Italy	5	7	5	4	6	7	5	2	1		1	1	2	2	1	1	2	1	1		1
Great Britain	2	1	5	1	2	1	6	7	8	4	9	8	5	6	9	6	9	8	9	7	7
Argentina	1	2	1	4	4	4	1	3	1		1										
Monaco	1																				
Thailand	1				1																
Switzerland		1	1	1										1	1	1	1	1	2	2	1
Belgium			1		1	1	2		1	1	3	1	1					1	2	1	1
Germany				1	2	2		1	1	1	2	1									1
Spain							2	1													
Brazil							2														1
USA								1	2	3	2	3	4	2	4	3	3	1	1		2
Australia								1	1	1	1	1	1	1	1	1	1	1	1	1	1
Sweden									1	1	1	1	1	1	1		1	1	1		1
New Zealand										1	1	1	1	2	2	2	2	3	3	3	3
South Africa													2	1	1						
Holland													1	1							
Mexico													1		1	1		1	1	1	1
Austria																1	1	1	1	1	1
Rhodesia																		1			
Number of drivers	16	13	16	12	19	17	21	19	19	15	21	17	19	17	22	16	20	21	24	18	25
Number of countries	6	5	6	6	7	6	7	8	9	8	9	8	10	9	10	8	8	12	11	8	13

with a gap of four years between the last two. The case of Germany is similar to that of Argentina, apart from the level of representation which remained extraordinarily modest for a country with such a large population. She participated from 1953 to 1961, with the exception of one year, only to disappear from the table for eight full years, before taking her place there again in 1970 .

For Spain one notes a brief appearance between two complete voids; for Brazil a lightning appearance also between two voids, but also a return (which seems destined to prolong itself) this year.

The United States made a late appearance, but from then on an almost continual participation has been evident but with marked ups and downs. In their turn the apparent stability of Australia and Sweden in the World Championship lists is in each case the result of the prolonged career of a single driver. New Zealand, on the other hand, had a sensational rise to success. She first appeared in the table in 1959 and her presence has continued and increased steadily since that date.

Again episodic appearances between interminable voids for South Africa, Holland, Rhodesia, and sustained participation but recent and on a very modest level for Mexico and Austria.

If this phenomenon is a purely natural one, how then can its fluctuations be explained?

Let us Widen the Panorama

Anybody at all versed in the study of evolutive phenomena will realize immediately that the period we have considered is much too short to permit any possible laws to manifest themselves clearly. To get a better perspective it would be necessary to observe in their totality the three-quarters of a century of existence of automobile competition, and even this would furnish us with very limited material.

But a major obstacle immediately presents itself. Since our World Championship was only created in 1950, how can we establish an equivalent list for the preceding years? In particular, upon what criterion should we base the selection of one race rather than another? Moreover the complete results of the races in those days are sometimes difficult to obtain. Yet another difficulty : in a sporting world much less populated than our own, the fifth and sixth places had infinitely less significance than they do at present. A reasonable solution to the problems would seem to be possible by retaining for the pre-1950 years all the international races open to what could be called the contemporary "top material", but only taking into account the first three placings in these more numerous races.

Finally, for reasons of space and easy reading (also because of the necessity to eliminate accidental factors), we have this time taken for consideration successive periods of three years each.

Having taken account of the stoppages produced by the two world wars, of the empty car sporting years between 1909 and 1911 and the transitory period of only two years in 1926 and 1927, the system brings us back to 21 columns, where again the countries are listed in order of appearance.

What we now arrive at can be seen in Table 2.

No more than this is needed to give the key to the puzzle to anyone who knows the general lines of the history of automobile competition.

It is a very simple key and one which we can acquire by reasoning, but the direct illustration given here is even more convincing.

The "System"

Even if one considers the existence of the champion as a natural phenomenon and if one thus classes him as capable of being born anywhere where there are men, he must, as we have seen earlier, go through a maturing process. And in order for the latter to be possible it is obviously necessary for the subject to be integrated into the automobile sport *system*.

In order better to understand this, let us suppose that a given individual unites all the qualities that define the ideal astronaut. If this man is neither an American nor a Soviet citizen, he will nevertheless never have the chance to be sent into space, for the astronaut *system* is at present limited to these two countries.

On more familiar ground, we should be aware of the fact that Fangio himself would never have become a GP driver if President Peron (for whom car racing was a plaything) had not integrated Argentina into the *system* by instituting *Temporadas* and inviting to them, at great expense, manufacturers, drivers and journalists. We begin to see to what a degree our table expresses "belonging to the *system*". From 1894 to 1896 car-racing was a sport exclusive to automobile pioneers. Since they were nearly all French so were the star drivers. From 1897 to 1902 the manufacturer gave way to a first generation of sporting personalities. But apart from the Ardennes circuit, inaugurated in 1902, racing organizations remained exclusively French. From then on car competition stayed in the hands of the French and the Paris Belgians. However, from the turn of the century on, some foreign participation (in very limited numbers because of the distance involved) was added to the original circle. The years 1903 to 1905 constituted a watershed. Car racing became more international and manufacturers returned to direct participation, their own testers and development men replacing the gentlemen-drivers of the preceding era. This had the automatic effect of superimposing the distribution by nationality of the drivers on that of the car industry, a situation which was to maintain itself up until 1925 and to illustrate the ups and downs

TABLE 2 **DRIVERS PLACED AMONG FIRST THREE IN LEADING EVENTS DURING THREE YEAR PERIOD**

	94 96	97 99	00 02	03 05	06 08	12 14	20 22	23 25	26 27	28 30	31 33	34 36	37 39	47 49	50 52	53 55	56 58	59 61	62 64	65 67	68 70
France	9	12	14	14	8	8	5	7	7	8	9	7	5	12	8	4	3	3	1	1	4
Belgium		2	3	4	4	2								1	1	2	2	3		1	2
Great Britain			2	1	1			1	1	2	4	2	1	5	7	2	12	11	10	11	11
USA			2				4	1	2				1				3	4	5	4	2
Germany			1	1	2	2				4	3	7	9			3	1	2	1		1
Italy				5	8	3	3	9	10	16	19	12	7	10	8	10	6	1	2	2	2
Hungary					1																
Poland								1			1										
Spain								1									2				
Monaco									1	1	1	1		1	1						
Rumania										1											
Austria											1	1	1							1	1
Switzerland													1	2	2	1			1	1	3
Argentina														3	2	6	3	1			
Thailand														1	1	1					
Brazil														1			2				1
Australia																	1	1	1	1	1
Sweden																	1	1	1	1	2
New Zealand																		1	2	3	3
South Africa																			2		
Mexico																			2	1	1
Holland																			1		
Rhodesia																				1	
Number of drivers	9	14	22	25	24	15	12	20	21	32	38	30	25	36	30	29	36	28	29	28	34

of each industry. The marked reduction in the number of stars between 1912 and 1914 is explained by the fact that after the void of 1909-1911 the sport was taken up again an a hierarchical basis and competition at the top was a very closed shop. The American breakthrough, immediately after the war of 1914-1918, came about because the hiatus of the war years was less long and marked in the United States. The aftermath of the First World War also explains the disappearance of the Germans. There was a new watershed with the 1925-6 period, when we see the sudden death of manufacturers' races. It was then for the first time Bugatti put a racing car on the general market. Also at that time sportsmen could buy material from factories that had retired from racing, and so the death throes of the traditional sport were veiled by the explosion of a new kind of purely sporting and much more widely open competition which greatly multiplied the number of races. In a first phase half of them were contested in Italy (where Fascism exploited the racing car), a quarter in France and a quarter in the rest of the countries involved. One automatically finds the same configuration in the distribution of prize-winning drivers.

If the Italian domination in numbers was even more accentuated in the 1931-3 period, it is because the mutation of competition driving had finished and caused the appearance of specialized teams and manufacturers with *Scuderia Ferrari* and *Maserati* in the top rank.

But all was to change between the years 1934-9 when Hitler's Germany, profiting from the lessons given by Italy, introduced motor sport into its "propaganda" in the powerful and shattering manner of the regime. Unlike Mussolini, Hitler did not do this to provide his people with a spectacle but for reasons of pride and at the same time to impress other nations. There was thus little point in racing in Germany so commandos with unbeatable cars were sent to all the foreign tracks.

Thus we see at that time the contingent of German drivers swell at the expense of the French and Italians, who were to shrink even more when the two countries virtually abandoned "formula racing"—which was replaced by sports-car racing in France and 1500cc single-seater racing in Italy—in order not to work for Hitler's propaganda.

After the War

Came 1947. Peace had been restored, the Germans had disappeared. The new Formula 1 cars were either Italian or French, and once again it was in those two countries—mostly in France—that races were held. The pre-war contingents were spontaneously regenerated.

However, as barriers between countries were torn down, Britain began to play a steadily growing part in racing on the Continent, and new countries appeared on the scene. Argentina, which had previously been quite unknown, entered the lists with a flourish. That was because Peron had adopted the methods employed by totalitarian countries. When he vacated the scene the presence of Argentina in the leading events came to an end.

The institution of the World Championship set well-defined territorial limits to racing at the highest level. On the other hand, after two years the cars, which were either pre-war, or derived from pre-war designs, had reached the end of their tether. To save the situation the *CSI* in 1952 threw the World Championship open to Formula 2 machines. That formula was the British drivers' happy hunting ground, so Britain inevitably took advantage of the exhaustion that had struck the French and Italians.

In 1954 a new Formula 1 gave racing a new balance of power. The superiority of the Italian drivers matched the numerical superiority of the Italian contingent. But if the machines were nearly all German, French or Italian, the internationalization of racing developed side by side with that of the world in general, which was changed beyond recognition by new rapid means of communications. The leading teams were glad to enlist foreign drivers with the result that the non-manufacturing countries added together were represented by a larger number of drivers than any one of the manufacturing countries taken by itself. Among the non-manufacturing countries, Argentina towered head and shoulders above the rest.

Then came the great turning point of 1956-1958. The rise of the lightweight, rear-engined car sounded the death-knell of the traditional classic design, and none of the drivers who had raced before 1956 succeeded in remaining in the field after 1961 (with the sole exception of Trintignant. On the other hand, some of those we still admire appeared on the scene in 1957. Last, but not least, Britain staged an irresistible invasion of Grand-Prix racing. Though this phenomenon coincided with the peak period of Vanwall and Cooper and the entry of Lotus on the scene, it was due first and foremost to a new dimension of the *system*.

In fact, now that it has become a tradition for competiting marques to enlist drivers of different nationalities and the territorial distribution of Grand-Prix races has expanded so that all countries are placed on the same level with not more than one Championship event each year, a new factor of decisive importance, namely driver training, has come to the fore.

A racing driver is born but...

Training has been indispensable from the very earliest times for, as the champions say themselves, "a racing driver is born but has to be made." And every driver gets his training for himself as he can and how he can, depending on available facilities.

What was needed was an organization to co-ordinate those facilities, as Count van der Straten had foreseen years ago. But only a big country can manage an organization of that sort on a nationwide scale. The first priority is to cream off every single individual who is interested in the sport and offer him a ladder on which to climb from the bottom to the top. Then and then alone is it a viable proposition.

That state of affairs was precisely what was achieved in Britain during the 1956-1958 period by the patient build-up of a comprehensive, homogeneous, organized system that stretched its tentacles to the most outlying parts of the country. Since then every Briton who is a born champion has been given a chance to become one. The result can be seen in the last five columns of Table 2.

It is because a system of the same kind is being built up in France that French drivers are once again coming to the fore. And it is because, now that racing has become a truly international sport, the British have thrown open their training system and their positions in the Formula 1 field (of which they make up three-quarters) to people from other countries that the latter can multiply on a par with the expansion of the means of communication.

Just take a look at the list of drivers in 1970 World Championship events. Jochen Rindt, Jacky Ickx, Jack Brabham, Denis Hulme, Chris Amon, Emerson Fittipaldi, Bruce McLaren and Reine Wisell are products of the British *system* neither more nor less than Jackie Stewart, Graham Hill, John Surtees, John Miles, Jack Oliver, Peter Gethin and Derek Bell, while Pedro Rodriguez, Rolf Stommelen, Johnny Servoz-Gavin, Dan Gurney and François Cévert may be compared with the students who went, or are still going, to university in Britain after getting their secondary schooling in their own country or elsewhere. This makes up 20 of the 25 names in the list.

It seems obvious, therefore, that the following principle may be laid down: *Grand Prix drivers are born in about the same proportions in all countries inhabited by the white race, but the chance of their coming to the fore is inversely proportional to their distance from the centre of the system.*

At the outset this *system* possessed only two dimensions—the motorcar manufacturers and the race organizers and, as we have seen, its centre of gravity slipped from France to Italy as those variables evolved. It has now been given a new dimension—training facilities. Since the first two have been virtually neutralized by the course of events, the third has become the decisive factor.

That is the reason why the centre of gravity of top-class racing is located in Britain and will be located there for many years to come. France, Italy and America are in a class by themselves. Although they have the advantage of the existence of a national body to organize car racing, each of them is hamstrung by the limits of its particular system.

Illustration

The clearest illustration of the principle and its corollary will be found in Table 3 below. It corresponds to Table 1 but, instead of the

TABLE 3

	50	51	52	53	54	55	56	57	58	59	60	64	62	63	64	65	66	67	68	69	70	Total
France			2		1		1											1	2		2	9
Italy	2	3			3	2	1	1			1	1	1	1							1	17
Great Britain			5		1		4	4	2	1	3	1	1	1	4	2	2	1	4		3	38
Argentina		1		2	1	1																5
Monaco																						
Thailand																						
Switzerland		1	1											1					1		1	5
Belgium			1		1		1				2							1				6
Germany				1	2			1						1							1	6
Spain							2															2
Brazil							2														1	3
USA								1	1	1	1				1	1	1				1	8
Australia								1														1
Sweden									1												1	2
New Zealand										1				1		1						3
South Africa													2									2
Mexico													1		1							2
Holland													1									1
Austria																1						1
Rhodesia																		1				1
Total	2	5	9	3	9	3	11	8	4	3	7	2	6	5	6	5	3	4	7		11	112

TABLE 4

	50	51	52	53	54	55	56	57	58	59	60	61	62	63	64	65	66	67	68	69	70	Total
France									1													1
Italy	1	1																				2
Great Britain					1		2		1				2		1		1					8
Argentina	1				1																	2
Monaco																						
Thailand																						
Switzerland																						
Belgium																				1		1
Germany												1										1
Spain																						
Brazil																						
USA												1			1							2
Australia										1												1
Sweden																						
New Zealand											1							1				2
South Africa																						
Mexico																					1	1
Holland																						
Austria																					1	1
Rhodesia																						
Total	2	1			2		2		2	1	1	2	2		2		1	1		1	2	22

TABLE 5

	50	51	52	53	54	55	56	57	58	59	60	61	62	63	64	65	66	67	68	69	70
G. Farina	■	■	■	■	■	■															
J. M. Fangio	■	■		■	■	■	■	■	■												
A. Ascari	■	■	■	■	■	■															
F. Gonzalez					■	■	■	■													
M. Hawthorn					■	■	■	■	■												
S. Moss							■	■	■	■	■	■									
P. Collins							■	■	■												
T. Brooks									■	■	■	■									
M. Trintignant									■	■											
J. Brabham										■	■	■	■	■	■	■	■	■	■	■	■
B. McLaren											■	■	■	■	■	■	■	■	■	■	■
P. Hill												■	■	■	■						
W. von Trips												■									
J. Clark													■	■	■	■	■	■	■		
G. Hill													■	■	■	■	■	■	■	■	■
J. Surtees															■	■	■	■	■	■	■
D. Gurney															■	■	■	■	■	■	■
J. Stewart																	■	■	■	■	■
D. Hulme																		■	■	■	■
J. Ickx																				■	■
J. Rindt																					■
P. Rodriguez																					■
Total	3	3	2	3	5	5	5	5	6	4	4	6	5	5	7	6	7	8	8	8	10

number of drivers of a given nationality named in the list of winners of World Championship events in a given year, it shows the number of *new elements* of each nationality who are mentioned for the first time in the list for that year.

Though Table 3 is sufficiently explicit and self-evident, its message is expressed far more clearly still in Table 4, which lists, by their nationality and the year of their first appearance in the field, the twenty-two crack drivers who have each won more than one Grand-Prix race and are therefore true champions.

As you can see from that Table, Britain, which built up the national system I have just referred to, is now for that very reason in a class of its own: it is the only country that produced more than two World Champions in the 21 years since the Championship was instituted.

What seems odd, is that, as the Table shows, those classic sources of champion drivers, France and Italy, dried-up prematurely and that their disappearance from the Table coincided precisely with the first appearance of the new countries.

It is obvious that if the appearance of new champions never occurs in more than two countries at a time, those countries cancel each other out. And if new countries enter the scene it is automatically at the expense of their predecessors. Nonetheless, the void one finds in Italy is something quite out of the ordinary. How is it that in a country that produced a host of crack drivers during a period of fifty years there has been such a dearth for the last twelve?

No doubt we shall discover what I would term a geometrical explanation of this phenomenon.

In fact, the total supply of racing drivers in any one year may be represented by a cone. At the apex there is room for only one man. Let us attribute the same number of points, namely 100, to the best driver of each year and so keep the height of the cone constant. If the base of the cone is expanded by increasing the number of new recruits, that expansion makes its impact felt at all levels. One of the results of this is that the rating of the 20 best drivers rises steadily. One can imagine that a 90-point driver might have found a place among the first twenty 35 or 40 years ago, whereas nowadays only a 98-point man can hope to do so. Very probably this is the explanation of why countries that had an excess of drivers when they monopolized motorcar racing are now in abeyance. This theory finds a practical demonstration in Table 5, which sets out the performance of the 22 champions I mentioned as having won at least two victories each. It shows that the number of champions in the field grows from year to year and, in fact, increased fivefold from 1952 to 1970. There is little doubt the same thing occurs at all levels. This pinpoints another fact, namely that it is far more difficult to win a Grand Prix race now than it was in the days of Fangio, Farina or Ascari. Consequently, one cannot compare the victories of drivers of different periods either in absolute or in percentage terms. Total numbers and percentages (which will be found elsewhere in these pages), though hard facts, serve only as pointers.

WORLD CHAMPIONSHIP 1950-1970

			50	51	52	53	54	55	56	57	58	59	60	61	62	63	64	65	66	67	68	69	70	Points
50	G. Farina	I	1	4	2	2	7	5																128,33
	J. M. Fangio	AR	2	1		3	1	1	1	1	13													279,14
	L. Fagioli	I	3	9																				32
	L. Rosier	F	4	10					19															18
	A. Ascari	I	5	2	1	1	19																	139,14
	B. Bira	TH	6				14																	8
	R. Parnell	GB	7	8																				9
	P. Whitehead	GB	7																					4
	L. Chiron	MC	7																					4
	D. Serafini	I	10																					3
	R. Sommer	F	10																					3
	Giraud-Cabantous	F	10	12																				5
	R. Manzon	F	10		6		10																	16
	P. Etancelin	F	10																					3
	F. Bonetto	I	15	7	12	8																		15,5
	E. Chaboud	F	16																					1
51	F. Gonzalez	AR		3	8	6	2	12		20														79,64
	L. Villoresi	I		5	7	5	15	12	19															49
	P. Taruffi	I		6	3			5																42
	C. Sanesi	I		10																				3
	E. de Graffenried	CH		12		7																		9
52	R. Fischer	CH			4																			10
	M. Hawthorn	GB			4	4	3		11	4	1													127,64
	J. Behra	F			8			8	4	9	10	17												51,14
	D. Poore	GB			10																			3
	K. Wharton	GB			10																			3
	M. Trintignant	F			12	10	4	4		16	6	5					16							74,33
	A. Brown	GB			12																			2
	E. Thompson	GB			12																			2
	P. Frère	B			12			11	7															11
53	O. Marimon	AR				9	10																	8,14
	O. Galvez	AR				10																		2
	H. Lang	D				10																		2
54	K. Kling	D					5	10																17
	H. Herrmann	D					6	17					24											10
	L. Musso	I					7	8	11	3	6													44
	R. Mieres	AR					7	7																13
	S. Moss	GB					10	2	2	2	2	3	3	3										188,64
	S. Mantovani	I					10																	4
	U. Maglioli	I					15	16																3,33
	E. Bayol	F					15																	2
	A. Pilette	B					15																	2
55	E. Castellotti	I						3	6															19,5
	C. Perdisa	I						12	15															5
	C. Menditeguy	AR						12		14			19											9
56	P. Collins	GB							3	8	9													47
	F. Godia	E							7															6
	J. Fairman	GB							10															5
	R. Flockart	GB							11				24											5
	H. Schell	F							15	6	4	12												32
	A. de Portago	E							15	20														4
	O. Gendebien	B							19		19	15	6	13										18
	Da Silva-Ramos	BR							19															2
	H. Gould	GB							19															2
	F. Landi	BR							25															1,5
	G. Gerini	I							25															1,5
57	T. Brooks	GB								5	3	2	11	10										74
	M. Gregory	US								6	17	8			18									22,5
	S. Lewis-Evans	GB								12	8													16
	W. von Trips	D								13	10	17	6	2										57
	G. Scarlatti	I								20														1
	R. Salvadori	GB								18	4			17										19
	J. Brabham	AUS								20	14	1	1	11	9	7	8	10	1	2	23	10	5	270
	B. Gerard	GB								20														1

			50	51	52	53	54	55	56	57	58	59	60	61	62	63	64	65	66	67	68	69	70	Points
58	P. Hill	US									10	4	5	1	6		19							98
	C. Allison	GB									14	17	12											11
	J. Bonnier	S									16	8	15	13	14	9	15		17	14	21			40
	C. Shelby	US									18													1,5
	G. Hill	GB									19		15	13	1	2	2	2	5	6	1	7	13	287
59	B. Mc Laren	NZ										6	2	7	3	6	7	8	14	14	5	3	14	160
	D. Gurney	US										7		3	5	5	6	4	12	8	21		22	133
	I. Ireland	GB										13	4	6	16	9	12							47
60	R. Ginther	US											8	5	8	2	4	7	11					107
	J. Clark	GB											8	7	2	1	3	1	6	3	11			274
	J. Surtees	GB											12	11	4	4	1	5	2	4	7	11	17	177
	W. Mairesse	B											15		14									7
	G. Cabianca	I											19											3
	H. Taylor	GB											19											3
	L. Bianchi	B											24								17			6
61	G. Baghetti	I												9	11									14
	J. Lewis	GB												13										3
62	T. Maggs	SA													7	8	12							26
	T. Taylor	GB													10	16	19							8
	L. Bandini	I													12	9	4	6	8					58
	R. Rodriguez	MX													12									4
	G. de Beaufort	NL													16	14								4
	N. Lederle	SA													18									1
63	G. Mitter	D														12								3
	J. Hall	GB														12								3
	J. Siffert	CH														14	10	11	14	11	7	9		49
	L. Scarfiotti	I														16			10	19	13			17
	C. Amon	NZ														16	16			4	10	12	7	59
64	P. Arundell	GB															8		17					12
	B. Anderson	GB															11		17	16				8
	M. Spence	GB															12	8	12	10				27
	W. Hansgen	US															16							2
	M. Hailwood	GB															19							1
	P. Rodriguez	MX															19	14		6	6	13	7	62
65	J. Stewart	GB																3	7	9	2	1	5	182
	D. Hulme	NZ																11	4	1	3	6	4	154
	J. Rindt	OE																13	3	11	12	4	1	109
	R. Bucknum	US																14						2
	R. Attwood	GB																14			13	13		11
66	M. Parkes	GB																	8	16				14
	B. Bondurant	US																	14					3
	J. Taylor	GB																	17					1
67	J. Love	RH																		11				6
	C. Irwin	GB																		16				2
	G. Ligier	F																		19				1
	J. Ickx	B																		19	4	2	2	105
68	J. P. Beltoise	F																			9	5	9	48
	J. Servoz-Gavin	F																			13	16	19	9
	J. Oliver	GB																			13	16	19	9
	V. Elford	GB																			17	13		8
	B. Redman	GB																			19			4
	P. Courage	GB																			19	8		20
	S. Moser	CH																			23	16		3
69																								
70	C. Regazzoni	CH																					3	33
	R. Stommelen	D																					11	10
	H. Pescarolo	F																					12	8
	M. Andretti	US																					15	4
	I. Giunti	I																					17	3
	E. Fittipaldi	BR																					10	12
	J. Miles	GB																					19	2
	F. Cevert	F																					22	1
	P. Gethin	GB																					22	1
	R. Wisell	S																					15	4
	D. Bell	GB																					22	1

This year (1971) the World Championship for Drivers attained its majority, so it seems to me a very good time to summarize in a special Table the performances of all those who competed over those 21 years.

The names of the drivers are listed in the order in which they entered the field and you will find, in the column for each year, the place each of them obtained in the relative Championship. I have omitted the American drivers who owed their victory in the World Championship to their placing in the 500 Miles of Indianapolis, which was, peculiarly, included among the Championship events for a certain number of years.

You will see at a glance from the Table that where the recruitment of drivers is concerned there have been fat years and lean years. For instance, there were eleven new names in 1956 and not a single one in 1969. You will also observe that only 50 drivers have competed for more than two years in Grand Prix races and that the number of those who have competed for several years has increased enormously since 1958.

The Table shows that 1957 marked the line of separation between two epochs. Not one of the drivers whose name appears before that year stayed the course after 1961 (except for Maurice Trintignant, who staged a come-back in 1964). On the other hand all the drivers who competed in 1970 started in 1957 or later. The Table also gives the total number of Championship points awarded to each driver, including those that were not taken into account for the placings in a given year because these latter are based on a limited number of events.

WORLD CHAMPIONSHIP ROLL OF HONOUR

From 1950 to 1970 thirty-two drivers shared the victories in the Grand Prix races that count for the World Championship. The next table sums up the careers of these outstanding drivers arranged in the descending order of the number of victories.
For each of them the Table gives the following information:

- How his career ended (K = killed; R = retired; D = died after retirement);
- The dates at which his career as Grand Prix driver began and ended (if it has ended);
- The number of Grand Prix races in which he competed (the figure in brackets refers, where relevant, to the number of cars driven in those races at the time when changing cars was permitted);
- The number of victories (and in brackets the number of those, if any, won after taking the wheel of a second car);
- The percentage of victories in terms of races run;
- The number and percentage of 1st, 2nd and 3rd places obtained (same conditions as for victories);
- The number and percentage of starts in pole position (in terms of the number of races run);
- The number of best laps chalked up and their percentage in terms of the number of starts;
- The total number of World Championship points that would have been awarded *at the rate in force at the present time* and the average number of points per race (calculated at the same rate).

World Championship Honours List		Racing years	Number of races	Wins		Placings (1-3)		Race finishes		Pole positions		Best laps		Championship points	
				N	%	N	%	N	%	N	%	N	%	Total	Per race
Jim Clark	K	60/68	72	25	34,7	32	44,4	47	65,3	33	45,8	28	38,8	274	3,80
Juan-Manuel Fangio	R	50/58	51 (58)	24 (2)	41,4	35 (4)	60,3	41 (5)	70,7	28	54,9	23	45,1	262	5,14
Stirling Moss	R	52/61	66 (71)	16 (1)	23,9	24 (3)	33,8	36 (4)	50,7	16	24,2	20	30,3	178	2,70
Jack Brabham	R	57/70	126	14	11,1	31	24,6	67	52,7	15	11,9	10	7,9	270	2,13
Graham Hill		58/70	124	14	11,3	36	29	63	50,8	13	10,5	10	8	287	2,16
Alberto Ascari	K	50/55	31 (35)	13	37,1	17 (2)	48,6	21 (2)	60,0	15	48,4	11	35,5	138	4,45
Jackie Stewart		65/70	63	12	19	23	36,5	33	52,4	6	9,5	6	9,5	182	2,89
Jacky Ickx'		67/70	35	6	17,1	14	40	21	60	7	20	8	22,9	105	3,00
John Surtees		60/70	98	6	6,1	24	24,5	43	43,5	8	8,2	11	11,2	177	1,80
Jochen Rindt	K	64/70	60	6	10,0	13	21,7	24	40,0	10	16,6	3	5,0	109	1,82
Denis Hulme		65/70	60	5	8,3	21	35	38	63,3	–	–	3	5	154	2,57
Nino Farina	D	50/55	32 (35)	5	14,3	19 (2)	54,3	26 (2)	74,3	7	20,0	5	15,6	128	3,84
Tony Brooks	R	56/61	38 (40)	5	12,5	9	23,7	20	50,0	3	7,9	3	7,9	74	1,95
Dan Gurney	R	59/70	86	4	4,6	19	22,1	41	45,3	3	3,5	6	7	133	1,55
Bruce McLaren	K	59/70	102	4	3,9	17	16,7	52	51,0	–	–	3	2,9	160	1,57
Peter Collins	K	52/58	32 (36)	3	8,3	7 (1)	19,4	14 (3)	38,9	–	–	–	–	42	1,31
Mike Hawthorn	D	52/58	44 (45)	3	6,7	18 (1)	40,0	28 (1)	62,2	5	11,4	6	13,6	123	2,80
Phil Hill	R	58/64	48	3	6,25	16	33,3	31	64,4	6	12,5	5	10,4	98	2,04
Froilan Gonzalez	R	51/60	26 (30)	2	6,66	12 (2)	40,0	16 (4)	53,3	3	11,5	5	19,2	61	2,34
Pedro Rodriguez		64/70	49	2	4,1	6	12,2	24	49,2	–	–	2	4,1	62	1,27
Maurice Trintignant	R	52/64	82 (84)	2	2,4	9 (2)	10,7	42 (2)	50,0	–	–	1	1,2	70	0,85
Taffy von Trips	K	58/61	27	2	7,5	6	22,2	17	63,6	2	7,5	–	–	57	2,11
Giancarlo Baghetti	R	61/67	21	1	4,8	1	4,8	9	42,9	–	–	1	4,8	14	0,67
Lorenzo Bandini	K	61/67	42	1	2,4	8	19,0	27	64,3	1	2,4	2	4,8	58	1,38
Joakim Bonnier		57/70	101	1	1	1	1	49	48,7	1	1	–	–	40	0,40
Emerson Fittipaldi		70/	5	1	20	1	20	4	80	–	–	–	–	12	2,40
Richie Ginther	R	60/66	52	1	1,9	14	26,9	36	69,2	–	–	3	5,8	107	2,06
Innes Ireland	R	59/66	50	1	2,6	4	8,0	26	52,0	–	–	–	–	47	0,94
Clay Regazzoni		70/	8	1	12,5	4	50	7	87,5	1	12,5	3	37,5	33	4,12
Lodovico Scarfiotti	K	63/68	10	1	10,0	1	10,0	6	60,0	–	–	1	10,0	17	1,70
Joseph Siffert		62/70	85	1	1,2	4	4,7	41	48,2	1	1,2	3	3,6	49	0,58
Piero Taruffi	R	51/55	18	1	5,6	5	27,9	10	55,6	–	–	1	5,6	42	2,33

THE GOLDEN LIST OF THE 1970 SEASON

Grand Prix	Pole position	Other driver on front row of grid	Ahead at the start	Number of laps leading the race	Winner	Seconds behind winner	Fastest lap
South Africa	Stewart	Amon Brabham	Stewart	Stewart 19 Brabham 61	Brabham	Hulme 8″1 Stewart 17″1	Surtees (6) Brabham (71)
Spain	Brabham	Hulme Stewart	Stewart	Stewart 90	Stewart	–	Brabham (19)
Monaco	Stewart	Amon	Amon	Stewart 27 Brabham 52 Rindt 1	Rindt	Brabham 23″1 Pescarolo 26″2	Rindt (80)
Belgium	Stewart	Rindt Amon	Rindt	Amon 4 Stewart 1 Rodriguez 23	Rodriguez	Amon 1″1	Rodriguez (28)
Holland	Rindt	Stewart Ickx	Ickx	Ickx 2 Rindt 78	Rindt	Stewart 30″	Ickx (22)
France	Ickx	Beltoise	Ickx	Ickx 14 Beltoise 11 Rindt 13	Rindt	Amon 7″61 Brabham 44″83 Hulme 45″46	Brabham (29)
Great Britain	Rindt	Brabham Ickx	Brabham	Ickx 6 Rindt 63 Brabham 11	Rindt	Brabham 32″9 Hulme 54″4 Regazzoni 54″8	Brabham (70)
Germany	Ickx	Rindt	Ickx	Ickx 31 Rindt 17 Regazzoni 2	Rindt	Ickx 0″7	Ickx (49)
Austria	Rindt	Regazzoni	Regazzoni	Regazzoni 1 Ickx 59	Ickx	Regazzoni 0″61	Ickx Regazzoni
Italy	Ickx	Rodriguez	Ickx	Ickx 5 Rodriguez 3 Stewart 16 Regazzoni 33 Oliver 10 Hulme 1	Regazzoni	Stewart 5″73 Beltoise 5″80 Hulme 6″15 Stommelen 6″41	Regazzoni (65)
Canada	Stewart	Ickx	Stewart	Stewart 31 Ickx 59	Ickx	Regazzoni 14″8 Amon 57″9	Regazzoni (75)
U.S.A.	Ickx	Stewart	Stewart	Stewart 82 Rodriguez 18 Fittipaldi 8	Fittipaldi	Rodriguez 36″4 Wisell 45″2	Ickx (105)
Mexico	Regazzoni	Stewart	Regazzoni	Regazzoni 1 Ickx 64	Ickx	Regazzoni 45″46 Hulme 45″97 Amon 47″05 Beltoise 50″09	Ickx

PANORAMA OF THE 1970 SEASON

Here the panorama of the season immediately behind us is placed in a different light.
The fact is that the prize list is not all. In the eyes of those for whom car racing is a way of life, and particularly of the team managers, who observe the drivers with an eagle eye in order to make a wise selection when the time arrives, there are two factors of no less importance. The first is the place occupied by a driver in the list of practice times; this is a true term of comparison if ever there was one. The second is the best place occupied during the race even, and indeed especially, if it was not confirmed by the place held at the finish.
These are the criteria by which drivers are weighed by those who give them their jobs. They will be found in the following Table, which shows, for each of the 43 drivers who competed for the 1970 World Championship and for each of the thirteen races that counted for the Championship, his place in the scale of practice times; his best place during the race (not counting the last lap); his placing at the finish.
You can examine this Table again and again; you can read it a hundred times and every time you will find a new point of interest, a new lesson. You can also use it to make up your personal list of drivers based on a formula of your own. You may be interested to learn, for instance, that one team manager compiles his list by giving 10 points for 1st place, 9 for 2nd, 8 for 3rd, and so on down to the tenth, whether occupied in practice, during the race or at the end. With this method he finds his own best ten.
Purists will further note that the Table gives the serial number of the car each driver used in each Grand Prix race.

ABBREVIATIONS

GP	Grand Prix	E	Practice
SA	South Africa	C	Race
E	Spain	RS	Result
M	Monaco		
B	Belgium		
NL	Netherlands		
F	France		
GB	Great Britain	R	Retired
D	Germany	NQ	Not Qualified
Œ	Austria	NS	Not Started
I	Italy		
CN	Canada		
US	United States		
MX	Mexico	N	Number of Firsts

Driver / Car	GP	SA	E	M	B	NL	F	GB	D	Œ	I	CN	US	MX	N
Chris Amon (NZ)	GP	SA	E	M	B	NL	F	GB	D	Œ	I	CN	US	MX	N
March-Ford 701/1	E	2	6	2	3	4	3	18	6	6	21	6	5	5	
	C	12	12	2	1	20	2	5	3	5	7	3	4	4	1
	RS	R	R	R	2	R	2	5	R	8	7	3	5	4	
Mario Andretti (US)	GP	SA	E	M	B	NL	F	GB	D	Œ	I	CN	US	MX	N
March-Ford 701/3	E	11	16					9	8	18					
	C	11	3					8	9	13					
	RS	R	3					R	R	R					
Derek Bell (GB)	GP	SA	E	M	B	NL	F	GB	D	Œ	I	CN	US	MX	N
Brabham-Ford BT 26/4 (B)	E				15								13		
Surtees-Ford TS7/002 (US)	C				17								5		
	RS				R								6		
J. P. Beltoise (F)	GP	SA	E	M	B	NL	F	GB	D	Œ	I	CN	US	MX	N
Matra MS120/01 (SA-E-M)	E	7	4	6	11	10	2	10	23	7	15	13	18	6	
Matra MS120/03	C	3	2	4	3	5	1	5	17	3	2	8	15	4	1
	RS	4	R	R	3	5	13	R	R	6	3	8	R	5	
Joakim Bonnier (S)	GP	SA	E	M	B	NL	F	GB	D	Œ	I	CN	US	MX	N
Mc Laren-Ford M7/C1	E										24		24		
	C										NQ		19		
	RS												R		
Jack Brabham (AUS)	GP	SA	E	M	B	NL	F	GB	D	Œ	I	CN	US	MX	N
Brabham-Ford BT 33/1	E	3	1	4	5	12	5	1	12	7	8	19	16	4	2
Brabham-Ford BT 33/2	C	1	2	1	3	8	3	1	20	5	7	12	10	3	3
(NL-Œ)	RS	1	R	2	R	11	3	2	R	13	R	R	10	R	1
François Cevert (F)	GP	SA	E	M	B	NL	F	GB	D	Œ	I	CN	US	MX	N
March-Ford 701/7	E					15	13	14	14	9	10	4	17	9	
March-Ford 701/4 (D-MX)	C					12	9	7	7	24	6	4	16	12	
	RS					R	11	7	7	R	6	9	R	R	
David Charlton (SA)	GP	SA	E	M	B	NL	F	GB	D	Œ	I	CN	US	MX	N
Lotus-Ford 49/08	E	12													
	C	6													
	RS	12													
Piers Courage (GB)	GP	SA	E	M	B	NL	F	GB	D	Œ	I	CN	US	MX	N
De Tomaso-Ford 505/1	E	20	13	9	12	9									
(SA-E)	C	15	NS	7	9	7									
De Tomaso-Ford 505/2	RS	R		R	R	R									
Andrea De Adamich (I)	GP	SA	E	M	B	NL	F	GB	D	Œ	I	CN	US	MX	N
Mc Laren-Alfa M7/D1	E		18	18		19	15	19	21	15	13	12	27		
(E-M-F-GB)	C		NQ	NQ		NQ	15	NS	NQ	12	8	8	NQ		
Mc Laren-Alfa M14/D1	RS						R			12	8	R			
Peter De Klerk (SA)	GP	SA	E	M	B	NL	F	GB	D	Œ	I	CN	US	MX	N
Brabham BT 26/3	E	21													
	C	11													
	RS	11													
Georges Eaton (CN)	GP	SA	E	M	B	NL	F	GB	D	Œ	I	CN	US	MX	N
BRM 139/02 (SA)	E	23	22	21		18	19	16		23	23	9	14		
BRM 153/03	C	13	NQ	NQ		13	12	19		11	10	9	12		
BRM 153/06	RS	R				R	12	R		11	R	10	R		
Emerson Fittipaldi (BR)	GP	SA	E	M	B	NL	F	GB	D	Œ	I	CN	US	MX	N
Lotus-Ford 49/10	E							22	13	16	25		3	18	
(GB-D-Œ)	C							8	4	12	NQ		1	16	1
Lotus-Ford 72/5(I-US-MX)	RS							8	4	15			1	R	1
Nanni Galli (I)	GP	SA	E	M	B	NL	F	GB	D	Œ	I	CN	US	MX	N
Mc Laren-Alfa M 7/D1	E										26				
	C										NQ				
	RS														
Peter Gethin (GB)	GP	SA	E	M	B	NL	F	GB	D	Œ	I	CN	US	MX	N
Mc Laren-Ford M14/A1	E					11			17	21	17	11	21	10	
Mc Laren-Ford M14/A2	C					10			20	8	9	6	13	8	
(NL)	RS					R			R	10	HC	6	14	R	

Ignazio Giunti (I)	GP	SA	E	M	B	NL	F	GB	D	Œ	I	CN	US	MX	N
Ferrari 002	E				8		11			4	5				
	C				5		9			4	5				
	RS				4		14			7	R				

Dan Gurney (US)	GP	SA	E	M	B	NL	F	GB	D	Œ	I	CN	US	MX	N
Mc Laren-Ford M14/A1	E					19	17	12							
	C					19	6	7							
	RS					R	6	R							

Hubert Hahne (D)	GP	SA	E	M	B	NL	F	GB	D	Œ	I	CN	US	MX	N
March-Ford 701/9									25						
									NQ						

Graham Hill (GB)	GP	SA	E	M	B	NL	F	GB	D	Œ	I	CN	US	MX	N
Lotus-Ford 49/7	E	19	15	12	16	21	20	23	21		18	20	10	8	
Lotus-Ford 72/4	C	6	4	5	9	12	9	5	9		NS	12	7	8	
(I-CN-US-MX)	RS	6	4	5	R	R	10	6	R			R	R	R	

Denis Hulme (NZ)	GP	SA	E	M	B	NL	F	GB	D	Œ	I	CN	US	MX	N
Mc Laren-Ford M14/A2	E	6	2	3			7	4	15	10	9	15	11	14	
Mc Laren-Ford M14/A1	C	2	2	3			4	3	3	6	1	6	6	3	1
(F-GB)	RS	2	R	4			4	3	3	R	4	R	7	3	

Gus Hutchison (US)	GP	SA	E	M	B	NL	F	GB	D	Œ	I	CN	US	MX	N
Brabham-Ford BT 26/3	E												22		
	C												18		
	RS												R		

Jacky Ickx (B)	GP	SA	E	M	B	NL	F	GB	D	Œ	I	CN	US	MX	N
Ferrari 001	E	5	7	5	4	3	1	3	1	3	1	2	1	3	4
Ferrari 002 (E)	C	2	5	4	3	1	1	1	1	1	1	1	2	1	8
Ferrari 003 (B-F-GB-D)	RS	R	R	R	8	3	R	R	2	1	R	1	4	1	3

John Love (RH)	GP	SA	E	M	B	NL	F	GB	D	Œ	F	CN	US	MX	N
Lotus-Ford 49/3	E	22													
	C	8													
	RS	8													

Pete Lovely (US)	GP	SA	E	M	B	NL	F	GB	D	Œ	I	CN	US	MX	N
Lotus-Ford 49/11						23	22	24					26		
						NQ	NQ	10					NQ		
								R							

Bruce Mc Laren (NZ)	GP	SA	E	M	B	NL	F	GB	D	Œ	I	CN	US	MX	N
Mc Laren-Ford M14/A1	E	10	11	10											
	C	4	2	10											
	RS	R	2	R											

John Miles (GB)	GP	SA	E	M	B	NL	F	GB	D	Œ	I	CN	US	MX	N
Lotus-Ford 49/10 (SA)	E	14	19	19	13	8	18	7	10	10	19				
Lotus-Ford 49/6 (M)	C	5	NQ	NQ	13	5	8	8	7	9	FF				
Lotus-Ford 72/1	RS	5			R	7	8	R	R	R					
(B-NL-F-GB)															
Lotus-Ford 72/3 (D-Œ-I)															

Silvio Moser (CH)	GP	SA	E	M	B	NL	F	GB	D	Œ	I	CN	US	MX	N
Bellasi-Ford F1/70	E					24	21		24	24	27				
	C					NQ	NQ		NQ	20	NQ				
	RS									R					

Jackie Oliver (GB)	GP	SA	E	M	B	NL	F	GB	D	Œ	I	CN	US	MX	N
BRM 153/1 (SA-E)	E	12	10	17	14	5	12	4	18	13	6	10	7	13	
BRM 153/3	C	4	6	7	8	3	15	3	7	5	1	8	5	7	1
BRM 153/4 (F)	RS	R	R	R	R	R	R	R	R	5	R	R	R	7	
BRM 153/6 (US-MX)															

Henry Pescarolo (F)	GP	SA	E	M	B	NL	F	GB	D	Œ	I	CN	US	MX	N
Matra MS 120/02	E	18	9	7	17	13	8	13	5	13	16	8	12	11	
Matra MS 120/01 (D)	C	7	3	3	4	8	5	8	4	9	10	7	8	9	
Matra MS 120/04 (MX)	RS	7	R	3	6	8	5	R	6	14	R	7	8	9	

Ronnie Peterson (S)	GP	SA	E	M	B	NL	F	GB	D	Œ	I	CN	US	MX	N
March-Ford 701/9 (M-B)	E			12	9	16	9	14	19		14	16	15		
March-Ford 701/8	C			7	8	9	7	7	11		9	14	9		
	RS			7	R	9	R	9	R		R	R	11		

Brian Redman (GB)	GP	SA	E	M	B	NL	F	GB	D	Œ	I	CN	US	MX	N
De Tomaso-Ford 505/3	E							25	20						
	C							NS	NQ						
	RS														

Clay Regazzoni (CH)	GP	SA	E	M	B	NL	F	GB	D	Œ	I	CN	US	MX	N
Ferrari 001 (D)	E					6		6	3	2	3	3	6	1	1
Ferrari 003 (NL-OE)	C					3		4	1	1	1	2	3	1	4
Ferrari 004	RS					4		4	R	2	1	2	13	2	1

Jochen Rindt (Œ)	GP	SA	E	M	B	NL	F	GB	D	Œ	I	CN	US	MX	N
Lotus-Ford 49/6 (SA)	E	4	8	8	2	1	6	1	2	1	12				3
Lotus-Ford 49/10 (M-B)	C	5	7	2	3	1	1	1	1	3	NS				4
Lotus-Ford 72/2	RS	13	R	1	R	1	1	1	1	R					5

Pedro Rodriguez (MX)	GP	SA	E	M	B	NL	E	GB	D	Œ	I	CN	US	MX	N
BRM 153/2 (SA-E-M-B)	E	16	5	20	6	7	10	16	8	22	2	7	4	7	
BRM 153/5	C	9	4	6	1	4	6	11	7	4	1	3	1	5	3
	RS	9	R	6	1	10	R	R	R	4	R	4	2	6	1

Tim Schenken (AUS)	GP	SA	E	M	B	NL	F	GB	D	Œ	I	CN	US	MX	N
De Tomaso-Ford 505/3	E									19	21	17	20		
	C									15	13	13	10		
	RS									R	R	R	R		

Johnny Servoz-Gavin (F)	GP	SA	E	M	B	NL	F	GB	D	Œ	I	CN	US	MX	N
	E	17	14	14											
	C	9	5	NQ											
	RS	R	5												

Joseph Siffert (CH)	GP	SA	E	M	B	NL	F	GB	D	Œ	I	CN	US	MX	N
March-Ford 701/4 (SA)	E	7	20	11	10	17	16	21	4	20	7	14	23	16	
March-Ford 701/5	C	5	NQ	3	7	12	9	10	3	9	7	11	9	14	
	RS	10		8	7	R	R	R	R	9	R	R	9	R	

A. Soler-Roig (E)	GP	SA	E	M	B	NL	F	GB	D	Œ	I	CN	US	MX	N
Lotus-Ford 49/10 (E-F)	E		21		18		23								
Lotus-Ford 72/2 (B)	C		NQ		NS		NQ								
	RS														

Jackie Stewart (GB)	GP	SA	E	M	B	NL	F	GB	D	Œ	I	CN	US	MX	N
March-Ford 701/2	E	1	3	1	1	2	4	8	7	4	4	1	2	2	4
(SA-E-D)															
March-Ford 701/4	C	1	1	1	1	2	3	5	6	14	1	1	1	2	7
Tyrell-Ford 001(CN-US-MX)	RS	3	1	R	R	2	9	R	R	R	2	R	R	R	1

Rolf Stommelen (D)	GP	SA	E	M	B	NL	F	GB	D	Œ	I	CN	US	MX	N
Brabham-Ford BT33/1	E	15	17	14	7	22	14	10	10	17	20	18	19	17	
(SA-E-M-B-M-F)															
Brabham-Ford BT33/3	C	12	6	NQ	5	NQ	7	NS	5	3	3	16	9	13	
	RS	R	R		5		7		5	3	5	R	12	R	

John Surtees (GB)	GP	SA	E	M	B	NL	F	GB	D	Œ	I	CN	US	MX	N
Mc Laren-Ford M7/C1	E	7	12	16		14	20		14	10	10	5	8	15	
(SA-EM- NL)	C	4	3	11		5	7		3	6	20	4	6	10	
Surtees-Ford TS7/001	RS	R	R	R		6	R		R	R	R	5	R	8	

Reine Wisell (S)	GP	SA	E	M	B	NL	F	GB	D	Œ	I	CN	US	MX	N
Lotus-Ford 72/2 (US)	E												9	12	
Lotus-Ford 72/3 (MX)	C												3	10	
	RS												3	R	

Peter Westbury (GB)	GP	SA	E	M	B	NL	F	GB	D	Œ	I	CN	US	MX	N
BRM P153/4	E												25		
	C												NQ		
	RS														

The Manufacturers' World

Porsche Reap What They Have Sown!

by Helmut Zwickl

It was a Porsche year that began at Daytona in January and ended on the Österreichring in October for it was marked by the Stuttgart firm's second consecutive victory in the Manufacturers' World Championship. What is more, the clean sweep at Le Mans, after two unsuccessful attempts for outright victory, put Porsche on top in the most exacting of all endurance tests.

This raised the question: Are long-distance races still real endurance tests? The answer must be an emphatic "Yes"! Let us consider Daytona. Competitors on that combination of speed track and road circuit maintain an average of 115 mph for the entire 24 hours. It means that from beginning to end the chassis is fatigued by the centrifugal force developed on bends banked to an angle of 31 degrees, one of which is entered at almost 190 mph, while the force of gravity presses the drivers into their seats and has the effect of making tired bodies feel as heavy as lead. At Sebring brake discs stay hot as stove plates for 12 hours. The *Targa Florio* is still the toughest test of roadholding, handling and stamina, as well as for dampers, gearboxes, tyres and engines—the latter must stand up to enormous variations in rpm—and all of it under the pitiless Sicilian sun whose fiery breath reduces the asphalt to the consistency of butter. For machines that are growing faster every day the Nürburgring is more than ever a test bench for chassis; and nowhere else do the engines run for so long on full load than at Le Mans.

Now that Formula I cars barely manage to last the two hours of a Grand Prix, in which the majority fail to cover the distance and are eliminated by the most absurd and futile breakdowns, a machine that can finish a race lasting 6, 12 or even 24 hours deserves the utmost respect. The time is past when long-distance races were won by keeping the throttle half-closed. Nowadays two-thirds of the distance are covered in the style of a two-hour Formula 1 Grand Prix; the pace gets hotter and more relentless as the cars can take more and more punishment. Le Mans is the last great exception in this respect: it is a law unto itself. For the drivers, too, long-distance races are genuine breaking-tests. One has simply to look at them after four laps of the *Targa Florio* to realize that, or watch how they age between two successive refuelling stops during the night at Le Mans. Only on the faces of the men who compete in the *Tour de France* cycle race will you see such marks of suffering after a grilling stage in the Pyrenees.

When at Zuffenhausen on April 21, 1969, the FIA Homologation Commission viewed a military-style parade of 25 Porsche 917s, the firm had already staked 5 ½ million marks (about £ ½ m or $1.2 m), counting only the 220.000 marks for the cost of materials for each machine, on victory. The seeds Porsche sowed in 1969 they reaped in 1970. And the harvest was magnificent—in spite of a skilled and experienced rival of almost equal value, named Ferrari.

The 24 hour race at Daytona was Porsche's honeymoon with John Wyer: Suddenly opponents turned into allies. Wyer, who had nothing more to expect from Ford, and his team, were to relieve Porsche of the cost of racing and the organization work it involved. Theirs cannot have been a love match; rather was it a marriage of convenience, and for two years (1970 and 1971) it was to give Porsche development time and to lessen their financial worries. But Porsche must have been too much the giving partner and JW Automotive Engineering, spoilt by the first marriage with Ford, too much the taker. The arrangement was that Wyer received the cars and all spares free and met the required fees for Rodriguez and Kinnunen. Porsche paid Siffert and Redman. Wyer could rely on generous assistance from Gulf. But Porsche did not withdraw from racing entirely. In the event of something going wrong with Wyer, Porsche-Salzburg Ltd. provided an emergency exit—a highly successful 'exit'.

When the 4 ½-litre 917 won its first great victory in a long-distance race, the Austrian 1,000 kilometres in August 1969, it was still a machine over which drivers had no real cause to enthuse. But during the tests on the Österreichring in late autumn of that year Wyer's team suggested abbreviating its tail. The aerodynamic correction improved the machine's roadholding enormously. A 30-hour preliminary training session at Daytona showed up braking problems that were only solved on the eve of the 24-hour race in 1970. It proved necessary to locate the brake fluid tank further away from the hot brake discs; aluminium was replaced by titanium for certain parts; the wheel suspension was strengthened and the lowest gear was fitted with a lock to avoid errors in shifting.

At Daytona Ferrari took up the Porsche challenge for the first time with the new 5-litre 512 S that had obtained homologation as a sports car just in time for the race. Except at the *Targa Florio* and the Nürburgring, lap times showed at the very start that the 3-litre prototypes didn't have a chance. Ferrari too had done some preliminary training at Daytona with Andretti, Schetty and Merzario, during which the cars had run mostly on wet roads and two of the 12-cylinder 48-valve engines had already broken

Championship 1970

down. In the race itself Andretti was never able to make up on the road section what he lost to the 917s on the banked oval track. "At 155 mph on the banked oval they simply left me standing," said Ferrari's fastest driver in astonishment at Daytona.
This first encounter between the 4 ½-litre 917 and the 5-litre 512 S (selling price 24 million lire, approximately £16,000 or $40,000) gave the rivals an opportunity to assess each other's potentiality at the beginning of the 1970 season. It indicated that though the Ferrari had a little more power than the Porsche's 560 HP, the latter weighed between 220 and 265 lb. less. At 1786 lb. the 917 entered by Porsche-Salzburg was only 25 lb. above the admissible minimum. Ferrari did not employ any titanium at all and several air vents on the tail made it aerodynamically inferior to the 917. For one reason or another at Daytona the Porsche 917 managed to go a tiny bit faster than the Ferrari. Joseph Siffert had broken his brake foot some weeks earlier at a go-kart demonstration in Berlin and it was still so sore that he could not really put all his weight on the pedal. He may perhaps have braked more than usual with the engine when changing down with the result that the life of the clutch was shortened. Be that as it may, at about 7.15 a.m. on the Sunday his car expired. Brian Redman climbed out of the cockpit and Porsche No. 1 was pushed to the pits by Wyer's mechanics. At that point David Yorke put Redman in the Rodriguez-Kinnunen machine (which was leading Andretti and Ickx's Ferrari by 12 laps) because it too was threatened with clutch trouble, which the experienced British driver was more likely to cope with than the fiery Mexican. All this time the Porsche-Stuttgart men who acted, so to say, as Grey Eminences, were at the back of the Wyler pit—Development Chief Ferry Piech was standing by the time recorder with Herr Falk, responsible for test driving, and engineer Bratenstein; Rico Steinemann was there too and two of Wyer's mechanics spoke the Swabian dialect. One of the group suddenly suggested changing the clutch on the Siffert/Redman machine. "It wouldn't take more than an hour and a half at the outside," Piech told Wyer. The latter ordered the 917 he had already written-off to be manhandled back to the pit and the two Zuffenhausen mechanics took charge of the lightning operation. A new clutch was fitted in 48 minutes and five minutes later Redman was back in the race. When Siffert took over from him an hour before the end an exhaust pipe was replaced and a wing fussily patched up. This cost Siffert five minutes and 50 seconds. All the same, seven minutes before the checquered flag was waved he managed to steal second place from Andretti. With a car that had already been written-off as a total loss and parked in the garage!
While Mario Andretti, thanks to his Indianapolis pit crew, gained up to 30 seconds on his rivals at each refuelling stop, Wyer's men used greater caution. As a result, the victorious Porsche driven by Rodriguez, Kinnunen and Redman spent a total of 38 minutes and 50 seconds out of the 24 hours at the pits,
The news that at Sebring Wyer's two 917s were both eliminated by the same hub fault and that Ferrari had won the 12-hour neck-to-neck struggle, caused great displeasure among the Zuffenhausen technicians. Trials on the Porsche test track at Weissach had shown that the new hubs fitted the Sebring cars could not stand up to the load they were on expected to bear. Before the race Porsche had told Wyer's people: "Fit the old hubs again; they will hold!" But the Britons had ignored the advice.
The long-awaited 5-litre version of the 917 was available for the 1,000-kilometre race at Monza. The bore of the flat 12-cylinder engine had been increased by one millimetre to 86 and a new crankshaft increased the stroke from 66 to 70.4 mm, so that total cylinder capacity was raised to 4,910 cubic centimetres. The chief advantage was the greater torque. As Porsche's Helmut Bott pointed out, there had never been a 5-litre (unsupercharged) engine of more than 600 HP.
For the *Targa Florio* Porsche had prepared the 908/3, an extra light tubular-chassis two-seater in which the driver's seat had been shifted so far forward that it was jokingly called the "VW Transporter". It derived from the 909 "mountain" two-seater that had made its debut at the Gaisberg event in 1968. The whole car cannot have weighed more than 1200 lb. That is extremely light for a machine designed to run in a long-distance race. But the methods used in Porsche's lightweight construction were very different from those employed by the small firms engaged on the building of British Formula 1 cars. Long trial runs over the bone-shaking test track at Weissach and Wolfsburg, where a car can be jolted to pieces at 55 mph for hours on end and even be made to jump over timber springboards, sooner or later show up any weak points. In this way breaking resistance had been raised to such a pitch that the "old" Porsche 908 was able to cover a total of 2,800 miles on the "jolt" course. No other makers of Grand Prix machines subject their Formula 1 cars to such

searching tests. It is only in training, or even in the race itself, that the Achilles heel of some Formula 1 cars is revealed. If something gives way it is made stronger next time. This degrades the driver to the level of a test puppet. Siffert & Co. were loud in their praise of the 908/3. And when on the north loop of the Nürburgring the Swiss driver, working like a navvy, did a lap time of 7:47.4 on the 5-litre 917 while chalking up an incredible 7:41 on the 908/3, which would also save one refuelling stop in 1,000 km, the 908/3 was once again given preference. Ferrari too made trial runs with the 5-litre 512 S. Jacky Ickx spotlighted the limit for that machine on the Ring: when he tried to better his lap time of 7:56 he very nearly flew off the track. As a result Porsche could count on the faster of the two rival 5-litre machines. It was John Wyer and his right-hand man David Yorke who organized the pit service for both Siffert/Redman's and Rodriguez/Kinnunen's Gulf 908/3s, but the Swabian technicians—and therefore Helmut Bott—who were there as "project attendants", had a finger in the pie. Wyer's fuelling methods robbed his two leading drivers Siffert and Rodriguez of their entire lead because both cars were refuelled fussily with a single hose instead of the two employed for the works Porsches.

Victories at Daytona, Brands Hatch, Monza, the *Targa Florio,* Spa and at the Nürburgring pushed Porsche's count up to 60 points. Ferrari had only 35, so after the 1,000 km race on the Nürburgring Porsche had the Championship in their pocket. But "Champion Constructor" is far from being a title of impact. The mass media can sell it only in a fancy wrapping, and even the most powerful publicity fails to give it the glamour that is linked with a victory at Le Mans. What had not happened to John Wyer with Ford happened with Porsche: he lost the 24 Hours of Le Mans. Three days before the race he had already given himself away in a highly suggestive speech. When Rico Steinemann said at a cocktail party for the press: "What counts is that a Porsche wins, it doesn't matter which," Wyer retorted in an "extra dry", bitterly earnest tone: "What counts is that no Wyer-Porsche is going to finish second." Not the usual Wyer accuracy.

Wyer and Yorke sent their three-car Armada into the fray without a proper plan: for once the two Britons' famous taut line was amazingly slack. At Porsche technical faults were always systematic, so this time the cards were shuffled. Wyer chose two 5-litre and one 4 ½-litre bob-tail 917s. That his cars at 2080 lb. were about 45 lb. heavier than the same type of machine driven by Herrmann and Attwood was due to a number of alterations introduced by the Britons. For instance, the twin pipes used for the oil conduits were removed and separate pipes fitted; the tail was reinforced and a fire-extinguishing plant installed. Neither the technicians nor the drivers were happy.

Would the tyres last? When the makers refused to give any guarantee beyond 190 mph Porsche explored the danger limit on their own test bench. It was found that Goodyear rear-wheel tyres could be relied on up to 245 mph but Firestone only up to 200 mph. Months earlier, against Porsche's wishes, Wyer had signed tyre contracts, so he had to mount Firestone whereas the machines that raced in the Salzburg colours used Goodyear. The bad experience gained in high-speed tests at Wolfsburg—both Kurt Ahrens and Willy Kauhsen had got caught unexpectedly in a shower with dry-weather tyres (result: two long-tail 917s out of action)—led to the decision to mount "intermediate" tyres at Le Mans.

One of the basic questions was: Will the brakes survive? During training the air-intake ports in the nose of the 917 were enlarged in order to help cool the front-wheel brakes. Ferrari kept 35 complete spare brake discs ready in their pit. Actually, when it began to rain hard at Le Mans all tyre and brake problems were washed away.

But the human problems were just as tough. The drivers, who tend to understatement, make light of many things and are never the first to mention hair-raising experiences, were at a loss for words to describe what happened during those hours. "I had never driven under such conditions before," Vic Elford said. "It was sometimes impossible to overtake a Porsche 911 on the long straight." Kurt Ahrens felt as if he was "sitting in a motorboat." Even Hans Herrmann, who was at his fifteenth Le Mans, got a shock: "You cannot see a thing," he said. "Your daren't use more than third gear on the straight; you cannot brake, accelerate or decelerate; in the puddles the car doesn't respond to the wheel at all. "During the rainy spells there were always some drivers who particularly distinguished themselves. On the Saturday evening, when it rained hard for the first time, van Lennep brought a Porsche 917 incredibly into third place in the general classification. On the Sunday morning the 3-litre prototype Alfa driven by Rolf Stommelen and Nanni Galli gained a vast amount of ground against the heavy guns. Months later Hans Herrmann confessed: "At Le Mans, during the wet spells, I made up my mind to chuck racing altogether. Even if I had not won I would have retired in any case after a race where in the rain one found oneself in situations so absolutely beyond control that the risk was really too great."

In 1970 the 3-litre prototypes, which had things all their own way the previous year, were rather put in the shade by the 5-litre sports cars where lap times and showmanship were concerned. But by and large it may be said that the traditional Porsche 908 two-seater was the private teams' most efficient weapon. Over and over again thanks to its sturdiness the matured, all-purpose design defeated the works prototypes fielded by Matra and Alfa Romeo, which certainly had about 70 hp more under the bonnet. Matra concentrated wholly on the 24 Hours of Le Mans. Nevertheless, the MS 650 two-seaters with their thundering V12 Formula 1 power plant were eliminated after seven hours. For the 3-litre Alfa 33-3, the engine of which could reach 9,500 rpm, a maximum speed of 8,600 rpm was fixed. But in spite of this precaution none of the Autodelta Alfas finished the course. In August a totally new, super-light Alfa Romeo prototype with a V8 engine that produced 420 was put through its first running tests.

For long-distance races where Grand Prix speeds must be maintained Joseph Siffert, Pedro Rodriguez, Jacky Ickx, and perhaps Mario Andretti as well, must be called in. They are the fastest drivers under all conditions and even in heavy traffic can chalk up incredible lap times. Almost on the same level, though occasionally a fraction slower, were Brian Redman, Vic Elford and the Finn Leo Kinnunen. The latter, at his first race with the Porsche 917, made sure once and for all of a place among the long-distance *élite* by establishing an unbelievable lap record in the *Targa Florio.*

Like low-flying fighters the victorious Gulf-Porsches of JW Automotive demonstrate their superiority near the end of the race. No. 2 is the winning Rodriguez-Kinnunen car, and No. 1 is second-place Siffert-Redman machine—after an incredible drive.

24 Hours of Daytona

Daytona, January 31, 1970

The 1970 Daytona 24 hours was of more than usual interest in that it marked the first of the events to contain the Porsches of John Wyer, whereas the year before the wily English team manager had been the thorn in the side of the works Porsche team with his JW Fords. JW Automotive took two Porsche 917s to race (and another as a spare), and Porsche Salzburg entered two.

The Porsche 917's chief adversaries in this the first 1970 race for the Group 5/6 Manufacturers' Championship were the Ferrari 512 Ss, and the works had entered three. The North American Racing Team run as usual by Luigi Chinetti had one 512 S for Dan Gurney and Chuck Parsons, and there was another—the first private 512 S to be delivered—for the *Scuderia Picchio Rosso*. Matra sent two Type 650 three-litre sport-prototypes for Jack Brabham-François Cevert and Jean-Pierre Beltoise-Henri Pescarolo. It was Brabham's first competition appearance for the French marque, and his first time at Daytona. Alfa-Romeo stayed away with their three-litre sport-prototypes, preferring to go back to Milan after their highly successful showing in the Buenos Aires 200 Miles two weeks before. So Matra's main opposition in the Group 6 category was to come from *NART*'s two Ferrari 312Ps. Only two Porsche 908s arrived. There was one Lola Mark 3b entered for Canadian George Eaton, three Ford GT 40s, and two Ferraris.

Around 30,000 people—a big crowd for the Sebring 24 hours—turned up on a cool, sunny day, and the first lap gave promise of a very exciting râce. Andretti and Siffert in Ferrari 512 S and Porsche 917 respectively, were

Ferrari 512S "office" is well-planned with small-diameter steering wheel and three spokes to render instruments easy to see. Both Porsche and Ferrari favour right-hand drive for racing. The Italian marque has even found room for the 'Prancing Horse'.

Rodriguez in close (Ferrari) company—but it couldn't happen to a cooler fella. Both he and his Finnish co-driver Leo Kinnunen, drove a model race, and led after three hours. The Mexican-Finnish combination was never again headed and finished 45 laps in front of the second-placed car.

Unlike any racing machine yet from Maranello the 5-litre Group 5 Ferrari presented a cluttered aspect to would-be overtakers. At one time the cars got progressively smoother each year to cheat the air-stream, now it all seems to be happening in reverse! A very fast car nevertheless.

side-by-side as they swept off the banking ahead of the other 62 runners. The Swiss driver however got ahead by the first curve and his team-mate Rodriguez followed him, relegating Andretti to third. The two Porsches and the Ferrari set a keen pace and Gurney moved his *NART* Ferrari into fourth, indicating a tough inter-marque scrap.

After the first refuelling stops however Siffert was some 25 seconds ahead of Rodriguez, and Andretti, who led the Ferrari armada. Gurney was fourth, two laps in arrears due to a pit-stop for an oil leak.

After the second pit-stops had been made for refuelling and driver-changes, Giunti went sideways in his Ferrari 512 S, hit the wall and smashed a rear suspension upright. The mechanics worked for two hours on the battered machine but it could not be repaired. And Ferrari mechanics don't give up easily! It looked as though the JW Porsches were invincible—after three hours Brian Redman led after changing-over with Siffert, and the Rodriguez-Kinnunen car was second. Highest-placed Salzburg 917 was that of Elford and Ahrens in fifth position.

Redman came crawling in on a punctured tyre, but even more serious was the broken brake pipe—torn by the whirling tyre tread. It took 17 minutes to put the car right and the British driver rejoined the race in eighth place.

As dusk took hold, Andretti's Ferrari, in third place, was black-flagged for inoperative rear lights, and Beltoise' Matra stopped with a broken rotor. Pescarolo sprinted out to the car with a new rotor and got it under way.

The Siffert-Redman car was going great guns after its stop and by 7pm was fourth. The Andretti rear light drama had given the Rodriguez-Kinnunen Porsche a five-lap lead. Then Jacky Ickx had a tyre go down on his Ferrari 512 S, clouted a wall, and was retired. Punctures were becoming a major problem. Forghieri, Ferrari's team manager, decided to put Ickx back to work, and made him Andretti's co-driver in place of Merzario. Beltoise and Pescarolo drove hard to put their Matra into 11th place, but the complete distributor than gave trouble and the car again fell back.

Brabham like the professional he is, had taken to the three-litre Matra and to Daytona, and around midnight took fourth place from Gurney in the five-litre Ferrari. The Andretti-Ickx Ferrari took 16 minutes to have the front brake discs changed. Then the Gurney-Parsons Ferrari 512S hit the *Scuderia Picchio*

No. 40, the 2-litre Porsche 906E of Loomis-Everett-Harrison did well to finish ninth overall, and the 3-litre Matra of Brabham and Cevert finished 10th after all sorts of ignition adventures. It was Brabham's first drive for the French marque, and his first visit to Daytona.

The Ferrari 512S No. 28 started the race with Andretti in charge, then his co-driver Merzario was changed for Ickx after the Belgian driver's car had hit a wall due to a puncture. The Ferrari had rear light trouble, and a broken rear crossmember, but still managed to finish third overall, 48 laps behind the winning Porsche.

Two stops for inoperative rear lights after being black-flagged, a 16-minute disc brake-changing session, and two more stops for chassis-welding which added-up to another 77 minutes would have deterred many drivers, but Andretti and Ickx kept at it to take their works Ferrari 512S on to third place. They covered 676 laps.

Rodriguez (left) waits with typical readiness to take over from Kinnunen (right). Leo Kinnunen, Finnish rally driver took easily to classic long-distance racing. Daytona was first race for Porsche.

With two hours to go the Matra mechanics display a singular lack of interest in the proceedings. The team was dogged with ignition troubles but Brabham and Cevert brought their Type 650 into 10th place.

Porsche new and old-boys, Wyer (left) and von Hanstein convince themselves its going to be all right.

Rosso 512S, bending the works car more than somewhat. It was repaired (repeatedly!) but fell back. The Salzburg 917 had a 42-minute stop for leaking fuel, the Parkes-Posey 312P developed a radiator leak, and so the drama went on through the night.

At breakfast-time the JW Rodriguez-Kinnunen Porsche was way out front with a 13-lap over the Andretti-Ickx Ferrari. Amazingly the Siffert-Redman 917 was third after a stop of more than an hour for a new clutch. They were then 39 laps behind the Ferrari. The second-place Ferrari had to make a 45-minute stop for the rear chassis-member to be welded, then it came in again. Surprisingly, it was still second when it rejoined the race. After more ignition trouble the Beltoise-Pescarolo Matra stopped, but Beltoise fitted some more bits and drove it to the pits. Meanwhile the Rodriguez-Kinnunen 917 headed the field with a lead of no less than 51 laps. Siffert pressed-on and was catching the second-place Ferrari. Even after a stop to straighten the Porsche after a wall-scraping episode, Siffert forced-on, passed the Ferrari and got on to the same lap. The Ferrari made its last pit-stop and was only 55 seconds ahead with 34 minutes to go. Leader Rodriguez was forgotten in the last-hour excitement. Siffert made a fantastic lap in 1m. 48.7s and was pushing the 917 like a Saturday five-lapper. With four minutes to go Siffert was on top of the Ferrari, and with two laps to go the Wyer car was second. And so JW won his first race for Porsche, and the first Championship event of the season. It was a 1-2 victory, and it also marked Wyer's third 24-hours race win in four starts.

The winning Ferrari 512S (No. 21) in close company with the Bucknum-Posey NART *512S Spyder. Giunti drives the victorious car here but he and Vaccarella were joined much later in the race by Andretti who drove furiously to take a 22.1-second win from the Revson-McQueen Porsche 908.* ▸

24
21

Sebring, March 21, 1970

Sebring 12-Hour Endurance Race

Second round of the 1970 Manufacturers Championship was obviously to be a battle between Porsche's and Ferrari's heavy metal, and as far as entries were concerned it looked like being a well-matched contest for the German cars numbered four 917s amongst their strength, and there were four Ferrari 512Ss. Two of the 917s were for the JW-Gulf camp, and there were two new cars for Porsche-Audi of America.

The four Ferrari 512Ss were all factory cars except the one car which was allocated to Luigi Chinetti's *North American Racing Team* hereinafter known as *NART*. The JW 917s were to be driven by the redoutable Siffert-Redman, Rodriguez-Kinnunen combinations and the Porsche-Audi machines by the powerful pairings—Elford-Ahrens and Herrmann-Lins.

The factory Ferraris were in the hands of Andretti-Merzario, Ickx-Schetty, and Giunti-Vaccarella. The *NART* car was manned by Posey and Bucknum, and with Porsche one-up on Ferrari after the Daytona affair, it promised to be a stern fight.

Wyer actually had one brand-new 917, the Daytona-winning car for Rodriguez and Kinnunen, and a spare. Both the Porsche-Audi cars were brand-new. Since Daytona, the JW-Gulf band had added extra air-intakes for crew and damper cooling, bigger wheel bearings, wider wheels and so on.

All four Ferrari 512S machines were new with rehashed streamlining, beefed-up chassis, yet with 80 lb. rumoured to be taken off. The latest fuel-injection equipment was said to boost the V12 engines by 40 bhp.

The sport-prototype brigade included three Alfa-Romeo three-litre *Tipo* 33/3s for Courage-de Adamich, Stommelen-Galli, and Gregory-Hezemans and, two Matra 650 Spyders for Pescarolo-Servoz-Gavin and Cevert-Gurney.

The lanky Californian was 'standing in' for his old team-mate Jack Brabham who was racing at Brands Hatch in the Formula 1 "Race of Champions" (which he very nearly won, but finished in fourth place).

Two three-litre Ferrari 312Ps were entered by *NART* for Parkes-Parsons and Adamowicz-Chinetti jnr, and extra zest was lent to the entire affair by the three Porsche 908s entered, with one car each, by AAW Finland (Laine-Lennep), International Martini Racing Germany (Larrousse-Attwood), and Solar Productions' car for Revson and McQueen. The last-named car was entered by McQueen's film company, and the actor himself was driving with his left foot in a special plaster cast after a cross-country motorcycle race crash some seven days before in which he finished fourth!

Lola was represented in the 1970 race by Udy and Hailwood with the Springbok-winning Mk 3b, and by Brown and Young in the Randy's Auto Body T70. There were also two Ford GT40s, one entered by Trevor Graham, the other by Auto Enterprises. Drivers, respectively, Forester-Hedges and Grant-Heppenstall. The field was completed by two Chevron B16s (Baker-Baker and Robinson-Kleinpeter), Corvettes, Camaros, 911Ss, MGBs, Fiats & c.

First day of the official 1970 practice went to Siffert who rushed the JW-Gulf 917 around in 2 m. 34.47 s. On the Friday Andretti took out the works Ferrari 512S and returned an exciting 2 m. 33. 5 s., earning his car pole pole position. The latest Ferrari was obviously very quick as well! The rolling start (the Le Mans start had been scrapped for the first time at Sebring) with 2 × 2 placings, had a Porsche 917 and a Ferrari 512S in the first three rows.

The bright sunny morning was blasted first by marching bands on show at the circuit, but the blast as the big field got away was more musical to race-fans ears. Andretti rushed away but Siffert wasn't far behind.

It seemed obvious that the two cars were in there as pace-setters, for the sprint pattern they were pursuing didn't seem to add-up to longevity. The Matras led the prototypes, but behind them the Ferraris and Alfa-Romeos were battling grimly.

In less than half-an-hour Siffert had smashed the lap record at 2 m. 33.11 s. in his efforts to pass the flying Ferrari, but Andretti was in the mood and held off the German air-cooled machine. The Italo-American dashed into his pit after 47 minutes of racing however, and indicated that partly-filled fuel tanks were some of the reason for the Ferrari's terrific showing. But only some.

Siffert was another seven minutes before he pulled-in for fuel—a job that the JW team managed far better than Ferrari, so after an hour's racing the Porsche, now in the hands of Redman, was out in front of the Porsches of Elford-Ahrens and Rodriguez-Kinnunen. The Ickx-Schetty Ferrari was fourth, and Matra led the prototypes with Gurney at the wheel in seventh place overall, just ahead of team-mate Pescarolo. None of the three-litre cars had refuelled. The Herrmann-Lins 908 went out with an over-revved engine. Then it all happened. Race-leader Redman shot into his pit with a loose ignition lead, Kinnunen passed Ahrens into the lead then suffered a puncture—so both 917s were passed by No. 19 with Andretti back in charge—and charging! Two and a quarter hours had passed and the Ickx-Schetty 512S was in second place. With three hours gone—quarter-distance—the Giunti/Vaccarella 512s had moved into third and the red cars looked set and sure. The last of the "Salzburg" 917s retired as the result of being involved in a stupid accident sparked off by one of the slowest cars. Elford limped to his pit after the multiple shunt, and his front wheel fell off. It seemed the beginning of the end for the Porsches, for the Siffert-Redman 917, hopelessly behind, made for the pits with wheel bearings sloppy in a front upright. In 35 minutes it was back in the race with a new upright from the practice chassis. Examination of the removed upright however indicated stretching bolts—and more trouble. Soon the Rodriguez-Kinnunen car was in with a sloppy front-end. The original troublesome upright had by then been repaired, so it was fitted to the car which shot off again into the race. But all was not lovely in the garden, for the Finnish driver clouted a Mustang with his tail (the car's, that is!), so he came in again for the tail to be transplanted from the spare car. In the middle of all the uproar, the other 917 came in for fuel but it wasn't necessary! The cooling fan had detached itself, and the motor had had its day—before the night stint had started.

So at half-distance it seemed that Ferrari had it made, and that they were fully avenging themselves for the Daytona debacle. The Andretti-Merzario car led with 131 laps to its credit, backed-up by Vaccarella-Giunti and Ickx-Schetty who had covered 130. The three-litre prototypes were now led by the Revson-McQueen 908, seven laps behind. Both the Matras had experienced electrical troubles, the Adamowicz-Chinetti Ferrari was out with overheating, but the Parkes-Parsons 312P was in fifth place.

The three Ferraris roared into the night looking invincible. But the *NART* car which had been damaged in the early multiple shunt, had fuel feed trouble, then the clutch became troublesome, so Chinetti snr pulled it out of the race. Then the motor of the Ickx-Schetty 512S died, and with four hours to go the Giunti-Vaccarella car punctured a tyre and the grinding drive to the pits on the wheel deranged the suspension—and it took the Ferrari mechanics 24 minutes to get it back into the contest. The three Alfas were experiencing troubles, and after another hour, Siffert's 917 broke another upright and was out. The Swiss was quickly popped into the other car with Rodriguez, and Kinnunen being given the day off, but a hub breakage happened and the Porsche dropped to fourth. Just when it looked as though it was to be a Ferrari victory, and with only 80 minutes to go, the leading 512S slowed, jammed in one gear. Then it seized and Merzario got out. Incredibly, JW's one remaining 917 was leading! Equally incredibly, the Revson-McQueen 908 was second.

Vaccarella came in for fuel and Forghieri put Andretti behind the wheel. It was an "impossible" task, but the Italo-American put on an amazing display. He knocked-off five seconds a lap, and with 22 minutes to go, passed the 908 into second place. It was terrific driving which put excitement back into the race after nearly 12 hours. Then the leading Porsche came in with broken hub studs, and it took the JW mechanics eight minutes to get it back into the race—but it was in fourth place.

So Ferrari won after all, 23.8 seconds ahead of the 908. It was a momentous drive by Andretti, but equally, the Revson-McQueen showing was great stuff. It was Ferrari's first Championship "sports car" win since 1967.

Schetty and Ickx whisper sweet nothings to each other during practice. They shared a works Ferrari 512 S and led the race in the early stages but were put out with a blown head gasket after seven hours. Their retirement reduced the Ferrari team to two cars—but one more was gone in another hour.

Luigi Chinetti, NART *boss doesn't look too pleased after his Ferrari 512S got caught up in a shunt—through no fault of his driver, Sam Posey. "Eh,* porca miseria, *what you do with these people''?*

Its not all the motor race at Sebring—the human race enters into it too. Jaguar owner studies chassis design and wonders how secure the knots are. After all, Lady Godiva came from Coventry—and had long hair.

Steve McQueen, who so nearly won the race with Peter Revson, adjusts the special cast on his left foot. He broke several bones in a motorcycle race prior to running at Sebring. The film actor drove extremely well and courageously.

Mario Andretti dominated the race with the works Ferrari 512S No. 19, and was leading with 80 minutes to go. Then the trasmission seized and the Italo-American was put in the Giunti-Vaccarella car, and won!

Siffert led the race in the early stages with the JW Porsche 917, and also set a new lap record at 122.265 mph. The car experienced front suspension and cooling troubles, and was finally retired. Note the reinforced nose section—a lesson learned from Daytona.

All three Alfa-Romeos T33-3s finished. This is the Courage-de Adamich car which finished eighth. The Gregory-Hezemans T33-3 took third place. The Courage-de Adamich car leads a Porsche 917 and a Matra.

Just before joining the fray Peter Revson adjusts the rear-view on the Solar Productions' Porsche 908 which was destined to take second place. ▶

Sandwich anyone? The winning Ferrari nicely bottled-up in between a Corvette and an Alfa at Green Park chicane. The Ferrari not only won—it was the only Ferrari finisher!

Latin revels. Andretti and his co-drivers celebrate their incredible victory with Moët. Should be Asti Spumante, surely! It was the first Ferrari win in a "sports car" classic for three years, and Andretti was the hero of the hour. Of the 12 hours! The Ferrari averaged 107.290 mph for the 248 laps.

Tribune di Cerda, May 3, 1970

Targa Florio

Sicilian as the *Targa Florio* is, it has become a German car preserve, Porsche having won every race from 1966 on, recording ten victories in all. Alfa-Romeo are second on an amassed victories basis with eight wins, and Ferrari follow with six. Over the last few years Ferrari participation has dwindled in the classic Sicilian event, and for 1970 the proud Italian marque was represented by one factory car only.

The 512 S in question was sent for Sicilian driver/schoolmaster Vaccarella so that he could keep his image with the locals—and of course because he probably knew the *Piccolo Madonie* circuit better than anyone else.

At one time the Sicilian led the race both on the road and on time, and the locals were consumed with joy, although in the end the Porsche phalanx triumphed, but the unsuitable Italian car came through to a well-deserved third.

Porsche, as usual, took the "Targa" very seriously, and left the ultra-powerful 917 s at home. Instead they turned-up with modified versions of their three-litre 909 *Bergspider* (open hill-climb) machines—which they had tested in Sicily some weeks before. The three-litre cars were designated 908/3 s, and it was obvious from the outset these neat and agile machines had been expressly designed to win the *Targa Florio*. It must have been an enormously expensive exercise, but it was well done and deserving of success. There were no less than five new cars, and in the end they finished 1-2-4-5, and Kinnunen in the second-placed car set a staggering new lap record at 33 m. 36 s.—a speed of 79.89 mph, and more than 90 seconds faster than Elford's 908 amazing record in 1969.

The new 908/3 s were for Elford-Herrmann (with Porsche KG Austria), three for John Wyer's Gulf-Porsche team with driver pairings, Rodriguez-Kinnunen, Siffert-Redman, and Attwood-Waldegaard. There was also a "spare" 908/3 and the original 909. As the 908/3 weighed some 90 lb. less than the 908, and had a shorter wheelbase it was expected to go well, and it did. Elford and Herrmann had brought a 917 as well, with which the latter driver lowered his own record (unofficially) at 35 m. 06.6 s, but he soon realised the potential of the 908/3 when he circulated at 34 m. 37.3 s, in spite of a sticking throttle—or maybe because of it! Vaccarella tried hard with the 512 S Ferrari but in spite of all his efforts and course knowledge, his best was 34 m. 46 s. Siffert was the real hero of the practice sessions with a fantastic 34 m 10 s., a time which put all others in the shade, and effectively demonstrated the potential of the Porsche 908/3. Fourth-fastest was Courage with one of the three Alfa 33/3 s, who recorded 35 m. 5.7 s. Courage was to share the Alfa 33/3 with de Adamich, the other two Autodelta machines being paired: Maglioli-Galli, and Gregory-Henzemans. Also in the same class were the AAW Racing Team's Porsche 908 for Laine and van Lennep, and the 908/2 of the Martini Racing Team for Larrousse and Lins. There were two works three-litre Abarth V8 s for Merzario and Ortner, and Casoni with Williams.

Amongst the two-litre prototypes were two privately-entered Ferrari Dinos for Piccolo-Calascibetta and "Cino"/Barbuscia, and there was a Porsche 907 for Alberti and Pinto.

One other Ferrari 512 S was entered by *Scuderia Filipinetti* for Parkes and Müller, but the big cars were not regarded as potential winners. After an early morning rain-shower, the start was delayed until 9.15 am (it should have started at 8.30 am) when 78 cars blasted away at odd intervals. Müller and Vaccarella were first away in the 512 S Ferraris and both found the circuit mud-strewn after the rain. Elford had one of his worst Targas ever, when only a few kilometres from Cerda he nudged a kerbstone, punctured a tyre and hit a wall. Three-times winner Maglioli also hit a wall before completing half a lap, so two stars were out very early in the proceedings.

On the first lap Siffert led on the road from Vaccarella, but on time it was Larrousse ahead of the pack in the Martini 908. Siffert was second, 13 seconds in arrears, and Kinnunen was third. Local-boy Vaccarella was seventh, and the Ferrari was still in that position when he handed over to Giunti on lap 2 during refuelling.

Refuelling stops were the order of the day and during the activity Giunti actually went into the lead on the road. Siffert thought he was in the lead, and wasn't! Giunti and Siffert both came in to the pits at the same time, and it was all a bit fraught. Vaccarella took-off four seconds quicker than the Porsche after the refuelling, and still led on the road—and the crowd was delirious. The race was actually being led on time by Rodriguez, 100 seconds ahead of Redman, so Porsches were well-placed. Vaccarella was third on time but he then put on a show, passing the Porsches and leading the lot (on the road) by lap 5. The Sicilian was going like the wind but he was 41 seconds behind the Mexican driver. By the time Vaccarella came in to hand over to Giunti, he had pulled the Ferrari up to the lead, both on the road and on time. He was 33 seconds, ahead of Laine who had worked himself into second, ahead of Redman. Rodriguez was back to fourth, and Gregory had crashed and turned over in his Alfa 33/3 so Courage was left to carry the Autodelta colours. Parkes and Muller ran along in eighth place with the *Filipinetti* 512 S and didn't seem able to improve on the placing.

Redman pulled out all the stops on lap 7, covered a *tour* at 34 m. 33.1 s, and put the 908/3 back in the lead. When he handed over to Siffert their car was 13 seconds ahead of Giunti. On laps 7 and 8 the Redman Porsche and Giunti Ferrari had only been feet apart so there was plenty of excitement for the crowd—particularly when they raced into the pits in very close company!

The German pit-team was a little quicker than the Italian, and it was Siffert who got away first with a new load of fuel, but Vaccarella was right behind him as they both roare back into the contest. As long as Siffert could keep the Porsche in front of the Ferrari, the German marque must win, for Vaccarella had to be more than 14 seconds ahead on time to lead. On that same lap Courage hit a tree with the remaining Alfa 33/3 so only seven cars were contesting the lead. Vaccarella was tired and Siffert had got more than a minute ahead. The Kinnunen-Rodriguez Porsche was third, the Laine-van Lennep Porsche fourth, the Larrousse-Lins Porsche fifth, and the Attwood-Waldegaard Porsche sixth! The Müller-Parkes 512 S was seventh and was the only other unlapped car.

Then Laine lost a front wheel, but kept going on the front brake disc! Vaccarella clouted a massive rock and bent the front suspension but kept going with a shuddering car, and the Larrousse-Lins car broke a universal joint. Poor Giunti was given the Ferrari for the last lap, the bent steering slowing him more than somewhat, but Kinnunen was flying and pushed the Porsche into second. Porsches finished 1-2-4-5, and Kinnunen staggered everyone with his near-80 mph record lap, but Vaccarella and Giunti did well to bring the big Ferrari into third. Engineer Piech had engineered the JW victory, so John Wyer congratulated him!

ALT
40

Larrousse and Lins finished 13th in their Porsche 908/2, entered by the Martini Racing Team. Here the car is shadowed by the Laine/Lennep 908 of AWW Racing Team, watched by a crowd of Sicilians—and wonder upon wonder, there's a safety barrier! Laine and Lennep finished fourth.

◂ *The Rodriguez/Kinnunen Porsche 908/3 roars past a typical Targa knot of spectators. Safety arrangements are sketchy, but the atmosphere is immense. It was this car in which Kinnunen set the amazing new lap record of 79.89 mph. The Finn knocked 1 ½ minutes off Elford's record—an almost unbelievable achievement.*

Guess who? Its local-boy Vaccarella—who else? And he's leading the race in the sole Ferrari works entry, on the first lap—on time and on the road. Enzo Ferrari entered just the one factory car so that Vaccarella could keep his image with his Sicilian public. He finally finished third.

Nino Vaccarella, Sicilian schoolmaster whose knowledge of the Targa course is unsurpassed, here leads Siffert's Porsche between Collesano and Campofelice. Siffert, with his co-driver Redman, went on to win comfortably from Rodriguez and Kinnunen. Real motor racing on a real circuit.

Siffert refuels the winning 908/3, and the Porsche mechanics are smiling already. The 908/3 was derived from the 909 Bergspider *(hill-climb car), and was ideal for the sinuous Targa Florio course.*

Courage and de Adamich were in the first nine until the Alfa T33-3 hit a tree on lap eight. Courage was unhurt. This picture also gives some idea of Targa Florio safety arrangments!

Attwood was paired with rallyman Waldegaard and between them they brought their Gulf-Porsche 908/3 into fifth place. Here the British driver corners fast between Collesano and Campofelice.

Jonathan Williams in the two-litre Alfa-Romeo T33-2 which he shared with Giorgio Alberti. It won the two-litre class and finished seventh—a very fine performance. The three works three-litre Alfas crashed.

Light and shade as Siffert flies through Campofelice en route to victory. It was the first time either the Swiss driver or Brian Redman had won the Sicilian classic. Porsches were 1-2-4-5.

The works Lancia Fulvio HF 1.6 of Claudio Maglioli and Amilcare Ballestriere near the Corde tribune. This combination won the Touring Car class, severely trouncing the Alfa-Romeo GTAs.

The Alpine-Renault 1300 driven by "Ro" in this photograph did not have a Wankel engine in spite of the driver's "name". The car was 20th overall and won the up-to -1300 GT class, co-driven by Giacomini.

Müller and Parkes did well to bring the private-entered Scuderia Filipinetti *Ferrari 512S coupé into sixth place, one lap behind the leaders. The roof bulge is to accommodate Parkes's head!*

ADAC-1000-km-Rennen

Nürburgring, May 31, 1970

The Nürburgring 1000 kilometres was another success story for Porsche, giving the German marque its sixth important victory of 1970, and making sure of the Constructors' Championship. This time however it wasn't the JW cars which brought home the bacon but the Austrian Salzburg team who were the heroes of the day. Their 908/3s finished first and second with Elford and Ahrens driving the winning car, and Attwood and Herrmann sharing the second-placed 908/3. Ferrari took third place with Surtees and Vaccarella sharing a 512 S, but the leading Porsches were the only cars on the same lap at the finish.

Both JW and Porsche Austria decided to use the Targa-type 908/3 machines, as their agility was considered a better bet on the tricky Nürburgring than the brute power of the 917s. It was a matter of great convenience too for Le Mans was but two weeks away, so the big cars which were so well suited to the Sarthe circuit could be readied almost without pressure.

The closeness of Le Mans was instrumental in Matra sending only one car for the German classic, and Alfa-Romeo who were to have originally entered three *Tipo* 33 s suddenly realised their cars were too heavy and sent one special lightweight T 33/3 for Courage and Stommelen. With revised suspension and the shedding of nearly 150 lb. great things were expected of the car, but a sole entry cannot normally be classed as serious opposition to a multi-car team. The Alfa entry was even further handicapped from being a contender for three-litre prototype honours in view of the Porsche teams' decision to race three-litre cars themselves.

With three five-litre 512 S Spiders, Ferrari looked well-fixed for Group 5 honours, but luck was not on their side for Schetty wrote off a car in practice, and Ickx slipped down some stairs and damaged his wrist too severely for him to race! Forghieri had to rehash his pairings a little, finally deciding on Surtees-Vaccarella and Giunti-Merzario with Schetty as reserve. Main opposition to the Ferraris were the private Porsche 917 s of Toivonen-Axelsson and Neuhaus-Kelleners, and the VDS Lola of Pilette and Gosselin. There was also a Ferrari 512 from *Scuderia Filipinetti* for Parkes and Müller.

It was soon evident it would be a very fast race for both JW 908/3 s, in the hands of Siffert and Rodriguez quickly lapped as fast as Ickx' outright Formula 1 record almost as the practice period opened. Siffert was the official fastest at 7 m. 43.3 s, Rodriguez was less than a second inferior, and third-fastest time also went to a Porsche 908/3 when Elford put the Salzburg car around the Eifel twists and turns at 7 m. 48.2 s. Surtees made best Ferrari time at 7 m. 57.1 s., and then Schetty lost the 512 on his practice run when it aquaplaned, left the road and was wrecked. Schetty was unhurt. Just before the end of the Saturday practice Hans Laine crashed in the *AWW* Porsche 908 whilst scrubbing-in new tyres and was trapped inside the burning car.

Although Koch stopped and tried to get the Finnish driver out, the Porsche burst into such a mass of flames that it was impossible to save the driver. It looked as though conditions were to be grim, for it rained all night before the race, but quite suddenly the downpour ceased. The surface was still wet however, and most cars prepared for the start with "intermediate" tyres. It was Rodriguez who rushed ahead at the start, and Giunti made a tremendous effort with the Ferrari 512, passing car after car and holding second place as the cars streamed through Adenau. First time past the pits the Mexican's Porsche was 14 seconds ahead of Giunti, who was in turn being pressured hard by Siffert in the second Gulf-Porsche. Surtees had passed Elford into fourth, so it was Porsche - Ferrari - Porsche - Ferrari - Porsche. After two laps Rodriguez had extended his lead to 19 seconds and Siffert had passed Giunti. The factory Ferraris were third and fourth. Siffert, in characteristic manner, started to close on Rodriguez, and Giunti's car stopped with a defunct metering unit. Surtees was being pressed hard by the sole Alfa 33/3.

Siffert was going as fast as he knew how and was within 11 seconds of the leader, and his pace had pulled him 20 seconds ahead of Elford.

Siffert grabbed the lead on lap 10, but on the next lap had to call-in for fuel. He made the pit just ahead of Rodriguez, and Elford brought the Salzburg car in 45 seconds after Siffert. Due to the JW cars having to share a hose, Ahrens got away at the same time as Kinnunen. The two drivers diced it out and Kinnunen got into trouble on an airborne section, and went into a bank, badly damaging the car. The Finn was unhurt.

So Ahrens led in the Salzburg Porsche, followed by Redman and Attwood. The Alfa 33/3 broke a rear damper and Courage retired as the sump was dragging on the track. Redman started to challenge Ahrens, and in two laps he had taken the lead with the Gulf-JW car. At 17 laps the JW car was 60 seconds ahead of the Salzburg entry. At half-distance the order was Redman-Siffert-Ahrens-Elford-Attwood-Herrmann - Parkes - Müller - Marko - Larrousse - Kelleners - Basche.

With a minute's lead Redman came in for fuel and to hand over to Siffert. The Swiss driver pressed the starter but the engine wouldn't fire, and Elford who had taken over from Ahrens, had refuelled and got away in the lead. It took ten minutes to get the reluctant JW Porsche to start, by which time Elford had lapped it, and the Herrmann-Attwood (which had also refuelled) was second. Siffert was really in trouble for he had got only as far as Hocheichen when the engine had tightened-up and he was out of the race. *All* the JW-Gulf Porsches were out of the race!

After that the race was dull. The factory Ferrari did pass the Larrousse-Marko Porsche 908 to take fourth place but it lost it when it stopped for fuel. Two laps later it repassed the Porsche, and started closing on the *Scuderia Filipinetti* car and put a little interest into the contest. With Surtees at the wheel the works 512 passed Müller into third place, but the two Salzburg 908/3 s were in first and second and seemed invulnerable. After the Siffert seizure (mechanical, not personal) the two leading Porsches made a pit-stop for oil, just as a precaution. The stop put the Ferrari a little nearer, but it was a lap behind at the finish. The British-entered Red Rose Chevron had experienced very hard luck, for after appearing to have the two-litre class sewn-up, was out at three-quarter distance with engine trouble.

To rub salt (from Salzburg?) into the wound, Ahrens lapped the Parkes-Müller Ferrari for the second time as he took the 908/3 into its last lap. It certainly demonstrated the *Porsche über Alles* theme and emphasised the Championship victory of the German marque. The second Salzburg car took the flag 5 m. 13 s. after the winner, and Ferraris took third and fourth. There were six Porsches in the first eight, Porsches had won the over two-litre G 6 class, and a Porsche had set a new lap record. Porsche won the two-litre prototype class with Wicky and Cabral driving a 907, but a Chevron took the two-litre Group 5 class with drivers Heavens and Garton.

BOSCH
Firestone
Shell
P 22

Elford (centre) and Ahrens (right), victors of the 1970 Nürburgring 1000 kilometres, look happily at their Salzburg 908/3 during the last practice session. Neither of the JW Gulf-Porsches finished.

◄ *Vic Elford presses on in the Salzburg Porsche 908/3 to clinch the Constructors' Championship for the marque. He and Ahrens played their part in bringing Stuttgart-Zuffenhausen's 1970 total to six Championship wins. The Elford-Ahrens car won and their team-mates Attwood and Herrmann took second place.*

Somehow this driver looks different — even disguised by overalls. It is the talented 27-year-old Hannelore Werner, fast female who is a dental mechanic by profession, sharing a turbo-blown Capri with Kranefuss. She retired.

▲
The start, from South Curve. The big, fast metal have already got around the curve and are heading for the Flugplatz, *the slower cars are way behind.*

Splendid showing by Wicky and de Cabral in their Porsche 907 gave them ninth position overall and a win in the up to two-litre Group 6 category.

After "his'' Ferrari had been wrecked in practice by Peter Schetty, John Surtees was paired with Nino Vaccarella. Both drivers did extremely well to place third after losing time with a tyre change, and a broken steering wheel.

A fourth place was netted for Ferrari by the Scuderia Filipinetti *512S coupé driven by Mike Parkes and Herbert Müller. In spite of the good placings for the Italian marque, the Swiss-entered car was twice lapped by the winning Porsche of smaller capacity. The Filipinetti car is seen here on the* Karussell.

Larrousse and Marko in the Martini Porsche 908 were models of consistency, and took an excellent fifth place. Martini 908s took fifth and sixth, the latter car being shared by Lins and Kauhsen.

Herrmann and Attwood drove an exemplary race to take second place in the other Salzburg Porsche 908/3. Both leading Porsches stopped for oil seven laps from the end of the 1000 km race.

First pit-stop: Redman is handing-over to Siffert. Their JW Gulf-Porsche 908/3 led for a significant part of the race, but finally went out with a seized engine.

The Siffert-Redman JW 908/3 exhibits its underwear and ability to fly. Both JW and Salzburg chose the lightweight, nimble 908/3s for the Nürburgring, in preference to the faster but less wieldy 917s. The drive is taken from the rear of the gearbox on this model, which puts the back wheels at "the corners".

Siffert lost the lead after a pit-stop when the starter proved reluctant. He finally went back into the race in third place, but got only as far as Hocheichen.

The winning Elford-Ahrens Salzburg Porsche 908/3 passes the abandoned Siffert-Redman JW 908/3. The second JW Porsche crashed in Kinnunen's hands when trying to overtake Ahrens, but Rodriguez had earlier set the fastest lap at a record 7 m. 50.4 s. Kinnunen, the "Flying Finn" was lucky to be unhurt in the crash.

Siffert gets uptight, both personally and behind Giunti as he tries to pass the Ferrari in the opening laps. The 908/3 led the race in the end, only to be put out with a seized engine. Another 908/3 won the race, a Salzburg machine driven by Elford and Ahrens. ►

Shell
57
55
22

Vingt-Quatre Heures du Mans

Le Mans, June 14, 1970

Le Mans 1970, first year without the traditional "run-and-jump" start, proved a win for Porsche at long last. The German marque had taken part in the classic 24-hours race for 19 years, and although they had come within an ace of winning in 1969, another year was to go by before they were victorious. But when they did win, they carried all before them with the first three places in general classification, five places out of the seven official finishers, and 12 places out of the 16 cars still running at the end of the 24 hours. In addition the third place (overall) Porsche 908 won the Sport Prototype class, a VW-Porsche 914-6 was victorious in the Grand Touring category, and Porsches won the Index of Performance, and the Index of Thermal Efficiency. To complete the German cars' domination, British driver Vic Elford set a new lap record with one of the "Salzburg" Porsche 917 s. at 3 m. 21 s.—a speed of 149.897 mph. It was a faster lap then even two years before when the speed-reducing "Ford Chicane" was added on the approach to the pit area, and faster than when there was no engine limit on the Sarthe circuit. As can be gathered from the one-make dominance, the race wasn't nearly so exciting as the 1969 event, and it was certainly one of the wettest ever seen on the 8.38-mile circuit.

The winning Porsche 917 was one of the 4 ½-litre Salzburg-entered machines, driven by Briton Richard Attwood and German Hans Herrmann. Forty-two year-old Herrmann had been the driver who had almost won the 1969 Le Mans (in a 908 Porsche) but who had been pipped by Jacky Ickx in the JW Ford. Herrmann had been racing since 1951 (he started with a Porsche!) and since that time had been a team driver for the 1954/55 Mercedes-Benz sports and Grand Prix team, had raced BRM for the British Racing Partnership, Porsche and others. After winning Le Mans he decided to retire, although this news took several weeks to filter through to the newspapers and magazines.

As has so often been the case over the years, the race was to be a battle between two marques—Porsche and Ferrari for 1970. The German firm had injected an enormous amount of money into the event, and Fiat had seen to it that Ferrari had a team of cars fast enough to give battle. With VW behind Porsche and Fiat backing Ferrari, it was high-speed puppetry controlled by big-time industry. Le Mans is a great international shop window, and not only does the winning marque reap sales benefits all over the world, but the country of origin also gains advantages in motor product sales.

Porsche's spirits were high for the 1970 *Grand Prix d'Endurance,* for Ferrari had enjoyed only one win (at Sebring) and although there were eleven Ferrari 512S cars to eight 917s, the German cars were prepared either by the works or by JW Automotive whereas the Italian machines were a mixture of factory cars and privately sponsored entries. John Wyer, team boss of the 1969-winning Ford GT 40, arrived with three 917s, all with the short abbreviated tails. The long-tailed, fully-aerodynamic bodies on which the factory had spend much time and money had proved unstable at speed on long corners, and were apt to be difficult in the wet. Two cars had been crashed beyond repair during testing, so Wyer put the short-tailed cars in a wind-tunnel and after adding a small wing at the rear of the body was able to reduce the spoiler in depth. Although not as fast in a straight line as the long-tailed "dolphins", they handled better and were less tiring. Siffert and Redman shared a five-litre, as did Rodriguez and Kinnunen. Hobbs and Hailwood shared a new 4½-litre.

Porsche Konstruktionen KG from Salzburg had three 917s, one of them with "dolphin" bodywork. The long-tailed car and one of the short cars had five-litre engines, the remaining machine being powered by a 4½-litre unit. Elford and Ahrens had the choice of a long or short-tail five-litre, and the other car was shared by Attwood and Herrmann. The "remaining" 917 was qualified by Porsche team manager Steinemann who had to find some racing overalls pretty quickly, as he had retired in 1968! One other dolphin-type 917 was entered by the Martini International Racing Team, and driven by Larrousse and Kauhsen. It was finished in a very mod green and blue colour scheme. Only the long-tailed machines were using the fifth speed, the short-tailed cars having five-speed gearboxes but finding four of them enough. Ferrari's phalanx consisted of four works 512S coupés, three 512Ss from *Scuderia Filipinetti,* two 512Ss from *NART*, one from *Ecurie Nationale Belge,* and one from the Spanish *Escuderia Montjuich*. Works Ferrari drivers were Ickx-Schetty, Vaccarella-Giunti, Regazzoni-Merzario, Bell-Peterson. The Filipinetti entries featured Parkes-Müller, Bonnier-Wisell, Manfredini-Moretti. The first two cars were genuine Filipinetti machines with long tails, the Manfredini-Moretti coupé being the *Scuderia Picchio Rosso* machine but entered by the Swiss équipe. *NART*'s drivers were Posey-Bucknum and Kelleners-Loos. The Belgian entry had de Fierlandt and Walker, and the Spanish car was driven by Fernandez and Spice. The works Ferraris were developing about 580 bhp, a comparable figure to the Porsche 917, but the Italian cars were still heavier. Group 6 was notable for a three-marque struggle, the contestants being the Matra V12s, the Alfa-Romeo V8s and the Porsche "flat-eights". The French marque had had all sorts of hold-ups and instead of fielding a team of three new cars, made do with a new *Type* 660 for Beltoise and Pescarolo, and two *Type* 650s for Brabham and Cevert, and Jabouille-Depailler. The latest version of the 12-cylinder engine was reputed to be developing a little less than 400 bhp. Autodelta, the Italian enterprise which does Alfa-Romeo's racing for them, brought four new 33/3 V8 Spiders for Courage-de Adamich, Stommelen-Galli, Gregory-Hezemans, and Zeccoli-Facetti. The new Alfas were some 90 lb. lighter than the 33/3s seen in earlier races, and featured such modifications as light-alloy radiators and titanium body brackets. Power-output was about 395 bhp. The Martini Racing Team had two 908/2 Porsche Spiders for Lins-Marko and Spoerry-Cortanze, and there was a third 908 running as a camera car for the Le Mans movie to be made by Steve McQueen's Solar Productions film company.

Another interesting entry was the much-modified Healey SR, which for the two previous years had raced with a Coventry-Climax V8 engine, but for 1970 had open bodywork and a Repco-Brabham V8.

Amongst the smaller cars the French Ligier JS 1 coupé with Cosworth-Ford FVC engine was of great interest, and Ligier himself was sharing the driving with Andruet. There were three Chevron B16s, a Wankel-powered Mazda B16, two Porsche 910s, and an armada of Porsche 911s. The GT class was notable for two seven-litre Chevrolet Corvette entries. One of the Stingrays was entered by rally/racing specialist Henri Greder and Jean-Pierre Rouget, the other *Ecurie Leopard* machine being driven by Bourdon and Aubriet. Both practice days were very hot, the first day's fastest time being put up by Sicilian Vaccarella in one of the factory 512 S Ferraris. He lapped at 3 m. 20 s., Porsche's fastest driver Rodriguez recording a best 3 m. 18.1 s. Elford experimented with long and short-tailed 917s, and the fastest three-litre on the first day was the Alfa 33/3 of Rolf Stommelen at 3 m. 33.8 s., closely followed by his team-mates' cars. The Matras did not go well.

On the Thursday Elford had had a change of gear ratio and with the 917 Dolphin he became the first driver to lap the circuit at less than 3 m. 20 s. He covered the lap at the staggering speed in spite of the Ford *chicane,* and was reported to have been nudging 227 mph on Mulsanne straight. The British driver was very happy with the handling of the streamliner. So, "Salzburg" was fastest, with Vaccarella still doing great things with the 512S and managing a lap at 3 m. 20.6 s. Siffert was fastest Gulf-JW driver with a searing 3 m. 21.1 s. Only one serious incident occurred during practice, and even then no-one was seriously hurt.

The incident occurred when Brabham was about to pass Spoerry in the Martini Porsche 908 after White House. Brabham's Matra was travelling at around 140 mph and he was closing on the Porsche which pulled to one side, ostensibly to let him through. When the Australian was alongside, Spoerry moved out and the two cars clouted each other. Brabham kept the Matra under control but

Pit-stop for eventual winners Herrmann and Attwood. It was a great victory for the German-British driving team and for the Salzburg-entered cars. The bob-tailed 917 averaged 119.29 mph for 2863 miles. ▶

AVIS
Firestone
CARBURATEURS
SOLEX
RSCHE 23
BOSC
LU
RANDS PIEDS
23
Shell

the Porsche left the track, crashed into a bank and flew to pieces. The engine went one way and the front suspension the other. The centre-section was on its own with Spoerry still strapped in, and a small fire broke out. The Porsche driver quickly got out as soon as his sled had come to a standstill, and ran away from the fire with only a cut leg! A very lucky man. Brabham had set fastest three-litre time until his unfortunate incident (at 3 m. 32.2 s.) but the Matra engineers weren't satisfied and the car was taken away for a new engine. Ligier made fastest two-litre time with his pretty coupé. After John Woolfe's tragic fatal accident with the Porsche 917 on the first lap of the 1969 race, the traditional "Le Mans" start had been abandoned. That unfortunate driver had started with his seat belts unsecured, so the 1970 starting procedure was that drivers sat in their cars with their harnesses secured and their engines switched-on. There were also 7½ miles more of barrier around the circuit, and the *Esses* and *Tertre Rouge* had been widened and resurfaced. The cars were positioned in front of the pits at a steep angle to minimise danger of collision as they drew away, and when Ferry Porsche lowered the flag the 51-car field was free to go. At 4 pm Porsche dropped the flag and two of his cars immediately blasted off, Elford and Siffert rushing away almost side by side. Ickx, who won in 1969 in a JW Ford, repeated his take-it-easy start in the Ferrari, letting most of the panic parade get away before setting off on the 24 hours' marathon. Brabham too was in no hurry and got away as though there was plenty of time. Which there was.

First time past the pits Elford led Siffert and Rodriguez—Porsches 1-2-3 from Salzburg-JW-JW. Merzario's Ferrari was next, followed by Vaccarella's.

Ferrari supporters groaned when Vaccarella, Ferrari's fastest man in practice, came limping in with bearing failure after 27 minutes of racing. By that time Elford had made a record lap at 3 m. 26., and continued to pull away from the field. Hezeman's Alfa was wheeled away with piston failure. After 50 minutes of racing Elford and Siffert came in for fuel and Rodriguez carried on, and so led the race. Elford and Siffert were both in and out in about 20 seconds, then Rodriguez came in, went out, and the order was as before.

Siffert was after the Salzburg 917 and in his efforts set a new lap record at 3 m. 22.6 s., whilst the Chevron-Mazda retired with reported seal failure.

Merzario's Ferrari was now in third place, but the leaders were still Elford and Siffert. After an hour-and-half conditions were drizzly and some wipers were going. By 5.45 pm the rain was more definite and a few cars came in to have wet tyres fitted. When the two leaders came in for their second stops they didn't change to rain tyres, but the Swiss got away first and not only led the race but proceeded to pull away from Elford. Rodriguez fell back, then retired with a broken fan shaft at Arnage. Siffert came in to have his wheel nuts tightened and Elford once more took the lead. The Parkes-Muller Ferrari came into its pit looking very much the worse for wear, and was pushed away. It had been involved in a shunt at Indianapolis, a multi-Ferrari affair which had involved the Bonnier-Wissell car, as well as Bell and Regazzoni. Wissell had slowed because he couldn't see through his oil-covered windscreen, Bell swerved to avoid him, Regazzoni tried to get in between at 150 mph and clouted the Swedish driver an enormous blow. Both cars were spinning all over the road when Parkes came along and ran into them, catching fire in the process. Marshals put out the fire and Parkes limped to the pits, and in the middle of it all Bell had over-revved his engine. So Porsche had four fewer Ferraris to fret about.

The rain got heavier and heavier, and an enormous storm carried on through most of the night. Everyone changed to rain tyres, and due to JW's superior pit-work, the Siffert-Redman 917 was once again in the lead. Conditions were ghastly, and Facetti spun his Alfa on the curve after the pits, clouted the protective barriers, and badly damaged the rear-end. While the driver was working on the back-end, Hailwood arrived with the JW 917 in third place, trying to maintain control through the slippery curve. There just wasn't room for all, and the ex-motorcycle champion hit the Alfa in the biggest possible way. Bourdon got out of control with his Stingray in the *Esses* and crashed, and the Healey clouted Martland's Chevron, and both had to stop for body repairs. Kelleners hit the barrier in the *Esses,* but got under way again. After four hours racing the rain let up a little, and the order was: Siffert-Redman (Porsche 917), Elford-Ahrens (Porsche 917), Piper-van Lennep (Porsche 917), Attwood-Hermann (Porsche 917), Larrousse-Kauhsen (Porsche 917), Ickx-Schetty (Ferrari 512S), Brabham-Cevert (Matra 650), Galli-Stommelen (Alfa T 33/3), Manfredini-Moretti (Ferrari 512S), Lins-Marko (Porsche 908).

Things looked rosey for Porsche, and it seemed as though Ickx and Schetty were carrying all the responsibilities and hopes for the Italian marque. Both drivers kept at it, and after six hours racing had pushed the red car into third place. The Matras were drinking oil, and spending much time in their pits. The Kelleners-Loos Ferrari was retired as it wouldn't handle on the streaming track. The biff at the barrier had obviously caused more than a bent snout. Elford too found the handling of his 917 peculiar, and finally a slow puncture was found. The trouble had let the JW-Gulf car get away in the lead, and the Ickx-Schetty 512 S now held second place. Elford had dropped to fifth. Courage spun in the Alfa T 33/3, damaged the rear-end, and was 13th by the time he got back into the race. Piper also spun his 917 whilst third, damaged the

◄ *On the Saturday afternoon while conditions were still reasonable, the Ferrari 512 S of Posey-Bucknum leads a team-mate and the Lola T 70 of Pilette and Gosselin. The Posey-Bucknum Ferrari finished fourth — first non-Porsche.*

The incredible 2.3-litre Porsche 911 S of Koob and Kreber finished seventh overall and covered 2256 miles. The car was timed at 158 mph on Mulsanne straight-no mean achievement for a GT coupé set-up for a 24-hours race. ►

Porsche 908 of Lins and Marko finished third at an average of 116.57 mph, and was the first three-litre Porsche home. The previous year a 908 almost won the 24-hours classic, but 1970 was the turn of the 4½-litre 917s.

Porsches at the pits in the appalling weather which prevailed for a major part of the race. The winning bob-tailed 'Salzburg' 917 is being refuelled and re-wheeled, while the Martini 917 langheck *of Larrousse and Kauhsen which took second place, pulls away. Out of seven 917 starters, only these two were running at the end- in first and second places! The victory also marked Porsche's first Le Mans victory after 19 years of trying.*

In spite of valiant efforts by Greder and Rouget their big Corvette was unclassified, having covered insufficient distance. It was in fact the seventh car past the flag having averaged 99.627 mph, and amassed a total mileage of 2391. The drivers handled the seven-litre car with restraint and skill.

Two more Porsches, the amazing 914-6 of Ballot-Lena and Chasseuil who finished sixth, won the GT sports class, and the 911S of Garant and Verrier which was not classified but running at the end.

Facetti does it all wrong in the Alfa 33-3 just as Beltoise and Mazzia blast past in Matra-Simca and Porsche 911 S respectively. The Alfa team had a most unsuccessful Le Mans, the 'Nanni Galli'/Stommelen car being disqualified for a pushstart, and Facetti's other team-mates retiring with mehanical troubles.

Ickx, Elford, and Siffert battle it out on the first day. Elford (No. 25) set up a staggering new Le Mans lap record at 149.90 mph with the Salzburg Porsche 917. ►

body and lights, and had fallen to 14th by the time they were reconstituted. Lins and Marko were leading Group 6 with their 908. Then Courage ran out of fuel, and van Lennep had a front tyre burst at 180 mph on the 917 but managed to bring the car to a halt. It was too bent to continue.

At a quarter-to-two in the morning, Ickx, who had complained of feeling tired, spun at the Ford Chicane, and hit a marshal who was killed. The Ferrari caught fire but the Belgian got out without injury. It was the end of the Ferrari challenge.

After ten hours racing the Siffert-Redman 917 was seven laps in the lead, and things looked good for JW, but motor racing is full of disappointments, and at 2 a.m. Siffert was in at the pit with 9600 on the rev-counter, and oil pouring from practically everywhere. First three cars were the 917s of Attwood-Herrmann, Larrousse-Kauhsen, and Elford-Ahrens, and the Lins-Marko 908 still led Group 6. The *Escuderia Montjuich* Ferrari retired with a split gearbox.

Meanwhile the Healey had spent a lot of time in its pit having the gearbox rebuilt but was back in the race and circulating.

The storm broke again and the rain bucketed down. At half-distance it was Attwood-Herrmann (Porsche 917), Larrousse-Kauhsen (Porsche 917), Elford-Ahrens (Porsche 917), Lins-Marko (Porsche 908), Galli-Stommelen (Alfa T33/3), Posey-Bucknum (Ferrari 512S).

Greder and Rouget were doing a great job keeping the Stingray in the Group 4 lead, treating the big car's transmission like velvet, but after 16 hours' the amazing VW-Porsche 914-6 had taken over. The Elford-Ahrens car was second but by 8.30 a.m. an inlet valve had broken and it was out of the race. The Galli-Stommelen Alfa was disqualified for receiving outside restarting help, and only the faultering Courage-de Adamich car was left. The Martini 908 held second but the 917 from the same stable was catching it. Then the Courage-de Adamich Alfa died.

With four hours to go it was Attwood-Herrmann (Porsche 917), Larrousse-Kauhsen (Porsche 917), Lins-Marko (Porsche 908), Posey-Bucknum (Ferrari 512S), de Fierlandt-Walker (Ferrari 512S), Adamowicz-Parsons (Ferrari 312). A huge storm broke on one side of the circuit, and some cars came in to change to ultra-wet tyres. Then the sun came out, and again there was much tyre-changing! The Attwood-Herrmann car came home five laps ahead of the Martini 917—the only 917 survivors. Third was the 908, and a long way behind, the two Ferrari survivors. The unfortunate Healey, after such a chequered race, stopped with ignition trouble, with two laps to go!

Early laps and Derek Bell in the works Ferrari 512 S leads the Porsche 917 of Herrmann-Attwood which was to win. Bell was soon in at the pits with a puncture. ►

Splashing through the pit area, the second-place Martini 917 of Larrousse-Kauhsen graphically illustrates the foul conditions which prevailed. ►

UNLOP
5
25

14
44
23
Shell
PORSCHE
7
Shell
Shell

AMPION
CHAMPION

Shell
23
GOODYEAR
BOSCH
PORSCHE

DUBONNET
CHAMPION
ARNAGE
5
11

▲ *Quartz-iodine lights illuminate incredibly and dazzle unbelievably. A contrast to the Le Mans of a few years ago when amber lights were compulsory.*

Doctor Forghieri will now take the motor racing class. Ferrari's team manager looks scholastic but is really only sheltering from the Sarthe rain. ▼

Pit No. 20 looks for their man Siffert, overdue when in the lead, but he is out after about ten hours' racing with a broken connecting rod. At that stage of the race no less than 23 cars had retired, and the weather was getting worse.

After 18 hours and 29 minutes the Courage-de Adamich Alfa 33-3 is pushed away with electric trouble and a broken piston. And you can't have it more final than that! It was the last of the Alfa 'works' entries.

◄ Above: *High-level shot of the winning 'bob-tail' Porsche 917 gives good idea of the amount of adhesion gained by body shape. The entire treatment is aimed at downward aerodynamic pressure, as well as wind-cheating qualities.* Below: *Saturday evening at Mulsanne. Rain and dusk falls as the Posey-Bucknum Ferrari 512 S 'leads' the similar car of Ickx-Schetty.*

Richard Attwood stands in front of the chequered flag as his co-driver Hans Herrmann brings the 917 into a well-deserved victory.

German Porsche supporter in the crowd holds his victory banner. Maybe he had also prepared Ferrari, Matra, and Alfa propaganda. But he is right!

Hans Herrmann squirts the traditional champagne over the well-wishers at the finish. The 42-year-old driver started racing in 1951, nearly won Le Mans in 1969, and announced his retirement soon after the 1970 race. He was a member of the 'invincible' Mercedes-Benz Formula 1 team in 1955, and also raced BRM in Grands Prix.

CAN-AM

Canadian-American Challenge-Cup

by Hunter Farnham

Starter Tex Hopkins leaps high to flag Denny Hulme's first 1970 Can-Am victory, at Watkins Glen.

The last time I talked with Bruce McLaren was May 30th, at Indianapolis. He said development work on Team McLaren's 1970 Can-Am car, the M8D, was considerably behind schedule. Because Denny Hulme's hands were heavily bandaged as a result of his Indy practice fire, the main testing for the M8D fell to the already overworked McLaren. Nevertheless, McLaren said he would be heading back to England immediately after the 500 to test the new Can-Am car at Goodwood. Three days later, June 2nd, McLaren was dead. The 32-year old New Zealander had been speeding around Goodwood in the new car. The rear engine cover came loose at high speed, and the car slewed off the track, out of control. McLaren died as a result of injuries received in the crash. His death was an overwhelming event in motor sports. Everyone connected with racing lost a friend, and a leader. The Can-Am series is a success today because of Bruce McLaren's successful designs, the over-powering racing team he led, and the inspiring example he set for competitors and spectators alike. We shall not see his like again, and are all poorer for his death.

Dan Gurney was signed as Team McLaren's second driver after McLaren's death. He drove brilliantly to beat Oliver at Mosport, but conflict between Gurney sponsor Castrol, and McLaren sponsor Gulf forced him out after Watkins Glen.

Young Canadian George Eaton led the the BRM team in the 1970 series, driving a BRM P154-Chevrolet. His best result was St. Jovite, where he finished third.

George Follmer, in the AVS Shadow, leading Jerry Titus at St. Jovite. The Shadow was destroyed after the race when a drunk, in a stolen car, smashed into its trailer. Although the car reappeared at Mid-Ohio, much modified, it was not as competitive as before in spite of quick Vic Elford being behind the wheel.

Koveleski (No. 54) pulls over in his McLaren M8b, to let Gurney and Stewart devour Adams' Ferrari. Stewart, in the foreground, was driving Jim Hall's revolutionary Chaparral 2J "reverse-hovercraft" and he surprised everyone by making fastest race lap before retiring. The lower pictures also show the 2J at speed in the race, its boxy outline, and the twin rear fans, driven by a 70 hp two-stroke twin-cylinder engine, which supply the suction which increase roadholding and cornering power.

Mosport Park

For the second straight year Mosport Park, in Canada, was the curtain raiser. The air at the race was noticeably subdued for McLaren's death affected driver and spectator alike. In spite of McLaren's death two orange McLarens were entered, the second for Dan Gurney. On paper they looked strongest but in practice Jackie Oliver's Autocoast Ti-22, the titanium based car which showed promise late in 1969, was 0″5 slower than that of Denis Hulme, and 1″3 behind pole-winner Gurney. Peter Revson was fourth, in the works Lola T-220 of Carl Haas, while Lothar Motschenbacher, in Hulme's 1969 car, and George Follmer, in the AVS-Shadow, filled row three.

The Shadow was a new approach to racing because it had a frontal profile half that of a McLaren M8D. Tiny 10-inch wheels kept the profile low. Less resistance meant more straight-line speed, and Follmer was over 190 mph down the Andretti Straight (next best was Gurney at 175 mph), but cornering was a diferent story entirely! George Eaton was quickest in row four, in Tony Southgate's BRM P154. Next was Bob Brown, quickest of the independents, in Gurney's 1968 "McLeagle". Other familiar names were Tony Dean, the "Giant Killer" in his Porsche 908, Jerry Titus, Canadian John Cordts, and New Zealand's Tasman Champ, Graeme Lawrence, in the "Spirit of Edmonton", owned by the citizens of Edmonton, Alberta. From the moment the flag dropped, however, it was business as usual for Team McLaren. Hulme led the first 44 laps, with Gurney and Oliver in his silage. Oliver passed Gurney after 22 laps, and an ailing Hulme on lap 44. All was not well with Hulme for his hands hurt badly, the engine was overheating, and his throttle was sticking. Hulme waved Gurney by, and the new McLaren recruit set out after Oliver, passing him on lap 60. From then on Gurney could not be caught, especially when Oliver was badly balked by Motschenbacher. Oliver finally shoved the balker off course, really damaging the American's car. But it was too late, and he was 16 seconds behind at the end, followed by Hulme, and "Giant Killer" Dean in his Porsche. Second level drivers filled the rest of the top 10, as Revson, Follmer, and Titus dropped out.

The initial race showed Team McLaren, as usual, the one to beat. Using 465 Chevrolet engines assembled at their new engine shop in Detroit, McLaren's organization was still tops. While some other teams (Eaton, Revson, Motschenbacher) were also using 465 Chevrolets, theirs were not as reliable as McLarens. Oliver, in fact, used a giant 494 Chevrolet.

St. Jovite

The St. Jovite race followed the same script, except that Oliver and the Autocoast Ti-22 were eliminated in a dramatic first lap accident. Cresting a rise on the Back Straight, Oliver's car became airborne, flipped, and was demolished. As the rest of the field slowed to miss the mess, Oliver struggled clear, miraculously unhurt. Gurney and Hulme were already gone. Gurney led the first seven laps, then Hulme took over for 14, but pitted with an overheating engine. Back out in 30 seconds, he soon took second from Motschenbacher, whose crew had completely rebuilt his car after its Mosport accident. Hulme's race ended after 50 laps, overheating did him in. Motschenbacher was second and George Eaton drove the collapsing BRM (suspension, loose seat, no tach) in to third, while Bob Brown was a good fourth in his McLeagle. With each race carrying a guaranteed $61,500 in prize money (plus accessory bonuses), and a Championship Fund of $200,000 for the top ten point scorers at the end of the year ($50,000 for first, $7,000 for tenth), it was obvious a reliable but not top-rank car, such as Dean's Porsche 908, or McCaig's 1969 McLaren M8C, could win a bundle through consistent finishes. So each race was primarily a two-event contest. The quick drivers ran off and hid, or didn't finish, while the majority of cars cluttered up the track, hoping to finish in the top ten.

Watkins Glen

1970's first US race was Watkins Glen. Mal Currie, the Executive-Director of the track, arranged for 13 of the Porsches, Lolas, and Ferraris from the previous day's 6-hour race to enter the Can-Am. The big news, however, was Jim Hall's new Chaparral 2J, with none other than World Champion Jackie Stewart at the wheel! Featuring a completely enclosed back, the car used the ground-effect principle to gain cornering advantage. An auxiliary engine provided power to drive two extractor fans, which sucked the air out from under the car, creating a partial vacuum. G.E.'s plastic-like Lexan skirts provided the necessary seal. Stewart was really impressed with the innovative car, and qualified third quickest, behind Hulme (using a 430 engine to combat overheating problems with the 465 Chevrolet), and Gurney. Revson, whose Lola was performing better, but still falling apart in the races, was fourth, while Andretti (Ferrari 512S) led the sportscars.

Race day was a scorcher and the track, already badly damaged from the last race, broke up even more during the pounding from the Can-Am cars. Hulme, whose car collected asphalt and grit in every pore, came home first, ahead of five Porsche 917s, and a Ferrari. Gurney, Stewart, and Revson put on a spirited fight for second early on, but each dropped out of contention with, respectively, over-heating, boiling brake fluid and vapor lock in the fan engine, and an oil leak. The Porsche Parade was lead by Siffert, who got within nine seconds of Hulme, after a planned fuel stop, only to spin off twice avoiding slower cars. The second best Can-Am car was Brown's McLeagle, in eighth. Thank heaven for the sportscars and their reliability!

Edmonton

The long trek to Edmonton, Alberta, produced few surprises. Team McLaren completed its first double of the year, as Hulme won from Gethin. Motschenbacher was a distant third, Brown fourth. But Gethin? The 30-year old Englishman took Gurney's place on the team when Gurney's ties to Castrol, and McLaren's ties to Gulf proved that oil on oil won't stop friction.

Mid-Ohio

Twisty, turny, Mid-Ohio was next to come. Motschenbacher broke the orange domination of the front row by ending up second quickest in practice, but Hulme blasted off into the lead when the flag dropped, and that was that. Motschenbacher led Revson and Gethin a merry chase for 27 laps until his brakes went spongy. Revson then took second, and Gethin third. The Lola driver, with confidence in his first Foltz prepared 465 Chevrolet, finished second, comfortably ahead of Motschenbacher, who took third when Gethin's engine died late in the race.

Road America Can-Am

A new wrinkle was added at the Road America Can-Am, the apparent winner was disqualified! Although Revson led lap one, the McLarens shot by him on lap two. That was it until lap 37 of 50, when Hulme spun in avoiding a slow car which "chopped" him in a corner. He pushed the starter button while corner workers moved him out of the turn, re-started, and led Gethin across the line, the apparent winner. The Stewards disqualified him for an illegal push start, however, declared Gethin the winner, and turned down team leader Teddy Mayer's protest. Mayer is now appealing the decision to ACCUS. Bob Bondurant, who came out of retirement to drive an old Lola T-160, with 427 Chevrolet, was second. None of the big names were in the top 10, except Gethin, and the slower, reliable drivers were again in clover as Causey, Wilson, Dean, etc., picked up valuable points.

Road Atlanta

Because the Bridgehampton track was all but washed away in a torrential summer rainstorm, the new, multi-million dollar, Road Atlanta racetrack, loveliest in the U.S.A., hosted race seven. The first time

Hulme after winning Watkins Glen. Although still bothered by his burns he triumphed over excessive heat, and a stiff challenge from the Porsche 917s.

The AVS Shadow, Mark 3. In the first two races the car's water and oil radiators were hidden inside the wing, with a horizontal two-inch slit channeling air to the radiators. The SCCA declared this arrangement illegal, however, and the radiators were repositioned on top of the body at Mid-Ohio. This effectively killed the low frontal area of the car (initially half that of a Team McLaren M8D), negating design advantages of the Shadow, with its tiny 10 and 12 inch wheels.

John Wyer's Gulf-Porsches provided Hulme's main challenge at Watkins Glen. Although all Porsches stopped for fuel, Siffert finished second, and Redman seventh after changing a flat.

◄ The Shadow reappeared at Mid-Ohio. With everything in miniature it would help to have both driver and crew about half normal size. But, as you see here, the mechanics tower over the miniature car, as did Elford when he drove it.

The first lap of race number five, Mid-Ohio, as the cars charge up to the Loop at the end of the Front Straight. Hulme leads Motschenbacher while Revson is narrowly in front of Gethin, in the second works McLaren M8D.

Ex-factory Mercedes mechanic, Lothar Motschenbacher drove his ex-Team McLaren M8B confidently throughout the season. Always quick, here he is on his way to third at Mid-Ohio after losing second to Revson because of failing brakes.

◄ *Pedro Rodriguez piloted three different cars in this year's Can-Am; the NART Ferrari pictured here at Mid-Ohio, a BRM P154, and a Porsche 917!*

Peter Revson, driving Carl Haas' semi-works Lola T220, was consistently quick throughout the season. But the team didn't start finishing races until switching to Foltz-prepared Chevrolets at Mid-Ohio, where Peter finished second.

The 1970 Can-Am was the fourth consecutive Championship for Team McLaren. Driving a quick, strong, conservative race car, Hulme won the title for the second time as the innovative challengers, the Chaparral 2J and the Shadow, fell by the wayside. Here Hulme is on his way to victory at Mid-Ohio.

The ground-effect Chaparral 2J was modified for its second appearance, at Road Atlanta. The auxiliary snowmobile engine driving the fans was fuel injected to improve reliability, and the fan belts were placed behind the car, protected by a belt cover named the "Martian bra"! (left). The front of the car (top) shows how airflow presses the car down. Although quickest in practice, Elford had auxiliary motor problems in the race and finished sixth.

Oscar Koveleski, President of the Polish Racing Driver's Association, took to the dirt at Road Atlanta in his ex-Team McLaren M8B when the car dropped oil on the course. Others followed...

Can-Am cars had penetrated the Deep South, NASCAR ace Lee Roy Yarbrough helped boost attendance by driving the Agapiou Brother's Ford G7A. Road Atlanta was by far the most bizarre race in Can-Am history! For starters, Vic Elford, driving the revised Chaparral 2J, won the pole position. It was the first time since Gurney was quickest at Riverside in 1967 that a Team McLaren had been off the pole! Hulme, however, was confident of a McLaren victory. If only he knew! Two orange streaks, followed by Revson, shot by Elford at the start. Up the curves, and down the hills they charged, leading a snake of other cars. Although Elford got by Revson on lap three, he could make no impression on the flying McLarens. On lap 10 Hulme made a rare driving error, smacking Gary Wilson from behind while over-taking in a turn. That put Gethin into the lead, from Elford, but the Chaparral soon stopped for attention to its auxiliary fan motor. Gethin proceeded to get it all wrong coming in to Turn 5, but saved himself as he went off the track on the left, bounced over some asphalt corner markers, and tore off the left front nosepiece—which the befuddled corner workers left sitting in the road for five minutes! When Gethin pitted, Revson led. Ten laps later the unlucky New Yorker had a monumental accident when a rear tire suddenly deflated at 170 mph. Bob Brown, now in the lead, arrived on the scene with his brakes hard on but could not avoid the wreck, smashing his car into Revson's at 30 mph. Although badly bruised, Revson had scrabbled to safety. With Revson and Brown out on the same lap George Eaton, in the fragile BRM, took over the hot seat! But Gethin was back on course, and reeling in the unreliable BRM. Eaton's lead lasted 19 laps, until his engine died. Gethin took over and another McLaren victory looked sure. But the Fates weren't through! Gethin pitted with gearbox problems, and was black flagged for speeding out of the pits. It made no difference as the gearbox packed-up on lap 66, and none other than Tony Dean led the rest of the way. TONY DEAN?! He snapped Team McLaren's 19-race winning streak, and won a cool $16,450. With all the quick drivers smashing up, the slower privateers had another field day with Causey, Kovoleski, and McCaig picking up points.

... principally Tom Dutton, who was smashed into by Ron Goldleaf before Dutton could restart his car. Neither driver was hurt, fortunately, but both cars were out of the race, and complete write offs.

Donnybrooke

Revson put his new, lengthened Lola T220 on the pole at Donnybrooke when Hulme and Gethin had practice problems. Chris Amon debuted the Robin Herd designed March 707, as a result of SCCA Pro Racing Director Jim Kaser's trip to Europe to drum up more competition. Although Amon's rear suspension went awry as he finished his quickest practice lap, he managed third fastest time, between Hulme and Gethin.

Practice was deceiving, however, for the orange cars reasserted their superiority with a one-two finish, Hulme over Gethin. Amon ran well in third, but ran out of gas at the end, losing third to Revson, and finishing fifth. A promising start, nevertheless, for the March. The series moved to California for the last two races, amidst rumors of the return of Autocoast and Oliver, and several European stars. But Hulme was secure at the head of the points table, and Gethin was only one point behind Motschenbacher.

Laguna Seca

The rumors were half right, for Oliver reappeared with a lower, longer, wider, more powerful Ti-22. But Elford's Chaparral was the practice sensation, almost two seconds quicker than anyone else! The Chaparral 2J was instantly favorite for the race. Ha! The car threw a rod Sunday morning and, because an engine change is really complicated, the car did not start. In the race it was McLarens as usual, and Hulme, using a new high silicon aluminium engine with no cylinder liners, beetled off into the lead, followed by Gethin, with Revson, Oliver, and Amon tagging along behind. Oliver managed to get around Revson on lap 35, and closed right up on Hulme when Gethin spun out and could not restart two laps later. But the young Englishman could not pass, nor force Hulme into a driving error, and the New Zealander won, 1″2 ahead, clinching his second Can-Am Championship with the victory. Revson was third, a lap down after a lecture for passing under the yellow flag, and brakeless Amon led a flag-to-flag fight between Rodriguez and Parsons, won by the Mexican. It was the best 1970 race to date, and everyone anticipated a super dust-up at Riverside in the finale.

Riverside

Riverside was, however, an anticlimax. Elford did his practice thing, in the smog, winning the pole by 2″2 from Denny Hulme, but the auxiliary motor crumped out when the race started and he was never a threat. Revson and Gethin retired early on, with cooling problems and a blown engine, and the race was a familiar orange procession, with Hulme holding Oliver at bay by four to eight seconds throughout. Amon ran third, ahead of Rodriguez and Motschenbacher, but finished fourth after a last lap stop for gas let Rodriguez move up. Bob Brown was sixth, and Tony Adamowicz was seventh, in the second Motschenbacher McLaren, while reliable Causey, Dean, and McCaig completed the top ten. Thus ended the 1970 Canadian-American Challenge Cup Series.

Conclusion

The final Championship point standings for the post-season $200,000 melon showed Hulme on top, with six wins and 132 points, second place Motschenbacher's 65 points. Gethin, who did seven races, was third (56), while top-of-the-old-reliables Dave Causey was fourth. Oliver, with three seconds in four races, was fifth, and Porsche 908 man Tony Dean, sixth. Gurney, Revson, Brown, and top Canadian Roger McCaig, filled the last four spots. Hulme's total winnings soared over $150,000 for the second straight year!

The appearance of several top-flight drivers, with competitive cars, at the end of 1970 augurs well for the 1971 series. There are also indications the sluggish American economy is moving up, which would make it easier for competitors to find sponsors. If the Ti-22, the March, the Chaparral, and Lola, develop well, and if there are some new faces and cars for 1971, the series could finally hit the big-time in terms of close fought, exciting competition.

The organizers, the SCCA and CASC, could help their cause in two ways. They have refused, so far, to address the problem of non-competitive cars participating in the series. The have been innumerable incidents of slower cars balking, chopping, and causing accidents with quicker cars. For 1971 the organizers must set an arbitrary limit on the number of starters in each race. This would move the "rolling chicanes" off course, and improve the racing. At the same time reducing the Championship Fund and payout at each race in order to offer starting money might lure more top-flight manufacturers, such as Porsche, Lotus, Ferrari, or Chrysler, into the ring. Keeping the Series at its present ten-race size, and following some of these suggestions would make the Can-Am the most exciting racing in the world.

Was 1970 the last year of Team McLaren's reign? They won, as usual, because, as usual, they were better prepared. But they also proved their class in 1970, for no team has suffered as much in one year and come back to finish such convincing winners of a major international championship. Their 1970 victory is a fine tribute to Bruce McLaren. For 1971 they are on their own, but don't bet against them—there's just too much talent in Colnbrook!

5
7
51
11
47
14
LOLA

George Eaton retired the BRM-Chevrolet at Watkins Glen but he's not quitting in this scene.

At Mid-Ohio Pedro Rodriguez stands around with Miss Ohio, Donna Sims. Promises, promises.

Jim Hall. He brought suction to motor racing (wings too) and started all kinds of trouble.

◄ Hulme leads Gethin and Revson on the pace lap at Road Atlanta, the first Can-Am race in the South. All three drivers retired, however, and the surprised winner was Dean in his Porsche 908!

Dan Gurney at Mosport where he won the first race of the series, in a works McLaren.

Denny Hulme has a look at new-boy Gethin's McLaren at Mid-Ohio. The New Zealander won but Gethin retired with engine trouble.

Andretti in 512 S Ferrari at Watkins Glen where he finished third the day before Can-Am race.

Vic Elford won distinction at Road Atlanta as first non-McLaren driver to gain 1970 pole.

Revson in at the pits at Mid-Ohio. He took his Lola into second, behind Hulme.

New Zealander Graeme Lawrence, Tasman Champ, drove "Spirit of Edmonton" in 1970 Can-Am series.

Sensation of Laguna Seca Can-Am was the performance of Oliver and the Ti22 "titanium" car. Winner Hulme is behind the Englishman.

Close-up of Oliver in the Norris Industries Ti22 Mk 2. He finished second at Laguna Seca, only 1.2 seconds behind Hulme's McLaren M8D.

Top : The Can-Am received a good boost at Donnybrooke when Chris Amon debuted the March 707. Designed by Robin Herd, former McLaren designer, the car had a fifth, and two fourths in the last three races. Centre : New Zealander Graeme Lawrence was the driver of the « Spirit of Edmonton", an updated McLaren M12 owned by the citizens of Edmonton, Alberta. His best finish was seventh at Road America. Bottom : After his car was destroyed in a spectacular accident at Road Atlanta Peter Revson raced a new, longer Lola T220 at Donnybrooke, and finished third! 1970 was Revson's best Can-Am year so far. ▸

A relaxed Hulme before the Road Atlanta race. Dean's Porsche won, and Elford made fastest practice lap with the Chaparral ! ▸

STP
OIL TREATMENT
77
Firestone
UNION

SPIRIT
EDMONTON
14
UNION
STP

L&M
LOLA
26

REYNOLDS
Coca-Cola
Gulf
BOSCH
GERMANY
SPARK PLUGS

Indianapolis 500-Mile Race

Indianapolis, May 30, 1970

Lovingly promoted as the World's Greatest Race, the Indianapolis 500 is THE biggest event of the year in spectacle-starved Indianapolis. A full month of parades, breakfasts, cocktail parties, and whoop-dee-festivities surrounding the annual classic are a diverting way to keep interest high for what is, essentially, a long, drawn-out prelude to a high-speed 500-mile endurance race.

For the first time at any race the prize and accessory money was more than a million dollars, $1,000,002 to be exact! But 1970 was different for another reason. For many years the 500 has been the only USAC 500-mile race. No longer. In September the new Ontario Speedway in California staged its first 500-mile race, and another is planned in Pennsylvania. No one is worrying about the future of the Speedway, but the Memorial Day Classic is no longer one of a kind.

The first year of the new decade brought little innovation to the Speedway. With four-wheel-drive and turbine power now outlawed, or contained by restrictive legislation, most of the cars were updated 1969, or earlier models. And, for the first time, every starter used a turbo-charged engine!

Andy Granatelli, however, had a new car for his driver, 1969-winner Mario Andretti. Far and away the most talented American driver, Andretti was pleased with his German-made McNamara, designed by Joseph Karasek. Unfortunately, a wheel bearing seized while Andretti was practicing, and the resultant crash destroyed the car. Some of its parts were used in building up a new McNamara, but, unlike the first car, the replacement was not designed specifically for Indy.

Dan Gurney, runner-up in 1968, and 1969, with his stock-block Eagle-Ford, reverted to a Len Terry design for his 1970 Eagle, and used an Offenhauser engine. Although stock-block engine size had been increased for 1970, Gurney felt they were no longer competitive with the turbo-charged engines. 1970 Eagles were supplied by Gurney to Bobby Unser, Gordon Johncock, and Lee Roy Yarbrough. But delivery was late and the drivers all drove older Eagles in the race. Once again the Eagle was the most popular chassis, nine started the race.

A most impressive debut at the Speedway was made by Bruce McLaren's McLarens. From the first day of practive, when all three cars were out and running (to the surprise of Indy regulars accustomed to seeing cars dribble into Gasoline Alley for the first two weeks in May), everyone talked about the cars, and the enthusiastic, detailed approach of the Kiwis. One of the most interesting details of the McLaren, unique in the field, was a hydraulic jack on the front suspension. By working levers in the cockpit the driver adjusted the front suspension to full/low fuel loads, and track conditions, Simple and straight forward in design, the McLaren was also an easy car for the mechanics to work on.

The Society of American Engineers, Indiana Chapter, was so impressed with the cars they presented Bruce McLaren a Certificate of Recognition. This singular honor for a first time entrant was richly deserved.

But if the McLarens were well-designed, there were unforeseen driver problems. Denis Hulme and Chris Amon were scheduled to drive. Hulme scratched from the race after he received third-degree burns to his feet, hands, and left arm, when a fuel tank vent cap flipped off, filling his car's cockpit with burning methanol during a practice run. While McLaren hunted for another driver Amon found he just couldn't get up to competitive speeds. Chrissy returned to Europe, leaving McLaren with no drivers. But eventually Peter Revson, who drove beautifully in 1969 taking his Brabham-Repco from 33rd to fifth, and Carl Williams, were chosen. Both took to the cars immediately and were soon turning laps in the high 160s.

There were other well-prepared cars in Gasoline Alley. Mark Donohue had a new, two-wheel drive Lola T-153, with Ford engine. Designer Eric Broadley was around to help with the car's development. As usual, the Penske people turned out an immaculate car. Former winner Parnelli Jones entered two George Bignotti-built P.J. Colts (based on Lolas). Using Ford power, the cars were exquisitely prepared for Al Unser, and Joe Leonard. A.J. Foyt's Coyote-Ford was also lovely, and efficient, as A.J. looked for his fourth Indianapolis win.

Jack Brabham, the man who started the rear-engine revolution in 1961, with the 2.7 litre Cooper-Climax, arrived late in May with a new Brabham, the BT 32. Lower and wider than the 1969 car, Brabham was using an Offenhauser engine for the first time. He qualified comfortably after three days of practice.

In spite of the presence of many competitive cars, Al Unser, in his P.J. Colt-Ford, "The Johnny Lightning Special," took charge of practice from the moment he arrived. Leading the USAC Championship coming into Indianapolis, many felt Al was out to atone for his disastrous 1969 Indy, which he sat out after breaking a leg while horsing around on a motorcycle! Unser was the only driver who seemed able to go over 170 mph at will. Everyone predicted record qualifying speeds this year, but it was not to be. Al Unser won the pole at 170.221 mph, 3 m. 31.49 s. for the 10-mile qualifying trip, a scant 1/100th of a second ahead of Johnny Rutherford in 1966 Eagle-Offenhauser! It was the closest race ever for the pole. A.J. Foyt took the outside position in the front row at 170.004 mph, while Donohue, Andretti, Bobby Unser, and Gurney also qualified the first day. Revson was quickest on Sunday, at 167.942 mph, but Lloyd Ruby, the amiable Texan who is Hard-Luck Champ of the Speedway, blew up three engines in two cars trying to qualify. Ruby qualified the next weekend, with Jack Brabham. When the bomb went off signalling the end of qualifying, the 33-car field had averaged 167.139 mph, a record. There was exactly 6.2 seconds, and 4.8 mph, between quickest qualifier Unser, and slow man Simon.

Showers on race day delayed the start. Then, on the pace lap, Malloy's Gerhardt had a torsion bar fail, sending the car into the wall.

After the debris was cleaned up the race got underway, an hour and ten minutes late. Johnny Rutherford led through the first two turns as Al Unser hung back to see what Johnny had. By the end of the lap Unser was in the lead. Except for brief periods during his first and second pit stops, when others led, no one came close to challenging the blue and gold "Johnny Lightning Special." Al Unser completely dominated the 54th running of the Indianapolis 500, leading 190 of the 200 laps!

The main interest in the first 50 laps was supplied by Lloyd Ruby. He started from the ninth row, but no one expected him to be down there for long. In characteristic style, Ruby came charging through the field. Tenth after five laps, and seventh after 22, Ruby passed McCluskey for fourth, and took Bobby Unser for third on lap 34. When the leaders changed during the first pit stops Ruby was ready. Unser and Rutherford went in, and then Foyt. Suddenly Ruby was in the lead, and the fans stood as one and cheered the brilliant performance. Leading at Indy is, however, the kiss of death for Ruby. In 1968 and 1969 he led, only to retire. This year he went out on lap 57 when oil leaking from a defective seal set his car on fire. Donohue then led, but passed the torch to Brabham, who was passed by Unser when he pitted. At 60 laps, 150 miles, Unser led from Foyt, followed by Rutherford, Bobby Unser, Leonard, and McCluskey. Donohue, Brabham, Muther, and Revson filled the top 10. Andretti was having an awful time with his McNamara, and had called at the pits several times. Describing himself as "an accident waiting to happen," he hung on grimly, fighting the car through the turns in very scary style. Gurney, too, was in trouble. His crew could find nothing wrong, however, and the big Californian pressed on just out of the top ten after his stops. Both McLarens were still going, but Revson's engine was fluffy, and Williams' car had lost fourth gear early on and was running in third, albeit almost as quickly. Donohue was going pretty well, but unable to challenge for the lead as he had set up the car with too much understeer. As the track became hotter and slicker the understeer intensified, and Donohue was doing well to keep the car on the track!

Only A.J. Foyt, then, looked able to keep pace with the leader. And, because Foyt is smart and prefers to tag along, and then blister the opposition in the last 100 miles, Indy railbirds were anticipating an exciting finish! Foyt's threat, never materialized. First, a goofed-up pit stop cost him dearly. Arriving for fuel, Foyt found his pit full of teammates' Coyotes. He had to go around. again, losing almost a full lap to Unser. And, secondly, during the annual end-of-the-race accident, his top gear disappeared, leaving him in low gear for the last 25 laps.

The inevitable accident, on lap 173 this year, was spectacular, but non-injurious. McCluskey, driving relief for Kenyon, lost a wheel and spun down the track hitting the wall, and catching fire. Bucknum spun to avoid McCluskey, and both cars came to rest in turn 3, with McCluskey's blazing merrily

Firestone
Ford
2
JOHNNY

◀ *Unser in the Bignotti-prepared Parnelli Jones Colt with turbo-charged Ford engine, not only fastest in practice, won and led for 191 of the 200 laps.*

▲ *Mark Donohue was on the second row of the grid at the start with his turbo-charged Lola-Ford T152, led for a few laps, and finally finished second.*

The consistent Gurney finished third with his Olsonite Eagle, powered by a turbo-charged Offenhauser. The previous year he finished second.

◄ *Al Unser, a member of the amazing speed family, won the 1970 Indianapolis 500, was second in 1967. His elder brother Bobby won the race in 1968.*

Unser rockets back into the race after making one of his lightning-fast pit-stops. McCluskey passes in his Scorpion with turbo-charged Ford engine.

away. The remaining cars took to the infield grass, and it was during this manoeuvre Foyt's transmission packed up. Brabham had to change all four tires after spinning to avoid the accident, and the resultant strain on a weak engine put him out at 175 laps, with a broken piston. But taking to the grass was a blessing for Andretti. Bouncing through the rough he heard a "POP!" Suddenly his car was handling perfectly! The right-rear drive shaft was finally back in place, and Andretti ran out the race turning laps at 165 mph, moving up two places to finish sixth.

Al Unser was an easy winner, earning $271,700, plus a $30,000 bonus from car sponsor Topper Toys, for his three-hour drive. Donohue, who inherited second when Foyt fell back, won over $86,000. Dan Gurney nursed his ailing Eagle into third ($59,000), giving him finishes of 2-2-3 for the past three years. Donnie Allison, NASCAR ace but Indy rookie, was fourth in a Foyt Coyote-Ford, and won Rookie-of-the-Year, while teammate Jim McElreath was fifth. Andretti, Grant, Muther, and Williams, in his "third gear" McLaren, were all ahead of Foyt, who finished tenth. Although missing his fourth Indianapolis victory, AJ had some consolation in having three of his four cars in the top ten. Indianapolis 1970 was not a vintage year. But for the first 50 laps it was a fine, exciting contest. Al Unser had by far the best car, and was best prepared for the race. He deserved to win.

FASTEST ON EARTH FOR BLUE FLAME

Its a Gas

The Land Speed Record was raised to 622.438 mph when brave young American Gary Gabelich blasted The Blue Flame rocket-car across Bonneville Salt Flats on 23 October 1970. Californian Gabelich made his runs just in time before autumn rains came to ruin the surface of the famous Utah salt flats. His first run through the measured mile was at 617.6 mph, and he improved it to 627.3 on his second. His average of 622.438 mph was a sizeable improvement on the 600.6 mph LSR set up by Craig Breedlove five years earlier in the turbocar Spirit of America. Gabelich's car is 38 feet long and weighs nearly three tons. Sponsored by the American Natural Gas industry its power-unit burned natural gas and hydrogen peroxide fuel, and developed 16.000 lb. thrust—equivalent to 58.000 horsepower. There are only three wheels and none of them are driven. Thirty-year-old Gabelich had been racing and hot-rodding since high school. A former test astronaut, he also took part in environmental control studies which called for living in space capsules for days under simulated zero gravity conditions. The Land Speed runs called for patience as well as skill and courage, for the team had been trying for six weeks to break the record, but mechanical problems and unsuitable weather held them back until late October. The World's Fastest Man on Wheels looks pleased with his efforts. Goodyear produced special bias-belted tyres which were tested at speeds up to 1000 mph. They were hand-made with a large number of plies and virtually no tread.

Polish champion Zasada in the Porsche 911 S near Nairobi. He led the Safari before the last leg but was forced out with engine trouble.

◀ *Herrmann's Datsun in the rising sun near Subukia on the first leg of the Safari. "Road" conditions are very different to the "Monte"!*

Hakan Lindberg with the fuel-injected Saab 96 fought for second overall place until he retired during the second stage of the Swedish Rally. ▶

FEV 1H

Jean-Claude Andruet, European rally champion, with the Alpine-Renault 1600 during the 1970 Tour de Corse. *Alpine-Renault came within an ace of winning the 1970 Rally Championship—a victory in the British RAC Rally would have clinched it.*

The victorious Ford Escort of Mikkola and Palm speeds through the dust and cactus in the London-Mexico Marathon. Sponsored by the Daily Mirror, *the event was described as the longest hardest rally ever. Only 23 cars reached Mexico.*

Jochen Rindt, World Champion 1970

RESULTS

Drivers' World Championship

European Trophy for Formula 2

Manufacturers' World Championship

Canadian-American Challenge Cup

European Hill-Climb Championship

European Rally Championship

South African GP 2.435 miles

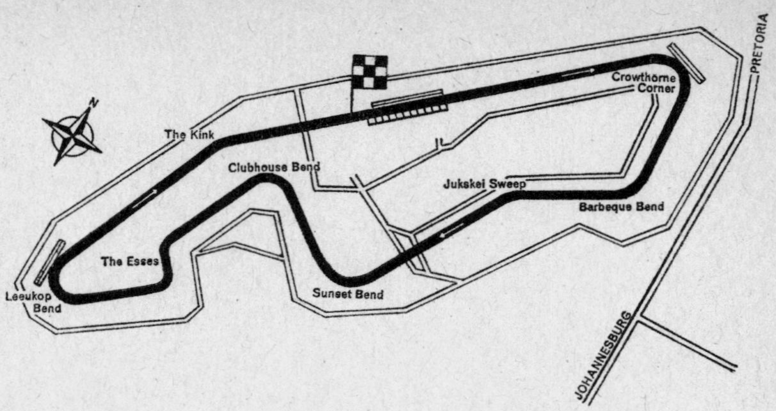

STARTING GRID

1. J. Stewart, March-Ford, V8, 1'19"3 — 15. C. Amon, March-Ford, V8, 1'19"3 — 12. J. Brabham, Brabham-Ford, V8, 1'19"6

9. J. Rindt, Lotus-Ford, V8, 1'19"9 — 17. J. Ickx, Ferrari, Flat-12, 1'20"0

6. D. Hulme, McLaren-Ford, V8, 1'20"1 — 7. J. Surtees, McLaren-Ford, V8, 1'20"2 — 3. J.-P. Beltoise, Matra-Simca, V12, 1'20"2

16. J. Siffert, March-Ford, V8, 1'20"2 — 5. B. McLaren, McLaren-Ford, V8, 1'20"3

8. M. Andretti, March-Ford, V8, 1'20"5 — 19. J. Oliver, BRM, V12, 1'20"9 — 25. D. Charlton, Lotus-Ford, V8, 1'20"9

10. J. Miles, Lotus-Ford, V8, 1'21"0 — 14. R. Stommelen, Brabham-Ford, V8, 1'21"2

20. P. Rodriguez, BRM, V12, 1'21"3 — 2. J. Servoz-Gavin, March-Ford, V8, 1'21"4 — 4. H. Pescarolo, Matra-Simca, V12, 1'21"5

11. G. Hill, Lotus-Ford, V8, 1'21"6 — 22. P. Courage, de Tomaso-Ford, V8, 1'22"0

24. P. de Klerk, Brabham-Ford, V8, 1'22"7 — 23. J. Love, Lotus-Ford, V8, 1'23"1 — 21. G. Eaton, BRM, V12, 1'24"4

RETIREMENTS

No.	Driver	Make	Lap	
15	Amon . . .	March-Ford	15	overheating
19	Oliver	BRM	23	gear selectors
14	Stommelen . .	Brabham-Ford	24	engine
8	Andretti	March-Ford	27	overheating
5	McLaren . . .	McLaren-Ford	40	engine
22	Courage . . .	de Tomaso-Ford	40	suspension
2	Servoz-Gavin .	March-Ford	58	engine
21	Eaton.	BRM	59	engine
7	Surtees. . . .	McLaren-Ford	60	piston
17	Ickx	Ferrari	61	engine
9*	Rindt	Lotus-Ford	73	engine
25*	Charlton . . .	Lotus-Ford	74	flat tyre

* = classified

RESULTS

Pos.	No.	Driver	Make	Laps	Time
1.	12	BRABHAM	Brabham-Ford	80	1.49'34"6
2.	6	HULME	McLaren-Ford	80	1.49'42"7
3.	1	STEWART	March-Ford	80	1.49'51"7
4.	3	BELTOISE	Matra-Simca	80	1.50'47"7
5.	10	MILES	Lotus-Ford	79	
6.	11	HILL	Lotus-Ford	79	
7.	4	PESCAROLO	Matra-Simca	78	
8.	23	LOVE	Lotus-Ford	78	
9.	20	RODRIGUEZ	BRM	76	
10.	16	SIFFERT	March-Ford	75	
11.	24	de KLERK	Brabham-Ford	75	
12.*	25	CHARLTON	Lotus-Ford	73	
13.*	9	RINDT	Lotus-Ford	72	

* = DNF but classified

Winner's average: 111.700 mph.
Fastest lap: J. Surtees, McLaren No. 7 and J. Brabham, Brabham-Ford No. 12, 1'20"8; average: 113,614 mph (new record).

FORMER WINNERS

Year	Drivers	Make	Circuit	Average (mph)
1934	STRAIGHT . . .	Maserati	East London	95.43
1936	« MARIO » . . .	Bugatti	East London	87.33
1937	FAIRFIELD . . .	ERA	East London	89.25
1938	MEYER	Riley	East London	86.53
1939	VILLORESI . . .	Maserati	East London	99.67
1960 (Jan.)	FRERE	Cooper	East London	84.88
1960 (Déc.)	MOSS	Porsche	East London	89.24
* 1961	CLARK	Lotus	East London	92.20
* 1962	G. HILL	BRM	East London	93.57
* 1963	CLARK	Lotus	East London	95.10
* 1965	CLARK	Lotus	East London	97.87
1966	SPENCE	Lotus	East London	97.75
* 1967	RODRIGUEZ . .	Cooper	Kyalami	97.09
* 1968	CLARK	Lotus	Kyalami	107.81
* 1969	STEWART . . .	Matra	Kyalami	110.62

* = Counted towards World Championship.

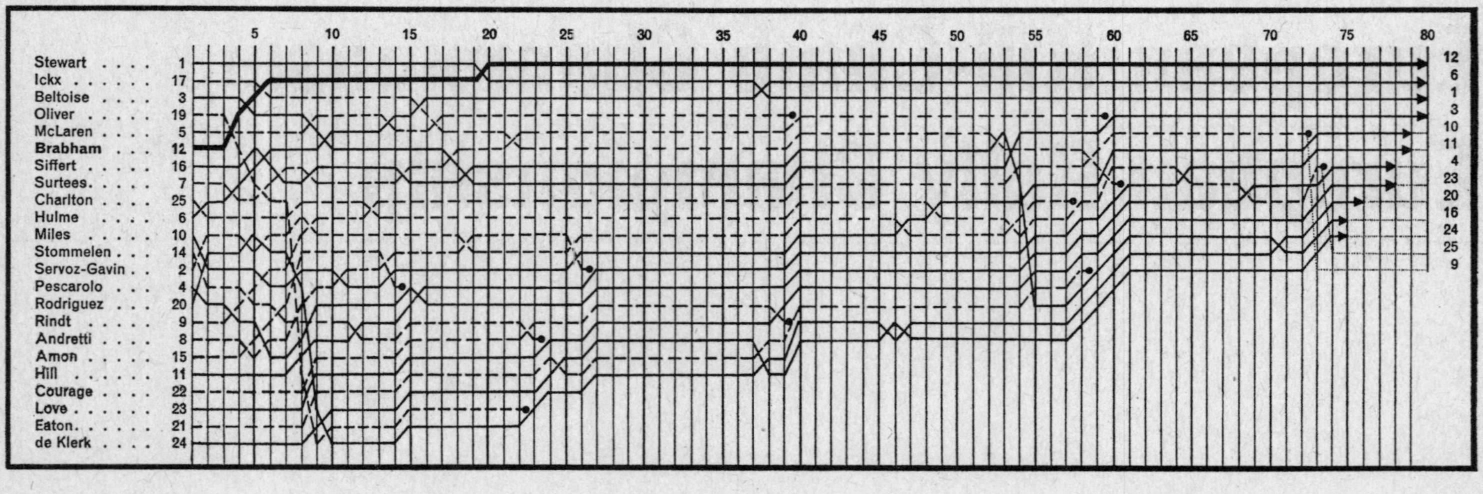

Gran Premio de España 2.112 miles

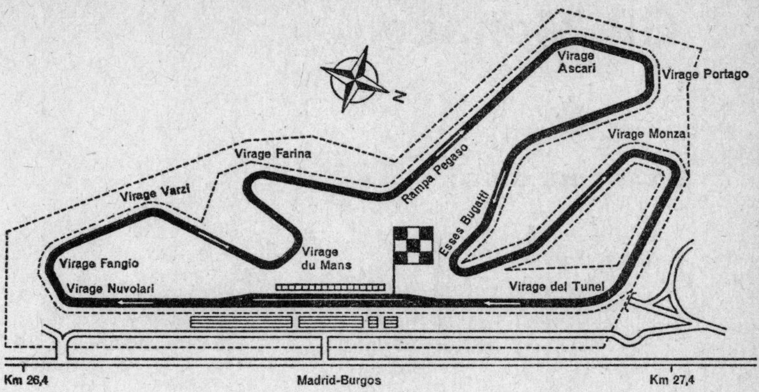

STARTING GRID

7. J. Brabham
Brabham-Ford
V8
1′23″9

5. D. Hulme
McLaren-Ford
V8
1′24″1

1. J. Stewart
March-Ford
V8
1′24″2

4. J.-P. Beltoise
Matra-Simca
V12
1′24″46

10. P. Rodriguez
BRM
V12
1′24″5

9. C. Amon
March-Ford
V8
1′24″65

2. J. Ickx
Ferrari
Flat-12
1′24″7

3. J. Rindt
Lotus-Ford
V8
1′24″8

22. H. Pescarolo
Matra-Simca
V12
1′24″9

15. J. Oliver
BRM
V12
1′25″0

11. B. McLaren
McLaren-Ford
V8
1′25″0

8. J. Surtees
McLaren-Ford
V8
1′25″2

12. P. Courage *
de Tomaso-Ford
V8
1′25″4

16. J. Servoz-Gavin
March-Ford
V8
1′25″46

6. G. Hill
Lotus-Ford
V8
1′25″54

18. M. Andretti
March-Ford
V8
1′25″7

24. R. Stommelen
Brabham-Ford
V8
No time

* = did not start

RETIREMENTS

No.	Driver	Make	Lap	
2	Ickx	Ferrari	1	accident
15	Oliver	BRM	1	accident
10	Rodriguez	BRM	5	withdrawn
3	Rindt	Lotus-Ford	10	ignition
59	Hulme	McLaren-Ford	11	engine
9	Amon	March-Ford	11	engine
4	Beltoise	Matra-Simca	32	engine
22	Pescarolo	Matra-Simca	34	engine
24	Stommelen	Brabham-Ford	44	engine
7	Brabham	Brabham-Ford	62	engine
8	Surtees.	McLaren-Ford	77	gearbox

FORMER WINNERS

Year	Drivers	Make	Circuit	Average (mph)
1923	DIVO	Sunbeam	Sitges	96.91
1924	SEGRAVE	Sunbeam	San Sebastian	64.08
1925	DIVO	Delage	San Sebastian	76.40
1926	GOUX	Bugatti	San Sebastian	76.40
1927	BENOIST	Delage	San Sebastian	80.52
1928	CHIRON	Bugatti	San Sebastian	80.58
1929	VARZI	Alfa Romeo	San Sebastian	71.52
1930	VARZI	Maserati	San Sebastian	86.82
1933	CHIRON	Alfa Romeo	San Sebastian	83.82
1934	FAGIOLI	Mercedes	San Sebastian	97.13
1935	CARACCIOLA. . . .	Mercedes	San Sebastian	102.40
1936	NUVOLARI	Alfa Romeo	Montjuich	69.20
1946	PELASSA	Maserati	Pedralbes	80.25
1948	VILLORESI	Maserati	Pedralbes	89.44
1950	ASCARI	Ferrari	Pedralbes	94.10
1951	FANGIO	Alfa Romeo	Pedralbes	98.76
1954	HAWTHORN	Ferrari	Pedralbes	98.01
1968	G. HILL	Lotus	Jarama	84.41
1969	STEWART.	Matra-Ford	Barcelona	92.91

RESULTS

Pos.	No.	Driver	Make	Laps	Time
1.	1	STEWART	March-Ford	90	2.10′58″2
2.	11	McLAREN	McLaren-Ford	89	2.11′02″4
3.	18	ANDRETTI	March-Ford	89	2.11′18″4
4.	6	HILL	Lotus-Ford	89	2.11′39″5
5.	16	SERVOZ-GAVIN . . .	March-Ford	88	2.12′05″3

Winner's average: 87.21 mph.

Fastest lap: J. Brabham, Brabham-Ford No. 7, 1′24″3; average: 90.33 mph (new record).

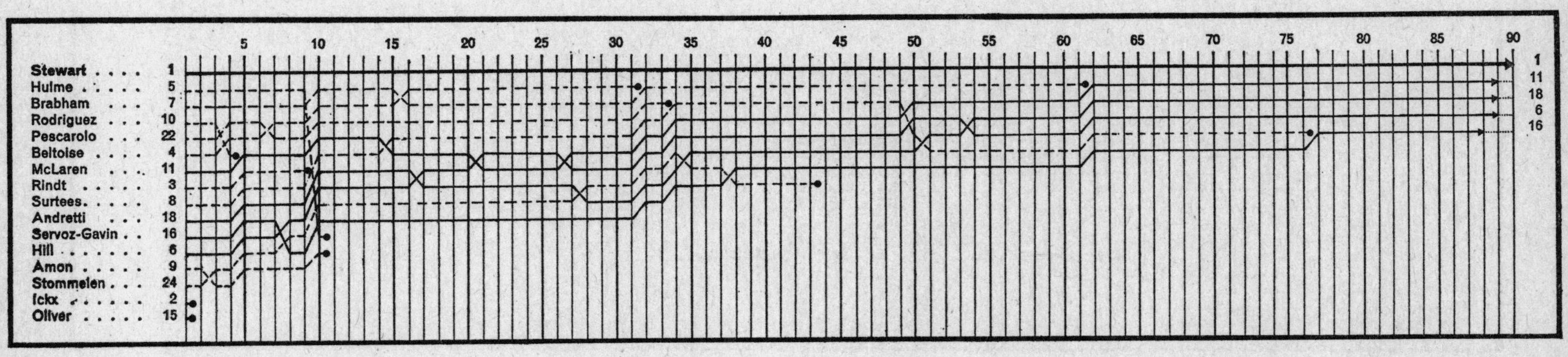

GP Monaco 1.95 miles

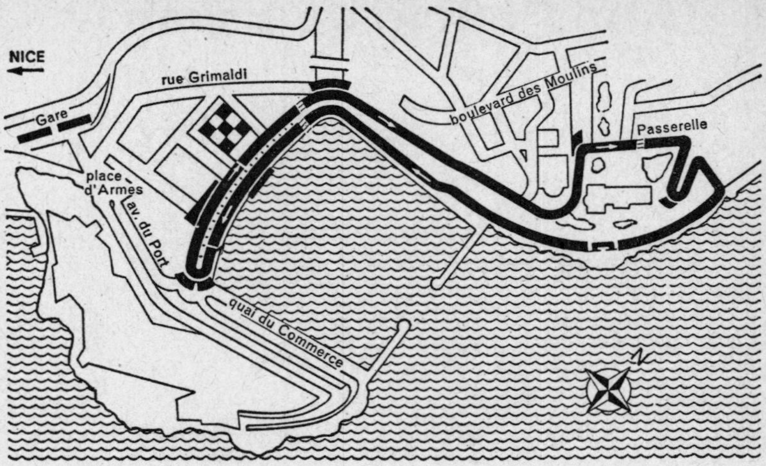

STARTING GRID

21. J. Stewart
March-Ford
V8
1'24"0

28. C. Amon
March-Ford
V8
1'24"6

11. D. Hulme
McLaren-Ford
11. D. Hulme
V8
1'25"1

5. J. Brabham
Brabham-Ford
5. J. Brabham
V8
1'25"4

26. J. Ickx
Ferrari
Flat-12
1'25"5

8. J.-P. Beltoise
Matra-Simca
V12
1'25"6

9. H. Pescarolo
Matra-Simca
V12
1'25"7

3. J. Rindt
Lotus-Ford
V8
1'25"9

24. P. Courage
de Tomaso-Ford
V8
1'26"1

12. B. McLaren
McLaren-Ford
V8
1'26"1

19. J. Siffert
March-Ford
V8
1'26"2

23. R. Peterson
March-Ford
V8
1'26"8

14. J. Surtees
McLaren-Ford
V8
1'27"4

16. J. Oliver
BRM
V12
1'27"5

17. P. Rodriguez
BRM
V12
1'27"8

1. G. Hill *
Lotus-Ford
V8
1'26"8

* = Hill used Miles' car for the race and so was at rear of the grid.

RESULTS

Pos.	No.	Driver	Make	Laps	Time
1.	3	RINDT	Lotus-Ford	80	1.54'36"6
2.	5	BRABHAM	Brabham-Ford	80	1.54'59"7
3.	9	PESCAROLO	Matra-Simca	80	1.55'28"0
4.	11	HULME	McLaren-Ford	80	1.56'04"9
5.	1	HILL	Lotus-Ford	79	
6.	17	RODRIGUEZ	BRM	78	
7.	23	PETERSON	March-Ford	78	
8.	19	SIFFERT	March-Ford	76	
*	24	COURAGE	de Tomaso	58	

* = not classified (less than 90 % of the total distance).

Winner's average: 81.84 mph.
Fastest lap: J. Rindt, Lotus-Ford No. 3, 1'23"2; average: 84.56 mph (new record).

RETIREMENTS

No.	Driver	Make	Lap	
26	Ickx	Ferrari	12	drive-shaft
14	Surtees. . . .	McLaren-Ford	15	oil pressure
12	McLaren . . .	McLaren-Ford	20	suspension after accident
8	Beltoise . . .	Matra-Simca	22	crown wheel and pinion
16	Oliver	BRM	43	engine
21	Stewart . . .	March-Ford	58	engine
28	Amon . . .	March-Ford	60	rear suspension

FORMER WINNERS

Year	Drivers	Make	Average (mph)
1929	« WILLIAMS »	Bugatti	49.66
1930	DREYFUS.	Bugatti	53.50
1931	CHIRON	Bugatti	53.94
1932	NUVOLARI	Alfa Romeo	55.67
1933	VARZI	Bugatti	56.91
1934	MOLL	Alfa Romeo	55.92
1935	FAGIOLI	Mercedes-Benz	58.03
1936	CARACCIOLA	Mercedes-Benz	51.52
1937	VON BRAUCHITSCH	Mercedes-Benz	63.11
1948	FARINA	Maserati	59.58
1950	FANGIO	Alfa Romeo	61.19
1952	MARZOTTO	Ferrari	58.03
1955	TRINTIGNANT	Ferrari	65.65
1956	MOSS	Maserati	64.79
1957	FANGIO	Maserati	64.54
1958	TRINTIGNANT	Cooper	67.82
1959	BRABHAM	Cooper	66.52
1960	MOSS	Lotus	67.27
1961	MOSS	Lotus	70.49
1962	McLAREN	Cooper	70.24
1963	G. HILL	BRM	72.23
1964	G. HILL	BRM	72.64
1965	G. HILL	BRM	74.30
1966	STEWART	BRM	77.29
1967	HULME	Brabham	76.68
1968	G. HILL	Lotus	77.81
1969	G. HILL	Lotus	80.18

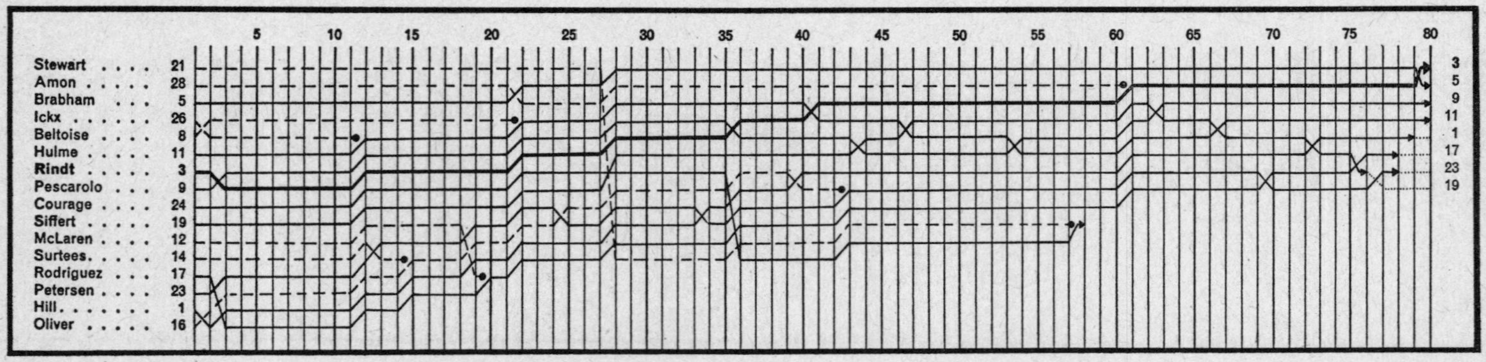

GP de Belgique 8.76 miles

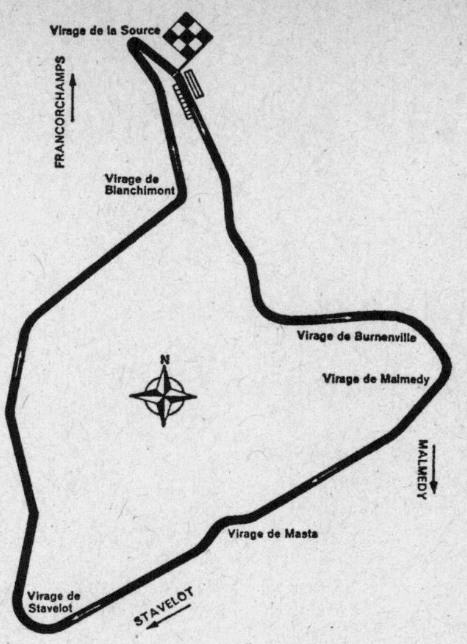

STARTING GRID

11. J. Stewart
March-Ford
V8
3'28"0

20. J. Rindt
Lotus-Ford
V8
3'30"1

10. C. Amon
March-Ford
V8
3'30"3

27. J. Ickx
Ferrari
Flat-12
3'30"7

18. J. Brabham
Brabham-Ford
V8
3'31"5

1. P. Rodriguez
BRM
V12
3'31"6

19. R. Stommelen
Brabham-Ford
V8
3'32"0

28. I. Giunti
Ferrari
Flat-12
3'32"4

14. R. Peterson
March-Ford
V8
3'32"8

9. J. Siffert
March-Ford
V8
3'32"9

25. J.-P. Beltoise
Matra-Simca
V12
3'32"9

7. P. Courage
de Tomaso-Ford
V8
3'33"0

21. J. Miles
Lotus-Ford
V8
3'33"8

2. J. Oliver
BRM
V12
3'34"2

8. D. Bell
Brabham-Ford
V8
3'36"2

23. G. Hill
Lotus-Ford
V8
3'37"0

26. H. Pescarolo
Matra-Simca
V12
3'37"1

RESULTS

Pos.	No.	Drivers	Make	Laps	Time
1.	1	RODRIGUEZ	BRM	28	1.38'09"9
2.	10	AMON	March-Ford	28	1.38'11"0
3.	25	BELTOISE	Matra-Simca	28	1.39'53"6
4.	28	GIUNTI	Ferrari	28	1.40'48"4
5.	19	STOMMELEN	Brabham-Ford	28	1.41'41"7
6.	26	PESCAROLO	Matra-Simca	27	
7.	9	SIFFERT	March-Ford	26	
8.	27	ICKX	Ferrari	26	
*	14	PETERSON	March-Ford	20	

* = not classified (less than 90 % of the total distance).

Winner's average: 157.210 mph
Fastest lap: C. Amon, March-Ford No. 10, 3'27"4; average: 152.076 mph (new record).

FORMER WINNERS

Year	Drivers	Make	Average (mph)
1925	ASCARI	Alfa Romeo	74.27
1930	CHIRON	Bugatti	71.96
1931	« WILLIAMS »	Bugatti	81.86
1933	NUVOLARI	Maserati	89.06
1934	DREYFUS	Bugatti	86.76
1935	CARACCIOLA	Mercedes-Benz	97.69
1937	HASSE	Auto-Union	103.88
1939	LANG	Mercedes-Benz	94.22
1946	CHABOUD	Delage	65.83
1947	WIMILLE	Alfa Romeo	95.10
1949	ROSIER	Talbot	96.77
1950	FANGIO	Alfa Romeo	109.79
1951	FARINA	Alfa Romeo	114.06
1952	ASCARI	Ferrari	102.89
1953	ASCARI	Ferrari	112.21
1954	FANGIO	Maserati	114.80
1955	FANGIO	Mercedes-Benz	118.56
1956	COLLINS	Ferrari	118.17
1958	BROOKS	Vanwall	129.63
1960	BRABHAM	Cooper	133.32
1961	P. HILL	Ferrari	127.86
1962	CLARK	Lotus	131.60
1963	CLARK	Lotus	113.84
1964	CLARK	Lotus	132.79
1965	CLARK	Lotus	117.16
1966	SURTEES	Ferrari	113.93
1967	GURNEY	Eagle	145.98
1968	McLAREN	McLaren	147.14

RETIREMENTS

No.	Driver	Make	Lap	
8	Bell	Brabham-Ford	1	gear shift lever
7	Courage	de Tomaso-Ford	5	engine
2	Oliver	BRM	8	engine
20	Rindt	Lotus-Ford	11	piston failure
21	Miles	Lotus-Ford	14	suspension
11	Stewart	March-Ford	15	engine
18	Brabham	Brabham-Ford	20	clutch failure
23	G. Hill	Lotus-Ford	20	engine

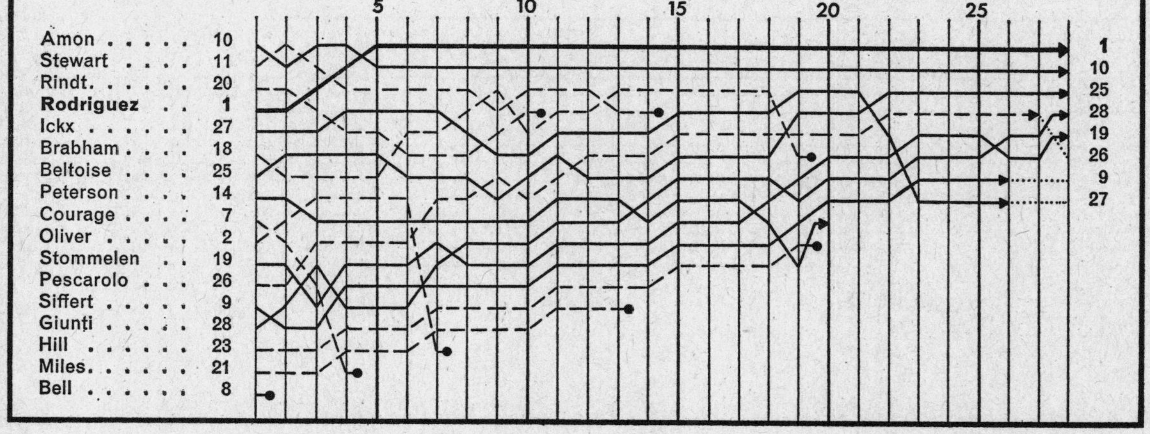

GP Nederland 2.6 miles

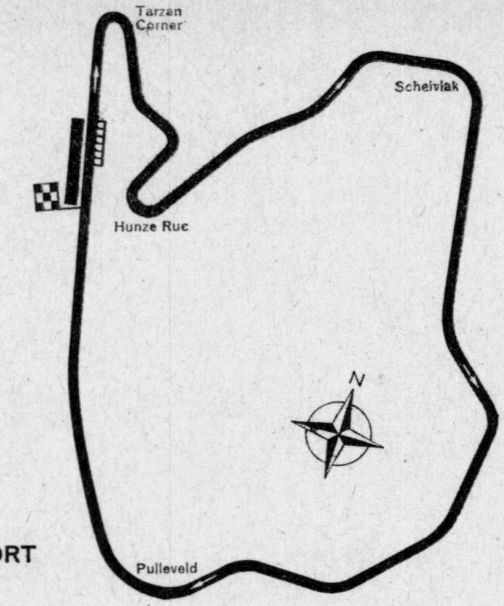

ZANDVOORT

STARTING GRID

25. J. Ickx
Ferrari
Flat-12
1'18"93

5. J. Stewart
March-Ford
V8
1'18"73

10. J. Rindt
Lotus-Ford
V8
1'18"30

2. J. Oliver
BRM
V12
1'19"30

8. C. Amon
March-Ford
V8
1'19"25

12. J. Miles
Lotus-Ford
V8
1'20"24

1. P. Rodriguez
BRM
V12
1'20"07

26. C. Regazzoni
Ferrari
Flat-12
1'19"48

23. J.-P. Beltoise
Matra-Simca
V12
1'20"38

4. P. Courage
de Tomaso-Ford
V8
1'20"32

24. H. Pescarolo
Matra-Simca
V12
1'20"89

18. J. Brabham
Brabham-Ford
V8
1'20"76

20. P. Gethin
McLaren-Ford
V8
1'20"41

6. F. Cervet
March-Ford
V8
1'21"18

16 J. Surtees
McLaren-Ford
V8
1'21"18

3. G. Eaton
BRM
V12
1'21"35

9. J. Siffert
March-Ford
V8
1'21"27

22. R. Peterson
March-Ford
V8
1'21"24

15. G. Hill
Lotus-Ford
V8
1'21"63

32. D. Gurney
McLaren-Ford
V8
1'21"36

RETIREMENTS

No.	Driver	Make	Lap	
8	Amon	March-Ford	1	clutch
32	Gurney	McLaren-Ford	3	engine
20	Gethin	McLaren-Ford	19	spun off
4	Courage	de Tomaso-Ford	23	accident
9	Siffert	March-Ford	23	engine
2	Oliver	BRM	24	engine
3	Eaton.	BRM	27	oil tank
6	Cevert	March-Ford	32	engine

RESULTS

Pos.	No.	Driver	Make	Laps	Time
1.	10	RINDT	Lotus-Ford	80	1.50'43"41
2.	5	STEWART.	March-Ford	80	1.51'13"41
3.	25	ICKX	Ferrari	79	
4.	26	REGAZZONI	Ferrari	79	
5.	23	BELTOISE	Matra-Simca	79	
6.	16	SURTEES	McLaren-Ford	79	
7.	12	MILES	Lotus-Ford	78	
8.	24	PESCAROLO	Matra-Simca	78	
9.	22	PETERSON	March-Ford	78	
10.	1	RODRIGUEZ	B.R.M.	77	
11.	18	BRABHAM	Brabham-Ford	76	
*	15	HILL	Lotus-Ford	71	

* = not classified (less than 90 % of the total distance).

Winner's average: 112.950 mph.
Fastest lap: J. Ickx, Ferrari No. 25, 1'19"23; average: 118.383 mph (new record).

FORMER WINNERS

Year	Drivers	Make	Average (mph)
1950	ROSIER	Talbot	76.45
1951	ROSIER	Talbot	78.28
1952	ASCARI	Ferrari	80.95
1953	ASCARI	Ferrari	80.86
1955	FANGIO	Mercedes	89.44
1958	MOSS	Vanwall	93.71
1959	BONNIER	BRM	83.24
1960	BRABHAM	Cooper	96.05
1961	VON TRIPS	Ferrari	95.98
1962	G. HILL	BRM	95.22
1963	CLARK	Lotus	97.30
1964	CLARK	Lotus	98.02
1965	CLARK	Lotus	100.86
1966	BRABHAM	Brabham	100.09
1967	CLARK	Lotus	103.44
1968	STEWART.	Matra	84.65
1969	STEWART.	Matra	111.04

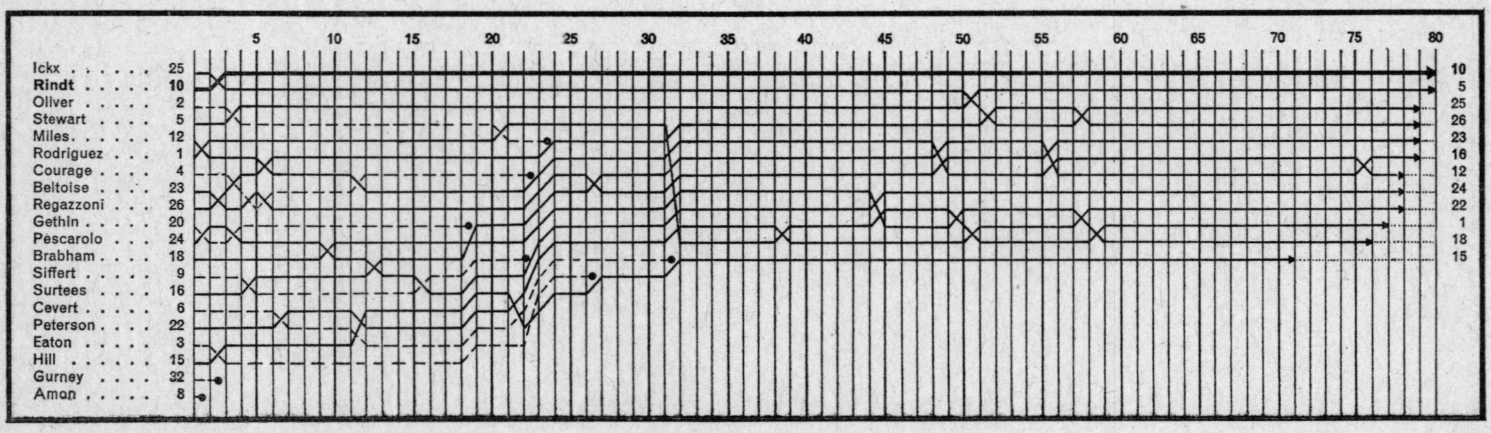

GP de France 5 miles

STARTING GRID

10. J. Ickx Ferrari Flat-12 2'58"22	21. J.-P. Beltoise Matra-Simca V12 2'58"70
14. C. Amon March-Ford V8 2'59"14	1. J. Stewart March-Ford V8 2'59"24
23. J. Brabham Brabham-Ford V8 2'59"67	6. J. Rindt Lotus-Ford V8 2'59"74
19. D. Hulme McLaren-Ford V8 3'00"42	20. H. Pescarolo Matra-Simca V12 3'00"59
18. R. Peterson March-Ford V8 3'01"21	3. P. Rodriguez BRM V12 3'01"29
11. I. Giunti Ferrari Flat-12 3'01"85	5. J. Oliver BRM V12 3'02"77
2. F. Cevert March-Ford V8 3'02"87	22. R. Stommelen Brabham-Ford V8 3'03"41
16. A. de Adamich McLaren-Alfa V8 3'03"48	12. J. Siffert March-Ford V8 3'03"78
1. D. Gurney McLaren-Ford V8 3'04"04	7. J. Miles Lotus-Ford V8 3'04"16
4. G. Eaton BRM V12 3'04"92	8. G. Hill Lotus-Ford V8 3'07"84

RESULTS

Year	No.	Drivers	Make	Laps	Time
1.	6	RINDT	Lotus-Ford	38	1.55'57"00
2.	14	AMON	March-Ford	38	1.56'04"61
3.	23	BRABHAM	Brabham-Ford	38	1.56'41"83
4.	19	HULME	McLaren-Ford	38	1.56'42"66
5.	20	PESCAROLO	Matra-Simca	38	1.57'16"42
6.	17	GURNEY	McLaren-Ford	38	1.57'16"65
7.	22	STOMMELEN	Brabham-Ford	38	1.58'17"16
8.	7	MILES	Lotus-Ford	38	1.58'44"17
9.	1	STEWART.	March-Ford	38	1.59'06"61
10.	8	HILL	Lotus-Ford	37	
11.	2	CEVERT	March-Ford	37	
12.	4	EATON	BRM	36	
13.**	21	BELTOISE	Matra-Simca	35	
14.	11	GIUNTI	Ferrari	35	
15.	16	de ADAMICH	McLaren-Alfa	29	

** = DNF but classified

Winner's average: 98.418 mph.
Fastest lap: J. Brabham, Brabham No. 23, 3'00"75; average: 99.686 mph (new record).

RETIREMENTS

No.	Driver	Make	Lap	
5	Oliver	BRM	6	ignition
3	Rodriguez	BRM	7	gearbox
10	Ickx	Ferrari	17	broken valve
18	Peterson	March-Ford	18	gearbox
12	Siffert	March-Ford	24	accident

FORMER WINNERS

Year	Drivers	Make	Circuit	Average (mph)
1906	SZISZ	Renault	Le Mans	62.74
1907	NAZZARO	Fiat	Dieppe	70.43
1908	LAUTENSCHLAGER .	Mercedes	Dieppe	68.88
1912	BOILLOT	Peugeot	Dieppe	68.32
1913	BOILLOT	Peugeot	Amiens	71.92
1914	LAUTENSCHLAGER .	Mercedes	Lyons	64.35
1921	MURPHY	Duesenberg	Le Mans	78.49
1922	NAZZARO	Fiat	Strasbourg	79.11
1923	SEGRAVE	Sunbeam	Tours	75.14
1924	CAMPARI	Alfa Romeo	Lyons	70.80
1925	BENOIST	Delage	Montlhéry	69.56
1926	GOUX	Bugatti	Miramas	67.85
1927	BENOIST	Delage	Montlhéry	78.12
1928	« WILLIAMS »	Bugatti	Comminges	84.63
1929	« WILLIAMS »	Bugatti	La Sarthe	82.46
1930	ETANCELIN	Bugatti	Pau	90.14
1931	CHIRON-VARZI . . .	Bugatti	Montlhéry	77.99
1932	NUVOLARI	Alfa Romeo	Reims	92.07
1933	CAMPARI	Maserati	Montlhéry	81.28
1934	CHIRON	Alfa Romeo	Montlhéry	84.81
1935	CARACCIOLA. . . .	Mercedes-Benz	Montlhéry	77.19
1936	WIMILLE-SOMMER .	Bugatti	Montlhéry	77.62
1937	CHIRON	Talbot	Montlhéry	82.27
1938	VON BRAUCHITSCH	Mercedes-Benz	Reims	100.87
1939	MÜLLER	Auto-Union	Reims	104.96
1947	CHIRON	Talbot	Lyons-Parilly	77.87
1948	WIMILLE.	Alfa Romeo	Reims	102.67
1949	CHIRON	Talbot	Reims	99.69
1950	FANGIO	Alfa Romeo	Reims	104.59
1951	FAGIOLI-FANGIO . .	Alfa Romeo	Reims	110.67
1952	ASCARI	Ferrari	Rouen-Les Essarts	79.91
1953	HAWTHORN	Ferrari	Reims	113.33
1954	FANGIO	Mercedes-Benz	Reims	115.69
1956	COLLINS	Ferrari	Reims	122.01
1957	FANGIO	Maserati	Rouen-Les Essarts	99.75
1958	HAWTHORN	Ferrari	Reims	125.11
1959	BROOKS	Ferrari	Reims	127.10
1960	BRABHAM	Cooper	Reims	131.50
1961	BAGHETTI	Ferrari	Reims	119.53
1962	GURNEY	Porsche	Rouen-Les Essarts	102.98
1963	CLARK	Lotus	Reims	124.99
1964	GURNEY	Brabham	Rouen-Les Essarts	108.77
1965	CLARK	Lotus	Clermont-Ferrand	89.20
1966	BRABHAM	Brabham	Reims	136.89
1967	BRABHAM	Brabham	Le Mans	98.92
1968	ICKX	Ferrari	Rouen-Les Essarts	109.39
1969	STEWART.	Matra-Ford	Clermont-Ferrand	97.71

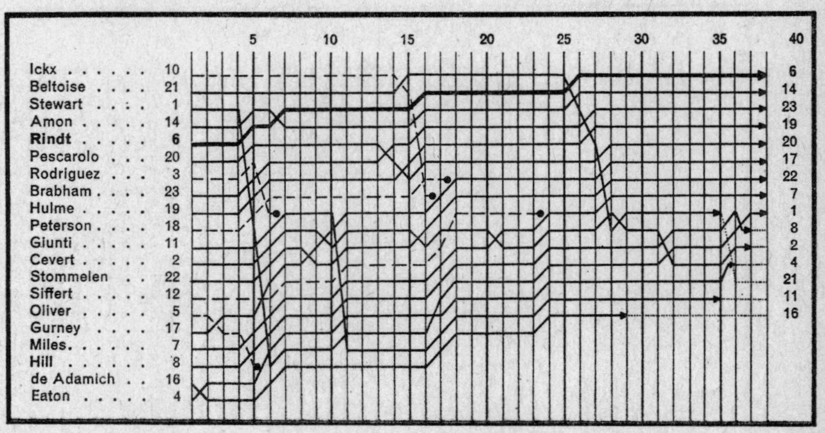

British GP 2.65 miles

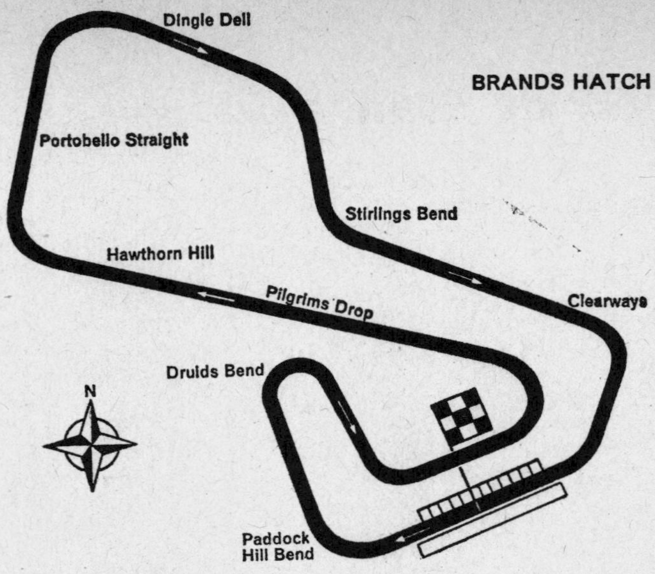

STARTING GRID

3. J. Ickx, Ferrari 312 B, Flat-12, 1'25"1 — 17. J. Brabham, Brabham-Ford, V8, 1'24"8 — 5. J. Rindt, Lotus-Ford, V8, 1'24"8

9. D. Hulme, McLaren-Ford, V8, 1'25"6 — 23. J. Oliver, BRM, V12, 1'25"6

1. J. Stewart, March-Ford, V8, 1'26"0 — 6. J. Miles, Lotus-Ford, V8, 1'25"9 — 4. C. Regazzoni, Ferrari 312 B, Flat-12, 1'25"8

7. J.-P. Beltoise, Matra-Simca, V12, 1'26"5 — 26. M. Andretti, March-Ford, V8, 1'26"2

27. R. Peterson, March-Ford, V8, 1'26"8 — 8. H. Pescarolo, Matra-Simca, V12, 1'26"7 — 10. D. Gurney, McLaren-Ford, V8, 1'26"6

22. P. Rodriguez, BRM, V12, 1'26"9 — 2. F. Cevert, March-Ford, V8, 1'26"8

11. A. de Adamich*, McLaren-Alfa, V8, 1'27"1 — 16. C. Amon, March-Ford, V8, 1'27"0 — 24. C. Eaton, BRM, V12, 1'26"9

15. J. Siffert, March-Ford, V8, 1'28"0 — 20. J. Surtees, Surtees-Ford, V8, 1'27"7

29. P. Lovely, Lotus-Ford, V8, 1'30"3 — 14. G. Hill, Lotus-Ford, V8, 1'28"4 — 28. E. Fittipaldi, Lotus-Ford, V8, 1'28"1

* = did not start

RESULTS

Pos.	No.	Driver	Make	Laps	Time
1.	5	RINDT	Lotus-Ford	80	1.57'02"0
2.	17	BRABHAM	Brabham-Ford	80	1.57'34"9
3.	9	HULME	McLaren-Ford	80	1.57'56"4
4.	4	REGAZZONI	Ferrari	80	1.57'56"8
5.	16	AMON	March-Ford	79	
6.	14	HILL	Lotus-Ford	79	
7.	2	CEVERT	March-Ford	79	
8.	28	FITTIPALDI	Lotus-Ford	78	
9.	27	PETERSON	March-Ford	72	
10.	29	LOVELY	Lotus-Ford	69	

Winner's average: 108.69 mph.
Fastest lap: J. Brabham, Brabham-Ford No. 17, 1'25"9; average: 111.06 mph.

RETIREMENTS

No.	Driver	Make	Lap	
3	Ickx	Ferrari	7	transmission
24	Eaton	BRM	11	oil pressure
6	Miles	Lotus 72	16	camshaft
15	Siffert	March-Ford	20	hub
26	Andretti	March-Ford	22	hub
7	Beltoise	Matra-Simca	25	wheel bearing
8	Pescarolo	Matra-Simca	42	left the road
20	Surtees	Surtees-Ford	52	engine
1	Stewart	March-Ford	53	fire
23	Oliver	BRM	55	engine
22	Rodriguez	BRM	59	left the road
10	Gurney	McLaren	61	oil pressure

FORMER WINNERS

Year	Drivers	Make	Circuit	Average (mph)
1926	SENECHAL-WAGNER	Delage	Brooklands	71.61
1927	BENOIST	Delage	Brooklands	85.59
1948	VILLORESI	Maserati	Silverstone	72.28
1949	DE GRAFFENRIED	Maserati	Silverstone	77.31
1950	FARINA	Alfa Romeo	Silverstone	90.95
1951	GONZALEZ	Ferrari	Silverstone	96.91
1952	ASCARI	Ferrari	Silverstone	90.92
1953	ASCARI	Ferrari	Silverstone	92.97
1954	GONZALEZ	Ferrari	Silverstone	89.70
1955	MOSS	Mercedes-Benz	Aintree	86.50
1956	FANGIO	Ferrari-Lancia	Silverstone	98.60
1957	BROOKS-MOSS	Vanwall	Aintree	86.80
1958	COLLINS	Ferrari	Silverstone	102.10
1959	BRABHAM	Cooper	Aintree	89.90
1960	BRABHAM	Cooper	Silverstone	108.70
1961	VON TRIPS	Ferrari	Aintree	83.91
1962	CLARK	Lotus	Aintree	92.25
1963	CLARK	Lotus	Silverstone	107.75
1964	CLARK	Lotus	Brand Hatch	94.14
1965	CLARK	Lotus	Silverstone	112.02
1966	BRABHAM	Brabham	Brands Hatch	95.49
1967	CLARK	Lotus	Silverstone	117.64
1968	SIFFERT	Lotus	Brands Hatch	104.82
1969	STEWART	Matra-Ford	Silverstone	127.25

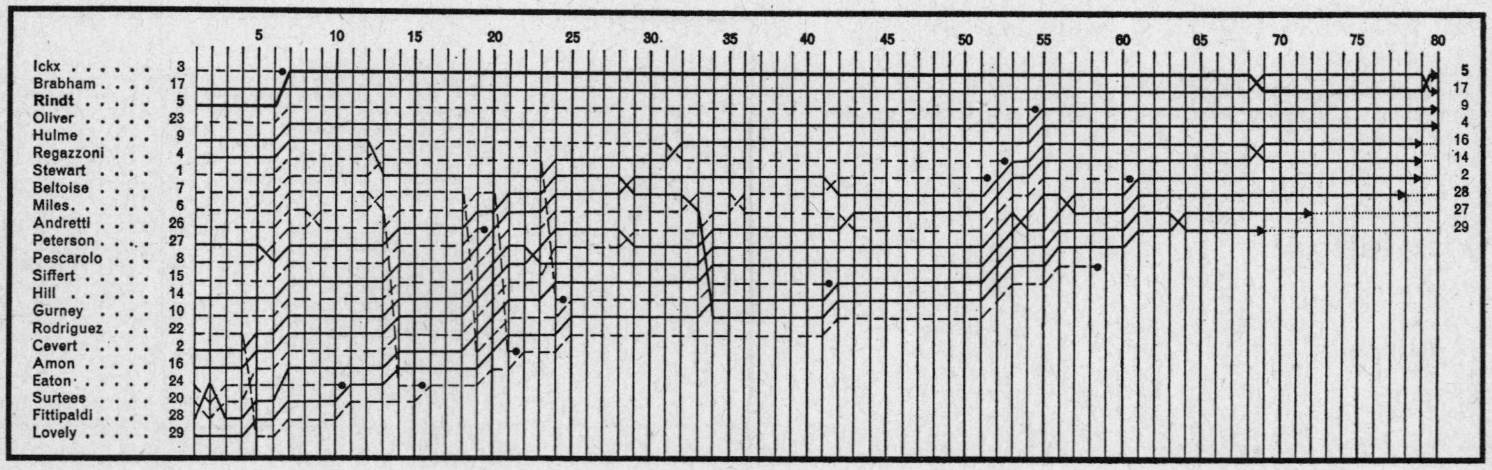

GP Deutschland 4.218 miles

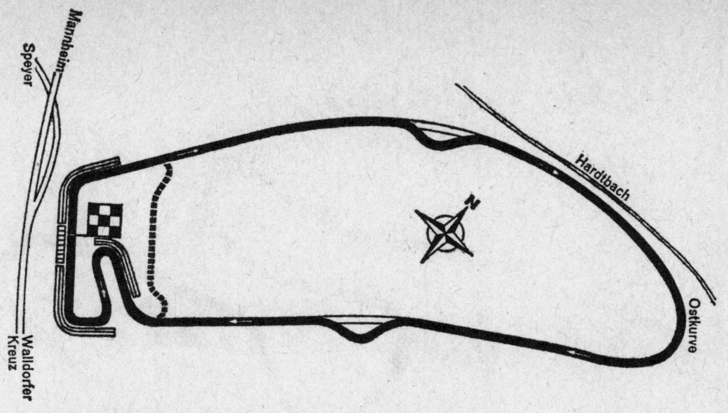

STARTING GRID

10. J. Ickx
Ferrari
Flat-12
1'59"5

2. J. Rindt
Lotus-Ford
V8
1'59"7

15. C. Regazzoni
Ferrari
V12
1'59"8

12. J. Siffert
March-Ford
V8
2'00"0

14. H. Pescarolo
Matra-Simca
V12
2'00"5

5. C. Amon
March-Ford
V8
2'00"9

1. J. Stewart
March-Ford
V8
2'01"0

6. P. Rodriguez
BRM
V12
2'01"1

11. M. Andretti
March-Ford
V8
2'01"5

16. J. Miles
Lotus-Ford
V8
2'01"6

21. R. Stommelen
Brabham-Ford
V8
2'01"6

3. J. Brabham
Brabham-Ford
V8
2'02"0

17. E. Fittipaldi
Lotus-Ford
V8
2'02"0

23. F. Cevert
March-Ford
V8
2'02"1

7. J. Surtees
Surtees-Ford
V8
2'02"1

4. D. Hulme
McLaren-Ford
V8
2'02"1

24. P. Gethin
McLaren-Ford
V8
2'02"2

18. J. Oliver
BRM
V12
2'02"3

22. R. Peterson
March-Ford
V8
2'02"4

9. G. Hill
Lotus-Ford
V8
2'03"0

8. J.-P. Beltoise
Matra-Simca
V12
2'05"2

RETIREMENTS

No.	Driver	Make	Lap	
24	Gethin	McLaren-Ford	4	engine
8	Beltoise	Matra-Simca	5	suspension
3	Brabham	Brabham-Ford	5	split oil union
18	Oliver	BRM	6	engine
6	Rodriguez	BRM	8	ignition
22	Peterson	March-Ford	12	engine
11	Andretti.	March-Ford	16	engine
1	Stewart	March-Ford	21	engine
16	Miles	Lotus-Ford	25	camshaft
15	Regazzoni	Ferrari	31	gearbox
5	Amon.	March-Ford	35	engine
9	Hill	Lotus-Ford	38	engine
7*	Surtees	Surtees-Ford	47	engine
12*	Siffert	March-Ford	48	ignition

* = classified

FORMER WINNERS

Year	Drivers	Make	Average (mph)
1926	CARACCIOLA.	Mercedes-Benz	83.76
1927	MERZ	Mercedes-Benz	63.24
1928	CARACCIOLA-WERNER	Mercedes-Benz	64.35
1929	CHIRON	Bugatti	66.27
1931	CARACCIOLA.	Mercedes-Benz	67.14
1932	CARACCIOLA.	Alfa Romeo	73.96
1934	STUCK	Auto-Union	76.26
1935	NUVOLARI	Alfa Romeo	75.08
1936	ROSEMEYER	Auto-Union	81.59
1937	CARACCIOLA.	Mercedes-Benz	82.58
1938	SEAMAN	Mercedes-Benz	80.47
1939	CARACCIOLA.	Mercedes-Benz	75.08
1950	ASCARI	Ferrari	77.50
1951	ASCARI	Ferrari	83.57
1952	ASCARI	Ferrari	82.02
1953	FARINA	Ferrari	83.70
1954	FANGIO	Mercedes-Benz	82.58
1956	FANGIO	Ferrari	85.37
1957	FANGIO	Maserati	88.59
1958	BROOKS	Vanwall	90.14
1959	BROOKS	Ferrari	143.03
1960	BONNIER	Porsche	80.10
1961	MOSS	Lotus	92.13
1962	G. HILL	BRM	80.10
1963	SURTEES	Ferrari	95.60
1964	SURTEES	Ferrari	96.56
1965	CLARK	Lotus	99.76
1966	BRABHAM	Brabham	86.75
1967	HULME	Brabham	101.47
1968	STEWART.	Matra	86.90
1969	ICKX	Brabham	108.43

RESULTS

Pos.	No.	Driver	Make	Laps	Time
1	2	RINDT	Lotus-Ford	50	1.42'00"3
2	10	ICKX	Ferrari	50	1.42'01"0
3	4	HULME	McLaren-Ford	50	1.43'22"1
4	17	FITTIPALDI . . .	Lotus-Ford	50	1.43'55"4
5	21	STOMMELEN . .	Brabham-Ford	49	
6	14	PESCAROLO . .	Matra-Simca	49	
7	23	CEVERT	March-Ford	49	
8**	12	SIFFERT	March-Ford	47	
9**	7	SURTEES	Surtees-Ford	46	

** = DNF but classified

Winner's average: 123.90 mph.
Fastest lap: J. Ickx, Ferrari 312 B No. 10, 2'00"5; average: 126.02 mph.

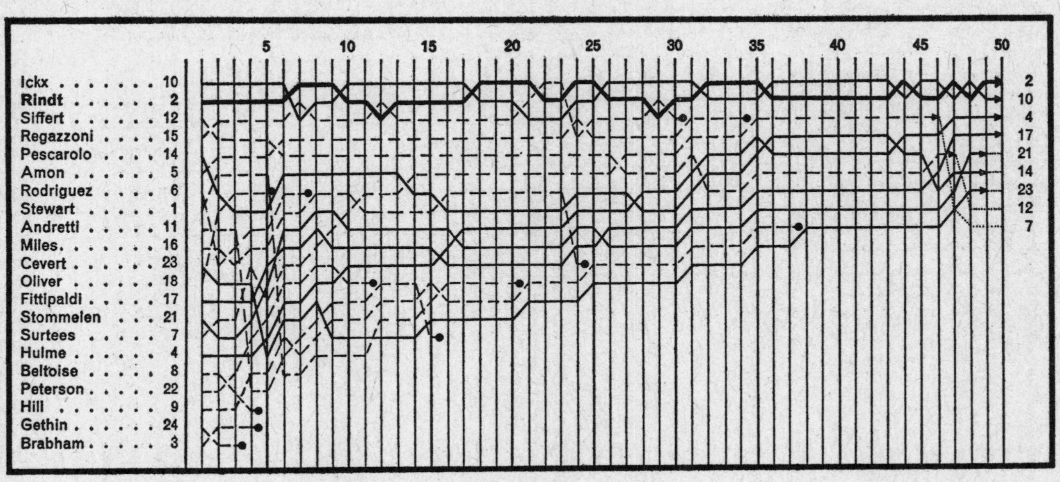

GP Österreich 3.734 miles

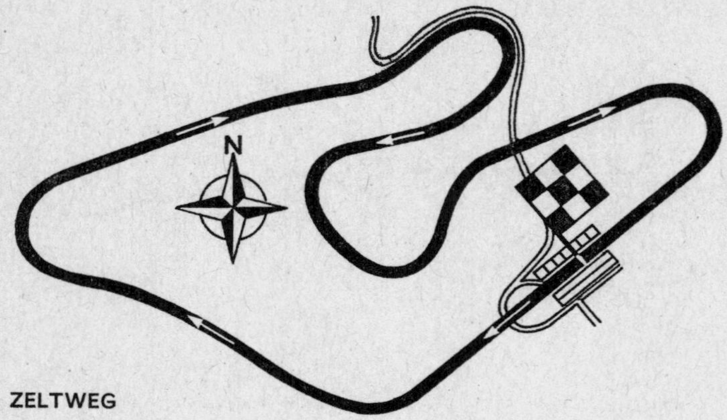

STARTING GRID

6. J. Rindt Lotus-Ford V8 1'39"2		27. C. Regazzoni Ferrari Flat-12 1'39"7
	12. J. Ickx Ferrari Flat-12 1'39"8	1. J. Stewart March-Ford V8 1'40"2
14. I. Giunti Ferrari Flat-12 1'40"3		4. C. Amon March-Ford V8 1'40"6
	19. J.-P. Beltoise Matra-Simca V12 1'40"8	10. J. Brabham Brabham-Ford V8 1'40"8
2. F. Cevert March-Ford V8 1'40"8		21. D. Hulme McLaren-Ford V8 1'41"4
	7. J. Miles Lotus-Ford V8 1'41"4	15. J. Surtees Surtees-Ford V8 1'41"5
20. H. Pescarolo Matra-Simca V12 1'41"7		16. J. Oliver BRM V12 1'41"7
	22. A. de Adamich McLaren-Alfa V8 1'41"8	8. E. Fittipaldi Lotus-Ford V8 1'41"9
11. R. Stommelen Brabham-Ford V8 1'42"1		5. M. Andretti March-Ford V8 1'42"3
	26. T. Schenken de Tomaso-Ford V8 1'42"4	3. J. Siffert March-Ford V8 1'42"5
23. P. Gethin McLaren-Ford V8 1'42"8		17. P. Rodriguez BRM V12 1'43"2
	18. G. Eaton BRM V12 1'45"0	24. S. Moser Bellasi-Ford V8 1'45"7

RESULTS

Pos.	No.	Driver	Make	Laps	Time
1.	12	ICKX	Ferrari	60	1.42'17"32
2.	27	REGAZZONI	Ferrari	60	1.42'17"93
3.	11	STOMMELEN	Brabham-Ford	60	1.43'45"20
4.	17	RODRIGUEZ	BRM	59	
5.	16	OLIVER	BRM	59	
6.	19	BELTOISE	Matra-Simca	59	
7.	14	GIUNTI	Ferrari	59	
8.	4	AMON	March-Ford	59	
9.	3	SIFFERT	March-Ford	59	
10.	23	GETHIN	McLaren-Ford	59	
11.	18	EATON	BRM	58	
12.	22	de ADAMICH	McLaren-Alfa	57	
13.	10	BRABHAM	Brabham-Ford	56	
14.	20	PESCAROLO	Matra-Simca	56	
15.	8	FITTIPALDI	Lotus-Ford	55	

Winner's average: 129.270 mph.

Fastest lap: J. Ickx and C. Regazzoni, Ferrari 312 B No. 12 and No. 27, 1'40"4; average: 131.705 mph.

RETIREMENTS

No.	Driver	Make	Lap	
2	Cevert	March-Ford	1	engine
7	Miles	Lotus-Ford	5	broken frontshaft
1	Stewart	March-Ford	8	fuel pump
5	Andretti.	March-Ford	14	left the road
24	Moser.	Bellasi-Ford	14	leaking radiator
6	Rindt	Lotus-Ford	22	engine
26	Schenken	Surtees-Ford	26	camshaft
15	Surtees	Surtees-Ford	28	valve spring
21	Hulme	McLaren-Ford	31	engine

FORMER WINNERS

Year	Drivers	Make	Average (mph)
1957	VOGEL	Porsche	132.0
1958	VON TRIPS	Porsche	121.5
1959	MARSH	Cooper F 2	131.1
1960	MOSS	Porsche F 2	141.0
1961	IRELAND	Lotus F 2	147.6
1963	BRABHAM	Brabham F 1	155.0
1964	BANDINI	Ferrari	159.6

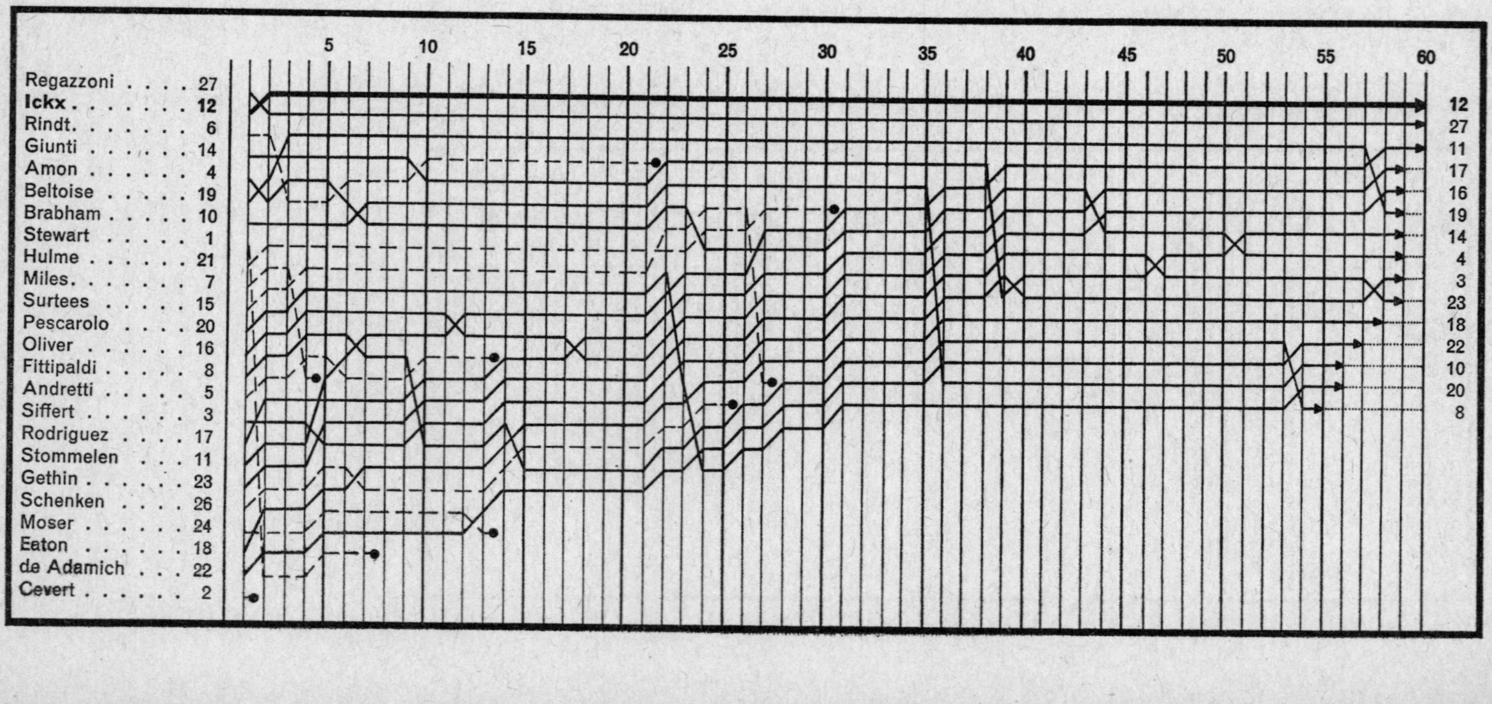

GP Italia 3.57 miles

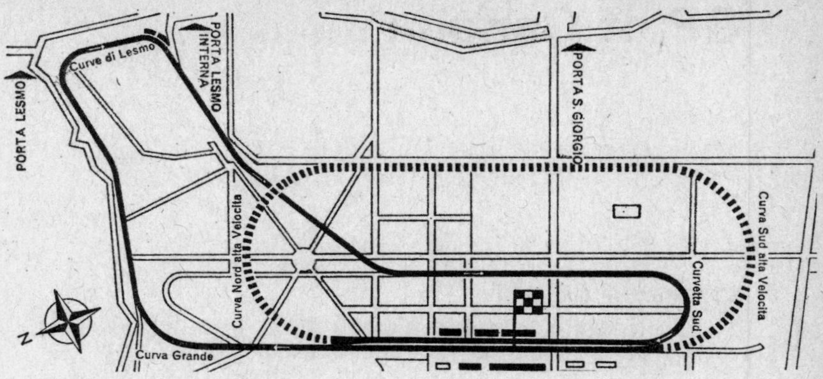

STARTING GRID

2. J. Ickx
Ferrari
Flat-12
1'24"14

10. P. Rodriguez
BRM
V12
1'24"36

4. C. Regazzoni
Ferrari
Flat-12
1'24"39

18. J. Stewart
March-Ford
V8
1'24"73

6. I. Giunti
Ferrari
Flat-12
1'24"74

8. J. Oliver
BRM
V12
1'24"77

50. J. Siffert
March-Ford
V8
1'25"09

44. J. Brabham
Brabham-Ford
V8
1'25"39

30. D. Hulme
McLaren-Ford
V8
1'25"47

14. J. Surtees
Surtees-Ford
V8
1'25"56

20. F. Cevert
March-Ford
V8
1'25"56

34. A. de Adamich
McLaren-Alfa
V8
1'25"91

52. R. Peterson
March-Ford
V8
1'25"93

40. J.-P. Beltoise
Matra-Simca
V12
1'26"01

42. H. Pescarolo
Matra-Simca
V12
1'26"04

32. P. Gethin
McLaren-Ford
V8
1'26"19

46. R. Stommelen
Brabham-Ford
V8
1'26"60

48. C. Amon
March-Ford
V8
1'26"67

54. T. Schenken
de Tomaso-Ford
V8
1'26"67

12. G. Eaton
BRM
V12
1'27"15

RETIREMENTS

No.	Driver	Make	Lap	
14	Surtees	Surtees-Ford	1	electrics
50	Siffert	March-Ford	3	engine
10	Rodriguez	BRM	13	engine
42	Pescarolo	Matra-Simca	15	valve spring
6	Giunti	Ferrari	15	engine
54	Schenken	de Tomaso-Ford	18	engine
12	Eaton	BRM	22	overheating
2	Ickx	Ferrari	26	clutch
44	Brabham	Brabham-Ford	32	accident
52	Peterson	March-Ford	36	engine
8	Oliver	BRM	37	engine

RESULTS

Pos.	No.	Driver	Make	Laps	Time
1.	4	REGAZZONI	Ferrari 312 B	68	1.39'06"88
2.	18	STEWART	March-Ford	68	1.39'12"61
3.	40	BELTOISE	Matra-Simca	68	1.39'12"68
4.	30	HULME	McLaren-Ford	68	1.39'13"03
5.	46	STOMMELEN	Brabham-Ford	68	1.39'13"29
6.	20	CEVERT	March-Ford	68	1.40'10"34
7.	48	AMON	March-Ford	67	
8.	34	de ADAMICH	McLaren-Alfa	61	
9.	32	GETHIN	McLaren-Ford	60	

Winner's: 147.07 mph.

Fastest lap: C. Regazzoni, Ferrari No. 4, 1'25"2; average: 147.07 mph

FORMER WINNERS

Year	Drivers	Make	Average (mph)
1921	GOUX	Ballot	89.73
1922	BORDINO	Fiat	86.70
1923	SALAMANO	Fiat	90.83
1924	ASCARI	Alfa Romeo	98.51
1925	BRILLI	Alfa Romeo	94.60
1926	CHARAVEL	Bugatti	85.68
1927	BENOIST	Delage	89.85
1928	CHIRON	Bugatti	99.13
1930	VARZI	Maserati	93.27
1931	CAMPARI-NUVOLARI	Alfa Romeo	96.57
1932	NUVOLARI	Alfa Romeo	103.86
1933	FAGIOLI	Alfa Romeo	108.33
1934	FAGIOLI-CARACCIOLA	Mercedes-Benz	65.20
1935	STUCK	Auto-Union	84.98
1936	ROSEMAYER	Auto-Union	83.91
1937	CARACCIOLA	Mercedes-Benz	81.41
1938	NUVOLARI	Auto-Union	96.54
1947	TROSSI	Alfa Romeo	70.17
1948	WIMILLE	Alfa Romeo	70.22
1949	ASCARI	Ferrari	104.79

Year	Drivers	Make	Average (mph)
1950	FARINA	Alfa Romeo	109.45
1951	ASCARI	Ferrari	115.26
1952	ASCARI	Ferrari	109.79
1953	FANGIO	Maserati	110.44
1954	FANGIO	Mercedes-Benz	111.73
1955	FANGIO	Mercedes-Benz	128.20
1956	MOSS	Maserati	129.44
1957	MOSS	Vanwall	120.00
1958	BROOKS	Vanwall	120.94
1959	MOSS	Cooper	124.10
1960	P. HILL	Ferrari	131.76
1961	P. HILL	Ferrari	129.81
1962	P. HILL	BRM	123.34
1963	CLARK	Lotus	127.45
1964	SURTEES	Ferrari	127.78
1965	STEWART	BRM	130.45
1966	SCARFIOTTI	Ferrari	135.48
1967	SURTEES	Honda	145.50
1968	HULME	McLaren-Ford	145.41
1969	STEWART	Matra-Ford	146.97

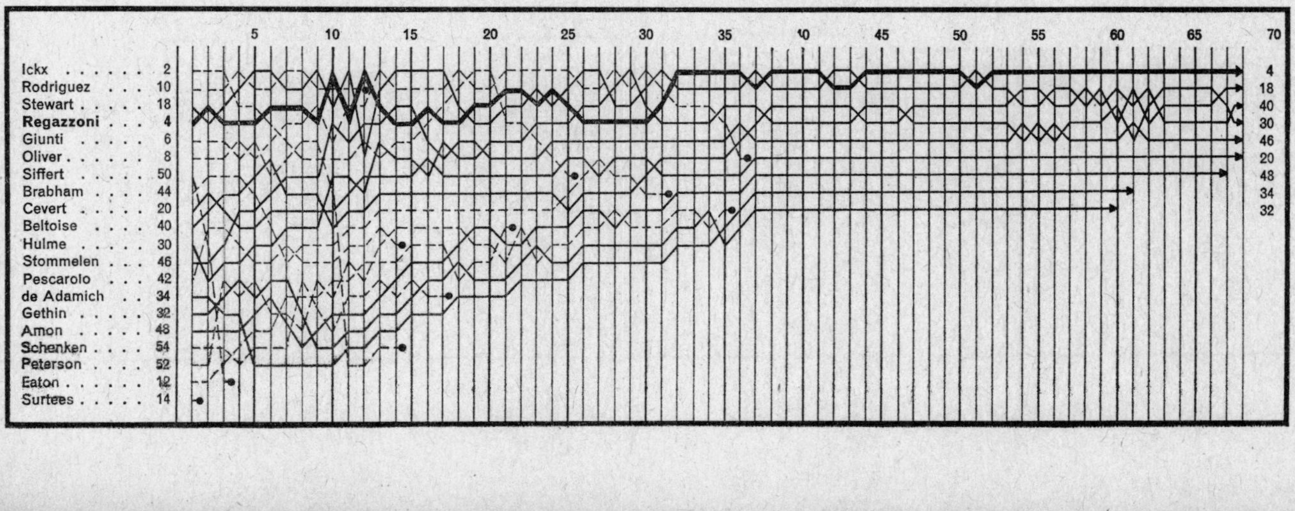

GP of Canada 2.65 miles

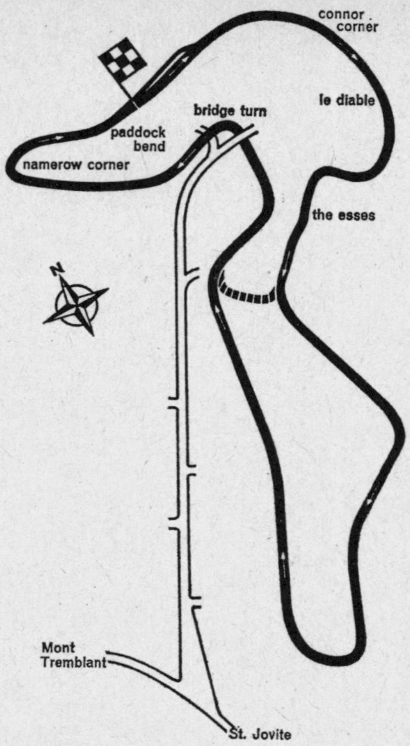

STARTING GRID

18. J. Ickx
Ferrari
Flat-12
1'31"6

3. J. Stewart
Tyrrell-Ford
V8
1'31"5

2. F. Cevert
March-Ford
V8
1'32"4

19. C. Regazzoni
Ferrari
Flat-12
1'31"9

20. C. Amon
March-Ford
V8
1'32"6

4. J. Surtees
Surtees-Ford
V8
1'32"6

24. H. Pescarolo
Matra-Simca
V12
1'32"9

14. P. Rodriguez
BRM
V12
1'32"7

15. J. Oliver
BRM
V12
1'33"1

16. G. Eaton
BRM
V12
1'32"9

8. A. de Adamich
McLaren-Alfa
V8
1'33"2

6. P. Gethin
McLaren-Ford
V8
1'33"2

21. J. Siffert
March-Ford
V8
1'33"5

23. J.-P. Beltoise
Matra-Simca
V12
1'33"4

26. R. Peterson
March-Ford
V8
1'34"4

5. D. Hulme
McLaren-Ford
V8
1'33"9

12. R. Stommelen
Brabham-Ford
V8
1'34"7

10. T. Schenken
de Tomaso-Ford
V8
1'34"6

9. G. Hill
Lotus-Ford
V8
1'35"8

11. J. Brabham
Brabham-Ford
V8
1'35"4

RETIREMENTS

No.	Driver	Make	Lap	
21	Siffert	March-Ford	23	engine
12	Stommelen	Brabham-Ford	24	steering
3	Stewart	Tyrrell-Ford	33	suspension
15	Oliver	BRM	53	stub axle
11	Brabham	Brabham-Ford	58	suspension
5	Hulme	McLaren-Ford	59	differential
26	Peterson	March-Ford	66	gas leak
8	de Adamich	McLaren-Alfa	70	oil pressure
9	Hill	Lotus-Ford	78	suspension
10	Schenken.	de Tomaso-Ford	80	suspension

RESULTS

Pos.	No.	Driver	Make	Laps	Time
1	18	ICKX	Ferrari	90	2.21'18"4
2	19	REGAZZONI	Ferrari	90	2.21'33"2
3	20	AMON	March-Ford	90	2.22'16"3
4	14	RODRIGUEZ	BRM	89	
5	4	SURTEES	Surtees-Ford	89	
6	6	GETHIN	McLaren-Ford	88	
7	24	PESCAROLO	Matra-Simca	87	
8	23	BELTOISE	Matra-Simca	85	
9	2	CEVERT.	March-Ford	85	
10	16	EATON	BRM	85	

Winner's average: 101.27 mph

Fastest lap: C. Regazzoni, Ferrari No. 19, 1'32"2; average : 103.47 mph.

FORMER WINNERS

Year	Driver	Make	Circuit	Average (mph)
1967	BRABHAM	Brabham	Mosport	82.72
1968	HULME	McLaren	Mt-Tremblant	97.25
1969	ICKX	Brabham	Mosport	112.76

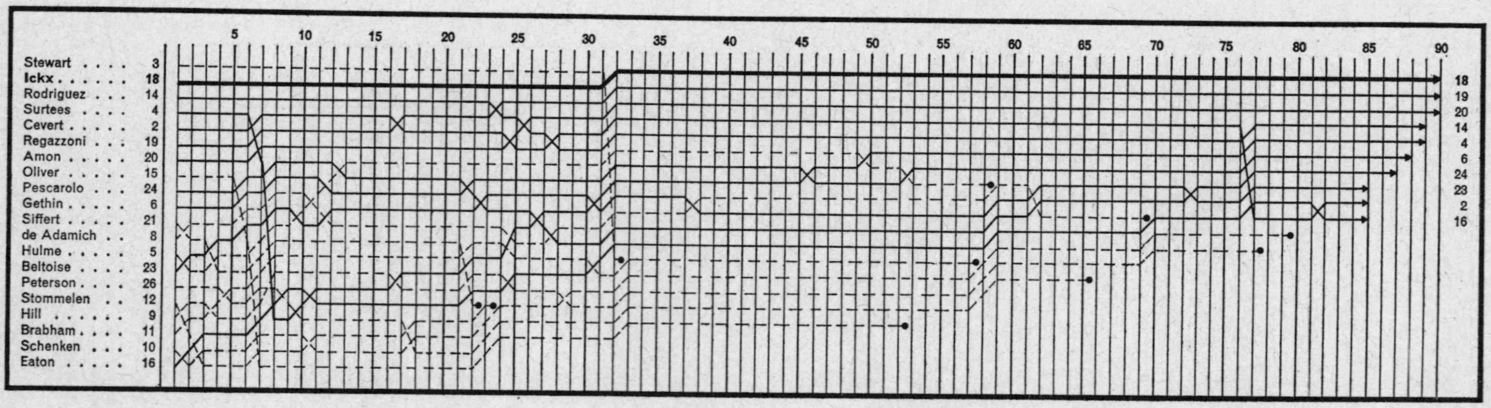

GP of the United States 2.3 miles

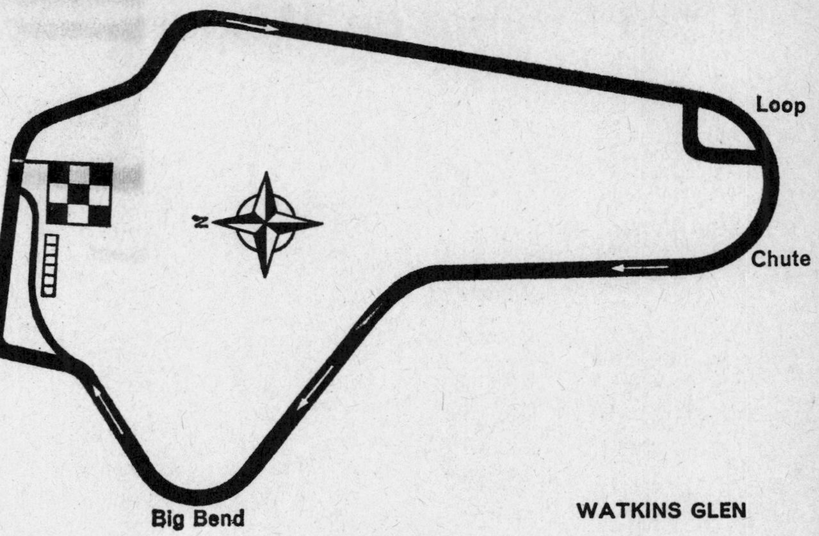

STARTING GRID

1. J. Stewart
Tyrrell-Ford
V8
1'03"62

3. J. Ickx
Ferrari
Flat-12
1'03"07

19, P. Rodriguez
BRM
V12
1'04"18

24. E. Fittipaldi
Lotus-Ford
V8
1'03"67

4. C. Regazzoni
Ferrari
Flat-12
1'04"30

12. C. Amon
March-Ford
V8
1'04"23

17. J. Surtees
Surtees-Ford
V8
1'04"52

20. J. Oliver
BRM
V12
1'04"37

14. G. Hill
Lotus-Ford
V8
1'04"81

23. R. Wisell
Lotus-Ford
V8
1'04"79

7. H. Pescarolo
Matra-Simca
V12
1'05"00

8. D. Hulme
McLaren-Ford
V8
1'04"84

21. G. Eaton
BRM
V12
1'05"14

18. D. Bell
Surtees-Ford
V8
1'05"00

15. J. Brabham
Brabham-Ford
V8
1'05"29

7. R. Peterson
March-Ford
V8
1'05"18

6. J.-P. Beltoise
Matra-Simca
V12
1'05"30

2. F. Cevert
March-Ford
V8
1'05"44

30. T. Schenken
de Tomaso-Ford
V8
1'06"08

16. R. Stommelen
Brabham-Ford
V8
1'05"77

31. G. Hutchison
Brabham-Ford
V8
1'06"22

9. P. Gethin
McLaren-Ford
V8
1'06"12

27. J. Bonnier
McLaren-Ford
V8
1'06"46

11. J. Siffert
March-Ford
V8
1'06"23

RESULTS

Pos.	No.	Driver	Make	Laps	Time
1	24	FITTIPALDI	Lotus-Ford	108	1.57'32"79
2	19	RODRIGUEZ	BRM	108	1.58'09"18
3	23	WISELL.	Lotus-Ford	108	1.58'17"96
4	3	ICKX	Ferrari 312 B	107	
5	12	AMON	March-Ford	107	
6	18	BELL	Surtees-Ford	107	
7	8	HULME	McLaren-Ford	106	
8	7	PESCAROLO	Matra-Simca	105	
9	11	SIFFERT	March-Ford	105	
10	15	BRABHAM	Brabham-Ford	105	
11	29	PETERSON	March-Ford	104	
12	16	STOMMELEN	Brabham-Ford	104	
13	4	REGAZZONI	Ferrari 312 B	101	
14	9	GETHIN	McLaren-Ford	100	

Winner's average: 126.79 mph

Fastest lap: J. Ickx, Ferrari No. 3, 1'02"74; average: 131.97 mph (new record).

RETIREMENTS

No.	Driver	Make	Lap	
17	Surtees	Surtees-Ford	7	flywheel
21	Eaton	BRM	11	engine
20	Oliver	BRM	15	engine
31	Hutchison	Brabham-Ford	22	fuel leak
6	Beltoise	Matra-Simca	28	suspension
27	Bonnier	McLaren-Ford	51	unknown
30	Schenken	de Tomaso-Ford	62	rear suspension
2	Cevert	March-Ford	63	lost rear wheel
14	Hill	Lotus-Ford	73	clutch
1	Stexart	Tyrrell-Ford	83	oil leak and engine

FORMER WINNERS

Year	Drivers	Make	Circuit	Average (mph)
1959	McLAREN	Cooper	Sebring	98.87
1960	MOSS	Lotus	Riverside	99.00
1961	IRELAND	Lotus	Watkins Glen	103.17
1962	CLARK	Lotus	Watkins Glen	108.61
1963	G. HILL	BRM	Watkins Glen	109.61
1964	G. HILL	BRM	Watkins Glen	111.10
1965	G. HILL	BRM	Watkins Glen	107.98
1966	CLARK	Lotus	Watkins Glen	114.94
1967	CLARK	Lotus	Watkins Glen	120.95
1968	STEWART.	Matra	Watkins Glen	124.86
1969	RINDT	Lotus	Watkins Glen	126.36

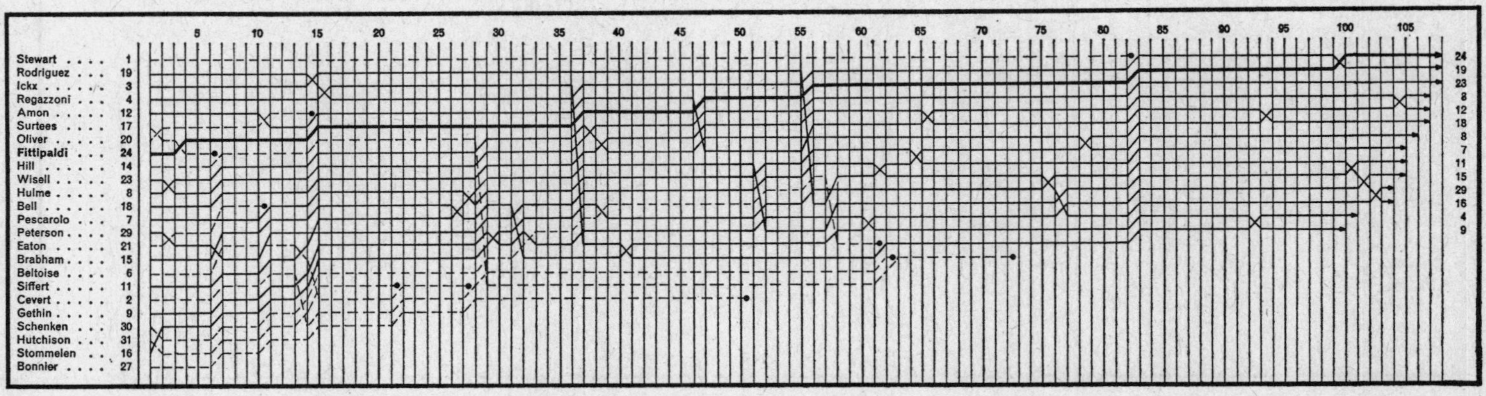

Gran Premio de México 3.07 miles

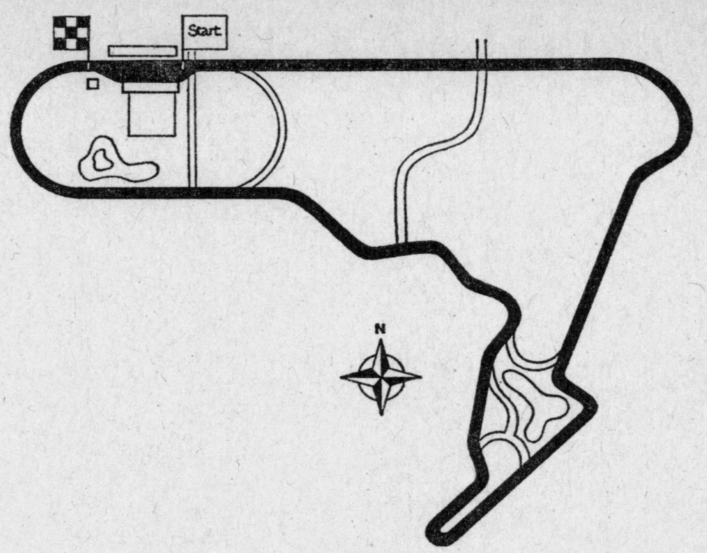

STARTING GRID

1. J. Stewart, Tyrrell-Ford, V8, 1'41"88
4. C. Regazzoni, Ferrari, Flat-12, 1'41"86
15. J. Brabham, Brabham-Ford, V8, 1'43"57
3. J. Ickx, Ferrari, Flat-12, 1'42"41
6. J.-P. Beltoise, Matra-Simca, V12, 1'43"82
12. C. Amon, March-Ford, V8, 1'43"71
14. G. Hill, Lotus-Ford, V8, 1'44"46
19. P. Rodriguez, BRM, V12, 1'44"01
9. P. Gethin, McLaren-Ford, V8, 1'44"46
2. F. Cevert, March-Ford, V8, 1'44"21
23. R. Wisell, Lotus-Ford, V8, 1'44"13
7. H. Pescarolo, Matra-Simca, V12, 1'44"55
8. D. Hulme, McLaren-Ford, V8, 1'44"95
20. J. Oliver, BRM, V12, 1'44"70
11. J. Siffert, March-Ford, V8, 1'46"15
17. J. Surtees, Surtees-Ford, V8, 1'45"03
24. E. Fittipaldi, Lotus-Ford, V8, 1'48"13
16. R. Stommelen, Brabham-Ford, V8, 1'46"30

RETIREMENTS

No.	Driver	Make	Laps	
24	Fittipaldi	Lotus-Ford	2	engine
11	Siffert	March-Ford	4	engine
14	Hill	Lotus-Ford	5	overheating
2	Cevert	March-Ford	9	engine
16	Stommelen	Brabham-Ford	16	engine
9	Gethin	McLaren-Ford	28	engine
1	Stewart	Tyrrell-Ford	34	accident
15	Brabham	Brabham-Ford	53	engine

RESULTS

Pos.	No.	Driver	Make	Laps	Time
1.	3	ICKX	Ferrari	65	1.53'28"36
2.	4	REGAZZONI	Ferrari	65	1.53'53"00
3.	8	HULME	McLaren-Ford	65	1.54'14"33
4.	12	AMON	March-Ford	65	1.54'15"41
5.	6	BELTOISE	Matra-Simca	65	1.54'18"47
6.	19	RODRIGUEZ	BRM	65	1.54'53"12
7.	20	OLIVER	BRM	64	
8.	17	SURTEES	Surtees-Ford	64	
9.	7	PESCAROLO	Matra-Simca	61	
*	23	WISELL.	Lotus-Ford	56	

* = not classified (less than 90 % of the total distance)

Winner's average: 106.78 mph.

Fastest lap: J. Ickx, Ferrari No. 3, 1'43"11; average: 108.49 mph (new record).

FORMER WINNERS

Year	Drivers	Make	Average (mph)
1962	CLARK	Lotus	90.33
1963	CLARK	Lotus	93.29
1964	GURNEY	Brabham	93.32
1965	GINTHER	Honda	94.26
1966	SURTEES	Cooper-Maserati	95.72
1967	CLARK	Lotus-Ford	101.42
1968	HILL	Lotus-Ford	103.80
1969	HULME	McLaren	106.15

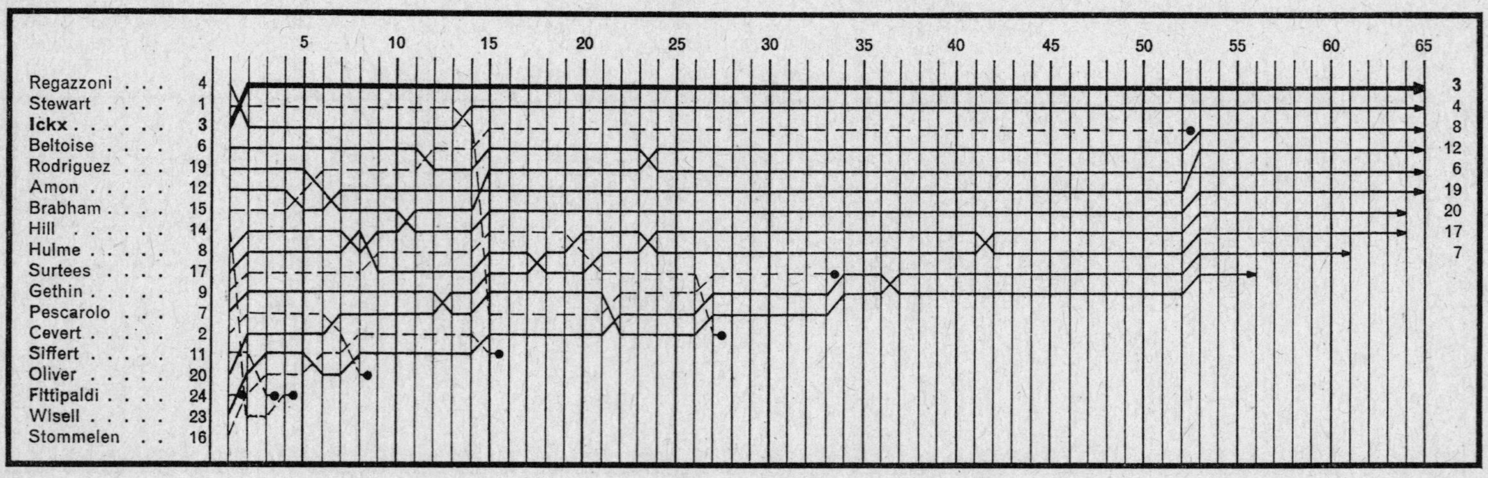

DRIVERS' WORLD CHAMPIONSHIP

FINAL CLASSIFICATION				South Africa	Spain	Monaco	Belgium	Holland	France	Great Britain	Total at the end of the first part of the Championship	Germany	Austria	Italy	Canada	USA	Mexico	Total *
1	† Jochen RINDT	A	Lotus-Ford . . .	–	–	9	–	9	9	9	**36**	9	–	–	–	–	–	**45**
2	Jacky ICKX	B	Ferrari	–	–	–	–	4	–	–	**4**	6	9	–	9	3	9	**40**
3	Clay REGAZZONI	CH	Ferrari	–	–	–	–	3	–	3	**6**	–	6	9	6	–	6	**33**
4	Denny HULME	NZ	McLaren-Ford . .	6	–	3	–	–	3	4	**16**	4	–	3	–	–	4	**27**
5	Jack BRABHAM	AUS	Brabham-Ford . .	9	–	6	–	–	4	6	**25**	–	–	–	–	–	–	**25**
5 ex.	Jackie STEWART . . .	GB	Tyrrell-Ford . . .	4	9	–	–	6	–	–	**19**	–	–	6	–	–	–	**25**
7	Chris AMON	NZ	March-Ford . . .	–	–	–	6	–	6	2	**14**	–	–	–	4	2	3	**23**
7 ex.	Pedro RODRIGUEZ . . .	MEX	BRM	–	–	1	9	–	–	–	**10**	–	3	–	3	6	1	**23**
9	Jean-Pierre BELTOISE .	F	Matra-Simca . .	3	–	–	4	2	–	–	**9**	–	1	4	–	–	2	**16**
10	Emerson FITTIPALDI . .	NZ	Lotus-Ford . . .	–	–	–	–	–	–	–	**0**	3	–	–	–	9	–	**12**
11	Rolf STOMMELEN . . .	D	Brabham-Ford . .	–	–	–	2	–	–	–	**2**	2	4	2	–	–	–	**10**
12	Henri PESCAROLO . . .	F	Matra-Simca . .	–	–	4	1	–	2	–	**7**	1	–	–	–	–	–	**8**
13	Graham HILL	GB	Lotus-Ford . . .	1	3	2	–	–	–	1	**7**	–	–	–	–	–	–	**7**
14	† Bruce McLAREN . . .	NZ	McLaren-Ford . .	–	6	–	–	–	–	–	**6**	–	–	–	–	–	–	**6**
15	Mario ANDRETTI	USA	March-Ford . . .	–	4	–	–	–	–	–	**4**	–	–	–	–	–	–	**4**
15 ex.	Reine WISELL	S	Lotus-Ford . . .	–	–	–	–	–	–	–	**0**	–	–	–	–	4	–	**4**
17	Ignazio GIUNTI	BR	March-Ford . . .	–	–	–	3	–	–	–	**3**	–	–	–	–	–	–	**3**
17 ex.	John SURTEES	GB	Surtees-Ford . .	–	–	–	–	1	–	–	**1**	–	–	–	2	–	–	**3**
19	John MILES	GB	Lotus-Ford . . .	2	–	–	–	–	–	–	**2**	–	–	–	–	–	–	**2**
19 ex.	Jackie OLIVER	GB	BRM	–	–	–	–	–	–	–	**0**	–	2	–	–	–	–	**2**
19 ex.	Johnny SERVOZ-GAVIN	F	March-Ford . . .	–	2	–	–	–	–	–	**2**	–	–	–	–	–	–	**2**
22	Derek BELL	GB	Brabham-Ford . .	–	–	–	–	–	–	–	**0**	–	–	–	–	1	–	**1**
22 ex.	François CEVERT	F	March-Ford . . .	–	–	–	–	–	–	–	**0**	–	–	1	–	–	–	**1**
22 ex.	Peter GETHIN	CH	McLaren-Ford . .	–	–	–	–	–	–	–	**0**	–	–	–	1	–	–	**1**
22 ex.	Dan GURNEY	USA	McLaren-Ford . .	–	–	–	–	–	–	1	**1**	–	–	–	–	–	–	**1**

* For classification, only the 5 best results of the first part of the Championship and the 4 best of the second part are retained.

EUROPEAN TROPHY FOR FORMULA 2

FINAL CLASSIFICATION				Thruxton	Hockenheim	Barcelona	Rouen	Mediterraneo	Tulln	Imola	Baden	Total*
1	G. REGAZZONI	CH	Tecno-Ford	2	9	–	9	9	–	9	6	**44**
2	D. BELL	GB	Brabham-Ford	9	4	9	2	3	6	4	1	**35**
3	E. FITTIPALDI	NZ	Lotus-Ford	–	2	4	6	4	–	6	3	**25**
4	R. PETERSON	S	March-Ford	–	–	–	3	–	4	3	4	**14**
4 ex.	D. QUESTER	D	BMW	3	–	2	–	–	–	–	9	**14**
6	F. CEVERT	F	Tecno-Ford	–	–	–	–	–	9	–	–	**9**
6 ex.	R. WIDDOWS	GB	Brabham-Ford	6	–	3	–	–	–	–	–	**9**
8	T. IKUZAWA	J	Lotus-Ford	–	6	–	–	–	2	–	–	**8**
9	P. WESTBURY	GB	Brabham-Ford	–	–	–	1	–	–	6	–	**7**
9 ex.	H. PESCAROLO	F	Brabham-Ford	–	–	6	–	–	–	–	–	**6**
9 ex.	T. SCHENKEN	AUS	Brabham-Ford	–	–	–	4	–	–	2	–	**6**
12	A. WALKER	GB	Brabham-Ford	4	–	–	–	–	1	–	–	**5**
13	V. BRAMBILLA	I	Brabham-Ford	–	–	–	–	–	3	–	–	**3**
13 ex.	H. HAHNE	D	BMW	–	3	–	–	–	–	–	–	**3**
13 ex.	C. REUTEMANN	RA	Brabham-Ford	–	–	1	–	–	–	–	2	**3**
16	J.-P. JABOUILLE	F	Pygmée-Ford	–	–	–	–	2	–	–	–	**2**
17	P. GAYDON	GB	Brabham-Ford	–	1	–	–	–	–	–	–	**1**
17 ex.	M. GOTH		Brabham-Ford	–	–	–	–	–	–	1	–	**1**
17 ex.	A. REID	GB	Brabham-Ford	1	–	–	–	–	–	–	–	**1**

* For classification, only the 6 best results are retained.

RESULTS F2

THRUXTON, Great Britain

March 30, 1970; distance: 108 miles

Pos.	Driver	Make
1.	RINDT	Lotus-Ford
2.	STEWART	Brabham-Ford
3.	BELL	Brabham-Ford
4.	WIDDOWS	Brabham-Ford
5.	WALKER	Brabham-Ford
6.	ICKX	BMW
7.	QUESTER	BMW
8.	REGAZZONI	Tecno-Ford
9.	REID	Brabham-Ford
10.	AMON	March-Ford
11.	PERROT	March-Ford
12.	IKUZAWA	Lotus-Ford

Winner's average: 112.73 mph; time: 57′41″0.

Fastest lap: Rindt, 1′14″0; average: 114.62 mph.

HOCKENHEIM, Germany

April 19, 1970; distance: 168.242 miles

Pos.	Driver	Make
1.	REGAZZONI	Tecno-Ford
2.	IKUZAWA	Lotus-Ford
3.	BELL	Brabham-Ford
4.	HAHNE	BMW
5.	FITTIPALDI	Lotus-Ford
6.	STOMMELEN	March-Ford
7.	GAYDON	Brabham-Ford
8.	REUTEMANN	Brabham-Ford
9.	WIDDOWS	Brabham-Ford
10.	PERROT	March-Ford
11.	GUTHRIE	March-Ford

Winner's average: 123.124 mph; time: 1.22′01″3.

Fastest lap: Dieter Quester, 1′58″7; average: 158.636 mph.

GRAN PREMIO DE BARCELONA, Spain

April 26, 1970; distance: 105.975 miles

Pos.	Driver	Make
1.	BELL	Brabham-Ford
2.	PESCAROLO	Brabham-Ford
3.	FITTIPALDI	Lotus-Ford
4.	WIDDOWS	Brabham-Ford
5.	QUESTER	BMW
6.	REUTEMANN	Brabham-Ford
7.	SOLER-ROIG	Lotus-Ford
8.	REGAZZONI	Tecno-Ford
9.	WESTBURY	Brabham-Ford
10.	BRAMBILLA	Brabham-Ford
11.	JABOUILLE	Pygmée-Ford
12.	STOMMELEN	March-Ford

Winner's average: 93.355 mph; Time: 1.08′07″6.

Fastest lap: Derek Bell, 1′29″5; average: 94.742 mph.

GRAN PREMIO MEDITERRANEO, Italy

August 23, 1970; distance: 186.65 miles

Pos.	Driver	Make
1.	REGAZZONI	Tecno-Ford
2.	SIFFERT	BMW
3.	ICKX	BMW
4.	WESTBURY	Brabham-Ford
5.	FITTIPALDI	Lotus-Ford
6.	STOMMELEN	Brabham-Ford
7.	BELL	Brabham-Ford
8.	JABOUILLE	Pygmee-Ford
9.	BRAMBILLA	Brabham-Ford
10.	SALVATI	Tecno-Ford
11.	REUTEMANN	Brabham-Ford
12.	QUESTER	BMW

Winner's average: 127.18 mph; time: 1.28′03″5.

Fastest lap: C. Regazzoni, 1′23″5; average: 129.79 mph.

GRAND PRIX DE ROUEN, France

June 28, 1970; distance: 101.624 miles

Pos.	Driver	Make
1.	SIFFERT	BMW 70
2.	REGAZZONI	Tecno-Ford
3.	FITTIPALDI	Lotus-Ford
4.	ICKX	BMW 70
5.	SCHENKEN	Brabham-Ford
6.	PETERSON	March-Ford
7.	BELL	Brabham-Ford
8.	BRABHAM	Brabham-Ford
9.	RINDT	Lotus-Ford
10.	WESTBURY	Brabham-Ford
11.	MAZET	Brabham-Ford
12.	REUTEMANN	Brabham-Ford
13.	JAUSSAUD	Brabham-Ford
14.	de ADAMICH	Brabham-Ford

Winner's average: 118.613 mph; time: 51′24″3.

Fastest lap: Schenken, 2′00″8; average: 121.141 mph.

TÜLLN-LANGENLEBARN, Austria

September 13, 1970; distance: 125 miles

Pos.	Driver	Make
1.	ICKX	BMW
2.	BRABHAM	Brabham-Ford
3.	CEVERT	Tecno-Ford
4.	BELL	Brabham-Ford
5.	PETERSON	March-Ford
6.	BRAMBILLA	Brabham-Ford
7.	IKUZAWA	Lotus-Ford
8.	WALKER	Brabham-Ford
9.	PERROT	March-Ford
10.	BRAMBILLA	Brabham-Ford
11.	SIFFERT	BMW
12.	WESTBURY	Brabham-Ford
13.	MAX	Tecno-Ford

Winner's average: 101.376 mph; time: 1.13′45″82.

Fastest lap: Cevert, 1′01″6; average: 103.892 mph.

GRAN PREMIO DI IMOLA, Italy

September 29, 1970; distance: 175 miles

Pos.	Driver	Make
1.	REGAZZONI	Tecno-Ford
2.	FITTIPALDI	Lotus-Ford
3.	BELL	Brabham-Ford
4.	PETERSON	March-Ford
5.	STOMMELEN	Brabham-Ford
6.	GOTH	Brabham-Ford
7.	IKUZAWA	Lotus-Ford
8.	BIRRELL	Brabham-Ford
9.	SCHENKEN	Brabham-Ford
10.	NELSON	Crosslé-Ford
11.	TERBECK	Brabham-Ford
12.	WALKER	Brabham-Ford
13.	REUTEMANN	Brabham-Ford

Winner's average: 115.306 mph, time: 1.30′50″3.

Fastest lap: Ickx, 1′35″5; average: 117.514 mph.

BADEN-WÜRTTEMBERG, Germany

October 11, 1970; distance: 147.637 miles

Pos.	Driver	Make
1.	QUESTER	BMW
2.	REGAZZONI	Tecno-Ford
3.	PETERSON	March-Ford
4.	FITTIPALDI	Lotus-Ford
5.	REUTEMANN	Brabham-Ford
6.	BELL	Brabham-Ford
7.	BASCHE	BMW
8.	BRAMBILLA	Brabham-Ford
9.	UNOLD	March-Ford
10.	WINGFIELD	Brabham-Ford
11.	POTOCKI	Lotus-Ford
12.	CULLEN	Brabham-Ford
13.	FREY	Tecno-Ford
14.	BRAMBILLA	Brabham-Ford
15.	BLADES	Lotus-Ford

Winner's average: 115.680 mph: time 1.16′34″4.

Fastest lap: Dieter Quester, 2′08″7; average: 117.991 mph.

Manufacturers' World Championship

Daytona 3.81 miles

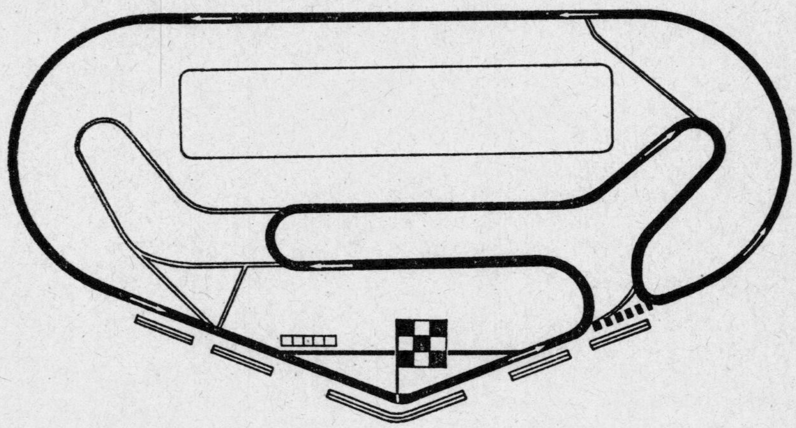

RESULTS

Pos.	No.	Drivers	Make	Cat.	cc	Laps
1**	2	RODRIGUEZ - KINNUNEN	Porsche 917	Sp	4500	724
2	1	SIFFERT - REDMAN	Porsche 917	Sp	4500	679
3	28	ANDRETTI - MERZARIO - ICKX	Ferrari 512 S	Sp	5000	676
4**	24	POSEY - PARKES	Ferrari 312 P	P	3000	647
5	23	ADAMOWICZ - PIPER	Ferrari 312 P	P	3000	632
6**	7	THOMPSON - MAHLER	Chevrolet Corvette	GT-O	7000	608
7	21	YOUNG - CHINETTI	Ferrari 275 LM	Sp	3300	603
8	18	WONDER - CUOMO	Ford GT-40	Sp	5000	579
9	40	LOOMIS - EVERETT	Porsche 906 E	P	2000	573
10	33	BRABHAM - CEVERT	Matra-Simca	P	3000	565
11	89	GOTTLEB - DOOLEY	Chevrolet Corvette	GT-O	7000	545
12**	12	MITCHELL - KEMP	Chevrolet Camaro	T-O	5000	535
13	6	de LORENZO - LANG	Chevrolet Corvette	GT-O	7000	534
14*	74	MEANEY - WRIGHT - BEAN	Porsche 911 S	GT-U	1991	533
15	90	COSTANZO - HEINZ	Chevrolet Corvette	GT-O	7000	521
16	14	CUOMO - GIMBLE - LISSBERG	Ford Mustang	T-O	5000	520
17	95	BROCKMAN - TREMBLAY	Chevrolet Camaro	T-O	5000	511
18	34	BELTOISE - PESCAROLO	Matra-Simca	P	2993	509
19	11	BOCK - DENT	Chevrolet Camaro	T-O	5000	507
20	78	BELPERCHE - LILLY - PICKETT	MG B	GT-U	1798	504
21	79	WALDRON - LANIER - BARROS	MG B	GT-U	1798	490
22*	48	TAYLOR - SHELDON	Alfa Romeo GTV	T-U	1779	478
23	38	FLEMING - JOHNSON	Fiat 124	T-U	1438	473
24	76	ADDISON - DAHM	Porsche 911 S	GT-U	1991	462
25	98	MASTANDREA - DROLET - RODGERS	Chevrolet Camaro	T-O	5000	409
26	83	COLLINS - WILSON	Ford Mustang	T-O	5000	407
27	71	WALLE - SPEAKMAN	TVR Vixen	GT-U	1600	364

O = + 2000 cc

U = 0-2000 cc

* = Class winners

** = Category winners

Distance covered by the winners: 2.758.44 miles; average: 114.866 mph.

RETIREMENTS OF MAJOR IMPORTANCE

No.	Drivers	Make	Laps	
55	Kearney-Roberts	Datsun PL	24	head gasket
86	Mollin-Riley	Volvo 122 S	54	engine
26	Vaccarella-Giunti	Ferrari 512 S	89	accident
27	Ickx-Schetty	Ferrari 512 S	115	accident
96	Gimondo-Dietrich	Chevrolet Camaro	130	brake system
22	Bucknum-Pickett	Ferrari 365 GTB	142	cooling system
0	Donohue-Revson	Javelin	205	no oil pressure
20	Cluxton-Tatun	Ferrari GBT 4	308	cooling system
3	Ahrens-Elford	Porsche 917	337	petrol storage tank
53	van Lennep-Laine	Porsche 908	385	engine
30	Manferedini-Moretti	Ferrari 512 S	412	suspension
25	Gurney-Parsons	Ferrari 512 S	464	gearbox

FORMER WINNERS

Year	Drivers	Make	Average (mph)
1959	MIERES - von DORY	Porsche	
1962	GURNEY	Lotus-Climax	103.66
1963	P. RODRIGUEZ	Ferrari	102.07
1964	P. RODRIGUEZ	Ferrari	98.20
1965	MILES - RUBY	Ford	99.94
1966	MILES - RUBY	Ford	108.01
1967	AMON - BANDINI	Ferrari	105.70
1968	ELFORD - NEERPASCH	Porsche	106.69
1969	DONOHUE - PARSONS	Lola-Chevrolet	99.27

Sebring 5.2 miles

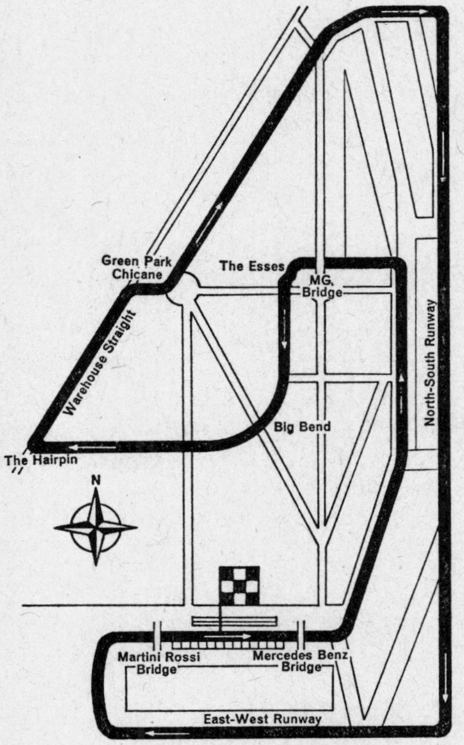

RESULTS

Pos.	No.	Drivers	Make	Cat.	cc	Laps
1**	21	ANDRETTI - VACCARELLA - GIUNTI	Ferrari 512 S	Sp	4994	248
2**	48	McQUEEN - REVSON	Porsche 908	P	2997	248
3	33	GREGORY - HEZEMANS	Alfa Romeo	P	2993	247
4	15	RODRIGUEZ - KINNUNEN - SIFFERT .	Gulf Porsche 917	Sp	4494	244
5	34	PESCAROLO - SERVOZ-GAVIN . . .	Matra-Simca 650	P	2999	242
6	22	PARKES - PARSONS	Ferrari 312 P	T	3000	240
7	46	LARROUSSE - KOCH - ATTWOOD .	Porsche 908	P	2997	236
8	31	COURAGE - de ADAMICH	Alfa Romeo	P	2993	231
9	32	STOMMELEN - GALLI	Alfa Romeo	P	2993	230
10**	1	de LORENZO - LANG	Chevrolet Corvette	GT	7000	219
11	3	JOHNSON - JOHNSON - GREENDYKE	Chevrolet Corvette	GT	7000	214
12	35	GURNEY - CEVERT	Matra-Simca 650	P	2999	213
13*	53	GREGG - HARRISON	Porsche	GT	1991	205
14**	40	GIMONDO - DIETRICH	Chevrolet Camaro	T	5000	203
15	52	DUVAL - BALLEY	Porsche 911 T	GT	1991	201
16	39	MITCHELL - KEMP	Chevrolet Camaro	T	5000	191
17	9	GROSSMAN - YENKO	Chevrolet Camaro	GT	7000	189
18	43	TREMBLAY - McDILL	Chevrolet Camaro	T	4997	187
19*	73	Miss SMITH - Miss GUTHRIE	Healey Sprite	P	1300	187
20	2	THOMPSON - MAHLER	Chevrolet Corvette	GT	7000	187
21	91	CORWIN - Miss MIMS	Chevrolet Camaro	T	4956	184
22	92	ELLIOTT - GWYNNE	Chevrolet Camaro	T	4956	182
23*	50	RAHAL - WISE - FRANK	Porsche 906	Sp	1991	181
24	37	COLLINS - WILSON	Ford Mustang	T	4655	175
25	57	BELPERCHE - GAMMON - MUMMERY .	MG B	GT	1798	175
26	58	SCOTT - LAINER - HOUSER	MG B	GT	1798	169
27	18	PETTY - HALLQUIST	Ford Mustang	T	5000	162
28*	80	KENNEDY - SAMM	Lancia Fulvia	T	1300	157

* = class winners ** = category winners

Distance covered by the winners: 1289.6 miles; average: 107.029 mph.

Fastest lap: L. Kinnunen, Porsche No. 14, 2'32"77; average: 122.537 mph (new record).

RETIREMENTS

No.	Drivers	Make	Laps	
27	De'udy-Hailwood	Lola Chevrolet T70	1	brakes
79	Taylor-Dyler-Drolet	Alfa Romeo GTV	2	engine
59	Smith-Donley-Buttari.	BMC	2	engine
60	Kilpatrick-Goodrich . . .	MG B	7	accident
7	Morehead-Vega .	American AMX	8	engine
86	Theall-Polimeni .	Volvo 122 S	8	piston
36	Cuomo-Gimbel-Lisberg	Ford Mustang	16	transmission
49	Greger-Schmalback . .	Porsche 910	22	engine
30	Forester-Hedges	Ford GT 40	22	engine
87	Whitaker-Slottag-Davidson	Volvo 122 S	25	oil pressure
17	Herrmann-Lins. .	Porsche 917	28	engine
45	Larrousse-Koch .	Porsche 908	31	starter
5	Schumacher-Petree	Chevrolet Corvette	34	—
74	Meaney-Bean .	Porsche	36	engine
62	Robinson-Kleinpeter	Chevron B 16	38	accident
41	Bock-Dent . . .	Chevrolet Camaro	40	oil fitting
88	Fleming-Johnson-Bowers	Fiat 124	47	disqualified
38	McLain-Boo-Floyd	Chevrolet Camaro	47	engine
67	Bandy-Stevenson	Lotus 47	48	rear hub carrier
23	Chinetti-Adamowicz . . .	Ferrari 312 P	56	overheating
16	Ahrens-Elford .	Porsche 917	61	accident
61	J. Baker-C. Baker-Richards-Rinzler	Chevron B16	70	broken crankshaft
69	Spruell-Theodoracopulos	Alfa Romeo	75	electrical trouble
77	Jennings-Tullius	Porsche 911 T	78	engine
82	Clark-Marsula . .	Lancia Fulvia	78	bent valve
55	Brennan-Blackburn . . .	MG B	84	broken oil line
24	Bucknum-Posey-Everett	Ferrari 512 S	92	fuel pump
26	de Ormes-Young	Lola-Chevrolet T70	114	transmission
29	Grant-Heppenstall-Marcus	Ford GT 40	117	broken rear axle
56	Woodner-O'Connor	MG Midget	122	oil pressure
20	Ickx-Schetty . . .	Ferrari 512 S	151	head gasket
4	Greenwood-Barker	Chevrolet Corvette	159	clutch
8	Heinz-Costanzo .	Chevrolet Corvette	191	—
14	Siffert-Redman .	Gulf P rsche 917	211	front end damage
19	Andretti-Merzario	Ferrari 512 S	227	gearbox
47	Laine-van Lennep	Porsche 908	229	—

FORMER WINNERS

Year	Drivers	Make	Average (mph)
1950	WACKER - BURRELL	Cadillac-Allard	66.95
1952	GREY - KULOK	Frazer-Nash	62.83
1953	FITCH - WALTERS	Cunningham	74.96
1954	MOSS - LLOYD	Osca	73.63
1955	HAWTHORN - WALTERS	Jaguar	78.86
1956	FANGIO - CASTELLOTTI	Ferrari	84.07
1957	FANGIO - BEHRA	Maserati	85.36
1958	COLLINS - P. HILL	Ferrari	86.60
1959	P. HILL - GENDEBIEN - GURNEY - DAIGH	Ferrari	81.49
1960	GENDEBIEN - HERRMANN	Porsche	87.44
1961	P. HILL - GENDEBIEN	Ferrari	90.21
1962	BONNIER - BIANCHI	Ferrari	88.28
1963	SURTEES - SCARFIOTTI	Ferrari	90.36
1964	PARKES - MAGLIOLI	Ferrari	92.36
1965	HALL - SHARP	Chaparral	84.75
1966	MILES - RUBY	Ford	98.63
1967	ANDRETTI - McLAREN	Ford	103.13
1968	HERRMANN - SIFFERT	Porsche	102.51
1969	ICKX - OLIVER	Ford	103.36

Targa Florio 44.7 miles

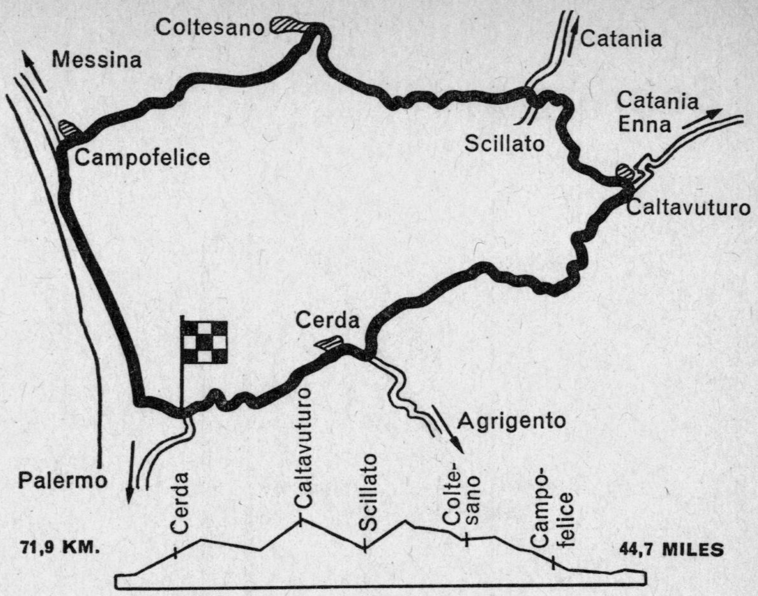

RESULTS

Pos.	No.	Drivers	Make	Cat.	cc	Laps	Time
1**	12	SIFFERT - REDMANN	Gulf-Porsche 908	P	2000-3000	11	6.35′30″0
2	40	RODRIGUEZ - KINNUNEN	Gulf-Porsche 908	P	2000-3000	11	6.37′12″5
3**	6	VACCARELLA - GIUNTI	Ferrari 512	Sp	2000-5000	11	6.39′05″2
4	18	LAINE - van LENNEP	Porsche 908	P	2000-3000	11	6.44′51″7
5	36	ATTWOOD - WALDEGARDE	Gulf-Porsche 908	P	2000-3000	11	6.45′01″6
6	4	MÜLLER - PARKES	Ferrari 512	Sp	2000-5000	10	
7*	56	ALBERTI - WILLIAMS	Alfa Romeo 33/3	P	1300-2000	10	
8*	94	« PAM » - « GIBI »	Fiat Abarth 2000	Sp	1600-2000	10	
9**	174	MUNARI - MAGLIOLI	Lancia Fulvia	GT	1300-1600	10	
10	98	VIRGILIO - TARAMAZZO	Fiat Abarth 2000	Sp	1600-2000	10	
11	58	Lo PICCOLO - CALASCIBETTA	Ferrari Dino	P	1300-2000	10	
12	60	NICODEMI - MORETTI	Porsche 907	P	1300-2000	10	
13	26	LARROUSSE - LINS	Porsche 908	P	2000-3000	9	
14*	140	MARCHIOLO - CASTRO	Porsche 911	GT	1600-2000	9	
15	138	de CADENET - OGIER	Porsche 911	GT	1600-2000	9	
16*	262	RUSPA - PELLEGRIN	Fiat Abarth	P	0-1000	9	
17	120	GARANT - CHENEVIERE	Porsche 911	GT	1600-2000	9	
18	190	RESTIVO - APACHE	Lancia Fulvia	GT	1300-1600	9	
19	260	LOCATELLI - GARGANO	A.M.S.	P	0-1000	9	
20*	278	« RO » - GIACOMINI	Alpine Renault	GT	0-1300	9	
21	286	« RADECH » - ARCOVITO	Lancia Fulvia	GT	0-1300	9	
22	172	PORETTI - BENEDINI	Alfa Romeo GTA	GT	1300-1600	9	
23	178	GALIMBERTI - « POCKER »	Lancia Fulvia	GT	1300-1600	9	
24*	154	de FRANCISCI - BALISTRERI	Alfa Romeo TZ	Sp	1300-1600	9	
25*	218	ZANETTI - PIANTA	Alfa Romeo	P	1000-1300	8	
26	214	SGARLATA - MAROTTA	Lancia TS	P	1000-1300	8	
27	152	GIUGNO - SUTERA	Alfa Romeo TZ	Sp	1300-1600	8	
28*	82	SANSON - PERRAMOND	Porsche 911	GT	+ 2000	8	
29	136	SELZ - GREUB	Porsche 911	GT	1600-2000	8	
30	162	FERRARO - VALENZA	Alfa Romeo	Sp	1300-1600	8	
31	274	« RAMON » - « ZERIMAR »	Lancia Fulvia	GT	0-1300	8	
32	184	RANDAZZO - PUCCI	Alfa Romeo GTA	GT	1300-1600	8	
33	142	GENTA - MONTICONE	Porsche 911	GT	1600-2000	8	
34*	236	GARUFI - « BLACK AND WHITE »	Fiat Abarth	Sp	0-1300	8	
35	64	« CINNO » - BARBUSCIA	Ferrari Dino	P	1300-2000	8	
36	112	BERRUTO - LICHERI	Porsche 911	GT	1600-2000	8	
37	292	MANTIA - Lo IACONO	Lancia Fulvia	GT	0-1300	8	
38	96	NICOLOSI - BONACCORSI	Porsche 906	Sp	1600-2000	8	
39	44	CHATHAM - HARVEY	MG C	P	2000-3000	8	
40	282	ANASTASIO - RATTAZZI	Lancia Fulvia	GT	0-1300	7	
41	28	de ADAMICH - COURAGE	Alfa Romeo 33-3	P	2000-3000	7	
42	90	TODARO - « CODONES »	Porsche 906	Sp	1600-2000	7	
43	200	PINTO - BALLESTRIERI	Lancia Fulvia	GT	1300-1600	7	
44	86	HALDI - « MIRAGE »	Porsche 911	GT	+ 2000	7	
45	62	NEGUS - HANSON	Chevron	P	1300-2000	7	
46	294	CUCINOTTA - PATTI	Lancia Fulvia	GT	0-1300	7	
47	194	SEBASTIANO - NARDINI	Lotus	GT	1300-1600	7	
48	252	SPATARO - BRUSCHI	Osca Maserati	P	0-1000	7	
49	122	SCHENETTI - ZERBINI	Porsche 911	GT	1600-2000	7	

** = category winners   * = class winners

Winners' average: 75.502 mph.
Fastest lap: L. Kinnunen, Porsche 908 No. 40, 33′36″0; average: 79.890 mph (new record).

FORMER WINNERS

Year	Drivers	Make	Average (mph)
1906	CAGNO	Itala	29.01
1907	NAZZARO	F.I.A.T.	33.48
1908	TRUCCO	Isotta-Fraschini	37.13
1909	CIUPPA	S.P.A.	33.91
1910	CARIOLATO	Franco	29.07
1911	CEIRANO	S.C.A.T.	29.01
1912	SNIPE - PEDRINI	S.C.A.T.	26.41
1913	NAZZARO	Nazzaro	33.66
1914	CEIRANO	S.C.A.T.	38.56
1919	BOILLOT	Peugeot	34.10
1920	MEREGALLI	Nazzaro	35.89
1921	MASETTI	Fiat	36.08
1922	MASETTI	Mercedes	39.06
1923	SIVOCCI	Alfa Romeo	36.64
1924	WERNER	Mercedes	40.92
1925	COSTANTINI	Bugatti	44.39
1926	COSTANTINI	Bugatti	45.57
1927	MATERASSI	Bugatti	44.02
1928	DIVO	Bugatti	45.50
1929	DIVO	Bugatti	46.23
1930	VARZI	Alfa Romeo	48.36
1931	NUVOLARI	Alfa Romeo	40.17
1932	NUVOLARI	Alfa Romeo	49.16
1933	BRIVIO	Alfa Romeo	47.43
1934	VARZI	Alfa Romeo	41.66
1935	BRIVIO	Alfa Romeo	49.15
1936	MAGISTRI	Lancia	41.97
1937	SEVERI	Maserati	72.91
1938	ROCCO	Maserati	70.86
1939	VILLORESI	Maserati	84.56
1940	VILLORESI	Maserati	88.16
1948	BIONDETTI - IGOR	Ferrari	54.99
1949	BIONDETTI - BENEDETTI	Ferrari	50.46
1950	BORNIGIA - BORNIGIA	Alfa Romeo	53.87
1951	CORTESE	Frazer-Nash	47.49
1952	BONETTO	Lancia	49.60
1953	MAGLIOLI	Lancia	49.97
1954	TARUFFI	Lancia	55.73
1955	MOSS - COLLINS	Mercedes-Benz	59.64
1956	MAGLIOLI	Porsche	56.35
1957	COLONNA	Fiat	
1958	MUSSO - GENDEBIEN	Ferrari	58.77
1959	BARTH - SEIDEL	Porsche	56.68
1960	BONNIER - G. HILL	Porsche	59.00
1961	VON TRIPS - GENDEBIEN	Ferrari	64.10
1962	R. RODRIGUEZ - MAIRESSE - GENDEBIEN	Ferrari	63.30
1963	BONNIER - ABATE	Porsche	64.41
1964	DAVIS - PUCCI	Porsche	61.48
1965	BANDINI - VACCARELLA	Ferrari	62.28
1966	MAIRESSE - MÜLLER	Porsche	63.73
1967	HAWKINS - STOMMELEN	Porsche	67.61
1968	ELFORD - MAGLIOLI	Porsche	75.25
1969	MITTER - SCHÜTZ	Porsche	72.99

ADAC-1000-km 14.17 miles

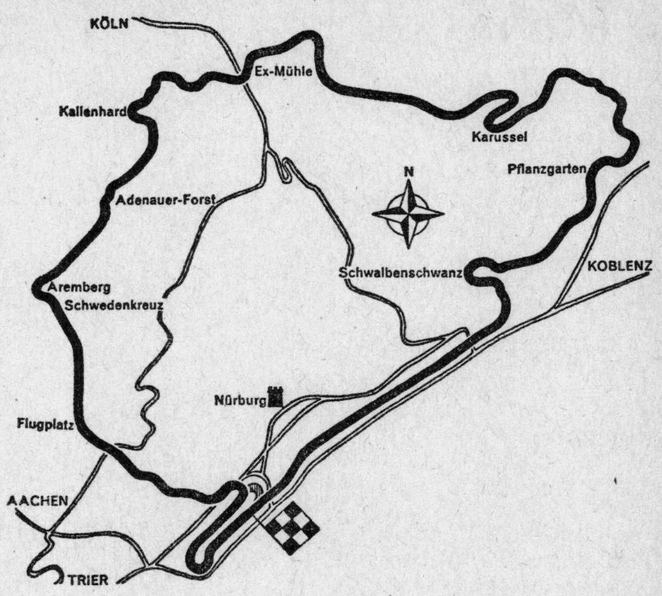

RESULTS

Pos.	No.	Drivers	Make	Cat.	cc	Laps	Time
1**	22	AHRENS - ELFORD	Porsche 908/3	P	2000-3000	44	6.05′21″2
2	15	HERRMANN - ATTWOOD	Porsche 908/3	P	2000-3000	44	6.10′34″8
3**	55	SURTEES - VACCARELLA	Ferrari 512 S	Sp	2000-5000	43	
4	58	MÜLLER - PARKES . . .	Ferrari 512 S	Sp	2000-5000	42	
5	1	LARROUSSE - MARKO . .	Porsche 908	P	2000-3000	42	
6	2	LINS - KAUHSEN	Porsche 908	P	2000-3000	42	
7	11	von WENDT - KOCH . . .	Porsche 908	P	2000-3000	41	
8	4	GREGER - LEUZE	Porsche 908	P	2000-3000	40	
9*	29	WICKY - de CABRAL . .	Porsche 907	P	1600-2000	39	
10	24	DEPREZ - VERNAEVE . .	Chevron-Mazda	P	1600-2000	39	
11	17	BASCHE - WERLICH - KELLENERS	Porsche 908	P	2000-3000	38	
12	10	FISCHHABER - SCHMID	Porsche	P	2000-3000	38	
13	31	KONIG - LANFRANCHI . .	Nomad BRM	P	1600-2000	37	
14**	79	FRÖHLICH - TOIVONEN .	Porsche 911 S	GT	+ 2000	37	
15	84	KREMER - HUBER	Porsche 911 S	GT	+ 2000	37	
16	85	SCHICKENTANZ - STUCK	Porsche 911 S	GT	+ 2000	37	
17*	67	HEAVENS - GARTON . .	Chevron BMW	Sp	1300-2000	37	
18*	92	LOOS - PESCH	Porsche 911 L	GT	1300-2000	36	
19	88	HUHN - SCHWARZ . . .	VW-Porsche 914	GT	1300-2000	36	
20	93	KAISER - STECKKÖNIG .	VW-Porsche 914	GT	1300-2000	36	
21	101	NOLTE - CHRISTMANN .	VW-Porsche 914	GT	1300-2000	36	
22	60	FORESTER - de CADENET	Ford GT 40	Sp	2000-5000	35	
23	96	QUIST - KRUMM	VW-Porsche 914	GT	1300-2000	35	
24	95	JACQUEMIN - SCHEEREN	Alpine Renault	GT	1300-2000	35	
25	83	HALDI - CHAPUIS	Porsche 911 S	GT	+ 2000	34	
26	91	BECKER - CLEVER . . .	Porsche 911 S	GT	1300-2000	34	
27*	42	WEIZINGER - BISTERFELD	Alfa Romeo GTA	P	1300-1600	34	
28	94	OTTO - KLASEN	Alfa Romeo GTA	GT	1300-2000	34	
29	97	WEIR - OGIER	Porsche 911 T	GT	1300-2000	32	
30	69	TANGYRE - WESTEY . .	Chevron BMW	Sp	1300-2000	32	
31	73	NEGUS - JOCELYNE . .	Chevron BMW	Sp	1300-2000	30	
32	43	ROBINSON - BLACKNEY	Unipower -BMC	P	1300-1600	29	
33	28	MYLIUS - BIRRELL	Gropa-Ford	P	1600-2000	28	
34	26	BRIDGES - LAWSON . . .	Chevron-Ford	P	1600-2000	28	

** category = winners * = class winners

Winners' average: 102.525 mph.

Fastest lap: P. Rodriguez, Porsche 908/3 No. 21, 7′50″4; average: 108.616 mph (new record).

RETIREMENTS

No.	Drivers	Make	Laps	
57	Giunti-Merzario . .	Ferrari 512 S	2	fuel injection
75	L'Amie-Reid	Porsche 910	4	left the road
14	Wilson-Daghorn . .	Lola-BRM	4	—
19	di Palma-Marincovich	Berta-Ford	5	broken water pipe
100	Becker-Theissen . .	Porsche 911 S	7	—
72	Blackie-Humble . .	Chevron-BMW	7	accident
54	Neuhaus-Kelleners .	Porsche 917	9	wheel bearing
6	Stommelen-Courage.	Alfa Romeo 333	11	damper
21	Rodriguez-Kinnunen	Porsche 908	11	left the road
12	Gaydon-Grant . . .	Brabham-Climax	12	—
16	Werner-Kranefuss .	Ford Capri	12	oil lack
32	Edwards-Enever . .	Astra-Ford	12	suspension
81	Peters-Eymann . .	Ford Shelby	13	engine
64	Doodwin-Taggert .	Chevron-BMW	15	left the road
23	Blatzheim-Kraus. .	Porsche 907	19	mechanical trouble
68	Bambord-Creasey . .	Chevron-BMW	20	fuel leak
70	Meier-Ilotte	Porsche 910	21	mechanical trouble
38	Richardson-Cowin. .	Daren-Ford	22	mechanical trouble
20	Siffert-Redman . . .	Porsche 908/3	22	no oil pressure
66	Killenberg-Bialas .	Chevron-BMW	24	—

FORMER WINNERS

Year	Drivers	Make	Average (mph)
1953	ASCARI - FARINA	Ferrari	74.52
1956	SCHELL - TARUFFI BEHRA - MOSS	Maserati	80.47
1957	BROOKS - CUNNINGHAM	Aston Martin	82.27
1958	MOSS - BRABHAM	Aston Martin	84.13
1959	MOSS - FAIRMAN	Aston Martin	82.33
1960	MOSS - GURNEY	Maserati	82.58
1961	GREGORY - CASSNER	Maserati	79.11
1962	P. HILL - GENDEBIEN	Ferrari	82.21
1963	SURTEES - MAIRESSE	Ferrari	82.52
1964	SCARFIOTTI - VACCARELLA . . .	Ferrari	86.99
1965	SURTEES - SCARFIOTTI	Ferrari	90.65
1966	P. HILL - BONNIER	Chaparral	89.30
1967	SCHÜTZ - BUZZETTA	Porsche	90.40
1968	SIFFERT - ELFORD	Porsche	95.04
1969	SIFFERT - REDMAN.	Porsche	100.97

Le Mans 8.34 miles

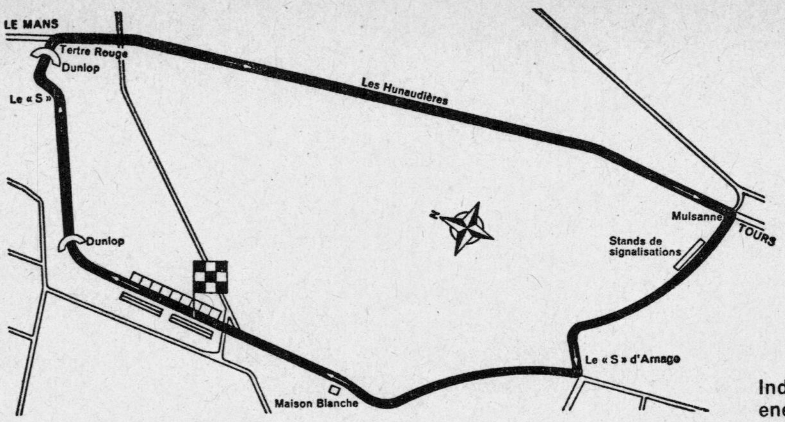

RESULTS

Pos.	No.	Drivers	Make	Cat.	cc	Distance in miles	Average mph	Index of perfor-mance	Index of energy (fuel consump-tion, speed and weight)
1**	23	ATTWOOD - HERRMANN	Porsche 917	Sp	4494	2863.154	119.298	1.132	0.77
2	3	LARROUSSE - KAUHSEN	Porsche 917	Sp	4494	2822.231	117.593	1.116	0.89
3**	27	LINS - MARKO	Porsche 908	P	2997	2797.892	116.578	1.151	0.79
4	11	POSEY - BUCKNUM	Ferrari 512 S	Sp	4993	2615.719	108.988	1.026	
5	12	de FIERLAND - WALKER	Ferrari 515 S	Sp	4994	2549.804	106.241	1.000	
6**	40	BALLOT-LENA - CHASSEUIL	Porsche 914/6	GT	1991	2382.494	99.270	1.041	0.80
7*	47	KREMER - KOOB	Porsche 911 S	GT	2253	2355.383	98.141	1.008	0.75
*	2	GREDER - ROUGET	Chevrolet-Corvette	GT	6998	2391.057	99.627		
*	29	LINGE - WILLIAMS	Porsche 908	Sp	2997	2359.826	98.326		
*	57	PARSONS - ADAMOWICZ	Ferrari 312 P	Sp	2989	2348.598	97.858		
*	62	MAUROY - MAZZIA	Porsche 911 S	GT	2195	2293.719	95.571		
*	42	VERRIER - GARANT	Porsche 911 TH	GT	1989	2263.483	94.311		
*	67	PAROT - DECHAUMEL	Porsche 911 S	GT	1990	2260.910	94.204		
*	45	LAURENT - MARCHE	Porsche 911 S	GT	2195	2191.994	91.333		
*	64	SAGE - GREUB	Porsche 911 S	GT	1991	2120.928	88.371		
*	66	SWIETLIK - LAGNIEZ	Porsche 911 S	GT	1991	1929.198	80.384		

** = category winners * = class winners
* = unclassified for not completing minimum allotted distance.
Fastest lap: Vix Elford, Porsche 917 No. 25, 3'21"; average: 149.896 mph (new record).

RETIREMENTS

No.	Drivers	Make	Hour	
37	Hezemans-Gregory	Alfa Romeo	1	piston failure
6	Vaccarella-Giunti	Ferrari 512 S	1	connecting rod
7	Bell-Peterson	Ferrari 512 S	3	accident
14	Bonnier-Wisell	Ferrari 512 S	3	accident
8	Merzario-Regazzoni	Ferrari 512 S	3	accident
15	Müller-Parkes	Ferrari 512 S	3	accident
48	Vernaeve-Deprez	Chevron-Mazda	3	seal failure
21	Rodriguez-Kinnunen	Porsche 917	3	connecting rod
38	Zeccoli-Facetti	Alfa Romeo	4	accident
22	Hobbs-Hailwood	Porsche 917	4	accident
1	Bourdon-Aubriet	Chevrolet-Corvette	4	accident
50	Ligier-Andruet	Ligier JS1	6	distributor
32	Brabham-Cevert	Matra-Simca	6	piston ring
10	Kelleners-Loos	Ferrari 512 S	6	handling problems
31	Beltoise-Pescarolo	Matra-Simca	6	piston ring
30	Jabouille-Depailler	Matra-Simca	7	engine
59	Egreteaud-Mesange	Porsche 911 S	7	—
4	Pilette-Gosselin	Lola-Chevrolet	9	gearbox
18	Van Lennep-Piper	Porsche 917	10	accident
5	Ickx-Schetty	Ferrari 512 S	10	accident
43	Gaban-Braillard	Porsche 911 S	10	—
9	Juncadella-Fernandez	Ferrari 512 S	10	accident
20	Siffert-Redman	Porsche 917	11	engine
63	Rey-Chenevière	Porsche 911 S	12	accident
16	Manfredini-Moretti	Ferrari 512 S	12	left rear driveshaft
46	Poirot-Kraus	Porsche 910	13	piston failure
60	Meier-Rouveyran	Porsche 910	14	brake failure
61	Wicky-Hanrioud	Porsche 907	16	accelerator pedal
65	Haldi-Blank	Porsche 911S	17	gearbox
25	Elford-Ahrens	Porsche 917	17	inlet valve
35	"Galli"-Stommelen	Alfa Romeo	17	disqualified
44	Baker-Martland	Chevron BMW	19	valve spring
36	de Adamich-Courage	Alfa Romeo	19	engine
49	Sailes-Hine	Chevron-Cosworth	23	—
34	Enever-Hedges	Healey-Repco	23	ignition

FORMER WINNERS

Year	Drivers	Make	Average (mph)
1923	LAGACHE - LEONARD	Chenard Walker	57.0
1924	DUFF - CLEMENT	Bentley	53.6
1925	DE COURCELLES - ROSSIGNOL	Lorraine	57.7
1926	BLOCH - ROSSIGNOL	Lorraine	65.9
1927	BENJAFIELD - DAVIS	Bentley	61.2
1928	BARNATO - RUBIN	Bentley	68.6
1929	BARNATO - BIRKIN	Bentley	73.4
1930	BARNATO - KIDSTON	Bentley	75.7
1931	HOWE - BIRKIN	Alfa Romeo	77.9
1932	SOMMER - CHINETTI	Alfa Romeo	76.3
1933	SOMMER - NUVOLARI	Alfa Romeo	81.2
1934	CHINETTI - ETANCELIN	Alfa Romeo	74.5
1935	HINDMARSCH - FONTES	Lagonda	77.6
1937	WIMILLE - BENOIST	Bugatti	84.9
1938	CHABOUD - TREMOULET	Delahaye	82.1
1939	WIMILLE - VEYRON	Bugatti	86.4
1949	CHINETTI - SELSDON	Ferrari	82.0
1950	ROSIER - ROSIER	Talbot	89.5
1951	WALKER - WHITEHEAD	Jaguar	93.2
1952	LANG - RIESS	Mercedes-Benz	69.4
1953	ROLT - HAMILTON	Jaguar	105.6
1954	GONZALES - TRINTIGNANT	Ferrari	104.9
1955	HAWTHORN - BUEB	Jaguar	106.8
1956	FLOCKHART - SANDERSON	Jaguar	104.2
1957	FLOCKHART - BUEB	Jaguar	113.5
1958	GENDEBIEN-P. HILL	Ferrari	105.9
1959	SALVADORI - SHELBY	Aston Martin	112.3
1960	GENDEBIEN - FRERE	Ferrari	108.9
1961	GENDEBIEN - P. HILL	Ferrari	115.6
1962	GENDEBIEN - P. HILL	Ferrari	114.9
1963	SCARFIOTTI - BANDINI	Ferrari	117.8
1964	GUICHET - VACCARELLA	Ferrari	121.6
1965	RINDT - GREGORY	Ferrari	120.8
1966	McLAREN - AMON	Ford	125.4
1967	GURNEY - FOYT	Ford	135.5
1968	RODRIGUEZ - BIANCHI	Ford	114.9
1969	ICKX - OLIVER	Ford	129.4

GENERAL CLASSIFICATION AND HOUR-BY-HOUR POSITIONS

No.	Drivers	Make	Class	cc	Start	1	2	3	4	5	6	7	8	9	10	11	12	13	14	15	16	17	18	19	20	21	22	23	24
1	BOURDON - AUBRIET . . .	Chevrolet Cor.	GT	6998	25	25	20	25	20	20	20	20	20	20	20	23	23	23	23	23	23	23	23	23	23	23	23	23	23
2	GREDER - ROUGET	Chevrolet Cor.	GT	6998	6	21	25	20	25	25	25	25	5	5	23	3	3	25	25	25	25	27	27	27	3	3	3	3	3
3	LARROUSSE - KAUHSEN . .	Porsche 917	S	4494	20	20	5	22	18	18	5	3	23	23	3	25	25	3	27	27	27	3	3	3	27	27	27	27	27
4	PILETTE - GOSSELIN	Lola Chevrolet	S	4995	8	22	22	18	23	5	3	5	3	3	25	27	27	27	3	3	3	11	11	11	11	11	11	11	11
5	ICKX - SCHETTY	Ferrari 512S	S	4994	21	18	18	5	3	23	18	23	25	25	27	35	35	35	35	35	35	12	12	12	12	12	12	21	12
6	VACCARELLA-GIUNTI . . .	Ferrari 512S	S	4994	5	5	8	23	5	3	23	35	27	27	35	11	11	11	11	11	11	57	57	57	57	57	40	40	40
7	BELL - PETERSON.	Ferrari 512S	S	4994	7	3	23	3	32	35	35	27	35	35	11	57	12	12	12	12	12	36	36	40	40	2	2	2	47
8	MERZARIO - REGAZZONI . .	Ferrari 512S	S	4994	15	8	3	35	35	32	27	4	11	11	12	12	57	57	57	57	57	40	40	2	40	40	47	47	2
9	JUNCADELLA - FERNANDEZ	Ferrari 512S	S	4994	14	23	7	27	16	31	36	11	4	12	57	2	2	36	36	36	36	2	47	47	47	47	57	29	29
10	KELLENERS - LOOS	Ferrari 512S	S	4994	22	7	16	36	27	27	4	57	12	9	2	36	36	2	2	40	40	47	2	29	29	29	29	57	57
11	POSEY - BUCKNUM	Ferrari 512S	S	4994	18	32	32	31	36	16	11	12	57	57	40	40	40	40	47	2	2	29	29	62	62	62	62	62	62
12	de FIERLAND - WALKER . .	Ferrari 512S	S	4994	3	36	36	30	31	36	57	9	9	18	36	47	47	47	40	47	47	62	62	67	67	42	42	42	42
14	BONNIER - WISELL	Ferrari 512S	S	4994	11	30	11	32	11	4	12	36	36	36	47	65	62	62	49	49	29	67	67	42	34	67	67	67	67
15	PARKES - MÜLLER	Ferrari 512S	S	4994	32	16	35	16	4	11	9	18	18	2	65	62	65	49	29	29	62	42	42	34	42	34	34	45	45
16	MANFREDINI - MORETTI . .	Ferrari 512S	S	4994	23	11	27	11	57	57	2	34	34	40	62	63	49	29	62	62	67	34	34	45	45	45	45	64	64
18	van LENNEP - PIPER.	Porsche 917	S	4494	16	4	30	4	30	12	34	2	2	47	63	49	42	42	67	67	42	45	45	64	64	64	64	66	66
20	SIFFERT - REDMAN	Porsche 917	S	4494	35	27	14	38	61	9	16	40	40	34	49	42	67	67	42	42	65	49	49	66	49	49	49		
21	RODRIGUEZ - KINNUNEN . .	Porsche 917	S	4494	10	14	4	10	9	50	40	47	47	62	42	67	29	61	65	61	34	44	44	49	66	66	66		
22	HOBBS - HAILWOOD	Porsche 917	S	4494	36	35	15	9	12	30	49	62	62	63	46	29	61	45	34	65	45	64	64						
23	HERRMANN - ATTWOOD. .	Porsche 917	S	4494	30	9	12	57	50	2	47	63	63	65	34	46	45	65	45	34	49	66	66						
25	ELFORD - AHRENS	Porsche 917	S	4494	31	12	38	61	40	40	62	43	49	49	67	45	34	34	61	45	64								
27	LINS - MARKO	Porsche 908	Sp	2997	27	38	31	12	2	61	43	49	65	43	29	61	60	64	64	64	44								
29	LINGE - WILLIAMS	Porsche 908	Sp	2997	37	15	9	50	47	47	63	65	43	42	45	34	64	66	66	44	66								
30	JABOUILLE - DEPAILLER . .	Matra 650	Sp	2999	9	61	10	60	65	34	65	42	42	46	61	60	46	60	44	66									
31	BELTOISE - PESCAROLO . .	Matra 660	Sp	2999	12	57	57	47	34	65	59	45	46	67	16	64	66	44											
32	BRABHAM - CEVERT	Matra 650	Sp	2999	38	31	61	2	63	63	30	60	45	29	60	66	44												
34	ENEVER - HEDGES	Healey-Repco	Sp	2993	4	10	34	63	44	62	42	46	67	45	64	44													
35	« GALLI » - STOMMELEN . .	Alfa Romeo	Sp	2992	57	34	50	44	62	49	45	67	29	16	66	16													
36	COURAGE - de ADAMICH .	Alfa Romeo	Sp	2992	61	50	60	34	49	43	60	29	61	61	44														
37	GREGORY - HEZEMANS. . .	Alfa Romeo	Sp	2992	50	48	44	65	43	59	67	16	16	66															
38	ZECCOLI - FACETTI . . .	Alfa Romeo	Sp	2992	29	44	47	67	10	44	46	61	66	64															
40	CHASSEUIL - BALLOT-LENA	Porsche 914/6	GT	1991	49	2	2	40	59	42	44	66	64	60															
42	VERRIER - GARANT	Porsche 911T	GT	1989	31	1	65	1	60	45	61	64	60	44															
43	GABAN - BRAILLARD . . .	Porsche 911S	GT	2195	1	60	63	59	45	60	29	44	44																
44	MARTLAND - BAKER	Chevron B16	Sp	1991	2	47	1	62	42	67	66																		
45	LAURENT - MARCHE	Porsche 911S	GT	2195	46	65	62	43	67	46	64																		
46	POIROT - KRAUS	Porsche 910	Sp	1991	44	63	67	49	66	10																			
47	KOOB - KREMER	Porsche 911S	GT	2253	60	40	40	42	46	29																			
48	DEPREZ - VERNAEVE	Chevron-Mazda	Sp	1964	65	62	66	45	29	66																			
49	SKAILES - HINE	Chevron B16	Sp	1991	63	67	45	66	64	64																			
50	LIGIER - ANDRUET	Ligier JS1	Sp	1791	48	66	59	46																					
57	ADAMOWICZ - PARSONS .	Ferrari 312 P	Sp	2989	43	45	49	29																					
59	EGRETAUD - TOURNOL . .	Porsche 911S	GT	2195	47	59	43	64																					
60	MEIER - ROUVEYRAN	Porsche 910	Sp	1991	64	42	21																						
61	WICKY - HANRIOUD	Porsche 907	Sp	2200	40	43	42																						
62	MAZZIA - MAUROY	Porsche 911S	GT	2195	62	49	48																						
63	CHENEVIERE - REY	Porsche 911S	GT	2195	67	46	46																						
64	SAGE - GREUB	Porsche 911S	GT	1991	59	64	29																						
65	HALDI - BLANK	Porsche 911S	GT	2195	42	29	64																						
66	LAGNIEZ - SWIETLIK	Porsche 911S	GT	1991	66																								
67	DECHAUMEL - PAROT . . .	Porsche 911S	GT	1991	45																								

BOAC 1000 km

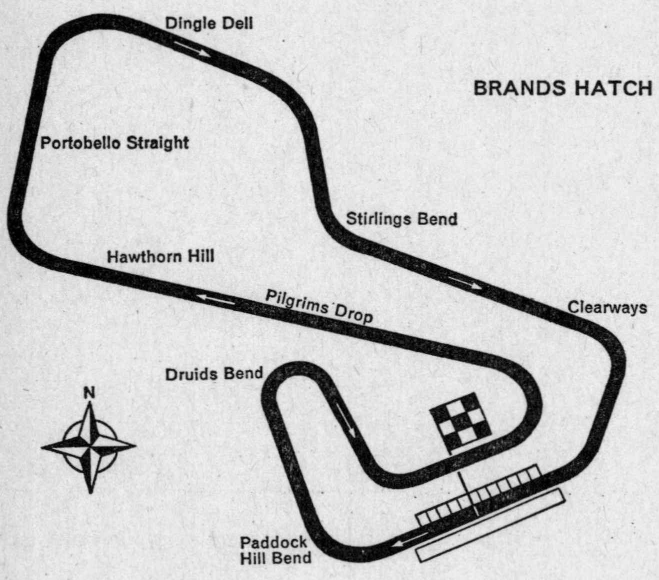

RESULTS

Pos.	Drivers	Make	Cat.	cc	Laps	Time
1**	RODRIGUEZ - KINNUNEN . . .	Porsche 917	Sp	4500	235	6.45'29"6
2	ELFORD - HULME	Porsche 917	Sp	4500	230	
3	ATTWOOD - HERRMANN . .	Porsche 917	Sp	4500	227	
4**	van LENNEP - LAINE	Porsche 908	P	3000	227	
5	AMON - MERZARIO	Ferrari 512 S	Sp	5000	225	
6	LARROUSSE - KOCH	Porsche 908	P	3000	217	
7	BONNIER - WISELL	Lola T 70	Sp	5000	217	
8	ICKX - OLIVER	Ferrari 512 S	Sp	5000	213	
9*	L'AMIE - REID	Porsche 910	Sp	2000	211	
10	LEPP - SILVERWOOD	Chevron B 8	Sp	2000	211	
11	BEUTTLER - GOLD	Porsche 910	Sp	2000	201	
12	BRABHAM - BELTOISE . . .	Matra-Simca 650	P	3000	201	
13	MÜLLER - PARKES	Ferrari 512 S	Sp	5000	197	
14	FRANEY - CLYDESDALE . . .	Chevron B 8	Sp	2000	197	
15*	BIRRELL - MYLIUS	Gropa CMC	P	1800	195	
16	NATHAN - BECKWITH	Astra RNR 2	P	1800	193	
17	BRIDGES - LAWSON	Chevron B 16	P	1800	189	
*	LANFRANCHY - MARK . . .	Nomad MK 2	P	2000	185	
*	de CADENET - del RIO	Porsche 908	P	3000	179	
*	SIFFERT - REDMAN	Porsche 917	Sp	4500	176	
*	PESCAROLO - SERVOZ-GAVIN	Matra-Simca 650	P	3000	161	

** = category winners * = class winners
* = not running at finish.

Winners' average: 92.15 mph.

FORMER WINNERS

Year	Drivers	Make	Average (mph)
1967	P. HILL - SPENCE	Chaparral	93.08
1968	ICKX - REDMAN	Ford	95.96
1969	SIFFERT - REDMAN.	Porsche 908	100.22

1000 km de Monza

RESULTS

Pos.	Drivers	Make	Cat.	cc	Laps	Time
1**	RODRIGUEZ - KINNUNEN . . .	Porsche 917	Sp	4500	174	4.18'01"7
2	GIUNTI - VACCARELLA . . .	Ferrari 512 S	Sp	5000	174	4.19'27"6
3	SURTEES - SCHETTY	Ferrari 512 S	Sp	5000	171	
4	AMON - MERZARIO	Ferrari 512 S	Sp	5000	171	
5**	BELTOISE - BRABHAM . . .	Matra-Simca 650	P	3000	169	
6	PESCAROLO - SERVOZ-GAVIN	Matra-Simca	P	3000	169	
7	GALLI - STOMMELEN	Alfa-Romeo 33-3	P	3000	166	
8	PARKES - MÜLLER	Ferrari 512 S	Sp	5000	163	
9	MORETTI - MANFREDINI . . .	Ferrari 512 S	Sp	5000	163	
10	NEUHAUS - KELLENERS . . .	Porsche 917	Sp	4500	162	
11	LAINE - van LENNEP	Porsche 917	Sp	4500	162	
12	SIFFERT - REDMAN	Porsche 917	Sp	4500	158	
13	de ADAMICH - COURAGE . .	Alfa Romeo 33-3	P	3000	158	
14	LARROUSSE - LINS	Porsche 908	P	3000	157	
15*	WICKY - CABRAL	Porsche 907	P	2000	144	
16	PILETTE - GOSSELIN	Lola-Chevrolet	Sp	5000	143	
17	BLATZHEIM - KRAUSE	Porsche 907	P	2000	139	
18	GREGORY - HEZEMANS. . . .	Alfa Romeo 33-3	P	3000	131	
19*	L'AMIE - NELSON	Porsche 910	Sp	2000	131	
20**	SCHENETTY - ZERBINI	Porsche 911 S	GT	2000	128	
21	GARANT - ILOTTE	Porsche 911 S	GT	2000	127	
22	RONDANINI - BONOMELLI .	Porsche 911 S	GT	2000	122	

** = category winners * = class winners

Winners' average: 144.561 mph.

Fastest lap: V. Elford, Porsche 917, 1'24"8; average: 151.678 mph (new record).

FORMER WINNERS

Year	Drivers	Make	Average (mph)
1965	PARKES - GUICHET	Ferrari	125.88
1966	SURTEES - PARKES	Ferrari	103.08
1967	BANDINI - AMON.	Ferrari	122.34
1968	HAWKINS - HOBBS	Ford	118.24
1969	SIFFERT - REDMAN.	Porsche	128.22

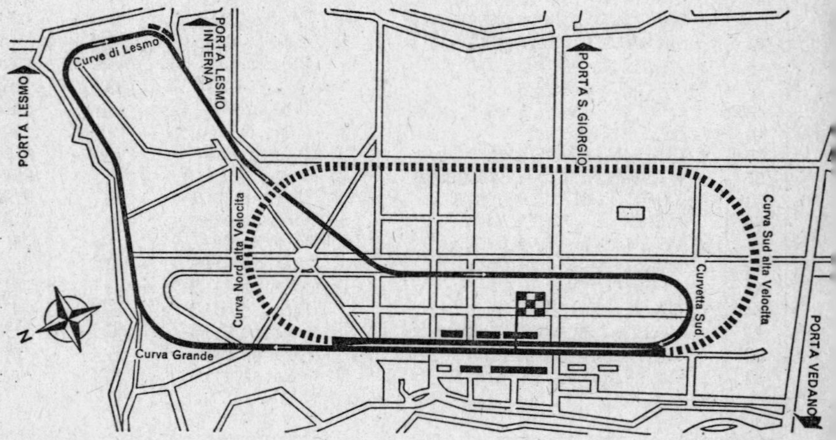

1000 km de Spa-Francorchamps

RESULTS

Pos.	Drivers	Make	Cat.	cc	Laps	Time
1**	SIFFERT - REDMAN	Porsche 917	Sp	5000	71	4.09′47″8
2	ICKX - SURTEES	Ferrari 512 S	Sp	5000	71	4.12′23″3
3	AHRENS - ELFORD	Porsche 917	Sp	5000	70	
4	GIUNTI - VACCARELLA	Ferrari 512 S	Sp	5000	68	
5	LAINE - van LENNEP	Porsche 917	Sp	4500	68	
6	ATTWOOD - HERRMANN	Porsche 917	Sp	4500	68	
7	SCHETTY - MERZARIO	Ferrari 512 S	Sp	5000	66	
8	BELL - de FIERLANT	Ferrari 512 S	Sp	5000	64	
9**	LARROUSSE - LINS	Porsche 908	P	3000	64	
10	BONNIER - WISELL	Lola-Chevrolet	Sp	5000	63	
11	DECHENT - MARKO	Porsche 908	P	3000	62	
12*	L'AMIE - NELSON	Porsche 910	Sp	2000	59	
13*	BLATZHEIM - KRAUS	Porsche 907	P	2000	59	
14	SADLER - VESTEY	Porsche 910	Sp	2000	56	
15	DEPREZ - VERNAEVE	Chevron-Mazda	P	2000	55	
16**	HALDI - CHENEVIERE	Porsche 911 S	GT	2000	55	
17	KELLENERS - NEUHAUS	Porsche 917	Sp	4500	54	
18	KREMER - von WENDT	Porsche 911 S	GT	2000	54	
19	JACQUEMIN - PALAYER	Alpine-Renault	GT	1500	52	
20	BUTSEL - MOERENHOUT	Porsche 911	GT	2000	52	
21	DUVIGNEAUD - DEMOULIN	Porsche 911 S	GT	2000	50	
22	GOODWIN - TAGGART	Chevron-BMW	Sp	2000	48	
23	WICKY - GARANT	Porsche 911 S	GT	2000	41	

** = category winners * = class winners

Winners' average: 149.414 mph.
Fastest lap: P. Rodriguez, Porsche 917, 3′16″5; average: 160.512 mph (new record).

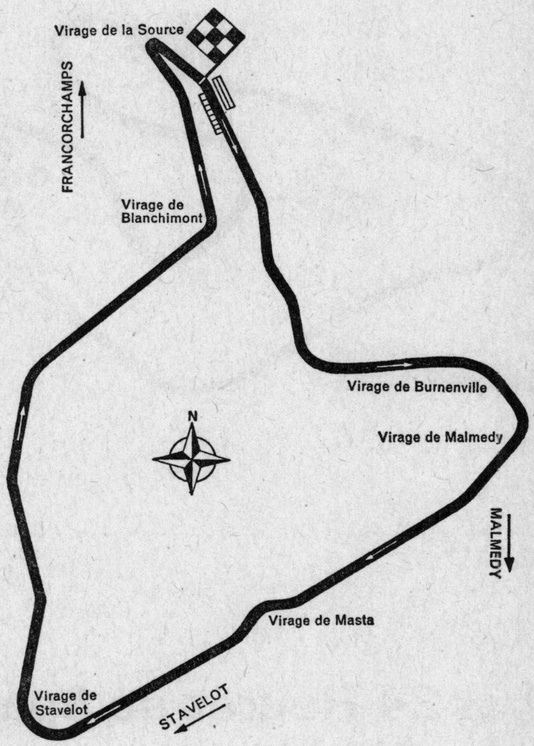

Six Hours of Watkins Glen

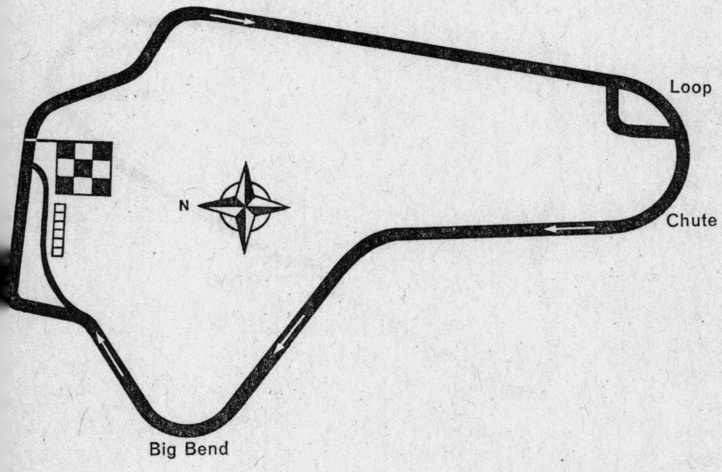

FORMER WINNERS

Year	Drivers	Make	Average (mph)
1968	ICKX - BIANCHI	Ford	109.5
1969	SIFFERT - REDMANN	Porsche	111.3

RESULTS

Pos.	Drivers	Make	Cat.	cc	Laps
1**	RODRIGUEZ - KINNUNEN	Porsche 917	Sp	5000	308
2	SIFFERT - REDMAN	Porsche 917	Sp	5000	308
3	ANDRETTI - GIUNTI	Ferrari 512 S	Sp	5000	305
4	HULME - ELFORD	Porsche 917	Sp	5000	302
5	ICKX - SCHETTY	Ferrari 512 S	Sp	5000	299
6	ATTWOOD - AHRENS	Porsche 917	Sp	5000	295
7**	MARKO - LINS	Porsche 908	P	3000	288
8	BONNIER - WISELL	Lola-Chevrolet T 70	Sp	5000	264
9	LARROUSSE - van LENNEP	Porsche 917	Sp	4500	260
10**	GROSSMAN - YENKO	Chevrolet-Camaro	GT	7000	243
11*	ROSEN - JACOBS	Porsche 906	Sp	2000	241
12	von FRANK - WISE - MANSFIELD	Porsche 906	Sp	2000	236
13*	JENNINGS - TULLIUS	Porsche 911	GT	2200	233
14	BANDY - CARGILL	Lotus-Ford 47	Sp	1600	233
15	PETERMAN - BARTLING - BREZINKA	Porsche 906	Sp	2000	231
16	WRIGHT - GRANT	Porsche 911 S	GT	2000	223
17*	RINZLER - CHRISTIAN - REYNOLDS	Chevron-Ford B 16	P	1800	223
18	GARANT - WICKY	Porsche 911	GT	2200	217
19	BAKER - RICHARDS	Chevron-Ford B 16	P	1800	206
20	MEANEY - BEHR	Porsche 914-6	GT	2000	181

** = category winners * = class winners

Winners' average: 117.81 mph.
Fastest lap: P. Rodriguez, Porsche 917 Nr. 2, 1′04″9; average: 127.58 mph (new record).

1000 km Österreichring

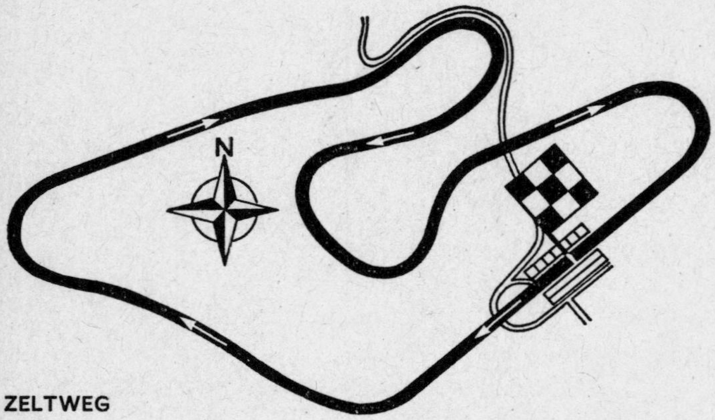

Pos.	Drivers	Make	Cat.	cc	Laps	Time
1 **	SIFFERT - REDMANN	Porsche 917	Sp	5000	170	5.08'04"67
2 **	de ADAMICH - PESCAROLO . .	Alfa Romeo T33/3	P	3000	168	
3	LARROUSSE - LINS	Porsche 908	P	3000	167	
4	ELFORD - ATTWOOD	Porsche 917	Sp	5000	162	
5	JÖST - PANKL	Porsche 908	P	3000	162	
6	LAUDA - PETER	Porsche 908	P	3000	161	
7	LOOS - PESCH	Ferrari 512S	Sp	5000	156	
8 *	WILSON - DAGHORN	Lola-Ford T210	P	1800	153	
9 *	MORESCHI - « PAM »	Abarth 2000 OT	Sp	2000	149	
10	HOFER - REIDL	Porsche 910	P	2000	146	
11	WEIR - de CADENET	Ford GT40	Sp	4700	141	
12 *	STECKKONIG-von HOHENZOLLERN	Porsche 914/6	GT	2000	139	

* = class winners ** = category winners

Winners's average: 121.49 mph.
Fastest lap: J. Ickx, Ferrari 512 M No. 31, 1'40"0; average: 132.24 mph (new record).

Les 24 Heures de Spa-Francorchamps

RESULTS

Pos.	Drivers	Make	cc	Distance in km
1*	HUBER - KELLENERS	BMW 2800 CS	+ 1600	4252.407
2	PINTO - BERGER	Alfa Romeo GTA	+ 1600	4240.195
3	ZECCOLI - FACETTI	Alfa Romeo GTA	+ 1600	4181.273
4	DEMOULIN - BOURGOIGNIE	Alfa Romeo GTA	+ 1600	4152.962
5	ENEVER - HINE	Mazda R 100	+ 1600	4057.736
6	MOORKENS - DEROM	BMW 2002 TI	+ 1600	3983.778
7	MATHAY - XHENCEVAL	BMW 2800 CS	+ 1600	3938.557
8*	MASONERI - GARANT	BMW 2800 GI	+ 1600	3895.665
9	WAUTERS - « CHAVAN »	Opel Commodore	+ 1600	3876.888
10	GOOSSENS - POLAK	Opel Commodore	+ 1600	3863.310
11*	KOOB - HERZOG.	BMW 1600 TI	1000-1600	3859.695
12	VERBEEK - SMET	Opel Commodore	+ 1600	3850.042
13	DEZY - PIZZINATO	Alfa Romeo GTA	1000-1600	3813.217
14	IMBERT - FOUQUET	Alfa Romeo GTA	1000-1600	3810.931
15	« PEDRO » - DUTOIT.	Opel Commodore	+ 1600	3806.780
16	COFFEY - MYERSCOUGH	Ford Escort	1000-1600	3777.085
17	DUVIGNEAUD - HOFMAN	Chevrolet Camaro	+ 1600	3774.788
18	LAGAE - DAMSEAUX	Alfa Romeo	+ 1600	3711.926
19	BLACKBURN - MOSS	Ford Capri 3000	+ 1600	3701.510
20	MONIN - SYLVAIN	BMW 2002 TI	+ 1600	3695.796
21	HENNE - BASCHE	Alfa Romeo 1300	1000-1600	3692.185
22	SAGE - SYDA	BMW 2002 TI	+ 1600	3559.065
23*	ABT - GRANO	Fiat Abarth	0-1000	3503.813
24	MOMBAERTS - MORAY	BMW 2002	+ 1600	3494.004
25	WISSKIRCHEN - KNOLZINGER	NSU TTS	0-1000	3485.262
26	BOUCHER - GUITTENY	NSU TTS	0-1000	3417.408
27*	COLLIGNON - « HEX »	Alfa Romeo GTV	1000-1600	3389.364
28	DONA - POKER	Alfa Romeo GTA	1000-1600	3253.472
29	DERNELLE - GUYETTE	BLMC Mini	0-1000	3113.153
30	SEARLE - NICHOLLS	Ford Escort	0-1000	2806.410

* = class winners

Winners average: 110.095 mph.

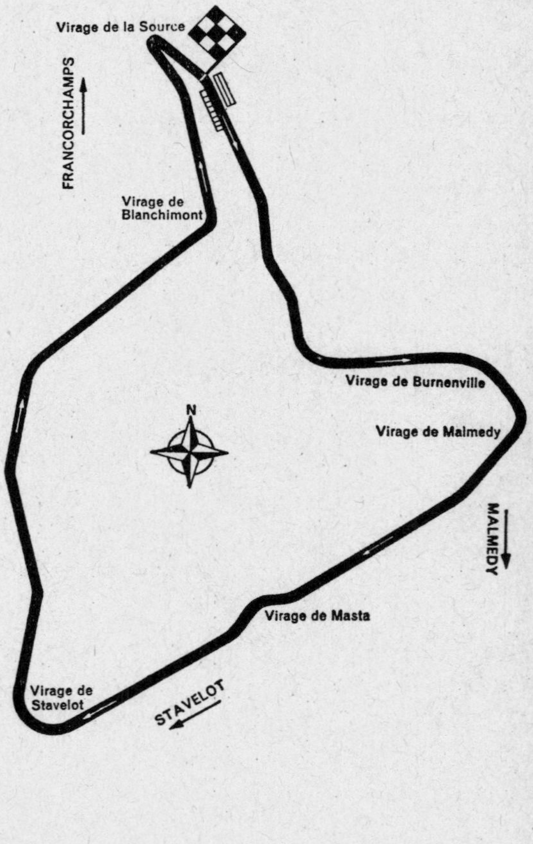

Indianapolis 500-Mile Race

STARTING GRID

2. Al Unser Colt-Ford TCF 3′31″49	18. Johnny Rutherford Eagle-Offy TCO 3′31″50	7. A.J. Foyt Coyote-Ford TCF 3′31″76
11. Roger McCluskey Scorpion-Ford TCF 3′32″75	66. Mark Donohue Lola-Ford TCF 3′33″13	10. Art Pollard King-Offy TCO 3′33″53
3. Bobby Unser Eagle-Ford TCF 3′33″64	1. Mario Andretti McNamara-Ford TCF 3′34″02	31. Jim Malloy Gerhardt-Offy TCO 3′34″42
84. George Snider Coyote-Ford TCF 3′34″72	48. Dan Gurney Eagle-Offy TCO 3′35″75	9. Mike Mosley Eagle-Offy TCO 3′36″02
27. Lee Roy Yarbrough Eagle-Ford TCF 3′36″14	97. Bruce Walkup Mongoose-Offy TCO 3′36″27	38. Rick Muther Hawk-Ford TCF 3′37″32
73. Peter Revson McLaren-Offy TCO 3′34″36	5. Gordon Johncock Gerhardt-Offy TCO 3′35″55	15. Joe Leonard Colt-Ford TCF 3′35″70
75. Carl Williams McLaren-Offy TCO 3′36″10	16. Gary Bettenhausen Gerhardt-Offy TCO 3′36″28	20. George Follmer Hawk-Ford TCF 3′3 6″80
23. Mel Kenyon Coyote-Offy TCO 3′36″99	83. Donnie Allison Eagle-Ford TCF 3′37″31	22. Wally Dallenbach Eagle-Offy TCO 3′37″39
25. Lloyd Ruby Mongoose-Offy TCO 3′33″15	32. Jack Brabham Brabham-Offy TCO 3′36″36	19. Ronnie Bucknum Cecil-Ford TCF 3′36″69
93. Greg Weld Gerhardt-Offy TCO 3′36″71	89. Jeer Grant Eagle-Offy TCO 3′36″89	58. Billy Vukovich Brabham-Offy TCO 3′37″19
44. Dick Simon Vollstedt-Ford TCF 3′37″19	67. Samy Sessions Eagle-Ford TCF 3′37″69	14. Jim McElreath Coyote-Ford TCF 3′35″80

TCO = Turbo-charged Offenhausers TCF = Turbo-charged Fords

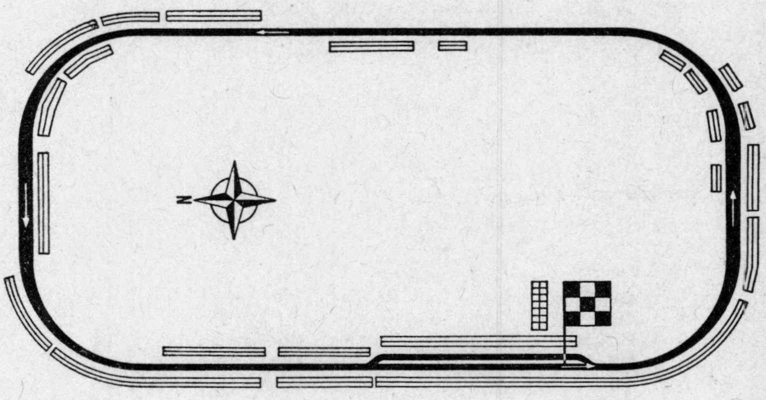

RESULTS

Pos.	No.	Driver	Car	Laps	Time
1	2	Al UNSER	Colt-Ford TCF	200	3.12′37″04
2	66	Mark DONOHUE	Lola-Ford TCF	200	3.13′09″23
3	48	Dan GURNEY	Eagle-Offy TCO	200	3.15′49″25
4	83	Donnie ALLISON	Eagle-Ford TCF	200	3.16′21″86
5	14	Jim McELREATH	Coyote-Ford TCF	200	3.17′07″95
6	1	Mario ANDRETTI	McNamara-Ford TCF	199	
7	89	Jerry GRANT	Eagle-Offy TCO	198	
8	38	Rick MUTHER	Hawk-Offy TCO	197	
9	75	Carl WILLIAMS	McLaren-Offy TCO	197	
10 *	7	A. J. FOYT, Jr.	Coyote-Ford TCF	195	
11	3	Bobby UNSER	Eagle-Ford TCF	192	
12	67	Sammy SESSIONS	Eagle-Ford TCF	190	
13 *	32	Jack BRABHAM	Brabham-Offy TCO	175	
14	44	Dick SIMON	Vollstedt-Ford TCF	168	
15 *	19	Ronnie BUCKNUM	Cecil-Ford TCF	162	
16 *	23	KENYON-McCLUSKEY	Coyote-Offy TCF	160	
17 *	22	Wally DALLENBACH	Eagle-Offy TCO	143	
18 *	18	Johnny RUTHERFORD	Eagle-Offy TCO	135	
19 *	27	Lee Roy YARBROUGH	Eagle-Ford TCF	107	
20 *	84	George SNIDER	Coyote-Ford TCF	105	
21 *	9	Mike MOSLEY	Eagle-Offy TCO	96	
22 *	73	Peter REVSON	McLaren-Offy TCO	87	
23 *	58	Billy VUKOVICH	Brabham-Offy TCO	78	
24 *	15	Joe LEONARD	Colt-Ford TCF	73	
25 *	11	Roger McCLUSKEY	Scorpion-Ford TCF	62	
26 *	16	Gary BETTENHAUSEN	Garhardt-Offy TCO	55	
27 *	25	Lloyd RUBY	Mongoose-Offy TCO	54	
28 *	5	Gordon JOHNCOCK	Gerhardt-Offy TCO	45	
29 *	97	Bruce WALKUP	Mongoose-Offy TCO	44	
30 *	10	Art POLLARD	Kings-Offy TCO	28	
31 *	20	George FOLLMER	Hawk-Ford TCF	18	
32 *	93	Greg WELD	Gerhardt-Offy TCO	12	
33 *	31	Jim MALLOY	Gerhardt-Offy TCO	0	

* = DNF Winner's average: 155.749 mph.

INDIANAPOLIS 500 MILE RACE ROLE OF HONOUR

Year	Drivers	Car name	Average (mph)
1911	Ray HARROUN	Marmon Wasp	74.59
1912	Joe DAWSON	National	78.72
1913	Jules GOUX	Peugeot	75.93
1914	René THOMAS	Delage	82.47
1915	Ralph DE PALMA	Mercedes	89.84
1916	Dario RESTA	Peugeot	84.00
1919	Howard WILCOX	Peugeot	88.05
1920	Gaston CHEVROLET	Monroe	88.62
1921	Tommy MILTON	Frontenac	89.62
1922	Jimmy MURPHY	Murphy Spl.	94.48
1923	Tommy MILTON	HCS Spl	90.95
1924	L. CORUM-J. BOYER	Duesenberg Spl.	98.23
1925	Pete DE PAOLO	Duesenberg Spl.	101.13
1926	Frank LOCKHART	Miller Spl.	95.90
1927	George SOUDERS	Duesenberg	97.55
1928	Louis MEYER	Miller Spl.	99.48
1929	Ray KEECH	Simplex Piston Ring Spl.	97.59
1930	Billy ARNOLD	Miller Hartz Spl.	100.45
1931	Louis SCHNEIDER	Bowes Seal Fast Spl.	96.63
1932	Fred FRAME	Miller Hartz Spl.	104.14
1933	Louis MEYER	Tydol Spl.	104.16
1934	Bill CUMMINGS	Boyle Spl.	104.86
1935	Kelly PETILLO	Gilmore Spl.	106.20
1936	Louis MEYER	Ring Free Spl.	109.06
1937	Wilbur SHAW	Shaw Gilmore Spl.	113.58
1938	Floyd ROBERTS	Burd Piston Ring Spl.	117.20
1939	Wilbur SHAW	Boyle Spl.	115.04
1940	Wilbur SHAW	Boyle Spl.	114.28
1941	Mauri ROSE-Floyd DAVIS	Hose Clamp Spl.	115.12
1946	George ROBSON	Thorne Spl.	114.82
1947	Mauri ROSE	Blue Crown Spark Plug Spl.	116.34
1948	Mauri ROSE	Blue Crown Spark Plug Spl.	119.81
1949	Bill HOLLAND	Blue Crown Spark Plug Spl.	121.33
1950	Johnny PARSONS	Kurtis-Kraft	124.00
1951	Lee WALLARD	Belanger Spl.	126.24
1952	Troy RUTTMAN	Agajanian Spl.	128.92
1953	Bill VUKOVICH	Fuel Injection Spl.	128.74
1954	Bill VUKOVICH	Fuel Injection Spl.	130.84
1955	Bob SWEIKERT	John Zink Spl.	128.21
1956	Pat FLAHERTY	John Zink Spl.	128.49
1957	Sam HANKS	Belond Exhaust Spl.	135.60
1958	Jimmy BRYAN	Belond AP	133.79
1959	Roger WARD	Leader Card Spl.	135.86
1960	Jim RATHMANN	Ken Paul SPl.	138.77
1961	A. J. FOYT	Bowes Seal Fast Spl.	139.13
1962	Roger WARD	Leader Card 500 Roadster Spl.	140.29
1963	Parnelli JONES	Agajanian Willard Battery Spl.	145.13
1964	A. J. FOYT	Sheraton Thompson	147.35
1965	Jim CLARK	Lotus 38-Ford	150.68
1966	Graham HILL	American Red Ball Spl.	144.31
1967	A. J. FOYT	Coyote-Ford	151.21
1968	Bobby UNSER	Eagle-Offy TC	152.88
1969	Mario ANDRETTI	Hawk-Ford TC	156.87

CANADIAN-AMERICAN CHALLENGE CUP

MOSPORT, Canada
June 14; distance: 197 miles

Pos.	Driver	Make	Laps	Time
1	GURNEY	McLaren-Chevrolet	80	1.47′05″6
2	OLIVER	Autocoast-Chevrolet	80	1.47′21″5
3	HULME	McLaren-Chevrolet	78	
4	DEAN	Porsche 908	73	
5	McCAIG	McLaren-Chevrolet	73	
6	DEWAR	McLaren-Chevrolet	72	
7	CAUSEY.	Lola-Chevrolet	70	
8	DURANT	Lola-Chevrolet	70	
9	DORAN	Lola-Chevrolet	68	
10	BREZINKA	McLaren-Chevrolet	67	

Winner's average: 110.214 mph.

Fastest lap: D. Gurney, McLaren, 1′18″0; average: 113.49 mph.

MT-TREMBLANT, Canada
June 28, 1970; distance: 198.75 miles

Pos.	Driver	Make	Laps	Time
1	GURNEY	McLaren-Chevrolet	75	2.01′45″7
2	MOTSCHENBACHER	McLaren-Chevrolet	75	2.01′56″2
3	EATON	BRM-Chevrolet	73	
4	BROWN	McLeagle-Chevrolet	71	
5	McCAIG	McLaren-Chevrolet	70	
6	KOVELESKI	McLaren-Chevrolet	69	
7	TITUS-REVSON . . .	McLaren-Chevrolet	68	
8	PARSONS	Lola-Chevrolet	67	
9	APEL	McLaren-Chevrolet	63	
10	PETERMANN	McLaren-Chevrolet	62	

Winner's average: 97.95 mph.

Fastest lap: D. Hulme, McLaren, 1′34″3; average: 101.17 mph.

WATKINS GLEN, USA
July 12, 1970; distance: 200.1 miles

Pos.	Driver	Make	Laps	Time
1	HULME	McLaren-Chevrolet	87	2.42′26″0
2	SIFFERT	Porsche 917	87	2.42′54″5
3	ATTWOOD	Porsche 917	85	
4	ELFORD	Porsche 917	85	
5	ANDRETTI	Ferrari 512 S	85	
6	van LENNEP	Porsche 917	83	
7	REDMAN	Porsche 917	82	
8	BROWN	McLeagle-Chevrolet	82	
9	GURNEY	McLaren-Chevrolet	81	
10	LARROUSSE	Porsche 908	81	
11	BONNIER	Lola-Chevrolet	80	
12	KOVELESKI	McLaren-Chevrolet	79	
13	CAUSEY.	Lola-Chevrolet	79	
14	BONDURANT	Lola-Chevrolet	76	
15	WILSON	Lola-Chevrolet	76	
16	DEAN	Porsche 908	75	
17	NAGEL	Lola-Chevrolet	74	
18	McCAIG	McLaren-Chevrolet	72	
19	REVSON	Lola-Chevrolet	72	
20	ADAMS	Ferrari 512 S	67	
21	PASQUALE	Lola-Chevrolet	67	

Winner's average: 118.56 mph.

Fastest lap: J. Stewart, Chaparral, 1′05″8; average: 125.85 mph

EDMONTON, Canada
July 26, 1970; distance: 202 miles

Pos.	Driver	Make	Laps	Time
1	HULME	McLaren-Chevrolet	80	1.54′05″5
2	GETHIN	McLaren-Chevrolet	80	1.54′39″0
3	MOTSCHENBACHER	McLaren-Chevrolet	79	
4	BROWN	McLeagle-Chevrolet	78	
5	CAUSEY.	Lola-Chevrolet	76	
6	WILSON	Lola-Chevrolet	76	
7	ADAMS	Ferrari 512 S	75	
8	McCAIG	McLaren-Chevrolet	74	
9	JANKE	McLaren-Chevrolet	70	
10	FREDERICK	McKee-Chevrolet	69	
11	DEAN	Porsche 908	68	

Winner's average: 106.31 mph.

Fastest lap: D. Hulme, McLaren, 1′23″9; average: 108.429 mph.

MID-OHIO, USA
August 23, 1970; distance: 192 miles

Pos.	Driver	Make	Laps	Time
1	HULME	McLaren-Chevrolet	80	2.01′03″3
2	REVSON	Lola-Chevrolet	80	2.02′16″3
3	MOTSCHENBACHER	McLaren-Chevrolet	79	
4	PARSONS	Lola-Chevrolet	77	
5	WILSON	Lola-Chevrolet	76	
6	McCAIG	McLaren-Chevrolet	74	
7	DURANT	Lola-Chevrolet	74	
8*	ADAMS - BONDURANT	Ferrari 512 S	72	
9*	GETHIN	McLaren-Chevrolet	71	
10	NAGEL	Lola-Ford	70	
11	RODRIGUEZ	Ferrari 512 S	70	
12	LAWRENCE	McLaren-Chevrolet	68	
13	SWINDELL	Lola-Chevrolet	68	
14	BREZINKA	McLaren-Chevrolet	67	

* = DNF

Winner's average: 95.163 mph.

Fastest lap: D. Hulme, McLaren, 1′28″8; average: 97.30 mph.

ROAD AMERICA, USA
August 30, 1970; distance: 200 miles

Pos.	Driver	Make	Laps	Time
1	GETHIN	McLaren-Chevrolet	50	1.54′16″1
2	BONDURANT	Lola-Chevrolet	49	
3	CAUSEY.	Lola-Chevrolet	48	
4	WILSON	Lola-Chevrolet	48	
5	DEAN	Porsche 908	48	
6*	BROWN	McLaren-Chevrolet	47	
7	RODRIGUEZ	Ferrari 512 S	47	
8	LAWRENCE	McLaren-Chevrolet	47	
9	DURANT	Lola-Chevrolet	46	
10	GOLDLEAF	McLaren-Chevrolet	46	
11	APEL	McLaren-Chevrolet	45	
12	THORNSJO	Lola-Chevrolet	41	

* = DNF

Winner's average: 105.016 mph.

Fastest lap: D. Hulme, McLaren, 2′12″4; average: 108.762 mph.

ROAD ATLANTA, USA

September 13, 1970; distance: 190 miles

Pos.	Driver	Make	Laps	Time
1.	DEAN	Porsche 908	75	1.49′45″88
2.	CAUSEY.	Lola-Chevrolet	75	1.50′57″09
3.	MOTSCHENBACHER	McLaren-Chevrolet	72	
4.	KOVELESKI	McLaren-Chevrolet	72	
5.	McCAIG	McLaren-Chevrolet	72	
6.	ELFORD	Chaparral-Chevrolet	69	
7.	GETHIN	McLaren-Chevrolet	66	
8.	DURANT	Lola T163	66	
9.	LAWRENCE	McLaren M12	62	
10.	DROLSOM	Lola T70	54	
11.	BREZINKA	McLaren M1C	52	

Winner's average: 103.45 mph.

Fastest lap: P. Revson (Lola TH220) and P. Gethin (McLaren), 1′18″05; average: 116.40 mph.

DONNYBROOKE, USA

September 27, 1970; distance: 210 miles

Pos.	Driver	Make	Laps	Time
1.	HULME	McLaren-Chevrolet	70	1.47′10″2
2.	GETHIN	McLaren-Chevrolet	70	1.48′10″2
3.	REVSON	Lola-Chevrolet	69	
4.	ADAMS	Ferrari 512 S	68	
5.	AMON	March-Chevrolet	67	
6.	MOTSCHENBACHER	McLaren-Chevrolet	66	
7.	DEAN	Porsche 908	66	
8.	CAUSEY.	Lola-Chevrolet	66	
9.	RODRIGUEZ	BRM-Chevrolet	66	
10.	GREGG	Lola-Chevrolet	66	
11.	LAWRENCE	McLaren-Chevrolet	65	
12.	KOVELESKI	McLaren-Chevrolet	64	
13.	DEWAR	McLaren-Chevrolet	63	
14.	KANTRUD	Lola-Chevrolet	63	
15.	McCAIG	McLaren-Chevrolet	62	
16.	CORDTS	Lola-Chevrolet	62	
17.	FREDERICK	McKee-Chevrolet	60	
18.	BREZINKA	McLaren-Chevrolet	59	
19.	ROSBACH	Lola-Chevrolet	59	
20.	ROE	McKee-Chevrolet	51	

Winner's average: 117.570 mph.

Fastest lap: D. Hulme, McLaren, 1′29″5; average: 120.67 mph.

LAGUNA SECA, USA

October 18, 1970; distance: 152 miles

Pos.	Driver	Make	Laps	Time
1.	HULME	McLaren-Chevrolet	80	1.25′58″8
2.	OLIVER	TRC-Chevrolet	80	1.26′00″0
3.	REVSON	Lola-Chevrolet	79	
4.	AMON	March-Chevrolet	78	
5.	RODRIGUEZ.	BRM-Chevrolet	78	
6.	PARSONS	Lola-Chevrolet	78	
7.	ADAMOWICZ	McLaren-Chevrolet	77	
8.	WILSON	Lola-Chevrolet	77	
9.	CAUSEY	Lola-Chevrolet	76	
10.	LAWRENCE	McLaren-Chevrolet	76	
11.	McCAIG.	McLaren-Chevrolet	75	
12.	GREGG	Lola-Chevrolet	75	
13.	BRENNAN	Genie-Chevrolet	73	
14.	LESLIE	McLaren-Chevrolet	72	
15.	DURANT	Lola-Chevrolet	71	
16.	JENSEN	Burnett-Chevrolet	71	
17.	GULDSTRAND	Lola-Chevrolet	66	

Winner's average: 105.068 mph.

Fastest lap: J. Oliver, TRC-Chevrolet, 1′02″4; average: 109.6 mph.

RIVERSIDE, USA

November 1, 1970: distance: 201 miles

Pos.	Driver	Make	Laps	Time
1.	HULME	McLaren-Chevrolet	61	1.40′27″4
2.	OLIVER	Norris Ti 22	61	1.40′35″6
3.	RODRIGUEZ	BRM-Chevrolet	59	
4.	AMON	March 707-Chevrolet	59	
5.	MOTSCHENBACHER . .	McLaren-Chevrolet	59	
6.	BROWN	McLaren-Chevrolet	57	
7.	ADAMOWICZ	McLaren-Chevrolet	57	
8.	CAUSEY	Lola-Chevrolet	56	
9.	DEAN	Porsche 908	56	
10.	McCAIG	McLaren-Chevrolet	56	
11.	HILLS	McLaren-Chevrolet	55	
12.	GULDSTRAND	Lola-Chevrolet	55	
13.	GREGG.	Lola-Chevrolet	54	
14.	McKITTERICK	Terry T10	54	
15.	SHELTON.	McLaren M2B	53	

Winner's average: 120.284 mph.

FINAL CLASSIFICATION

				Mosport	St. Jovite	Watkins Glen	Edmonton	Mid-Ohio	Road America	Road Atlanta	Donnybrooke	Laguna Seca	Riverside	Total *
1	Denis HULME	NZ	McLaren-Chevrolet	12	—	20	20	20	—	—	20	20	20	**132**
2	Lothar MOTSCHENBACHER	USA	McLaren-Chevrolet	—	15	—	12	12	—	12	6	—	8	**65**
3	Peter GETHIN.	GB	McLaren-Chevrolet	—	—	—	15	2	20	4	15	—	—	**56**
4	Dave CAUSEY	USA	Lola-Chevrolet	4	2	—	8	—	12	15	3	2	3	**47**
5	Jackie OLIVER	GB	Norris-Chevrolet	15	—	—	—	—	—	—	—	15	15	**45**
6	Tony DEAN	USA	Porsche 908	10	—	—	—	—	8	20	4	—	2	**44**
7	Dan GURNEY	USA	McLaren-Chevrolet	20	20	2	—	—	—	—	—	—	—	**42**
8	Peter REVSON	USA	Lola-Chevrolet	—	—	—	—	15	—	—	12	12	—	**39**
9	Bob BROWN	USA	McLaren-Chevrolet	—	10	3	10	—	6	—	—	—	6	**35**
10	Roger McCAIG	CDN	McLaren-Chevrolet	8	8	—	3	6	—	8	—	—	1	**34**

* For classification, only the four best of the first five results and the four best of the second five are retained.

EUROPEAN HILL-CLIMB CHAMPIONSHIP

Extract from the Regulations of the International Automobile Federation

Art. 2. Eligible cars

Group 2: Special touring cars
Group 4: Special grand touring cars
Group 5: Sportscars

Art. 3. Type of events

The qualifying events counting for the European Championship must have a minimum run of 5 km and a difference of level of at least 350 metres between the starting point and the finish line. In the events of 10 km or more, the difference will be at least 500 m. There will be only one or two climbs according to the provisions of the specific regulations.

Art. 4. Classification and prizes

For each qualifying event will be established a general overall classification, all groups amalgamated, as well as supplementary classifications per group of cars (Groups 2, 4 and 5).

For each qualifying event, a driver shall be granted points for his place in the general overall classification. Moreover, he will receive points for his place in the supplementary classifications per groups of cars, in compliance with the following scale:

Numbers of starters in the group concerned	Number of points attributed Place 1st	2nd	3rd	4th	5th	6th
2	1					
3 or 4	2	1				
5 or 6	3	2	1			
7 or 8	4	3	2	1		
9 or 10	6	4	3	2	1	
11 and over	9	6	4	3	2	1

There will be no granting of points for a classification per group of cars if less than 5 vehicles have actually started in the group concerned.

MONTSENY, Spain

May 24; distance: 10 miles

Sport		1 run
1. M. CASONI (I), Abarth 2000	63.935 mph	9'30"28
2. « RICCARDONE » (I), Abarth 2000		9'44"42
3. G. TARAMAZZO (I), Abarth 2000		10'04"65
4. M. JUNCOSA (E), Abarth 1000		10'39"85
Special grand touring		
1. C. HALDI (CH), Porsche 911 S		10'36"43
2. S. GREGER (D), Porsche 914		10'46"89
3. W. BARTELS (D), Porsche 911 T		11'08"66
4. J. SOLÉ (E), Seat 850		13'39"76
Special touring		
1. E. FURTMAYR (D), BMW 2002		10'31"51
2. P. KELLER (D), BMW 2002 TI		10'48"27
3. J. BÄBLER (E), BMW 2002		10'55"85
4. J. Mª PALOMO (E), Seat 1430		11'28"67
5. L. LÓPEZ MIR (E), BLMC		12'43"67
6. « JORGE CHI » (E), Abarth 850		13'04"50

TRENTO-BONDONE, Italy

July 5, 1970; distance: 10.75 miles

Sport		1 run
1. F. PILONE (I) Abarth	54.597 mph	11'48"82
2. « RICCARDONE » (I) Abarth		11'50"29
3. L. TARAMAZZO (I) Abarth		11'50"53
4. « GI-BI » (I) Abarth		12'18"38
5. K. FEDERHOFER (D) Abarth		12'55"49
6. L. MORESCHI (I) Abarth		12'58"27
Special grand touring		
1. C. HALDI (CH) Porsche 911		12'33"98
2. E. BONOMELLI (I) Porsche 911		12'43"67
3. S. GREGER (D) Porsche 914		12'50"08
4. G. C. RONDANINI (I) Porsche 2400		12'59"76
5. G. C. GALIMBERTI (I) Lancia Fulvia HF		13'12"31
6. A. de PAOLI (I) Opel GT 1900		13'14"80
Special touring		
1. J. MASS (D) Ford Capri		12'38"34
2. E. FURTMAYR (D) BMW 2800 CS		12'39"27
3. D. SCHMID (D) BMW 2002 TI		12'56"28
4. P. MATTLI (CH) BMW 2002 TI		13'13"94
5. R. RICCI (I) BMW 2002 TI		13'24"78
6. G. POZZO (I) Alfa Romeo GTA		13'26"55

MONT-VENTOUX, France

June 22, 1970; distance: 13.4 miles

Sport		1 run
1. J. ORTNER (A), Abarth 2000		12'00"8
2. A. FINKEL (F), Abarth 2000		12'34"9
3. « POGO » (I), Abarth 2000		13'56"3
4. « CYPRIEN » (F), Abarth 2000		14'40"8
Special grand touring		
1. S. GREGER (D), Porsche 911		12'08"7
2. J. ORTELLI (F), Alpine 110		12'25"9
3. F. ALESI (F), Alpine 110		12'26"5
4. S. FROHDE (S), Porsche 911		12'29"8
5. H. BALAS (F), Porsche		12'46"5
6. C. HALDI (CH), Porsche		13'07"2
Special touring		
1. E. FURTMAYR (D), BMW 2800	72.407 mph	11'07"3
2. J. MASS (D), Ford Capri		11'11"3
3. S. DINI (I), Alfa Romeo		11'17"5
4. P. KELLER (CH), BMW 2001		11'38"4
5. D. SCHMIDT (D), BMW 2002		11'47"4
6. M. MOGA (F), Ford Mustang		12'16"0

FREIBURG-SCHAUINSLAND, Germany

July 26, 1970; distance: 6.96 miles

Sport		2 runs
1. J. ORTNER (A) Abarth	71.681 mph	11'38"97
2. F. PILONE (I) Abarth		11'57"91
3. K. FEDERHOFER (D) Abarth		13'13"45
4. R. WEILAND (D) Ferrari		14'29"71
Special grand touring		
1. S. FROHDE (S) Porsche 911 T		12'51"45
2. C. HALDI (CH) Porsche 911 S		12'36"25
3. S. GREGER (D) Porsche 914/6		13'00"39
4. P. ETTMÜLLER (CH) Alpine-Renault		13'10"86
5. W. BARTELS (D) Porsche 911 S		13'14"02
6. R. GÖRING (D) Porsche 911 T		13'17"53
Special touring		
1. J. MASS (D) Ford Capri		12'49"49
2. P. KELLER (CH) BMW		13'03"05
3. A. KREBS (D) BMW		13'12"94
4. G. SCHÖCHLIN (D) BMW		13'15"29
5. J. POHLMANN (D) BMW		13'47"60
6. G. BELLOF (D) BMW-Alpine		13'55"76

CESANA-SESTRIERE, Italy

July 12, 1970; distance: 6.44 miles

Sport		1 run
1. J. ORTNER (A), Abarth	75.679 mph	5'07"4
2. F. PILONE (I), Abarth		5'12"6
3. « POGO » (I), Abarth		5'13"0
4. G. TARAMAZZO (I), Abarth		5'16"3
5. « GI-BI » (I), Abarth		5'20"1
6. G. VARESE (I), Abarth		5'46"0

Special grand touring

1. C. HALDI (CH), Porsche	5'37"3
2. E. BONOMELLI (I), Porsche	5'40"9
3. S. GREGER (D), Porsche	5'43"7
4. M. ILOTTE (I), Porsche	5'47"6
5. R. RUSPA (I), Alfa Romeo GTA	5'56"3
6. F. GENTA (I), Porsche	5'56"5

Special touring

1. E. FURTMAYR (D), BMW 2800	5'38"2
2. J. MASS (D), Ford	5'44"0
3. A. ROSSELLI (I), Alfa Romeo	5'45"6
4. P. KELLER (CH), BMW 2002	5'48"9
5. P. de LEONIBUS (I), Alfa Romeo GTA	5'54"8
6. « GAP » (I), BMW 2002	6'04"3

MONT-DORE, France

August 9, 1970; distance: 3.10 miles

Sport		2 runs
1. J. ORTNER (A), Abarth 2000	60.90 mph	6'14"4
2. F. PILONE (I), Abarth		6'34"5
3. A. FINKEL (F), Abarth		6'45"3
4. H. HAZARD (F), Porsche 910		6'53"6
5. A. BERSANO (I), Abarth 1000		7'51"8

Special grand touring

1. C. HALDI (CH), Porsche 911 S	6'36"0
2. S. GREGER (D), Chevrolet Corvette	6'48"2
3. H. BALLAS (F), Porsche 911 S	6'50"3
4. A. CLEMENT (F), Alpine 1600	6'51"3
5. R. CHARRIERE (F), Alpine 1600	6'57"8
6. J. VIGNAUD (F), Alpine 1600	7'02"2

Special touring

1. P. KELLER (CH), BMW 2002 TI	6'37"2
2. E. FURTMAYR (D), BMW 2800 CS	6'38"7
3. J. MAAS (D), Ford Capri	6'40"7
4. E. HERMAN (F), BMC Cooper	7'19"0
5. R. BOUBET (F), Cooper 1300	7'24"2
6. M. HAZARD (F), BMW 2002 TI	7'26"0

DOBRATSCH, Austria

September 27, 1970; distance: 4 miles

Sport		2 runs
1. J. ORTNER (A), Abarth	77.56 mph	6'02"8
2. F. PILONE (I), Abarth		6'05"8
3. « PAM » (I), Abarth		6'10"1
4. « RICCARDONE » (I), Abarth		6'10"2
5. H. WENGERT (D), Abarth		6'14"9
6. C. REISCH (A), Alfa Romeo		6'19"4

Special grand touring

1. B. CHENEVIÈRE (CH), Porsche	6'49"2
2. M. ILOTTE (I), Porsche	6'52"6
3. W. BARTELS (D), Porsche	7'02"2

Special touring

1. E. FURTMAYR (D), BMW 2800	6'46"3
2. H. MASS (D), Ford	6'47"3
3. G. KRAMMER (A), Alfa Romeo	7'06"2
4. K. WENDLINGER (A), Abarth	7'24"7
5. A. JOSL (A), NSU	7'26"2
6. W. RUDOLPH (A), NSU	7'26"9

	FINAL CLASSIFICATION			Montseny	Mont-Ventoux	Cesana-Sestriere	Trento-Bondone	Freiburg-Schauinsland	Mont-Dore	Dobratsch	overall total	retained total*
1	Johannes ORTNER	A	Abarth	—	4	18	—	12	12	18	64	**64**
2	Franco PILONE	I	Abarth	—	—	12	18	8	8	12	58	**58**
3	Claude HALDI	CH	Porsche	5	—	10	11	13	10	—	49	**49**
4	Ernst FURTMAYR	D	BMW	12	15	9	6	—	5	6	53	**48**
5	Jochen MASS	D	Ford	—	10	6	10	12	3	4	45	**42**
6	Paul KELLER	CH	BMW	6	5	3	—	6	7	—	27	**27**
7	« RICCARDONE »	I	Abarth	6	—	—	12	—	—	6	24	**24**
8	Sepp GREGER	D	Porsche	2	4	4	4	5	—	—	19	**19**
9	Luigi TARAMAZZO	I	Abarth	4	—	6	8	—	—	—	18	**18**
10	« GI-BI »	I	Abarth	—	—	4	6	—	—	—	10	**10**

*** For classification, only the 5 best results are retained.**

EUROPEAN RALLY CHAMPIONSHIP

39th RALLYE DE MONTE-CARLO

January 16 to 24, 1970

First 15 positions overall

	Drivers	Make	Points
1.	WALDEGÄRD - HELMER (S) . . .	Porsche 911	19 744
2.	LARROUSSE - GELIN (F)	Porsche 911	19 863
3.	NICOLAS - ROURE (F)	Alpine	19 814
4.	ANDERSSON - THORSELIUS (S) .	Porsche 911	20 175
5.	CLARK - PORTER (GB)	Ford Escort	20 291
6.	BALLESTRIERI - AUDETTO (I) . .	Lancia HF	20 417
7.	MAKINEN - LIDDON (GB)	Ford Escort	20 599
8.	BARBASIO - MANNUCCI (I) . . .	Lancia HF	20 772
9.	CHARRIERE - CASTEL (F)	Alpine	21 819
10.	PIANTA - PALEARI (I)	Lancia 1600	22 178
11.	RAGNOTTI - THIMONIER (F) . . .	Opel Kadett	22 401
12.	WALTER - RACK (D)	Porsche 911	22 544
13.	HANRIOUD - PERAY (F)	BMW 2002	22 545
14.	POUDEROUX - VINCENT (F) . . .	Citroën DS	22 671
15.	CHRIS - CROUS (F)	Renault R	22 709

21st KAK-RALLYT: SWEDISH RALLY

February 11 to 15, 1970

First 15 positions overall

	Drivers	Make	Points
1.	WALDEGÄRD - HELMER (S)	Porsche 911 S	44 450
2.	BLOMQVIST S. - REINIKE (S)	Saab V4	45 846
3.	NASENIUS - CEDERBERG (S)	Opel Kadett	46 773
4.	BLOMQVIST G. - BLOMQVIST I. (S) .	Opel Kadett	47 184
5.	LARSSON - LUNDBLAD (S)	Porsche 911 S	47 517
6.	GULLBERT - WÄHLIN (S)	BMW 2002 TI	47 840
7.	KULLÄNG - KARLSSON (S)	Opel Kadett	47 933
8.	FROHM - OTTOSSON (S)	Ford Escort TC	47 978
9.	ANDERSSON R. - ANDERSSON C. (S)	Volvo 142	48 670
10.	OLSSON O. - TÖRNQVIST (S)	BMW 2002 TI	48 791
11.	CARLSSON - OLSSON A. (S)	Volvo 122	49 948
12.	DANIELSSON - JOHANSSON (S) . .	Opel Kadett	50 031
13.	ÄHLIN - FREDRIKSSON (S)	Opel Kadett	50 848
14.	KEDEMARK - STÄHLGREN (S)	Triumph 2,5 PI	51 316
15.	HOLMSTRÖM - WESTERLUND (S) . .	BMW 2002	52 183

1st SAN REMO-SESTRIERE: ITALIAN RALLY

March 3 to 6, 1970

First 15 positions overall

	Drivers	Make	Points
1.	THERIER - CALLEWAERT (F).	Alpine Renault	810.5
2.	KALLSTRÖM - HAGGBOM (S)	Lancia Fulvia HF	1 037.7
3.	VINATIER - JACOB (F)	Alpine Renault	1 600.0
4.	TRANA - ANDREASSON (S)	Saab	1 796.0
5.	PIANTA - KUSTER (I)	Lancia Fulvia HF	2 146.0
6.	SMANIA - ZANCHETTI (I)	Fiat 125 S	2 859.7
7.	CECCATO - EISENDLE (I)	Fiat 125 S	3 013.5
8.	LINDBERG - HERTZ (S).	Saab	3 130.0
9.	PAGANELLI - RUSSO (I)	Fiat 124	3 488.4
10.	TECILLA - SCABINI (I)	Fiat 125 S	3 679.0
11.	SONDA - TURRI (I).	Fiat 125 S	4 048.5
12.	BENETTI - VIGLINO (I)	Renault-Gordini	4 439.5
13.	INNOCENTE - FREGNAN (I)	Lancia Fulvia HF	6 617.9
14.	BOLOGNA - RAVIOLA (I)	Lancia Fulvia HF	6 958.5
15.	ZAMBELLI - PIZZO (I)	Fiat 125 S	10 394.0

23rd RALLYE LYON-CHARBONNIÈRES/ STUTTGART-SOLITUDE

March 13 to 15, 1970

First 15 positions overall

	Drivers	Make	Time
1.	ANDRUET - STONE (F-GB)	Alpine	3′00″40
2.	HALDI - CHAPUIS (CH)	Porsche 911 S	3′16″01
3.	HENRY - SALDER (F)	Alpine	3′16″56
4.	WARMBOLD - BIEBINGER (D)	Opel Kadett	3′23″14
5.	BEIN - MAHMEL (D)	BMW 2002 TI	3′33″25
6.	CHARRIERE - CASTEL (F)	Alpine	3′33″26
7.	RAGNOTTI - THIMONNIER (F)	Opel Kadett	3′34″44
8.	PALAYER - DENIS (F)	BMW	3′36″10
9.	DIRAND - VAUTRIN (F)	BMW 2002 TI	3′36″53
10.	BEAUMONT - GRANDRIVE (F)	Opel Kadett	3′42″56
11.	DARMICHE - DEMANGE (F)	Alpine	3′48″24
12.	KLEINT H. - KLAPPROTH (D)	Ford Escort GT	3′50″04
13.	LABAUNE - « LHA-KHES » (F)	Porsche 911 S	3′50″57
14.	WEBER H. - GOTTSCHICK (D)	NSU GT S	3′51″06
15.	EYMANN - FUCHS (D)	BMW	3′54″44

10th PNEUMANT RALLYE — RALLYE DDR

March 18 to 21, 1970

Overall classification

	Drivers	Make	Points
1.	HOMMEL - BORK (DDR)	Wartburg 353	256.67
2.	SMORAWINSKI - ZEMBRZUSKI (PL)	BMW 2002 TI	293.87
3.	CALLESJÖ - OLSSON (S)	Ford Capri 2300 GT	451.70
4.	STREHLOW - MALSCH (DDR) . . .	Wartburg 353	635.39
5.	ASMUS - PIEHLER (DDR).	Trabant 601	651.16
6.	NOWICKI - KOMOROWSKI (PL) . .	Renault-Gordini R8	875.81
7.	NIELSEN - LIND - ISAKSEN (DK) . .	BMW 2002 TI	899.32
8.	ULLMANN - LANGE (DDR)	Trabant 601 S	970.97
9.	F. KRAMER - G. KRAMER (DDR) . .	Trabant 601	1385.78
10.	EHRLICH - SCHÖNE (DDR)	Wartburg 311	1720.40
11.	SUHR - HIDDEL (DDR)	Wartburg 353	1778.81

18th EAST AFRICAN SAFARI

March 26 to 30, 1970

First 15 positions overall

	Drivers	Make	Points
1.	HERRMANN - SCHULLER (EAK-D) . . .	Datsun 1600 SSS	395
2.	JOGINDER - RANYARD (EAK)	Datsun 1600 SSS	446
3.	SHANKLAND - ROTHWELL (EAT) . . .	Peugeot 504	489
4.	DIN - MUGHAL (EAU)	Datsun 1600 SSS	509
5.	MICHAELIDES - ROBINSON (EAK) . .	Volvo 122 S	670
6.	MANDEVILLE - ALLISON (EAK)	Triumph	670
7.	KIRKLAND - ROSE (EAK)	Datsun 1600 SSS	698
8.	HARRIS - AUSTIN (EAK)	Peugeot 504	762
9.	ESPOSITO - RANDALL (EAK)	Alfa Romeo Giulia	810
10.	NOWICKI - CLIFF (EAK)	Peugeot 504	866
11.	SHAH - T. SINGH (EAK)	Datsun 1600 SSS	905
12.	KUNER - SULEMAN - SALIM (EAK). . .	Datsun 1600 SSS	919
13.	D. SINGH - DHANJI (EAK)	Saab 96	946
14.	REMTULLA - JIVANI (EAK)	Peugeot 404	946
15.	H. SINGH - M. SINGH - MANGAT (EAK)	Peugeot 404	955

GALLAHER CIRCUIT OF IRELAND RALLY

March 27 to 31, 1970

First 15 positions overall

	Drivers	Make	Penalty marks
1.	CLARK – PORTER (GB)	Ford Escort TC	566.5
2.	SCLATER – VALENTINE (IRL)	Ford Escort TC	723.7
3.	HENRIKSSON – CARLSTRÖM (S)	Opel Kadett	741.6
4.	McBURNEY – SMITH (IRL)	BMW 2002 TI	786.1
5.	JONSSON – QUIST (S)	Saab 96	830.9
6.	BLOXHAM – HARPER (IRL)	BMW 2002 TI	837.5
7.	BOYD – CRAWFORD (IRL)	Ford Escort TC	878.5
8.	DOLAN – O'BRIEN (IRL)	Ford Escort TC	890.0
9.	FOWKES – O'GORMAN (IRL)	Lotus Cortina	896.3
10.	DANIELLSSON – JOHANSSON (S)	Opel Kadett	932.5
11.	SYREN – LARSSON (IRL)	BMW 2002	953.8
12.	JOHNSTON – ALLEN (IRL)	BLMC-Cooper S	957.7
13.	THOMPSON – ISLEY (IRL)	Vauxhall Viva GT	991.2
14.	RIDOUT – COLLEY (IRL)	Ford Escort TC	995.4
15.	O'GORMAN – CONWAY (IRL)	Ford Escort TC	1009.3

3th RALLYE DELL'ISOLA D'ELBA

April 3 to 4, 1970

First 15 positions overall

	Drivers	Make	Points
1.	PAGANELLI - RUSSO (I)	Fiat 124 S	193.0
2.	CECCATO - EISENDLE (I)	Fiat 125 S	380.0
3.	BISULLI - ZANUCCOLI (I)	Fiat 125	569.7
4.	TECILLA - SCABINI (I)	Fiat 125 S	607.5
5.	SONDA - TURRI (I)	Fiat 125 S	739.6
6.	TROMBOTTO - BOSSOLA (I)	Fiat 124 S	786.6
7.	SMANIA - ZANCHETTI (I)	Fiat 125 S	917.5
8.	GIUBAR - SCALABRINI (I)	Fiat 124	2218.5
9.	SQUILLACE - BETTINI (I)	Lancia Fulvia	2406.0
10.	« POPO » - ZANUSSI (I)	Lancia HF	2850.5
11.	LO BELLO - LO BELLO (I)	Lancia Fulvia	2985.0
12.	BARTOLETTI - BARTOLETTI (I)	Fiat 128	3057.7
13.	MISCHIATTI - TAGLIERETTI (I)	Fiat 850	3204.5
14.	GIORGI - RICCIONI (I)	Lancia 1300	3426.0
15.	VIGLIETTA - « POL » (I)	Citroën DS	3752.5

22nd INTERNATIONALE TULPENRALLYE

May 3 to 9, 1970

First 15 positions overall

	Drivers	Make	Points
1.	van GRIEKEN - VERBUNT (NL)	BMW 2002 TI	963.4
2.	RAGNOTTI - THIMONIER (F)	Opel Kadett	1040.9
3.	BARBASIO - MANNUCCI (I)	Lancia Fulvia HF	1152.7
4.	PON - WIEDENHOFF (NL)	VW 1600	1261.0
5.	BEAUMONT - FOUQUET (F)	Opel GT	1276.5
6.	BORJESSON - STERNER (NL)	Opel Kadett	1313.0
7.	KLAUSE - GODICHARD (NL)	Renault-Gordini	1368.4
8.	GULIKER - SCHOONDERBEEK (NL)	BMW 2002 TI	1391.9
9.	SIGURDSON - BERGLUND (NL)	Saab V4	1393.0
10.	PALMER - SPOKES (GB)	Porsche 911	1462.8
11.	GASTSONIDES - BUWALDA (NL)	Daf 55	1553.1
12.	W. LUYBREGTS - J. LUYBREGTS (NL)	Daf 55	1749.6
13.	VEDER - MOUWES (NL)	BMW 2002 TI	1750.0
14.	EDWARDS - DRUMMOND-WALKER (NL)	Ford Escort TC	1809.6
15.	D. de WILD - W. de WILD (NL)	Vauxhall Viva	1821.3

41st INTERNATIONALE ÖSTERREICHISCHE ALPENFAHRT

May 6 to 10, 1970

First 15 positions overall

	Drivers	Make	Points
1.	WALDEGÄRD - NYSTRÖM (S)	Porsche 911 S	9 016.8
2.	LINDBERG - ANDREASSON (S)	Saab V 4	9 250.0
3.	PIOT - TODT (F)	Ford Escort TC	9 297.6
4.	BOYD - CRAWFORD (GB)	Ford Escort TC	10 038.8
5.	DARNICHE - MAHÉ (F)	Alpine Renault	10 067.3
6.	LUX - SIEBERT (A)	VW 1500	10 530.1
7.	WURZ - ZÖGL (A)	Ford Escort TC	10 563.9
8.	Rich. ZELENKA - Rob. ZELENKA (A)	Ford Escort TC	10 727.7
9.	KALLSTRÖM - HAGGBOM (S)	Lancia Fulvia HF	10 734.4
10.	RUSSLING - EGGENBERGER (A)	Porsche 911	10 816.0
11.	BOCHNICEK - KERNMAYER (A)	Citroën DS 21	11 268.5
12.	ELTZ - NESTINGER (A)	VW 1500	11 360.4
13.	TROMBOTTO - BOSSOLA (I)	Fiat 124	11 748.5
14.	KAJA - BREZA (A)	BMW 2002 TI	11 887.1
15.	BINDER - STREIT (A)	NSU 1000 TTS	11 942.3

32nd INTERNATIONALE RALLYE WIESBADEN DEUTSCHLAND RALLYE

May 22 to 24, 1970

First 15 positions overall

	Drivers	Make	Points
1.	WARMBOLD - BIEBINGER (D)	Opel Kadett	20
2.	HUBACEK - RIEGER (CS)	Renault-Gordini	120
3.	RICHTER - POLLAND (D)	BMW 2002 TI	140
4.	RACK - KOEHLER (D)	Porsche 911 S	190
5.	MIERSCH - AGETHEN (D)	Opel Kadett	206
6.	KLEINT - KLAPPROTH (D)	Ford Capri	210
7.	SCHONS - ZWEIBAEUMER (D)	Ford Capri	266
8.	MEMMEL - RAUCH (D)	Opel Kadett	292
9.	BEIN - MEHMEL (D)	BMW-Alpina	360
10.	KOMORNICKI - KRUPA (PL)	Alpine Renault	386
11.	ROSER - LOIBNEGGER (A)	Alpine Renault	416
12.	P. BRINK - H.-J. BRINK (D)	Porsche 911 S	434
13.	LEYEN - SCHNEIDER (D)	Renault-Gordini	449
14.	HAINBACK - HERTWECK (D)	Opel Kadett	480
15.	STOEHR - KROENINGER (D)	BMW 2002 TI	504

14th INTERNATIONALE BODENSEE-NEUSIEDLERSEE — RALLYE

May 28 to 30, 1970

First 15 positions overall

	Drivers	Make	Points
1.	GASS - FREY (D)	Porsche 911 S-C	4126.5
2.	BEIN - MEHMEL (D)	BMW Alpina 2002	4250.6
3.	SCHINDLER - HRUSCHKA (A)	Porsche 914/6	4254.4
4.	NEGER - STERNECKER (A)	BMW 2002 TI	4416.9
5.	R. ZELENKA - R. ZELENKA (A)	Ford Escort TC	4422.2
6.	UTZ - BRUST (D)	BMW 2002 TI	4442.2
7.	NEUKOM - HOPF (A)	BMW 2002 TI	4460.0
8.	BARBASIO - MANNUCCI (I)	Lancia HF 1600	4485.6
9.	WARMBOLD - BIEBINGER (D)	Opel Kadett	4561.1
10.	LUX - SIEBERTH (A)	VW 1500	4576.9
11.	RYSZARD - KOMOROWSKI (PL)	Renault-Gordini	4581.4
12.	WURZ - ZOEGL (A)	Ford Escort TC	4583.0
13.	DIETMAYER - QUIDENUS (A)	BMW 2002 TI	4587.7
14.	FISCHER - RADER (A)	VW 1500	4591.3
15.	FESSL - PIPPAN (A)	Renault-Gordini	4598.4

18th ACROPOLIS RALLY

May 27 to June 2, 1970

Overall positions

	Drivers	Make	Points
1.	THERIER - CALLEWAERT (F)	Alpine Renault	108.1
2.	VINATIER - STONE (F-GB)	Alpine Renault	385.4
3.	ANDERSSON - PORTER (S-GB)	Ford Escort TC	387.4
4.	PIOT - TODT (F-GB)	Ford Escort TC	943.6
5.	LINDBERG - REINICKE (S)	Fiat 125 S	1192.9
6.	NICOLAS - VERON (F)	Alpine Renault	1406.3
7.	« SIROKO » - ANDRIOPOULOS (GR)	Opel Kadett	2765.3
8.	PSIHAS - NOMIKOS (GR)	Toyota Coronna	3898.4
9.	SIPAHI - ZORLU (TR)	BMW 2002	7476.0
10.	« DAFFY » - VOURDOUBAKIS (GR)	Humbert Scepter	8027.3
11.	KASSIMATIS - MOSHOVAKOS (GR)	Toyota Corolla 1100	8198.1
12.	MICHAILIDIS - BOSENCE (GB)	Sunbeam IMP	12336.5
13.	S. GREWS - Mrs S. GREWS (USA)	Saab 96 V4	18375.2

17th RALLYE DE LORRAINE

May 30 to 31, 1970

First 15 positions overall

	Drivers	Make	Time
1.	ANDRUET - VIAL (F)	Alpine Renault	1.14′54″1
2.	ROUSSELY - BERGUET (F)	Alpine A 110	1.15′20″0
3.	HENRY - LAUER (F)	Alpine A 110	1.16′04″2
4.	BARAILLER - FLAVIGNY (F)	Alfa Romeo	1.19′22″1
5.	BALLOT-LENA - MORENAS (F)	Porsche 911	1.20′27″0
6.	RAGNOTTI - THIMONIER (F)	Opel Kadett	1.22′52″2
7.	NUSBAUMER - HERVIEU (F)	Alpine A 110	1.23′01″0
8.	BEAUMONT - GRANDRIVE Mlle (F)	Opel GT	1.24′05″0
9.	« PEDRO » - SYMENS (B)	BMW 2002	1.25′31″2
10.	PALAYER Mme - PERIER Mlle (F)	Porsche 911 S	1.25′48″0
11.	VITTORI - AUBERTIN (F)	Alpine A 110	1.28′51″4
12.	BUGNOT - MARTIN (F)	Citroën DS 21	1.29′26″0
13.	« SIAL » - THULLIEZ (F)	Renault R8 G	1.30′44″1
14.	KRAUSE - GODICHARD (F)	Renault R8 G	1.33′06″2
15.	TOUBEAU - « CHAVAN » (B)	Porsche 911	1.33′38″3

SCOTTISH RALLY

June 6 to 12, 1970

Overall positions

	Drivers	Make	Points
1.	CULCHETH - SYER	Triumph 2.5 PI	2857
2.	HOPKIRK - NASH	Mini Clubman	3269
3.	McBURNEY - SMITH	BRM 2002 TI	3729
4.	C. GREWER - I. GREWER	Volvo 122 S	4251
5.	TAYLOR - McIVER	Ford Escort TC	4396
6.	WILSON - KNOX	Hillman Hunter	4543
7.	SMITH - DOYLE	Wolseley Hornet	4592
8.	BROWN - PARKER	BLMC-Cooper S	4688
9.	PILCHER - CLARK	Ford-Lotus Cortina	4696
10.	ROBERTSON - LINDSAY	Saab V4	5038
11.	BORGESSON - FAHLSTROM	Volkswagen 1600 L	5274
12.	WAREING - HARRIS	Escort GT	5397

38th RALLYE INTERNATIONAL DE GENÈVE

June 18 to 21, 1970

First 15 positions overall

	Drivers	Make	Points
1.	ANDRUET - VERON (F)	Alpine Renault A 110	8.698
2.	NICOLAS - TODT (F)	Alpine Renault A 110	9.033
3.	MAURIN - MOURIER (F)	Alpine Renault A 110	9.447
4.	HALDI - CHAPUIS (CH)	Porsche 911 S	9.460
5.	BARBASIO - MANNUCCI (I)	Lancia Fulvia HF	9.553
6.	RAGNOTTI - THIMONIER (F)	Opel Kadett R	9.789
7.	PALAYER - DEROLLAND (F)	Porsche 911 S	9.885
8.	« BEAUMONT » - FOUQUET (F)	Opel GT	10.123
9.	MEIER - BIANCHI (CH)	Porsche 911 R	10.157
10.	HANRIOUD - CHEVALLIER (F)	BMW 2002 TI	10.206
11.	J.-C. GAMET - M. GAMET (F)	NSU	10.302
12.	FATIO - HOFMANN (CH)	Alfa Romeo GTA	10.352
13.	J.-M. MARTIN - P. MARTIN (F)	Citroën DS 21	10.788
14.	VOGELSANG - GUENIN (CH)	Opel Kadett R	11.047
15.	MAURIS - GRASSO (CH)	Renault R8 Gordini	11.125

11th RALLYE VLATAVA: MOLDAU RALLY

July 3 to 5, 1970

Fist 15 positions overall

	Drivers	Make	Points
1.	STAEPELAERE - AERTS (B)	Ford Escort TC	7083
2.	KALLSTRÖM - HAGGBOM (S)	Lancia Fulvia	7090
3.	ROSER - LOIBNEGGER	Alpine Renault	7380
4.	HUBACEK - RIEGER (CS)	Renault-Gordini	7531
5.	KEC - STEAUER (CS)	Renault	8020
6.	BRUNCLIK - KAVKA (CS)	Skoda 100	8034
7.	GULLBERG - BERGMANN (S)	BMW 2002 TI	8153
8.	BRITH - JANSSON (S)	Opel Kadett	8212
9.	VITASEK - ROUDNICKY (CS)	Skoda 110	8470
10.	FREIENSTEIN - MÜHLING (D)	BMW 2002	8558
11.	GULMBACHER - ERNST (DDR)	Wartburg 353	8628
12.	JOHANSSON - SÖDERBERG (S)	Opel Kadett	8642
13.	BOLD - POMEZNY (CS)	Skoda 100 L	8656
14.	COBURN - SPOKES (GB)	Vauxhall Viva GT	8698
15.	JELINEK - SOUKUP (CS)	Skoda 110	9054

30th RAJD POLSKI: POLISH RALLY

July 16 to 19, 1970

First 15 positions overall

	Drivers	Make	Time
1.	ANDRUET - VERON (F)	Alpine Renault	7.491.46
2.	ZASADA - ZASADA (PL)	Porsche 911 S	7.537.79
3.	STAEPELAERE - AERTS (B)	Ford Cortina	8.498.53
4.	BIEN - KRZESIWO (PL)	Porsche 911	8.864.06
5.	KEC - KLIMA (CS)	Renault-Gordini	8.954.24
6.	LINDBERG - CALSTROM (S)	Fiat 125 S	9.237.30
7.	SUNDBERG - JONSSON (S)	Lancia Fulvia	9.643.46
8.	NOWICKI - MAGIERA (PL)	Renault-Gordini	10.952.00
9.	SOCHACKI - LESZCZUK (PL)	Fiat 125 S	11.826.66
10.	SYBERG - SYBERG (DK)	Opel Kadett	11.951.57
11.	WOJTYNA - CZEKALA (PL)	BMW 2002	12.141.42
12.	HOMMEL - BORK (DDR)	Wartburg 353	12.527.10
13.	MUCHA - BORKOWSKI (PL)	Fiat 125 P	12.572.97
14.	HEUSER - VOGT (D)	Opel Kadett	13.044.21
15.	JAROMIN - BRODACKI (PL)	Fiat 125	13.170.63

7th INTERNATIONALE DONAU RALLY

July 29 to 31, 1970

First 15 positions overall

	Drivers	Make	Points
1.	JANGER - WESSIAK (A)	Porsche 911 S	5185
2.	SCHINDLER - HRUSCHKA (A)	Porsche 914/6	5383
3.	HOLLIER - SHORT (GB)	Alpine Renault	5573
4.	BOSCH - MALLAT (A)	VW 1500	5793
5.	FISCHER - RADER (A)	VW 1500	5828
6.	LUX - SIEBERT (A)	VW 1500	5888
7.	PÖLTINGER - HARTINGER (A)	Porsche 914/6	5946
8.	MAIER-KAIBIC - PUCHER (A)	Ford Escort TC	5993
9.	WARMBOLD - KLAPPROTH (D)	Opel Kadett	6161
10.	FERJANCZ - ZSEMBERY (H)	Renault 8 Gordini	6220
11.	ROTARU - RADULESCU (R)	Renault 8 Gordini	6252
12.	KOMORNICKI - KRUPA (PL)	Alpine Renault	6585
13.	TCHOUBRIKOV - KURKTCHIEV (BG)	Alpine Renault	6589
14.	FALL - LIDDON (GB)	Ford Escort TC	7565
15.	POPESCU - VEZEANU (R)	Renault 8 Gordini	9002

20th JYVÄSKYLÄN SUURAJOT: 1000 LAKES RALLY

August 20 to 23, 1970

Fist 15 positions overall

	Drivers	Make	Points
1.	MIKKOLA - PALM (SF-S)	Ford Escort TC	16.612
2.	MÄKINEN - LIDDON (SF-GB)	Ford Escort TC	16.798
3.	LAMPINEN - DAVENPORT (SF-GB)	Lancia Fulvia HF	16.802
4.	MAJANDER - AHAVA (SF)	Volvo 142	17.228
5.	SOUTULAHTI - KESKITALO (SF)	Volvo 142	17.247
6.	LUSENIUS - HALME (SF)	Renault Gordini	17.545
7.	KÄRHÄ - ALANEN (SF)	Isuzu 1600 GT	17.711
8.	PÄÄKKÖNEN - TIUKKANEN (SF)	Sunbeam 900	17.749
9.	VALTAHARJU - PAALAMA (SF)	Opel Kadett	18·001
10.	NUUTTILA - NUUTTILA (SF)	Opel Kadett	18.174
11.	HALONEN - HÄRKÖNEN (SF)	Opel Kadett	18.180
12.	P. LEHTONEN - K. M. LEHTONEN (SF)	Saab 96	18.399
13.	LINDROOS - SAARTELA (SF)	Isuzu 1600 GT	18.500
14.	TÖTTERMAN - RÖNNQVIST (SF)	Skoda S 100	19.063
15.	KOSKINEN - LEINO (SF)	Volvo 122 S	19.177

RALLYE SAN MARTINO DI CASTROZZA

August 28 to 30, 1970

Overall classification

	Drivers	Make	Points
1.	KALLSTRÖM - HAGGBOM (S)	Lancia 1600 HF	69.5
2.	BARBASIO - MANNUCCI (I)	Lancia 1600 HF	100.0
3.	CAVALLARI - SALVAY (I)	Lancia 1600 HF	229.5
4.	PAGANELLI - RUSSO (I)	Fiat 124	251.0
5.	CECATO - EISENDLE (I)	Fiat 125 S	315.5

15th TOUR DE FRANCE

September 19 to 27, 1970

First 15 positions overall

	Drivers	Make	Time
1.	BELTOISE - TODT (F)	Matra-Simca 650	10.44'03"5
2.	PESCAROLO - RIVES (F)	Matra-Simca 650	10.48'18"0
3.	LARROUSSE - GELIN (F)	Porsche	11.20'13"4
4.	CHASSEUIL - BARON (F)	Porsche 911 S	11.31'50"1
5.	REY - JACQUEMIN (F)	Porsche	11.43'26"7
6.	BALLOT-LENA - MORENAS (F)	Porsche 914-6	12.14'32"5
7.	PIANTA - ALEMANI (I)	Alfa Romeo	12.22'18"6
8.	BALAS - IMBERT (F)	Porsche 914-6	12.28'27"5
9.	HANRIOUD - VIOLLET (F)	Porsche 911 S	12.28'30"9
10.	SELZ - COCHET (CH)	Porsche 911 S	12.30'06"9
11.	PONTI - VETSCH (CH)	Porsche 911 S	12.31'42"7
12.	POIROT - SOUKRY (F)	Porsche 907	12.34'20"0
13.	BELLIARD - BEAUGEARD (F)	Porsche 911 S	12.35'37"4
14.	DIEUDONNÉ - CURIEN (B)	Alfa Romeo GT	12.42'18"9
15.	PALAYER - DEROLLAND (F)	Porsche 911 S	12.46'56"8

THREE-TOWNS-RALLY: MUNICH - VIENNA - BUDAPEST

October 1 to 3, 1970

First 15 positions overall

	Drivers	Make	Points
1.	ANDRUET - VERON (F)	Alpine Renault	4007.8
2.	NICOLAS - CALLEWAERT (F)	Alpine Renault	4041.8
3.	STAEPELAERE - AERTS (B)	Ford Escort	4333.6
4.	WARMBOLD - STRUNZ (D)	Opel Kadett	4347.3
5.	JANGER - WESSIAK (A)	Porsche 911	4451.3
6.	ROSER - LOIBNEGGER (A)	Alpine GT	4540.6
7.	FERJANCZ - ZSEMBERY (H)	Renault-Gordini	4679.3
8.	FISCHER - RADER (A)	VW 1500	4807.8
9.	KOMORNICKI - KRUPA (PL)	Alpine Renault	4832.4
10.	BOSCH - MALAT (A)	VW 1500	4878.3
11.	ZELENKA - ZELENKA (A)	Ford Escort	4987.6
12.	LUX - SIEBERT (A)	VW 1500	5084.5
13.	SCHINDLER - HRUSCHKA (A)	Porsche 914	5123.9
14.	FISCHER - WIESER (A)	BMW 2002	5280.7
15.	DIETMAYER - MOSER (A)	BMW 2002 TI	5288.9

4th TAP INTERNATIONAL RALLY (PORTUGAL)

October 1 to 4, 1970

First 15 positions overall

	Drivers	Make	Points
1.	LAMPINEN - DAVENPORT (SF-GB)	Lancia	7099
2.	MUNARI - BERNACCHINI (I)	Lancia	7486
3.	WALDEGAARD - THORSZELIUS (S)	Porsche	7929
4.	LAMPREIA - MELVILLE (P)	Datsun	8786
5.	ROMAOZINHO - SIMOES (P)	Citroën	9121
6.	PEIXINHO - BANDEIRA (P)	Alfa Romeo	10.021
7.	NUNES - FONSECA (P)	Porsche	10.041
8.	SALVI - ARNAUD (I)	Porsche	10.052
9.	CHAVAN - LOYENS (B)	Datsun	10.140
10.	FIDLER - HUGHES (GB)	Ford	10.160
11.	GULLBERG - BERGGREN (S)	BMW 2002	10.470
12.	GREDER - GELIN (F)	Opel	10.741
13.	ALBINO - GRADE (P)	Datsun	10.807
14.	BEAUMONT - RIVE (F)	Opel	11.148
15.	BOTELHO - ANTONIO (P)	Citroën	11.240

RAC RALLY: GREAT BRITAIN RALLY

November 13 to 18, 1970

First 15 positions overall

	Drivers	Make	Time
1.	KÄLLSTRÖM - HÄGGBOM (S)	Lancia Fulvia	5.41'50"
2.	ERIKSSON - JOHANSSON (S)	Opel Kadett	5.44'18"
3.	NASENIUS - CEDEBERG (S)	Opel Kadett	5.53'18"
4.	HENRIKSSON - CARLSTRÖM (S)	Opel Kadett	5.56'08"
5.	COWAN - CARDNO (GB)	Alpine Renault	5.60'20"
6.	LARROUSSE - WOOD (F-GB)	Porsche 911 S	5.61'04"
7.	AALTONEN - EASTER (GB)	Datsun	5.67'19"
8.	CULCHETH - SYER (GB)	Ford Escort TC	5.80'53"
9.	JÖNSSON - QUIST (S)	Saab V4	5.83'41"
10.	KLEINT - RÖHR (D)	Ford Capri	5.90'33"
11.	SPARROW - RAEBURN (GB)	Cooper S	5.96'45"
12.	HALDI - GRETNER (CH)	Porsche 914/6	6.05'41"

7th RALLYE DER 1000 MINUTEN, Austria

October 16 to 18, 1970

First 15 positions overall

	Drivers	Make	Points
1.	LAMPINEN - MANNUCCI (SF-I)	Lancia Fulvia HF	4.477.2
2.	JANGER - WESSIAK (A)	Porsche 911 S	4.533.5
3.	PAGANELLI - RUSSO (I)	Fiat 124	4.549.0
4.	KÄLLSTRÖM - HAGGBOM (S)	Lancia Fulvia HF	4.729.1
5.	FISCHER - RADER (A)	VW 1302 S	4.743.2
6.	BOCHNICEK - KERNMAYER (A)	Citroën DS 21	4.789.9
7.	TROMBOTTO - MACALUSO (I)	Fiat 124	4.965.3
8.	DIETMAYER - MOSER (A)	BMW 2002 TI	5.031.8
9.	PÖLTINGER - HARTINGER (A)	VW Porsche 914/6	5.072.7
10.	KERSCHBAUM - SEDLACEK (A)	BMW 2002 TI	5.148.9
11.	BALLESTRIERI - AUDETTO (I)	Lancia Fulvia HF	5.242.3
12.	PETZL - SCHULZ (A)	Citroën DS 21	5.276.7
13.	MÜLLER - ZÖGL (A)	BMW Alpina 2002	5.335.3
14.	JÄGER - GOTTLIEB (A)	Alfa Romeo CS	5.378.3
15.	BOSCH - MALAT (A)	VW 1500	5.430.1

SPANISH RALLY

October 22 to 25, 1970

Overall positions

	Drivers	Make	Points
1.	NICOLAS - STONE (F-GB)	Alpine Renault 1600	9 892.6
2.	RUIZ-GIMENEZ - CASTENEDA (E)	Porsche 911 S	10 092.7
3.	DARNICHE - CALLEWAERT (F)	Alpine Renault 1600	10 201.0
4.	PINTO - « KILROI » (I)	Lancia 1600	10 286.9
5.	REVERTER - PABON (E)	Porsche 911 R	10 377.7
6.	STAEPELAERE - AERTS (B)	Ford Escort TC	10 380.5
7.	RAGNOTTI - THIMONIER (F)	Opel Kadett 1900 S	10 825.0
8.	KOMORNICKI - KRUPA (PL)	Alpine Renault	10 906.7
9.	van DULKEN - ANTOLINE	Renault 8	12 059.7
10.	RASILLA - « GAVAL » (E)	Renault 8	12 252.4

15th TOUR DE CORSE

November 7 to 8, 1970

First 15 positions overall

	Drivers	Make	Time
1.	DARNICHE - DEMANGE (F)	Alpine Renault 1600	4.19'03"7
2.	ANDRUET - VIAL (F)	Alpine Renault 1600	4.23'05"2
3.	MANZAGOL - OLIVA (F)	Alpine Renault 1600	4.31'22"6
4.	CHASSEUIL - BARON (F)	Porsche 911 S	4.36'28"1
5.	VINATIER - MURAC (F)	Alpine Renault 1800	4.37'17"9
6.	PIOT - PORTER (F-GB)	Ford Escort 1800	4.48'09"8
7.	JACQUEMIN - ROUFF (B)	Alpine Renault 1600	4.56'54"8
8.	HENRY - LAPORTE	Opel Kadett	5.10'17"6
9.	MAUBLANC - PEYRUSSON	BMW 2002 TI	5.19'10"5
10.	BALLOT-LÉNA - MORENAS	Porsche 911 S	5.28'00"7
11.	HALDI - REFUVEILLE	Porsche 911 S	5.34'00"7
12.	« BEAUMONT » - de LAGRANRIVE (F)	Opel GT	5.46'36"3
13.	VALABRÈGUE - JAUBERT	Opel Kadett	5.51'27"6
14.	SIMONETTI - ALBERTI	Alpine Renault	5.53'49"4
15.	ALESI - BRUNET DEBAINES	Opel Kadett	5.55'34"5

TOUR DE BELGIQUE

November 20 to 22, 1970

Overall classification

	Drivers	Make	Points
1.	STAEPELAERE - AERTS (B)	Ford	63.7
2.	PAGANELLI - RUSSO (I)	Fiat 124	212.8
3.	BERTINCHAMPS - DEPREZ	Alfa Romeo	303.0
4.	BALLESTRIERI - AUDETTO (I) . .	Lancia Fulvia	305.7
5.	TRICOT - LUX (B)	Opel Commodore	504.1
6.	BARBASIO - MANNUCI (I)	Lancia Fulvia	624.9
7.	ANDRIENSSENS - DAEMERS (B) . .	BMW 2002	635.1
8.	TROMBOTTO - ZANUCCOLI (I) . .	Fiat 124	854.1
9.	VAHUNESSEL - DEMAY (B)	Porsche 911 S	925.1
10.	DIDI - LOPEZ	Fiat 903	1 055.6

EUROPEAN RALLY CHAMPIONSHIP FOR MANUFACTURERS

1. Porsche	28 points
2. Alpine-Renault	26 points
3. Lancia	16 points
4. Saab	15 points
5. Ford	10 points

EUROPEAN RALLY CHAMPIONSHIP FOR DRIVERS

FINAL CLASSIFICATION	Stuttgart-Solitude	DDR	Ireland	Tulpenrally	Wiesbaden	Bodensee	Lorraine	Scottish Rally	Genève	Moldau	Polish Rally	Donau	1000 Lakes	San Martino	Tour de France	Munich-Vienna	TAP	Isola d'Elba	1000 Minutes	Spanish Rally	Tour de Corse	Tour de Belgique	Total
1. Andruet (F) . .	13						13		13		10					13					8		**70**
2. Aerts (B) . . .										13	10					10				9		13	**55**
2. Staepelaere (B)										13	10					10				9		13	**55**
4. Warmbold (D) .	9				13	9						9				6							**46**
5. Ragnotti (F) . .	9			11			9		9											6			**44**
5. Thimonier (F) .	9			11			9		9											6			**44**
7. Biebienger (D) .	9				13	9																	**31**
8. Paganelli (I) . .														3				13	4			5	**25**
8. Russo (I) . . .														3				13	4			5	**25**
10. Stone (GB) . .	13																			10			**23**

LONDON-MEXICO CITY
DAILY MIRROR WORLD CUP RALLY 1970

	Drivers	Make	Points
1.	MIKKOLA - PALM (SF-S)	Ford Escort	9.07′
2.	CULCHETH - SYER (GB)	Triumph 2500	10.25′
3.	AALTONEN - LIDDON (SF-GB)	Ford Escort	10.46′
4.	HOPKIRK - NASH - JOHNSTON (GB) . . .	Triumph 2500	12.26′
5.	MAKINEN - STAEPELAERE (SF-B)	Ford Escort	14.31′
6.	GREAVES - FALL (GB)	Ford Escort	19.31′
7.	VANSON - TURCAT - LEPRINCE (GB-F). .	Citroën DS 21	22.03′
8.	ZASADA - WACHOWSKI (PL)	Ford Escort	23.59′
9.	REDGRAVE - COOPER - TREEBOROUGH	Morris 1800	24.42′
10.	SMITH Miss - WATSON Mrs - DEROLLAND Miss (GB).	Austin Maxi	30.35′
11.	TUBMAN - WELINSKI - McAULEY (AUS) .	Austin 1800	32.36′
12.	POTAPCHIK - BAZHENOV - LESOVSKI	Moskvitch	34.06′
13.	BENDEK - HUBNER - BURGOA (BOL) . . .	BMW 2002 TI	35.14′
14.	CHANNON - COOPER (GB)	Ford Cortina	36.43′
15.	REES - LLEWELLIN - WASHINGTON (GB) .	Hillman	37.50′

LONDON-SYDNEY MARATHON 1969
DAILY EXPRESS - DAILY TELEGRAPH RALLY

	Drivers	Make	Points
1.	COWAN - COYLE - MALKIN (GB). . .	Hillman Hunter	50
2.	HOPKIRK - NASH - POOLE (GB) . . .	BLMC 1800	56
3.	VAUGHAN - FORSYTH - ELLIS (AUS)	Ford Falcon GT	62
4.	ZASADA - WACHOWSKI (PL)	Porsche 911 S	65
5.	HODGSON - RUTHERFORD (AUS) . .	Ford Falcon GT	70
6.	AALTONEN - LIDDON - EASTER (SF-GB)	BLMC 1800	71
7.	KLEINT - KLAPPROTH (D)	Ford 20 M RS	91
8.	NEYRET - TERRAMORSI	Citroën DS-21	125
9.	CLARK - ANDERSSON (GB-S)	Ford Cortina Lotus	144
10.	TUBMANN - FORREST	Volvo 144 S	148
11.	FERGUSON - CHIVAS - JOHNSSON .	Holden GTS	169
12.	WELINSKI - LISTER.	Volvo 144 S	171
13.	WHITEFORD - PERKINS - HAWKER .	Holden GT S	173
14.	HERMANN - SCHULLER	Porsche 911 S	195
15.	SLOTEMAKER - JANSSEN	Daf 55	208

Photographic acknowledgements

Follow the pictures clockwise, beginning at the left-hand corner on each page.

Jacket: Yves Debraine • Back of the jacket: DPPI • 47-53: Montagu Motor Museum (8 photos), Arnold Farrar (19 photos) • 54: usine • 63: usine, usine, usine, Bernard Cahier • 64-67: usine • 68: usine, usine, Jean Fondin • 69-75: usine • 76: usine, usine, Rudolf Karpat, Rudolf Karpat, Rudolf Karpat • 77: DPPI, usine, usine, usine, usine, usine • 78: usine, usine, Ami Guichard, usine, usine • 79: usine • 80: Ami Guichard, usine, usine, Ami Guichard, Ami Guichard • 81: Ami Guichard, usine • 82-84: DPPI • 85: DPPI, DPPI, usine, DPPI, DPPI, DPPI • 86: usine • 87: usine, usine, DPPI, Automobil Revue • 88: Bernard Cahier • 90: Yves Debraine, Ami Guichard, Ami Guichard, Ami Guichard, Ami Guichard • 91-94: Ami Guichard • 95: Yves Debraine, Ami Guichard, Ami Guichard, Ami Guichard, Ami Guichard, Ami Guichard • 96-97: Ami Guichard • 98: DPPI • 107: Josef Reinhard • 108: Josef Reinhard, Philippe Toussaint • 109: Alton Berns, Alton Berns, Philippe Toussaint • 110: Bernard Cahier, Yves Debraine, Yves Debraine • 111: Carl Imber, Bernard Cahier • 112: Geoffrey Goddard, Yves Debraine • 113: Yves Debraine • 114-115: L'Auto-journal • 116: Yves Debraine • 117: Bernard Cahier, Yves Debraine • 118: Eric della Faille • 119: Bernard Cahier • 120: Geoffrey Goddard • 121: Eric della Faille, Carl Imber, Geoffrey Goddard • 122: Michael Cooper, Eric della Faille, Michael Cooper, Geoffrey Goddard • 123: Bernard Cahier • 124: Bernard Cahier, Remy Stohler, Karl Heinz Fiebig, Michael Cooper • 125: Michael Cooper, Bernard Cahier • 126: Geoffrey Goddard, Yves Debraine • 127: Yves Debraine • 128-129: DPPI • 130: Yves Debraine • 131: Philippe Toussaint • 132: Geoffrey Goddard, Eric della Faille, Bernard Cahier • 133: Michael Cooper • 134: Geoffrey Goddard, Michael Cooper • 135: Michael Hewett, Lynton Money, Geoffrey Goddard • 136: Hans G. Isenberg, Hermann Pickartz • 137: Geoffrey Goddard • 138: Hermann Pickartz, Georges A. Spozio • 139: Hans G. Isenberg, Geoffrey Goddard, Hans G. Isenberg • 140: Geoffrey Goddard, Bernard Cahier, Geoffrey Goddard • 141: Geoffrey Goddard • 142: Geoffrey Goddard, Bernard Cahier, Geoffrey Goddard • 143: Yves Debraine • 144-145: Bernard Cahier • 146: Josef Reinhard, Bernard Cahier, Josef Reinhard • 147: DPPI • 148: DPPI • 149: DPPI, Pete Lyons • 150: William H. Murenbeeld, DPPI, DPPI • 151: Pete Lyons • 152: DPPI • 153: Pete Lyons, DPPI, DPPI • 154: DPPI • 155-157: Bernard Cahier • 158: Remy Stohler • 159: Gérard Flocon, Bernard Cahier, Gérard Flocon, Gérard Flocon, Gérard Flocon • 160: Gérard Flocon • 161: Gérard Flocon, Hans G. Isenberg, Gérad Flocon, Bernard Cahier, Geoffrey Goddard • 162: usine, Gérard Flocon, Geoffrey Goddard, Gérard Flocon, Hans G. Isenberg, Geoffrey Goddard • 163: DPPI • 164-165: Année Automobile • 179: DPPI • 180: Eric della Faille, J. J. Mollitt, Bob d'Olivo • 181: Bob d'Olivo, DPPI, Bob d'Olivo • 182: DPPI, Eric della Faille, DPPI, Eric della Faille • 183: Bill Warner • 185: Bernard Cahier, J. J. Mollitt, Bill Warner, Bill Warner • 186: Bernard Cahier, Bill Warner, Bill Warner • 187: Bill Warner • 188: Bill Warner • 190: Georges A. Spozio • 191: Eric della Faille, Geoffrey Goddard • 192: Eric della Faille, Geoffrey Goddard, Geoffrey Goddard • 193: Bernard Cahier, Bernard Cahier, Geoffrey Goddard • 194: Geoffrey Goddard, Georges A. Spozio, Bernard Cahier • 196-197: Yves Debraine • 198: Yves Debraine, Remy Stohler, Yves Debraine • 199: Werner Eisele, Yves Debraine, Kunibert Söntgerath • 200: Yves Debraine, Hermann Pickartz, Kunibert Söntgerath, Kunibert Söntgerath • 201: Kunibert Söntgerath • 203: Ami Guichard • 204: Yves Debraine • 205: Pierre Guex, Eric della Faille, Pierre Guex • 206: Bernard Cahier, Geoffrey Goddard, Bernard Cahier • 207: Yves Debraine • 208-209: Thomas Zimmermann • 210: Yves Debraine, Ami Guichard • 211: Yves Debraine • 212: Bernard Cahier, Werner Eisele, Werner Eisele • 213: William H. Murenbeeld • 214: Alice Bixler, William H. Murenbeeld, William H. Murenbeeld • 215: Hunter Farnham, J. J. Mollitt, Hunter Farnham • 217: J. J. Mollitt, Gero Hoschek, William H. Murenbeeld • 218-219-220: Hunter Farnham • 222: Bill Warner • 223: Gero Hoschek Gero Hoschek, Hunter Farnham, Hunter Farnham, Hunter Farnham, Hunter Farnham, Hunter Farnham, Gero Hoschek, William H. Murenbeeld • 224: J. J. Mollitt, Bernard Cahier • 225: DPPI • 226: Hunter Farnham • 228: Bob d'Olivo • 229: Bob d'Olivo, Richard George • 230: Richard George, Bob d'Olivo • 231: B. Cahier • 232: Africapix • 233: Gérard Flocon • 234: usine • 235: DPPI • 236: Michael Cooper.

PRINTING

Advertisements, text, black and white illustrations

PRESSES CENTRALES LAUSANNE S. A.

Colour illustrations

OFFSET JEAN GENOUD, LAUSANNE

BINDING

MAURICE BUSENHART, LAUSANNE

PRINTED IN SWITZERLAND